"Each of Vern Poythress's books has beer particular subject, whether science, herm method, gender-neutral Bible translation, or the Mosaic law. Not only are these books expertly researched and cogently argued, but they are explicitly Christian in their starting point, method, and conclusion (to use a phrase of Cornelius Van Til). Poythress does not merely claim that these disciplines allow a place for God, or that a theistic worldview provides useful context, or that engagement in such studies is somehow useful to Christians. Rather, he comes right in your face with the claims of Christ: All of these studies are grounded in the nature and work of the triune God, and nothing can be rightly understood apart from him. God is not merely a possibility, not merely a conclusion, but the starting point for any understanding at all.

"So in the present book on language, Poythress shows that the foundation of human speech is the speech between the Father, Son, and Holy Spirit, so that without God meaningful language would be impossible. He makes this audacious claim, not as a mere preacher but as one who has gained an expert knowledge of linguistics as well as biblical theology. This book is essential for anyone who would pursue an understanding of language. It is also a great help to those who are troubled by contemporary challenges to the very possibility of meaningful communication. And to those who wonder how the word of God can possibly be expressed in human speech, Poythress shows us that without the word of God human speech is impossible."

**John M. Frame,** Professor of Systematic Theology and Philosophy,
Reformed Theological Seminary, Orlando

"In this remarkable volume, Vern Poythress takes the reader on a theological adventure into the depths of language, showing that God's gift of language reveals important things about humankind and about God himself. Poythress argues that the intricacies of language present both a general revelation of the triune nature of God and the means for special revelation of himself in the words of Scripture. The complexities and sophistication of human discourse reflect the inherently communicative nature of God, in whose image people are created. The gifts of language and Scripture are testimonies to God's love and are tools for sharing that love in every language and culture of the earth."

**Richard Brown,** International Translation Consultant,
Wycliffe Bible Translators

"If you were to ask me to propose one person to guide me through a thoroughly Christian view of language, Vern Poythress would be my first choice. His detailed knowledge of both the Bible and linguistics, his creative ability to see connections, his determination to be true to God, and his engaging personal manner, all come through in this book. I came away with a fresh appreciation for our creaturely dependence on the triune God, and renewed thankfulness to God for his remarkable gift of language."

**C. John ("Jack") Collins,** Professor of Old Testament,
Covenant Theological Seminary

"This book represents a lifetime of theological thinking about the significance of language: about God's involvement with language, the nature of language itself from phonemes to literary genres, and the diverse ways humans interact with one another, and with God, through language. Here one finds not only a biblical but a systematic theology of language built on the insight that human language reflects the triune God, sometimes in surprising ways. And, as if thirty-six chapters were not enough, Poythress includes significant appendices analyzing language in postmodernism, translation theory, speech acts, deconstruction, and more. There is nothing like this book on the market!"

**Kevin J. Vanhoozer,** Research Professor of Systematic Theology, Trinity Evangelical Divinity School

"Vern Poythress presents a compelling, textured Biblical theology of human and divine communication. By looking through the right end of the telescope, starting with God rather than human understanding, he plumbs the depths of God's role as guarantor and sustainer and as the locus within which meaning and interaction have their being. Poythress's treatment is woven together as what appears to be an exhaustive corpus, analyzing multitudinous facets of God's role in language and how this role affects how we should understand and practice communication. He brings added depth through rigorous analysis of theoretical and philosophical developments relating to the study of language and culture."

**Chris Simmons,** Executive Director, The Gospel and Culture Project

"This fascinating and remarkably insightful book is the product of a lifetime of profound thinking about the amazing complexity of language as created by God to reflect his own character and give him glory. Poythress's multiple perspectives on language will enable readers to understand the Bible more deeply and also to avoid the mistakes of various non-Christian theories of language that influence society today. This book is a wonderful resource in many ways."

**Wayne Grudem,** Research Professor of Bible and Theology, Phoenix Seminary

# In the Beginning Was the Word

## Language—A God-Centered Approach

Vern Sheridan Poythress

WHEATON, ILLINOIS

*In the Beginning Was the Word: Language—A God-Centered Approach*
Copyright © 2009 by Vern S. Poythress
Published by Crossway Books
     a publishing ministry of Good News Publishers
     1300 Crescent Street
     Wheaton, Illinois 60187

Page and typesetting design: Lakeside Design Plus
Cover design: Studio Gearbox

First printing 2009

Scripture quotations are from The Holy Bible, English Standard Version®, copyright © 2001 by Crossway Bibles, a publishing ministry of Good News Publishers. Used by permission. All rights reserved.

Emphasis in Scripture quotations added by author.

Printed in the United States of America

| Trade paperback ISBN: | 978-1-4335-0179-1 |
| PDF ISBN: | 978-1-4335-1239-1 |
| Mobipocket ISBN: | 978-1-4335-1240-7 |

**Library of Congress Cataloging-in-Publication Data**
Poythress, Vern S.
  In the beginning was the word : language : a God-centered approach / Vern Sheridan Poythress.
    p. cm.
  Includes bibliographical references (p.   ) and indexes.
  ISBN 978-1-4335-0179-1 (tpb)
  1. Communication—Religious aspects—Christianity. 2. Language and languages—Religious aspects—Christianity. I. Title.
BV4319.P69 2009
230.01'4—dc22

                             2009001552

| SH | | | 19 | 18 | | 17 | 16 | 15 | 14 | 13 | 12 | 11 | 10 | 09 |
| 14 | 13 | 12 | 11 | | 10 | 9 | 8 | 7 | 6 | 5 | 4 | 3 | 2 | 1 |

to my teacher Dr. John M. Frame
who first taught me about
the divine character of God's word

and

to my teacher the late Dr. Kenneth L. Pike
who first taught me
that human language reflects
God in his Triunity

and

to my friends in Wycliffe Bible Translators
who have daily lived out being disciples of Christ
as they have played a role in making disciples of all nations

# Contents

# The Importance of Language

By the word of the LORD the heavens were made,
and by the breath of his mouth all their host.

—Psalm 33:6

Language is wonderful and mysterious. It is so because it is a gift of God to us. It reflects and reveals him.

How does language reflect God? According to the Bible, God himself can speak, and does speak. We are made like him, and that is why we can speak. When we use language, we rely on resources and powers that find their origin in God. In fact, as we shall see, language reflects God in his Trinitarian character. We can appreciate language more deeply, and use it more wisely, if we come to know God and understand the relation of God to the language we use.

Because I am a follower of Christ, I trust in the Bible as the word of God.[1] The Bible is a foundational resource for my thinking about language. From time to time we will look briefly at other views of language. But my primary purpose is helping people increase their appreciation for language, using the Bible for guidance. If you as a reader are not yet convinced about the Bible, I would still invite you to think with me about language. The actual character of language does, I believe, confirm what the Bible says.

---

1. Interested readers may consult many works that show at length that the Bible is the word of God. See, among others, Benjamin B. Warfield, *The Inspiration and Authority of the Bible* (reprint; Philadelphia: Presbyterian & Reformed, 1967); D. A. Carson and John Woodbridge, eds., *Scripture and Truth* (Grand Rapids, MI: Zondervan, 1983). It is an important issue, so important that it deserves much more space than we could take here.

## The Central Role of Language

Language has a central role in human living. We spend a lot of our time talking and listening. Education constantly uses language. Television, radio, newspapers, and the Internet use language. Friendships are cemented and maintained through language.[2] All these are sources of meaning in our lives.

Some tasks, such as washing dishes, do not demand using language. But even they gain significance from what we say and think about them. We wash dishes because through language we have learned about bacteria, sickness, and how washing helps protect health. And washing dishes can be more pleasant if we are talking with a friend while doing it.

We could go on. Many of the most significant and precious moments in life gain significance through language. So examining language itself could contribute significantly to reorienting our lives. That is why we are going to take a long look at language and its meaning.

## The Importance of Language in the Bible

The Bible confirms the importance of language. It says that in the beginning God created the world using language: "And God *said*, 'Let there be light,' and there was light" (Gen. 1:3).[3]

The first recorded interaction between God and man involved God *speaking in language* concerning man's task:

> And God blessed them. And God *said* to them, "Be fruitful and multiply and fill the earth and subdue it and have dominion over the fish of the sea and over the birds of the heavens and over every living thing that moves on the earth" (Gen. 1:28).

Adam and Eve fell into sin through the serpent's use of language to tempt them: the serpent *said*, "You will not surely die" (Gen. 3:4). Shortly afterward, God gave hope to Adam and Eve through a promise of redemption, and the promise was expressed in language:

> The LORD God *said* to the serpent, . . .

---

2. "Without the signposts of speech, the social beehive would disintegrate immediately" (Eugen Rosenstock-Huessy, *Speech and Reality* [Norwich, VT: Argo, 1970], 16).

3. Bible quotations are from the English Standard Version (ESV).

"I will put enmity between you [the serpent] and the woman,
    and between your offspring and her offspring;
he shall bruise your head,
    and you shall bruise his heel" (Gen. 3:14–15).

One of the principal aspects of Jesus' earthly ministry was teaching and pro-claiming a message.[4] He used language; he had much to say. And he made plain the importance of his teaching:

"Everyone then who hears these *words of mine* [Jesus' words] and does them will be like a wise man who built his house on the rock. And the rain fell, and the floods came, and the winds blew and beat on that house, but it did not fall, because it had been founded on the rock. And everyone who hears these *words of mine* and does not do them will be like a foolish man who built his house on the sand. And the rain fell, and the floods came, and the winds blew and beat against that house, and it fell, and great was the fall of it" (Matt. 7:24–27).

Jesus raised Lazarus from the dead by issuing a verbal command: "Lazarus, come out" (John 11:43). Jesus' words have power. The future resurrection of the body will take place through the power of Jesus' words: ". . . for an hour is coming when all who are in the tombs will hear his [Jesus'] *voice* and come out, those who have done good to the resurrection of life, and those who have done evil to the resurrection of judgment" (John 5:28–29).[5]

At the last judgment people will be judged according to their *words*:

I tell you, on the day of judgment people will give account for every careless *word* they speak, for by your *words* you will be justified, and by your *words* you will be condemned (Matt. 12:36–37).

And how can we escape condemnation? The answer to condemnation is found in the gospel, the good news concerning what Christ has done to save us. That good news is a *verbal message*. Through this *message*, given in *language*, people come to believe in Christ and to receive God's salvation:

For I am not ashamed of the *gospel*, for it is the power of God for salvation to everyone who believes, to the Jew first and also to the Greek. For in it the righteousness of God is revealed from faith for faith, as it is written, "The righteous shall live by faith" (Rom. 1:16–17).

---

4. Mark 1:38–39: "And he said to them, 'Let us go on to the next towns, that I may *preach* there also, for that is *why* I came out.' And he went throughout all Galilee, *preaching* in their synagogues and casting out demons."

5. Note also the illustration of the power of the prophetic word when Ezekiel is told to prophesy and in response dead bones come to life (Ezek. 37:4–10).

But what does it *say*? "The *word* is near you, in your *mouth* and in your heart" (that is, the *word* of faith that we *proclaim*); because, if you *confess* with your mouth that Jesus is Lord and believe in your heart that God raised him from the dead, you will be saved (Rom. 10:8–9).

How then will they *call* on him in whom they have not believed? And how are they to believe in him of whom they have never *heard*? And how are they to *hear* without someone *preaching*? And how are they to *preach* unless they are sent? As it is *written*, "How beautiful are the feet of those who *preach* the *good news*!" But they have not all obeyed the *gospel*. For Isaiah *says*, "Lord, who has believed what he has *heard* from us?" So faith comes from *hearing*, and *hearing* through the *word* of Christ (Rom. 10:14–17).

Words, then, have a central role, according to the Bible. And of course the Bible itself is composed of words.

We may note still one more role of language. Jesus Christ himself has a close relation to language. The Gospel of John calls Christ "the Word," and begins by speaking of his eternal existence with God:

In the beginning was the Word, and the Word was with God, and the Word was God. He was in the beginning with God. All things were made through him, and without him was not any thing made that was made (John 1:1–3).

These verses in John allude to the opening chapter in Genesis, when God created the universe by speaking. So the "Word" in John 1:1, that is, Christ before his incarnation, was the source of the speech of God in Genesis. Christ is thus the origin of language itself. Moreover, Christ says concerning himself, "I am the way, and *the truth*, and the life" (John 14:6). He identifies himself with "the truth," showing a connection with truth in language. And he says that God's word is *truth* and the source of holiness for disciples:

Sanctify them in the *truth*; your *word* is *truth*. As you sent me into the world, so I have sent them into the world. And for their sake I consecrate myself, that they also may be sanctified in *truth* (John 17:17–19).

God himself is true: "Whoever receives his testimony sets his seal to this, that God *is true*" (John 3:33).

## Language in Our Conduct

Language, then, has a significant role in God's relation to human beings from creation onward. Appreciating language properly can contribute to our well-being in relation to God.

Language affects not only the big issues concerning who God is, and how to be reconciled to him, but the smaller issues of how to conduct our lives. The book of Proverbs contains any number of illustrations of the importance of language in our conduct:

The *lips* of the righteous know what is acceptable,
>    but the *mouth* of the wicked, what is perverse (Prov. 10:32).

There is one whose rash *words* are like sword thrusts,
>    but the *tongue* of the wise brings healing (Prov. 12:18).

A wise son *hears* his father's *instruction,*
>    but a *scoffer* does not *listen* to *rebuke* (Prov. 13:1).

Whoever guards his *mouth* preserves his life;
>    he who opens wide his *lips* comes to ruin (Prov. 13:3).

By *insolence* comes nothing but strife,
>    but with those who *take advice* is wisdom (Prov. 13:10).

Poverty and disgrace come to him who ignores *instruction,*
>    but whoever *heeds reproof* is honored (Prov. 13:18).

By the *mouth* of a fool comes a rod for his back,
>    but the *lips* of the wise will preserve them (Prov. 14:3).

Leave the presence of a fool,
>    for there you do not meet *words* of knowledge (Prov. 14:7).

In all toil there is profit,
>    but mere *talk* tends only to poverty (Prov. 14:23).

A *truthful witness* saves lives,
>    but one who *breathes out lies* is deceitful (Prov. 14:25).

A soft *answer* turns away wrath,
>    but a harsh *word* stirs up anger (Prov. 15:1).

Which of us would not benefit from greater wisdom in how to speak and how to listen?

# God's Involvement
# with Language

# Language and the Trinity

"I do as the Father has commanded me."

—John 14:31

Language has a close relation to the Trinitarian character of God. In fact, the Trinitarian character of God is the deepest starting point for understanding language. So we need to look at what the Bible teaches about God in his Trinitarian character.

## The Trinity

The Bible teaches that God is one God, and that he exists in three persons, the Father, the Son, and the Holy Spirit. I will not undertake to defend orthodox Trinitarian doctrine in detail, because this has already been done many times.[1] Let me mention briefly only a small number of evidences.

In addressing the polytheism of surrounding nations, the Old Testament makes it clear that there is only one true God, the God of Israel, who is the only Creator (Genesis 1; see Deut. 6:4; 32:39; Isa. 40:18–28). The New Testament introduces further revelation about the distinction of persons in God, but it everywhere presupposes the unity of one God, as revealed in the Old Testament. The New Testament does not repudiate but reinforces the Old Testament. "Hear, O Israel: The Lord our God, the Lord is *one*" (Mark 12:29). "You believe that God is *one*; you do well" (James 2:19).

---

1. For a recent discussion, see John M. Frame, *The Doctrine of God* (Phillipsburg, NJ: Presbyterian & Reformed, 2002), 619–735.

Second, in the New Testament the deity of Christ the Son of God is dramatically affirmed by applying to him Old Testament verses that use the tetragrammaton, the sacred name of God: "Everyone who calls on the name of the *Lord* will be saved" (Rom. 10:13; from Joel 2:32, which has the tetragrammaton).[2] We also find explicit affirmations that Jesus is God in John 1:1 ("... and the Word was God") and John 20:28. The Holy Spirit is God, according to Acts 5:3–4.[3] The distinction between the persons is regularly evident in John, when it expresses the relation of two persons as a Father-and-Son relation, and when the Spirit is described as *another* Helper, indicating that he is distinct from the Son (John 14:16).

## God Speaks to Himself

The New Testament indicates that the persons of the Trinity speak to one another. This speaking on the part of God is significant for our thinking about language. Not only is God a member of a language community that includes human beings, but the persons of the Trinity function as members of a language community among themselves. Language does not have as its sole purpose human-human communication, or even divine-human communication, but also divine-divine communication. Approaches that conceive of language *only* with reference to human beings are accordingly reductionistic.

What is the evidence for divine-divine communication? First consider John 16:13–15:

> When the Spirit of truth comes, he will guide you into all the truth, for he will not speak on his own authority, but whatever *he hears* he will speak, and he will declare to you the things that are to come. He will glorify me, for he will take what is mine and declare it to you. All that the Father has is mine; therefore I said that he will take what is mine and declare it to you.

The principal role of the Holy Spirit in these verses is to speak to the disciples of Christ. But we need to notice the basis for that speaking: "Whatever *he hears* he will speak." The Spirit is first a hearer. And whom does he hear? The subsequent explanation brings in both the Father and the Son. The Spirit hears the Father, and hears about "what is mine," that is, what is the Son's. Conceivably the Son as

---

2. The tetragrammaton is *YHWH* (Hebrew יהוה, "Jehovah"), often translated in Greek as *kurios*, "Lord").

3. Acts 5:3–4 indicates that to lie to the Holy Spirit is to lie to God: "But Peter said, 'Ananias, why has Satan filled your heart to lie to the *Holy Spirit* and to keep back for yourself part of the proceeds of the land? While it remained unsold, did it not remain your own? And after it was sold, was it not at your disposal? Why is it that you have contrived this deed in your heart? You have not lied to men but to *God*.'"

well as the Father is speaking to the Spirit. But in any case we have divine-divine communication between at least two persons of the Trinity.

Consider next John 17. In John 17 we have a long discourse where the Son speaks to the Father. This discourse is often called the "high priestly prayer," because Jesus is interceding on behalf of the disciples. The label "prayer" invites us to think of this passage in connection with Jesus' human nature. As high priest he shares our humanity, and so is able to represent us (Heb. 2:10–18; 4:15). Doubtless this is one aspect of what is going on in John 17. Some translations even use the *word* "pray" when they translate the Greek word that has the general meaning "ask" (17:9, 20). But Christ as a whole *person* is communing with the Father. The words we have in John 17 show us what he asks, not only with respect to his *human* nature but with respect to his *divine* nature as well. Consider, for example, that he talks about "the glory that I had with you before the world existed" (John 17:5). The word "I" in that verse must include the divine nature of Christ, because the "glory that I had with you" was the glory *before* his incarnation ("before the world existed"), a glory therefore with respect to his *divine* nature but not his *human* nature. Similarly John 17:24 says that "you [God the Father] loved me before the foundation of the world."[4]

We conclude, then, that John 17 presents not merely human communication but also *divine* communication between the divine persons of the Father and the Son. That communication takes place through language. And so language is something used among the persons of the Trinity.

Of course the language recorded in John 17 is *also* language accessible to us as human beings. But it is given to us as human beings precisely so that we may know that the communication that it represents exceeds human grasp, and is divine communication. This particular piece of language in John 17 is not "merely" human, as modernist theologians sometimes claim concerning language in general. It is *also* divine. And because God is God, and is greater than we are, we can never plumb to the bottom the depths of divine communication.

## Distinct Roles of the Persons of the Trinity in Language: Speaker, Speech, Breath

We need to consider another striking biblical claim about language. John 1:1 calls the second person of the Trinity "the Word":

In the beginning was the Word, and the Word was with God, and the Word was God.

---

4. For further discussion of this passage, and the implications for divine language, see Vern S. Poythress, *God-Centered Biblical Interpretation* (Phillipsburg, NJ: Presbyterian & Reformed, 1999), 16–25.

One of the backgrounds to John 1:1 is Genesis 1, where God creates the world by speaking. "And God said, 'Let there be light,' and there was light" (Gen. 1:3). The eternal Word in John 1:1 is analogically related to the creational words that God spoke in calling the world into existence in Genesis 1, and to the words of Scripture, which are the word of God (2 Tim. 3:16). All three of these—eternal Word, creational words, and the Bible—are forms of the word of God. The latter two both make manifest the wisdom of God that has its source in the eternal Word (Col. 2:3; 1 Cor. 1:30).[5]

Without going into detail about these different forms, let us start with the most basic form, namely, the eternal Word, the second person of the Trinity. Calling him "the Word" indicates a relation between the Trinitarian character of God and language. In this analogical relation, God the Father is the speaker, while God the Son is the speech, "the Word." Is there a role for the Holy Spirit? John 1:1–18 does not directly mention the Spirit, but the background passage in Genesis 1 does include the presence of the Spirit in Genesis 1:2. The Spirit "was hovering over the face of the waters." Psalm 104, which reflects back on Genesis 1 and praises God for his works of creation, also includes a role for the Spirit:

> When you hide your face, they [animals] are dismayed;
>     when you take away their breath, they die and return to their dust.
> When you send forth *your Spirit*, they are created,
>     and you renew the face of the ground (Ps. 104:29–30).

The Spirit of God gives life to a new generation of animals and plants ("renew the face of the ground"). The Spirit is their empowerer. We can even see a close relation between the breath of animals, which represents their life, and the power of the Spirit of God "breathing" life into them. The connection is made explicit in Job 33:4:

> The *Spirit* of God has made me,
>     and the *breath* of the Almighty gives me life.

The Hebrew word for "spirit" is *ruach*, which can also mean "breath" or "wind." In most contexts it has only one of these three meanings, but the potential is there to invoke more than one, as happens in Job 33:4 above. In Ezekiel 37 we meet all three meanings in a passage that relates all three meanings to one another: "spirit" (37:1, 14), "wind" (37:9), and "breath" (37:5, 6, 9, 10; but closely related to "spirit" coming into dead bodies). The third person of the Trinity is named "Spirit" partly to suggest a close relation between him and the picture of the "breath" of God.

---

5. See ibid., 27–50.

Putting these passages together with John 1:1, we can obtain a coherent picture of the persons of the Trinity as the origin of speech and language. God the Father is speaker, God the Son is the speech, and God the Spirit is the breath carrying the speech to its destination. The Spirit is also the power who brings about its effects.

## Personal Indwelling

The persons of the Trinity are distinct from one another. But they also mutually indwell one another. Jesus says, "Believe me that I am *in* the Father and the Father is *in* me" (John 14:11). The Father dwells in the Son and the Son in the Father.

Jesus asks the Father, concerning his disciples, "that they may all be one, just as you, Father, are in me, and I in you, that they also may be in us, . . ." (John 17:21). Jesus also promises that the Holy Spirit will dwell in believers (John 14:17), and this indwelling will be an indwelling of the Son as well (John 14:20). We may conclude that the Son dwells in the Spirit. This indwelling is called *coinherence* or *perichoresis*.[6]

We can see one way in which coinherence is expressed when we think about the roles of the three persons of the Trinity in language. The Father's wisdom is expressed in the Word. This expression in the Word shows that the Father dwells in the Son. The Father's thought is in the Son. In addition, the Father's word is in the Father even before he expresses it to the world. That implies that the Son dwells in the Father. And the Spirit, as the breath of God, works in power in conformity with the character of the Word. The Spirit is in the Son and the Son is in the Spirit. The Spirit carries out the purpose of the Father, and manifests the power of the Father, which implies that the Father dwells in the Spirit and the Spirit in the Father.

## Speaker, Speech, and Audience

Let us now consider the implications for three foci in communication, namely, speakers, speeches, and hearers. The Trinitarian original has God the Father as speaker and God the Son as discourse, as we have already seen. Who is the audience? There is no human audience for divine speech until the world is created. But John 16:13 mentions the Spirit as one who "hears": "whatever he hears he will speak." The discussion of John 16:13 is in the context of redemption, where the speech will eventually go out and be received by the disciples of Christ. But the idea of the Spirit's hearing can be generalized, because it is surely in harmony with who the Spirit is as an eternal person of the Trinity.

---

6. See ibid., 36–42.

The Spirit is the "breath" of God, according to our earlier argument. But the breath carries the message to a destination in personal recipients. If these are believing human recipients, we know that the Spirit in some ways stands "with" these recipients and enables them faithfully to hear ("illumination"; see 1 John 2:20–27; 1 Cor. 2:14–16). Behind these activities of the Spirit in redemption stands the character of the Spirit as an eternal person of the Trinity. The revelation in redemption invites us to think of the Spirit as recipient (audience) for the Word of God eternally.

In this respect also the persons of the Trinity coinhere. The Spirit receives the Word, and with the Word receives the message and the mind of the Father. The Spirit thus shares in the message of the Word and of the Father, and this sharing is an aspect of the mutual indwelling of the persons.

## Enjoying and Relying on God's Presence and His Goodness

God has impressed his Trinitarian character on language. Whenever we use language, we rely on what he has given us. We also rely on the mutual indwelling of the persons of the Trinity. Because of this indwelling, our use of language holds together. In the use of language, we live in the presence of God who through the Spirit gives us life and through the Spirit empowers our use of language. Tacitly, we are trusting in God's faithfulness and consistency and wisdom. This is true even when non-Christians use language. But they have suppressed awareness of their dependence on God, as Romans 1:19–21 indicates:

> For what can be known about God is plain to them, because God has shown it to them. For his invisible attributes, namely, his eternal power and divine nature, have been clearly perceived, ever since the creation of the world, in the things that have been made. So they are without excuse. For although they knew God, they did not honor him as God or give thanks to him, but they became futile in their thinking, and their foolish hearts were darkened.

# God Speaking

For he spoke, and it came to be;
he commanded, and it stood firm.
—Psalm 33:9

God is infinitely wise, and infinitely deep in his knowledge. If God makes himself known in the textures of language, it means that language itself may have not only one but many indications of its source in God. We should be on the lookout for many ways in which God shows the imprint of his presence. We will gradually explore a number of those ways.

## Acts of Creation

In Genesis 1 the Bible gives the primary account of God's acts in creating the world. God created by speaking:

And God *said*, "Let there be light," and there was light (Gen. 1:3).

And God *said*, "Let there be an expanse in the midst of the waters, and let it separate the waters from the waters." And God made the expanse . . . (Gen. 1:6–7).

Genesis 1 contains no less than eight commandments of this type (Gen. 1:3, 6, 9, 11, 14, 20, 24, 26). In addition, there are two speeches of blessing (Gen. 1:22, 28–30) and three places where God assigns names (Gen. 1:5, 8, 10).[1]

---

1. I am aware that many modern people do not think that Genesis 1–3 recounts real events in time and space. I differ with them. Vern S. Poythress, *Redeeming Science: A God-Centered Approach* (Wheaton, IL: Crossway, 2006), chapter 6, gives some account of Genesis as a literary whole, and

Clearly, God's speaking has a central role in creation. This is confirmed by later statements that indicate that the whole work of creation takes place by speaking:

> By the *word* of the LORD the heavens were made,
>     and by the *breath of his mouth* all their host (Ps. 33:6).

In the beginning was the Word, and the Word was with God, and the Word was God. He was in the beginning with God. All things were made through him, and without him was not any thing made that was made (John 1:1–3).

God also brings about his acts of providence and judgment by speaking:

> Who has *spoken* and it came to pass,
>     unless the Lord has *commanded* it?
> Is it not from the *mouth* of the Most High
>     that good and bad come? (Lam. 3:37–38).

In Lamentations 3:38 the expression "good and bad" is comprehensive, so we may conclude that everything that happens in creation, providence, and redemption happens by God speaking. Of course this is not the only way that the Bible describes God as interacting with the world. But it is a legitimate way—one perspective on his acts.[2]

These activities of God speaking are important for us. If indeed God spoke to create the world, then the world from its beginning, and down to its roots, is structured by God's language. Language is not an alien imposition on the world but the very key to its being and its meaning. And if God governs the world even today through his word, then language, God's language, is also the deepest key to history and to the development of events.

## Three Aspects of God's Speaking

We can further analyze God's speaking in terms of three aspects or motifs: meaning, control, and presence. Why these three? These are not the only possibilities. Any attribute of God might be used as a perspective on what it means for

---

why it is correct from the standpoint of literary analysis to see Genesis as recounting real events. Chapters 2–3 of the same book give some indications of why we need to trust the Bible. The harmony between Genesis and modern scientific evidence is discussed in chapters 7–10.

2. On perspectives, see Vern S. Poythress, *Symphonic Theology: The Validity of Multiple Perspectives in Theology* (Grand Rapids, MI: Zondervan, 1987; reprinted, Phillipsburg, NJ: Presbyterian & Reformed, 2001); John M. Frame, *Perspectives on the Word of God: An Introduction to Christian Ethics* (Phillipsburg, NJ: Presbyterian & Reformed, 1990); Frame, *The Doctrine of the Knowledge of God* (Phillipsburg, NJ: Presbyterian & Reformed, 1987); Frame, *The Doctrine of the Christian Life* (Phillipsburg, NJ: Presbyterian & Reformed, 2008).

God to speak. I pick these three terms because they will prove useful in several respects.

First, the three terms are closely related to attributes of God: Meaning is related to the fact that God knows everything (God's "omniscience"). Control expresses the fact that God has boundless power and rules over everything (God's "omnipotence"). Presence says that God is present everywhere—his "omnipresence." Using these three aspects, we can trace implications of the character of God for thinking about language.

Second, the three terms are closely related to the triad of lordship that John M. Frame has widely employed in his books. In his book *Doctrine of the Knowledge of God* Frame introduces three terms—"authority," "control," and "presence"—to describe God's relation to us as covenant Lord.[3] I have substituted "meaning" for "authority" because meaning is particularly important when we consider language, and because meaning is one implication of authority. One significant way in which God expresses his authority over us is by expressing his commandments to us in concrete *meanings* (such as the Ten Commandments). God has authority to specify the meaning of what he creates. And, derivatively, human speakers and authors exercise authority over language in their speaking and writing.

Frame introduced his three terms to try to articulate clearly the biblical teaching concerning God's transcendence and immanence, and to contrast it with various nonbiblical alternatives.[4] All this is pertinent to the study of language as well, because the same issues arise. Thus we can build on Frame's work, rather than doing everything afresh.

Finally, we can see a relation between these three terms and the roles of the persons of the Trinity. The Father is closely associated with being the source of meaning. Meaning originates from the plan of the Father. As executor of the Father's will, the Son is closely associated with control. The Father speaks specific orders in his word, which is the Word of the Son. By means of the Son, the Father carries out his will. And the Holy Spirit is closely associated with the presence of God. In Genesis 1:2 the Spirit hovering over the waters expresses the presence of God in creation. Since persons of the Trinity are coinherent, we expect that the three perspectives on communication, namely, meaning, control, and presence, will also be derivatively coinherent.

## Meaning, Control, and Presence in God's Acts of Creation

Let us now illustrate how meaning, control, and presence are expressed in the acts in which God speaks to create the world. The primary record of God's creative

---

3. Frame, *Doctrine of the Knowledge of God*, especially 15–18.

4. See appendix C.

acts is found in Genesis 1. God repeatedly speaks. And the words he speaks have *meaning*. Each of God's utterances in Genesis 1 has specific meaning, and each specifies what will come forth. Sometimes the utterances include specifications as to how the newly created thing is to function. "Let the earth sprout vegetation, plants yielding seed, and fruit trees bearing fruit in which is their seed, each according to its kind, on the earth" (Gen. 1:11). There are many specific meanings here, about trees, about fruit, about seeds that are in the fruit, about "each according to its kind," and about the process of sprouting, yielding seed, and so on. The word of God is specific in its meaning.

Second, God's words exert *control*. God's word controls the world that he creates. The immensity of his power is clearly exhibited in the immensity of the effects that his word has. As Psalm 148:5 summarizes it, "He commanded and they were created." God's word exhibits his own omnipotence.

Third, the word of God manifests the *presence* of God. The presence of God is made strikingly evident by the fact that God's word has the attributes of God. It has divine power, or omnipotence, as is evident from its power to bring forth created things that match its specification. It has divine wisdom, as is evident from the wisdom displayed in the completed creation. It has divine goodness, as is evident from the goodness of the created product (Gen. 1:31). God's word shows us God. To put it another way, the word of God is God speaking, not a "something" detached and unrelated to God himself. The close relation between God and his speaking anticipates the truth in John 1:1, where the Bible proclaims that "the Word was God."[5]

These three aspects of the word of God, namely, its meaning, control, and presence, are coinherent. They are not neatly separable, as though some parts of his word have meaning, other parts exert control, and still other parts exhibit God's presence. Rather, all three aspects are there in everything that God speaks. They are coinherent because they reflect the coinherence or mutual indwelling of the three persons of the Trinity.

We can also see that the three aspects of the word of God are coinherent by remembering that the three aspects are related to attributes of God—omniscience, omnipotence, and omnipresence. These three attributes of God are not neatly separable. They are not "parts" of God, but each characterizes all of God. God's omnipotence is an omniscient omnipotence, and his omnipresence is an omniscient, omnipotent omnipresence. For God to be present is to be present with his power and knowledge, thus implying control and meaning. God's control, in his

---

5. For further reflections on the divine attributes of God's word, and for the relation of the plurality of "words" to the one "Word," the second person of the Trinity, see Vern S. Poythress, *God-Centered Biblical Interpretation* (Phillipsburg, NJ: Presbyterian & Reformed, 1999), chapter 3. John Frame's class lectures at Westminster Seminary first drew my attention to the divine attributes of the word of God.

omnipotence, is never an irrational control but is always exercised in accordance with his wisdom and his meaning. We could obviously extend these observations to encompass other attributes of God.

The coinherence of aspects is evident in God's speeches in creation. Consider "Let there be light" (Gen. 1:3). The utterance brings about the creation of light, exhibiting God's control or omnipotence. And the result is light, not something else. It has all the meaning of light. We can say that the created thing and its meaning correspond to the meaning of God's utterance. Control impresses the meaning in God's mind on the world of light, and the meaning that God has in mind specifies beforehand what the control will accomplish. Control and meaning go together. Meaning exhibits the wisdom of God, and therefore expresses his *presence* in wisdom. So God is present in light, by displaying his wisdom. Conversely, God's presence, because it is the presence of God in his fullness, always includes the presence of his control and his meaning (see chart 3.1).

| Aspects of God's Word | Related Attribute of God | Illustration |
|---|---|---|
| meaning | omniscience | light is specified *as light* |
| control | omnipotence | God's command makes light exist |
| presence | omnipresence | God shows his goodness, power, and purity in light |

CHART 3.1

## God's Word to Human Beings

The three aspects of the word of God—meaning, control, and presence—also characterize the words that God speaks to human beings. This result is to be expected, since the three aspects express God's attributes and his lordship. His lordship belongs to everything he does, including all his interactions with human beings.

The Bible contains two early instances of God's communication to human beings before the fall:

> And God said to them, "Be fruitful and multiply and fill the earth and subdue it and have dominion over the fish of the sea and over the birds of the heavens and over every living thing that moves on the earth." And God said, "Behold, I have given you every plant yielding seed that is on the face of all the earth, and every tree with seed in its fruit. You shall have them for food. And to every beast of the earth and to every bird of the heavens and to everything that creeps on the earth, everything that has the breath of life, I have given every green plant for food" (Gen. 1:28–30).

And the LORD God commanded the man, saying, "You may surely eat of every tree of the garden, but of the tree of the knowledge of good and evil you shall not eat, for in the day that you eat of it you shall surely die" (Gen. 2:16–17).

Let us focus on the second of these two speeches (Gen. 2:16–17). The distinction made between the tree of the knowledge of good and evil and the other trees is obviously a use of *meaning*, distinguishing one thing from another. That may be the most obvious expression of meaning, but of course the whole speech is full of meaning, and each word within it has meaning: "tree," "eat," "you," and so on. Next, the threat of death expresses God's *control* over the consequences.

Finally, consider the theme of God's *presence*. God gave the trees and their fruit to man. He expresses his bounty, and therefore the speech expresses his presence in his goodness. In fact, every aspect of the speech expresses God's presence. God is making known to man some of the contents of his mind and his plan. It is *his* mind and *his* plan, and so man comes to know God himself in some of the ways that God thinks.

We could multiply examples expressing the three aspects of the word of God, if we extended these observations to the word of God spoken after the fall. Every word of God manifests his lordship, and therefore includes all three aspects in a unity.

When we as human beings listen to the Bible, we are listening to God's word. We experience his meaning, his control, and his presence. We learn specific information and hear specific commands (meaning); we are transformed as our minds are renewed (control; Rom. 12:1–2); and we have spiritual communion with him (presence).

## The Origin of Language

In the midst of this richness, let us not forget the obvious. Language originates with God, not with man.

# CHAPTER 4

# God's Creation of Man

Blessed are you, O Lord;
teach me your statutes!
With my lips I declare
all the rules of your mouth.

—Psalm 119:12–13

Genesis 1 says that God created man in his own image (Gen. 1:26–27). What are the implications for our thinking about language?

Genesis 1 implies that man is *like* God. He is like God in any number of respects, and the declaration in Genesis 1:26–27 about being made in the image of God invites us to find likenesses. God is personal, and man is clearly personal. As an aspect of his personal character, God is able to speak and use language. Human beings likewise are able to speak and use language.[1] Human language and human use of language come about only because God has created human beings with certain capacities, and those capacities reflect capacities in God himself. That is, God is the "archetype," the original. Man is an "ectype," derivative, creaturely, but still imaging God. So we should expect that human language would reflect divine language in any number of ways.

---

1. But the capacity to use language can be damaged by genetic defects, developmental defects, injuries, mental derangement, dementia, etc. These deviations from what human beings might be show the unsatisfactory character of this present fallen world. The fall will come up for discussion at a later point.

## Adam's Naming the Animals

After Adam was created, his first active accomplishment, as recorded in Genesis 2, involved a use of language. He named the animals:

> Now out of the ground the LORD God had formed every beast of the field and every bird of the heavens and brought them to the man to see what he would call them. And whatever the man called every living creature, that was its name. The man gave names to all livestock and to the birds of the heavens and to every beast of the field. But for Adam there was not found a helper fit for him (Gen. 2:19–20).

In Genesis 1 God gave names to some of the created things: "God called the light Day, and the darkness he called Night" (Gen. 1:5); "And God called the expanse Heaven" (Gen. 1:8); "God called the dry land Earth, and the waters that were gathered together he called Seas" (Gen. 1:10). It follows that in Genesis 2 Adam was imitating God in the process of naming.

## Meaning, Control, and Presence

Man's speech shows meaning, control, and presence. In this respect it images the meaning, control, and presence of God's speech. Naming the animals clearly expresses meaning, in distinguishing different kinds of animals from one another and in expressing the commonality belonging to a group of animals of the same kind.

The making of a name is also an act expressing control over language. "And whatever the man called every living creature, that was its name" (Gen. 2:19). The man established a name for the creature, and from then on that was its name. The man thereby controlled the future of language. In addition, the man exerted control over the animals themselves. In Hebrew culture, naming was not equally everyone's privilege. The power to name belonged to the one who had *authority* to do it. God's naming of created things in Genesis 1 expressed his authority and sovereignty over those things. Likewise, Adam's naming the animals went together with the fact that he had been given dominion over them (Gen. 1:28).

Finally, does Adam's naming express presence? God is omnipresent, and therefore present in every event on earth. But is there also a derivative presence, a presence of Adam as a person in the speeches that he makes? Clearly there is. The speeches express his desires, his thoughts, and his purposes. He intends to name the animals, as an act of his person. And in the lingual act of naming, he expresses that personal intention. It is *Adam* acting, not a robot that happens to have the shape of Adam. So Adam's act of naming expresses his personality. Adam is present in his speech. For correlations between God and the image of God in man, see fig. 4.1.

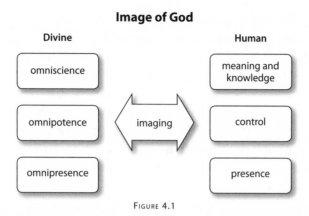

FIGURE 4.1

Human speech depends vitally on all three of these aspects. Without meaning, speech is empty. Without control, it does not accomplish anything, and makes no difference. Without presence, the speech is disconnected from the speaker, and again loses its point. We depend on the fact that we are made in the image of God.

## Speaker, Expression, and Breath

We can see still another analogy between God's speech and human speech. In the Trinity, the language in John 1:1 represents the Father as the speaker, the Son as the speech (the Word), and the Holy Spirit as the breath. This triad in speech is clearly analogous to what happens in human speech. We have a human speaker, his speech, and the breath or other medium that carries the speech to its destination. (See chart 4.1.)

| Divine Speech | Human Speech |
|---|---|
| The Father speaks | speaker |
| The Word (the Son is the discourse) | discourse |
| The Spirit as "breath" | travels to destination |

CHART 4.1

## Coinherence in Human Communication

The language of human beings reflects God's Trinitarian character in another way, namely, in its *coinherence*. The persons of the Trinity dwell in one another. How is this indwelling reflected in man as the image of God?

God is unique, and so the indwelling within the Godhead is also unique. But the Trinitarian indwelling is also analogous to an indwelling in believers about which Jesus speaks: "that they [believers] may all be one, just as you, Father, are *in* me, and I *in* you, that they also may be *in* us, so that the world may believe that you have sent me" (John 17:21). Similarly, within language we can see an analogue to the unique indwelling in the Godhead. If we call the original indwelling within the Godhead *archetypal* coinherence, that is, original coinherence, then this human reflection of it is an *ectypal* coinherence, a derivative coinherence.

Within God, the archetypal coinherence among the persons of the Trinity is displayed in the fact that the Father as the speaker, the Son as the Word spoken, and the Spirit as the "breath" function together in producing God's speech.[2] All three persons participate fully in the entire utterance, and the speech is, as it were, "indwelt" by all three persons.

Now let us consider the analogue, the ectypal indwelling within human speech. Speech presupposes a speaker. A speech without a speaker is virtually an impossibility. Suppose that we found out that something that initially sounded like a speech had been generated by the sound of the waves, or by thunder. We might conclude that it was pure coincidence, and then we would say that, despite appearances, the alleged "speech" turned out to have no meaning, and not to be a speech at all. Or we might decide that it was a miraculous speech from God, and then we would have a speaker, namely, God. Or we might personify the waves or the thunder, or claim that the speech came from a spirit within the waves or the thunder, in which case we would still have a personal speaker.

Thus, a speech is dependent on a speaker, and can be coherently understood only on those terms. The speech must "dwell in" a speaker in order to be a speech. But, conversely, a speaker presupposes a speech. If we are to know what the speaker means, we cannot climb inside his head; we rely on his speech or on some alternate, speech-like mode of communication (like gestures). A speaker is accessible through his speech. He "dwells in" his speech.

And the speech will express the purpose of the speaker to accomplish something, to persuade or amuse or inform someone (even if, as in the exceptional case of soliloquy, the "someone" is actually the speaker himself). The speech goes to its destination through breath, or through some breath-like medium of communication. Without a medium and a transfer, there is no speech at all. The speech must "dwell in" its breath or its medium. Conversely, without the meaning content, there is no speech at all. The breath must "dwell in" a speech and its meaning in order to be a speech at all. Without a speaker and his intentions, there is no speech at all. The breath must issue from a speaker, and "dwell in" the speaker. Each starting point points us toward the *whole* speech, not simply a part of it. But each starting point or perspective is different. As shown in the following

---

2. See chapter 2.

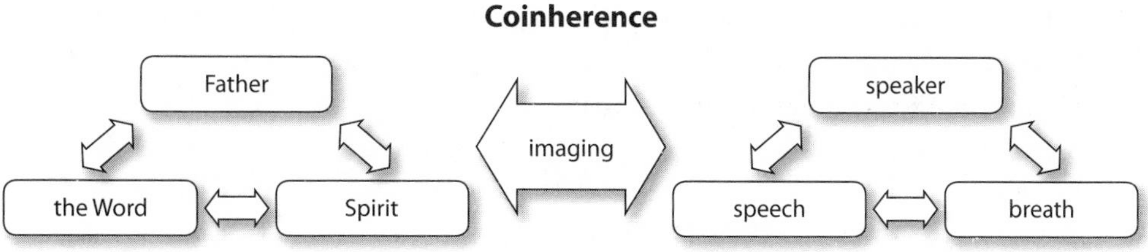

**Coinherence**

FIGURE 4.2

illustration (fig. 4.2), this is an analogue within created speakers to the mutual indwelling of the persons of the Trinity.

## Author, Text, and Reader

With a slight shift of focus, we can expand our horizon to talk about implications for the way we think about three foci in communication: speakers, speeches, and audiences. If we include written as well as oral communication, we may include authors, texts, and readers.[3]

In the Trinity as archetype, the Father is the speaker, the Son is the discourse, and the Holy Spirit is the hearer. The persons of the Trinity indwell one another in communication.[4]

By analogy (see chart 4.2), there will be a kind of mutual indwelling in human communication. Human speakers express their intentions in speeches that effectively communicate with audiences. And the audiences, when they understand, achieve a measure of coinherence with the truths and intentions and expressions of the speakers. An understanding audience "indwells" the ideas of the speaker.

| Roles of Persons in the Trinity | Roles of Human Persons |
| --- | --- |
| Father as speaker | speaker |
| Son as discourse | speech |
| Spirit as hearer | audience |

CHART 4.2

Unlike the Godhead, finite human beings may sometimes fail in communication. A person in an audience misunderstands a speaker and his discourse. Or the speaker is inept and fails clearly to express his meaning. Or the speaker attempts to deceive his audience, and the speech does not match what he knows. Even in these failures the impulse and expectation are there, among users of language,

---

3. Later we will consider some differences between oral and written communication. But there are clearly many similarities.

4. See chapter 2.

to try to interpret communication. This hope for good communication has of course a perfect model in God, whose communication never fails to express his meaning and to accomplish his purpose:

> So shall my word be that goes out from my mouth;
>     it shall not return to me empty,
> but it shall accomplish that which I purpose,
>     and shall succeed in the thing for which I sent it (Isa. 55:11).

We are made in the image of God. As we grow up within the context of his providential control, we learn to exercise our image-bearing nature through analogical imitation of God. We imitate him when we endeavor to exercise dominion over the world (based on Gen. 1:28–30). We also imitate him in human communication, which goes from speaker to discourse to audience. Even our failures presuppose an underlying desire for true communication, such as we find in God. Even when human communication fails, speaker and audience rely on the God-given standards for true communication in trying to assess the failure.

Even when communication succeeds, it may not succeed *totally*. The speaker may not succeed in expressing in an ideal way everything that he wanted to express. And the audience may not take in every nuance. Nevertheless, there is still a kind of "coinherence." The audience *does* succeed in understanding. We understand enough to cooperate with one another and take the next step forward in mutual aid, in understanding, and in joint tasks. That is how God designed us and the language that we use. We do not need to be a god—to have exhaustive, infinite, and perfect understanding—in order to have genuine understanding.

## Dorothy Sayers's View of Creativity

These reflections based on the Bible find confirmation in what Dorothy Sayers has written about artistic creation. Dorothy Sayers wrote detective stories, so she had firsthand experience with artistic creation. She saw that the creation of man in the image of God is the basis for human ability to create artistic works.[5] Artistic creation imitates the creative activity of God.

Sayers finds in the process of artistic creation an analogy to the Trinitarian character of God. She observes that any act of human creation has three coinherent aspects, which she names "Idea," "Energy," and "Power." "The Creative Idea" is the idea of the creative work as a whole, even before it comes to expression. "This

---

5. Dorothy L. Sayers, *The Mind of the Maker* (New York: Harcourt, Brace, 1941). See especially, "The Image of God," 19–31.

is the image of the Father."[6] "The Creative Energy" or "Activity" is the process of working out the idea, both mentally and on paper. Sayers describes it as "working in time from the beginning to the end, with sweat and passion. . . . this is the image of the Word."[7] Third is "the Creative Power," "the meaning of the work and its response in the lively soul: . . . this is the image of the indwelling Spirit."[8]

Sayers uses her three terms to describe what happens within an author's mind as he works out his ideas mentally, even if they are never put to paper. In this internal process, the "Power" is the author's experience of receiving the work back, as he takes the position of an observer of his own idea and work. But Sayers also applies the terms to a work that goes out into the world, gets printed in a book, and gets read by readers. Then the readers experience its Power. At this stage, the term "Power" is obviously related most closely to the audience or readership, while the Idea is attached to the author, and the Energy or Activity to the Discourse itself. Thus Sayers is advocating a variation on what we observed, namely, that the process of communication, from author to text to reader, has a Trinitarian original. Communication goes from the Father to the Word to the Spirit.

Sayers also observes that each of the three aspects—Idea, Activity, and Power—is intelligible only in the context of the others. She affirms the coinherence or indwelling of each in the others.

## The Distinctiveness of God as Creator and Sovereign

We have so far emphasized the similarities between God and man in the use of language. But there are also differences. Man is made in the image of God, but he is not God. The Bible, unlike various forms of pantheism and panentheism, maintains a clear distinction between God and human beings. God is the Creator, while human beings are creatures. Adam is not supposed to exercise an independent judgment concerning the tree of the knowledge of good and evil, nor he is the author or semi-author of the tree's unique character and the prohibition (Gen. 2:17). He must obey a restriction originating in God and not in him. Man is not semidivine but is completely subject to God's authority. Human beings are not to worship sun, moon, stars, or animals, as some of the pagan nations surrounding Israel did. They are to worship God alone.

So there will be distinctions also in human use of language in comparison with God's use. God's language, "Let there be light," is all-powerful (omnipotent). Human use of language exercises *control*, but not exhaustive control. A human being shows "potence"—"power," if you will—but not all power. He expresses

---

6. Ibid., 37. The context of Sayers's work is worth reading, for a fuller explanation of the distinctions among the three aspects.

7. Ibid.

8. Ibid., 37–38.

meaning, but not meaning of which he knows the infinite depths. He is not all-knowing, omniscient. He is present in his speech, but is not capable in the context of his bodily presence and bodily limitations of sending out his speech equally to every place in the universe. He is present, in the body, but not everywhere present (omnipresent).

## Harmony in Human Language Functions, Due to God

Human beings, then, are limited; they are finite. The limitations might appear to be a problem, if human beings had to make themselves self-existent, autonomous, and totally independent of God. How then could they guarantee that human language, in its meaning, control, and presence, would function reliably? For example, how can we know that our word for "dog" matches the character of the world out there, the world in which we meet dogs?

In a God-created world, a world that God pronounced "very good" (Gen. 1:31), we know there is harmony. First of all, human beings were created to be in personal harmony with God. But in addition, God gave them the gift of language in complete harmony with who they were. He made the world of light and dry land and plants and animals in harmony with human nature. He gave human beings dominion over this world, and we may infer that this dominion, rather than being the sometimes exploitative and cruel dominion exercised by fallen human beings, was a dominion in harmony not only with the character of God and with the character of human beings, but also with the character of the world. And it was in harmony with the character of language. Our word for "dog," and our thinking about dogs, is in harmony with the world of dogs.

A human being's knowledge of his own language and language use is finite. He cannot remember in detail how he learned the word "dog." He does not see to the very bottom. But he does not need to see to the very bottom. The key to a solution is in his personal fellowship with God. Before the fall of man and his rebellion against God, there was no barrier to personal fellowship between God and man. Adam knew God. He heard the word of God. And the sense of God's presence and God's goodness was imprinted firmly on his mind. He relied on God and trusted that God was good. And so he could confidently assume that the language that God gave him, and the world of his environment, were suitable for him. He knew that his word for "dog" was designed by God as a fitting help for his task. He could go forward in confidence not because he was omnipotent, omniscient, and omnipresent, but because God as the infinite God guaranteed the harmony of his finite functioning in dependence on God.

Adam's meanings were not meanings imposed on alien material, but meanings from a mind made in the image of God, and therefore a mind in tune with the world.

When Adam named the animals, his control did not smash the world and destroy what the world was "in itself." Rather, God designed Adam's control to be a blessing not only to himself but to the world: "to work it [the garden] and keep it" (Gen. 2:15). Adam's control through language was not a distortion of the world but a naming that drew the world toward the destiny planned by God from the beginning.

The presence of language was not something that Adam and Eve could "climb out of" to see the world as it really is. But they did not need to climb out of it, because, on the basis of the good creating activity of God, they were already in harmony with the world as it really is.

In short, difficulties that some of us modern human beings may feel very keenly, because we are alienated from God, created no substantive difficulty while human beings lived in fellowship with God—in harmony with God, with the world that God created, and with the language that God had given.

## Language as Shared

A particular human language is normally not the exclusive possession of only one human being. Native speakers of English share English with all other native speakers, and to a lesser extent with those for whom English is a second language. Language has a communal dimension built into it.

Linguistic analysis has customarily paid attention to the community of human speakers. But the Bible presents an important difference. It begins not with a human speaker but with God as the divine speaker: "Let there be light" (Gen. 1:3). Later on, human beings appear on the scene. But the very first recorded lingual communications involving a human being also involve God. God addresses human beings in Genesis 1:28–30 and 2:16–17.

Adam and Eve share language not only with each other but also with God. From the beginning, as part of God's design for creation, language is given to human beings for divine-human communication as well as human-human communication. Tellingly, there was divine-human communication even before human-human communication was possible. God communicated to Adam in Genesis 2:16–17 *before* Eve was created, *before* Adam had any other human being with whom to communicate.

So human language is not merely for human beings. God spoke in the initial communications to Adam. He would continue to speak to Adam and Eve, and Adam and Eve and their descendants would continue to speak to him. The conversation would have continued in a harmonious personal relationship, over the years, if Adam and Eve had not sinned. Even though they did sin, God still continued to speak with them (Gen. 3:9–19). So God is part of the community of language users. One of the purposes of language—in fact, a central, predominant purpose—is to be a vehicle for personal communication and communion between God and human beings.

If, then, we believe the narrative in Genesis, we have a clear basis for confidence about language. Language is not only capable of expressing knowledge of God, but God designed it specifically for this purpose, and his design is masterful. Language is supremely capable of doing what God himself designed it to do. A word like the word for "dog" is masterfully designed to facilitate our thinking and communicating about dogs and their relation to the larger context that God designed.

## Modern Approaches to Language

We may contrast this view with most modernist and postmodernist thinking about language.[9] In the twentieth century, structural linguistics has mostly assumed *from the beginning*, in the foundation of the discipline, that language and communication are *purely human*, that is, that God either does not exist or that he can be factored out of the picture. The same goes for the sociological study of human communication. Otherwise, how could these disciplines hope to be scientific?

But the aspiration of such disciplines to be scientific is itself loaded. To begin with, it may be loaded with the assumption that somehow human beings can be treated exactly as if they were on the same level as animals or rocks or other creatures over which human beings are granted dominion. It ignores the fact that we are made in the image of God. But even more seriously, it ignores the possibility that our modern conception of science, taken from the existing state of the natural sciences, has already been distorted by a systematic human flight in the direction of denying the presence of God in science.[10] The aspiration to be "scientific" may already have introduced biases.

So, according to this modernist viewpoint, God is emphatically *not* a participant in lingual and social communication. But from a biblical point of view, the move to exclude God ignores *the* single most important fact about communication and the most weighty ontological fact about language. It has distorted the subject matter that we study, and so we can only anticipate a multitude of repercussions when it comes to the detailed analysis of the subject.

---

9. On modernism and postmodernism, see appendix A.

10. See Vern S. Poythress, *Redeeming Science: A God-Centered Approach* (Wheaton, IL: Crossway, 2006).

# God Sustaining Language

The LORD has established his throne in the heavens,
and his kingdom rules over all.
—Psalm 103:19

Now let us look at God's relation to the present day and its processes. God's faithfulness guarantees that there will be a stability to the things that he has created. And this stability extends to human beings. We have the same bodies and the same memories from one day to the next—though, of course, there are also gradual changes. One aspect of this stability is that we are persons, and that we have the capacity to use and understand language.

God's governance over our world extends even to details: "You [God] cause the grass to grow for the livestock and plants for man to cultivate" (Ps. 104:14). Scientists explore the regular patterns in God's governance, regularities that are based on God's faithfulness and consistency.[1] God controls even seemingly random events: "The lot is cast into the lap, but its every decision is from the LORD" (Prov. 16:33; see also 1 Kings 22:20, 34). God controls everything: "The LORD has established his throne in the heavens, and his kingdom rules over *all*" (Ps. 103:19). "Who has spoken and it came to pass, unless the Lord has commanded it? Is it not from the mouth of the Most High that good and bad come?" (Lam. 3:37–38).

We can conclude, then, that God's control extends to language as well, and to its details. God controls and specifies the meaning of "go" in English. He controls

---

1. See Vern S. Poythress, *Redeeming Science: A God-Centered Approach* (Wheaton, IL: Crossway, 2006), especially chapter 1, pp. 13–31, and chapters 13–14, pp. 177–195.

and specifies the meaning of each word—not only in English but in Hindi, Vietnamese, Italian, and every other language, living or dead. He also controlled the original splitting apart of the distinct languages of the world, as the account of Babel shows (Gen. 11:1–9).

God's control over human affairs does raise a concern. How can God's control be consistent with human responsibility, and with human sin?[2] The Bible nowhere fully explains how, but it does show that God is in control of human affairs. In the first sermon in the book of Acts, Peter declares, "This Jesus, delivered up according to the definite plan and foreknowledge of God, you crucified and killed by the hands of lawless men" (Acts 2:23). The expression "the definite plan and foreknowledge of God" indicates that God brought about all the events in accordance with his plan. The mention of "lawless men" indicates, however, that human beings like Herod, Pontius Pilate, and the Jewish leaders who brought about the crucifixion were responsible for their unjust deeds.

God brought about salvation through Christ's crucifixion, and his purposes were wholly good. The human beings had evil motives. Acts 4:27–28 expresses similar principles: "For truly in this city there were gathered together against your holy servant Jesus, whom you anointed, both Herod and Pontius Pilate, along with the Gentiles and the peoples of Israel, to do *whatever your hand and your plan had predestined* to take place."

There are two levels of action here. Theologians have classically spoken of "primary cause" and "secondary cause." God as creator and ruler is the *primary cause* of the events of Christ's crucifixion. Human beings like Pilate acted on the level of *secondary cause*. Both of the two are real and valid. But they are not on the same level, as though God were merely another human being, with greater power, who wrestled with the other human beings in order to force things to go his way instead of their way. No, God as creator is simply not on the level of his creatures. We are not able fully to conceptualize how he acts, because we are finite and he is infinite. We could discuss these matters at much greater length, but we must leave that to other books.[3] It is enough for the present for us to understand that God's control does not undermine the genuineness of human participation and human responsibility.

---

2. It has become fashionable in some religious circles nowadays not only to refashion the role of the Bible but to refashion the conception of God, in order for it to match various modern expectations and sensibilities. I believe that such refashioning is a great mistake, for reasons that will become clear when later on we discuss the fall of mankind and the contrast between Christian and non-Christian thinking about God.

3. For further discussion of God's sovereignty and providential control, see Poythress, *Redeeming Science*, 181–183, 193–195; John M. Frame, *The Doctrine of God* (Phillipsburg, NJ: Presbyterian & Reformed, 2002), 47–79; and other Reformed theological books on God.

## Authority, Good and Bad

We should briefly consider one other issue related to God's control. Nowadays many Americans and Europeans distrust authority. And they have some good reasons for distrust. Parents, politicians, governments, employers, advertisers, and religious leaders have grievously disappointed them. People with power have run roughshod over those under them.

God is the biggest authority of all. So is his authority the most dangerous? In one sense, yes. People can falsely appeal to God's authority in order to manipulate others. Such manipulation is particularly dangerous because people *claiming* to have God's authority can try to make their ideas and actions unchallengeable. Manipulation can then be all the more oppressive. But such manipulation misuses God's name.

So what should we do? Should we repudiate all authority? That is one temptation. But if we abolished governmental authorities, those who are powerful would have no governmental restraint and might further exploit the weak. Rather, we should respond by seeking good exercise of authority in order to drive out the bad. God is the ultimate *good* authority. But as fallen humans we start out with distorted ideas about God, and distorted hopes for what we think is a good life. We have been disappointed in God, because we do not know or understand or love him.

I cannot here undertake to address every aspect of this disappointment with and this alienation from God. A classic book from Billy Graham, *Peace with God*, has helped many.[4] Many other books that explain the teaching of the Bible could be cited. And of course there is the Bible itself, which I would recommend if you are struggling in this area. At the heart of the Bible is the record of Christ's life, found in the four Gospels, Matthew, Mark, Luke, and John. Knowing Christ enables us to know God as he really is, and to overcome our alienation from him.

Here we can focus only on one part of the whole picture, namely, language. God has authority over language, and it is good authority.

4. Billy Graham, *Peace with God* (Waco, TX: Word, 1984).

# Creativity in Language

"Behold, the former things have come to pass,
and new things I now declare;
before they spring forth
I tell you of them."

—Isaiah 42:9

Human speech involves creativity. And this creativity derives from God. Let us look at creativity more closely, because it is an emphasis complementary to the fact that God is in control.

## Creativity among Human Beings

Creativity is an important aspect of human life. Dorothy Sayers sees a clear analogy between God's activity as Creator and the human creativity of an artist. But she also observes that artists are not unique in their exercise of creativity; rather, they show in a more dramatic form the kind of creativity that belongs to workers of all kinds.[1]

Because we are made in the image of God, we are made to be creative, each of us in his own sphere. None of us is a carbon copy of anyone else. And we all meet challenges in our circumstances that have never before appeared in exactly the same way. Challenges arise about how to deal both with people and with material things in the environment. God expects us to be creative in meeting those challenges:

---

1. Dorothy L. Sayers, *The Mind of the Maker* (New York: Harcourt, Brace, 1941), 179–216.

Look carefully then how you walk, not as unwise but as wise, making the best use of the time, because the days are evil. Therefore do not be foolish, but understand what the will of the Lord is. And do not get drunk with wine, for that is debauchery, but be filled with the Spirit, . . . (Eph. 5:15–18).

God gives us moral rules for living, as summarized in the Ten Commandments. But his commandments call for application to our specific circumstances, and in the application we need God's wisdom to be insightful about the circumstances, and to be creative in exercising love.[2] Human creativity, rightly understood, does not produce tension with God's rules but acts in harmony with the rules in reaching out to new situations and needs. God's rules and God's creativity are in harmony. And so likewise it ought to be with us. Being filled with the Holy Spirit, the very Spirit of God, gives us power from God both to keep his rules and to be creative, with the creativity that the Holy Spirit brings.

## Creativity in Language

Creativity has a place in language. In speaking, we speak in a language such as English that already is there and follows certain rules. But we also exercise creativity. We say things that have never been said before. Even when we speak a sentence that has already been said before, we say it in new circumstances, and in that way we are creative. We are speaking within our fresh circumstances in a way that has never occurred before and never will occur again.

There are literally millions of possibilities for what we could say. The *Oxford English Dictionary*, second edition, contains over 600,000 definitions.[3] Even with a very basic vocabulary of 4,000 words, there are millions of ways of forming a single sentence. Suppose, within the small vocabulary of 4,000 words, we have 1,000 common nouns and 1,000 transitive verbs (verbs that can take an object). We then start with a simple sentence: "The woman saw the dog on the street." Suppose that 1,000 different nouns can replace "woman," 1,000 different verbs can replace "saw," 1,000 different nouns can replace "dog," and 1,000 different nouns can replace "street." The total number of possible ways to revise that sentence is then 1,000 x 1,000 x 1,000 x 1,000, or one trillion.

Actually, many of these combinations will result in nonsense statements such as "The box obeyed the leaf on the sky." But this simple calculation still illustrates

---

2. See John M. Frame, *The Doctrine of the Christian Life* (Phillipsburg, NJ: Presbyterian & Reformed, 2008), especially with regard to the perspectival relation among rules (normative perspective), situations (situational perspective), and motives (love, the existential perspective). The existential perspective shows the value of human creativity.

3. J. A. Simpson and E. S. C. Weiner, eds., *Oxford English Dictionary*, 2nd ed. (Oxford/New York: Oxford University Press, 1989). The statistic is from <http://en.wikipedia.org/wiki/English_vocabulary#Number_of_words_in_English>.

the way in which each choice multiplies the number of possibilities, and very soon the total number of possibilities becomes astronomical. And a single sentence is only the beginning, since we then have the opportunity of choosing to put sentences together into longer discourses.[4] God, through the gift of language, offers us incredibly vast choice, and with it incredible scope for creativity and diversity among different human beings and different things they say. Language in this way provides a small-scale picture of the creativity and diversity in human nature as a whole.

God has provided all the richness of the millions of choices. Without his presence and his action, there would be no words, no choices to make among words, and no constructions making sentences; more fundamentally still, there would be no human beings to make the choices.

Human beings really do make these choices, minute by minute, day after day, every time they speak. Their choices are real, and they are significant. Sometimes the significance of any one choice may seem very small. But it is there, and God sees it. "For a man's ways are before the eyes of the LORD, and he ponders all his paths" (Prov. 5:21). Sometimes the choices are weighty:

> "And if it is evil in your eyes to serve the LORD, *choose* this day whom you will serve, whether the gods your fathers served in the region beyond the River, or the gods of the Amorites in whose land you dwell. But as for me and my house, we will serve the LORD." ...
>
> And the people said to Joshua, "No, but we will serve the LORD." Then Joshua said to the people, "You are witnesses against yourselves that you have *chosen* the LORD, to serve him." And they said, "We are witnesses" (Josh. 24:15, 21–22).

This creativity in our speech is closely related to the motif of control. We exercise control by choosing to say one thing and not another. Our ability to control

---

4. Consider a medium-sized book of about 100,000 words. Its sentences will include some "connective" words like "of" and "a," for which there may not be many substitutes. But, if we allow for some fairly nonsensical sentences, at least a third of the words may have at least 1,000 substitutes: 1,000 possible nouns could substitute for a particular noun, or 1,000 verbs for a verb. The total number of possible books of 100,000 words is then something in the range of $10^{100,000}$ (the number 1 followed by 100,000 zeros), an unimaginably large number. By comparison, the estimated number of protons in the observable universe is about $10^{78}$.

People have speculated about the possibility that monkeys typing at random on typewriters could, given enough time, produce the complete works of Shakespeare. But if each proton in the universe were to become a monkey, and each monkey were to produce one whole book per day, after a trillion years we would have only $4 \times 10^{92}$ books. This entire process would have to be repeated something like $2 \times 10^{99,907}$ times to get close to the total of $10^{100,000}$ possible books. (And this picture presumes that monkeys type nothing except actual words, rather than random sequences of letters.)

reflects God's ability. It is God, first of all, who chooses to speak creatively. He chooses to say one thing, "Let there be light," and not another, "Let there be unicorns." His creativity is the basis for our own lesser creativity. Interestingly, his creativity is not at odds with his control. Rather, it illustrates his control. God controls his own speech when he chooses to say one thing rather than another. And through his speech he controls the world, choosing to create horses rather than unicorns.

## Roots of Creativity in the Trinity

God's creativity is rooted in his Trinitarian character. Remember that John 1:1 identifies the second person of the Trinity as "the Word." The context of John 1:1 alludes to creation in Genesis 1. The one, eternal Word is behind the particular words that God spoke in creation, and the choices that he made. God's choices in creation were choices that took place in the fellowship between the Father and the Son. The New Testament indicates that the Son as well as the Father is an agent in creation (1 Cor. 8:6; Col. 1:16; Heb. 1:2).

The Father and the Son and the Holy Spirit are in control and are creative in their acts of creating the world and its creatures. At the same time, the Father and the Son are in perfect harmony, in their love for one another, through their mutual indwelling in the Holy Spirit. The Son says, "I always do the things that are pleasing to him" (John 8:29). And, "the Son can do nothing of his own accord, but only what he sees the Father doing. For whatever the Father does, that the Son does likewise" (John 5:19).[5] The same holds with respect to the speech of the Son: "For I have not *spoken* on my own authority, but the Father who sent me has himself given me a commandment—what to *say* and what to *speak*" (John 12:49).

In fact, the most basic biblical representations of the relation of the Father and the Son imply both freedom and harmony. The designation of the persons as "Father" and "Son" shows that they are persons, distinct from one another. Each is God; each therefore has infinite creativity[6] in deciding divine action. Each has creativity when he speaks. On the other hand, the designation of the

---

5. These and other key passages about the relation between the Father and the Son occur in the context of redemptive action by the Son. But we can infer by analogy that similar truths hold concerning the original relation between the Father and the Son in creating the world. We must be careful here, because the redemptive passages are considering the Son in his incarnation, when he is man as well as God. But they are still consistent with who the Son is as God.

6. Sometimes people have construed God's freedom to mean that God could do anything whatsoever, anything we could imagine. But this is not taught in the Bible. For example, God cannot lie (Titus 1:2). He cannot deny himself (2 Tim. 2:13). God cannot do anything inconsistent with his character. But he can do anything he wishes, anything he pleases (Ps. 135:6). His wishes, of course, are always consistent with his character.

Son as "the Word" indicates that he is analogous to a person's speech. The Father, as omnipotent speaker, speaks the Word, who is in *exact* conformity with the Father's intention and will. Similarly, according to Hebrews, "He [the Son] is the radiance of the glory of God and the *exact* imprint of his nature" (Heb. 1:3). Passages such as John 5:19 show the Son during his incarnate state exactly carrying out the will of the Father. Hebrews 1:3 and John 1:1 imply that, even before his incarnation, the Son exactly conformed to the Father's will. In addition, the Father's speech harmonizes with his love for the Son. The Father purposes to glorify the Son (John 8:54; 13:31–32; 17:1–5), and to sum up all things in him (Eph. 1:10, 22). The Son purposes to glorify the Father (John 17:4).

Thus two things go together in the Trinity: (1) The Son has the infinite creativity of God himself; and (2) the Son has infinite conformity to the will of his Father. These are true both when the Son speaks and when he acts in other ways. How can this be so? We do not fully know, because we are describing the infinitude of God himself. But we know that it is so. And we can to some extent even see *how* it is so. The Father delights in the Son and in honoring the Son. The Son *delights* in the Father, and so delights in his Father's will. He has no attraction to any kind of independence that would do otherwise. "Jesus said to them, 'My food is to do the will of him who sent me and to accomplish his work'" (John 4:34). The Father and the Son are in everlasting harmony, in the presence of the Holy Spirit. Their harmony is an expression of the theme of presence. The conformity of the Son is also an expression of the theme of control—control by the Father. The Father as God sovereignly controls all things, including the actions of the Son in history. The Son as sovereign God freely decides and creatively speaks, and his speech is always in harmony with the Father. We affirm the control of the Father, and also the creative speech on the part of the Son.

## The Son in His Humanity

Now let us begin to think about *human* decision making. The Son during his time on earth honored the Father in both his divine nature and his human nature. The will of the divine Son was in full conformity to the will of his Father, and the human will of his human nature submitted to the will of the Father, even when it took him to the cross:

> And going a little farther he fell on his face and prayed, saying, "My Father, if it be possible, let this cup pass from me; nevertheless, not as I will, but as you will." . . . Again, for the second time, he went away and prayed, "My Father, if this cannot pass unless I drink it, your will be done" (Matt. 26:39, 42).

"For this reason the Father loves me, because I lay down my life that I may take it up again. No one takes it from me, but I lay it down of my own accord. I have authority to lay it down, and I have authority to take it up again. This charge I have received from my Father" (John 10:17–18).

"Now is my soul troubled. And what shall I say? 'Father, save me from this hour'? But for this purpose I have come to this hour. Father, glorify your name." Then a voice came from heaven: "I have glorified it, and I will glorify it again" (John 12:27–28).

Jesus is fully man as well as fully God. He had to be fully man in order to represent us as the last Adam, and in order to be our sin-bearer. And he had to be a *willing* sin-bearer:

> When he was reviled, he did not revile in return; when he suffered, he did not threaten, but continued entrusting himself to him who judges justly. He himself bore our sins in his body on the tree, that we might die to sin and live to righteousness (1 Pet. 2:23–24).

Jesus freely entered into the path that the Father laid before him. Through his work he brought into being a "new creation" (2 Cor. 5:17). At the same time, his path of suffering and the coming of new creation had been prophesied beforehand, in Isaiah 53 and other passages that predicted his sufferings and subsequent glory (Isa. 53:11–12; 59:19; 60:1; 65:17).

## Human Creativity in Harmony with God

Among other things, Jesus offers a model for understanding human creativity. His work was unique. He alone was able to begin the new creation by rising from the dead. But in an analogous way we too can be creative as we enter into fellowship with him. The key to creativity is fellowship with God, who is the unique Creator. Jesus brought forth the new creation of eternal life by being in fellowship with the Father, obeying the will of the Father, and being filled with the Holy Spirit (Rom. 8:11; Acts 2:33).

Through Jesus we have our fellowship restored with God (2 Cor. 5:18). Then we can be creative, in imitation of God's creativity. We are stimulated because we begin to understand God, and the vastness of God's mind opens up new directions and new thoughts. We blossom as whole people, who are no longer slaves to sin (Rom. 6:20–21). And if we blossom as whole people, we blossom as speakers as well. We learn to be creative in what we say, because through renewal in the Holy Spirit we become creative in what we think. "God's love has been poured into our hearts through the Holy Spirit who has been given to us" (Rom. 5:5).

By contrast, those who rebel against God like to think that creativity comes from being independent of God. But such independence is nothing more than slavery to sin (Rom. 6:20–21).

God planned beforehand the earthly life of Christ, as is evident from the way in which it fulfills many Old Testament texts. Jesus talks repeatedly about what "must" take place (Matt. 16:21; 26:54; Luke 24:26). So it is with us, by analogy. All our days are planned by God beforehand: "in your book were written, every one of them, the days that were formed for me, when as yet there were none of them" (Ps. 139:16). God planned our good works beforehand: "For we are his workmanship, created in Christ Jesus for *good works*, which God *prepared beforehand*, that we should walk in them" (Eph. 2:10). Such planning includes our speech: "Even before a word is on my tongue, behold, O Lord, you know it altogether" (Ps. 139:4).

Such planning on God's part is consistent with creative human action. Jesus willingly obeyed his Father and carried out his will. He made decisions throughout his life, decisions to follow God's way rather than a selfish way. We see his creativity in the unexpected ways that he dealt with social outcasts. We see it also in the way that he rejected the typical worldly routes to power, and was willing to go to the cross.

The analogy between God and a human creative artist can perhaps be helpful. If a human creative artist writes a novel, he commissions the characters in the novel to act creatively, in accordance with the personalities that they possess by virtue of his creative activity. The characters make decisions, and act creatively, and produce consequences. At the same time, the author controls the entire novel. The analogy is imperfect, but it points back to the deeper reality, where God the Father commissions his Son to make choices, and these choices always harmonize with the Father's plan.

We also are called on to obey willingly. The good works are prepared "that we should *walk* in them." In fact, the presence of God encourages and empowers our working:

> Therefore, my beloved, as you have always obeyed, so now, not only as in my presence but much more in my absence, *work out* your own salvation with fear and trembling, for it is God who works in you, both to will and to work for his good pleasure (Phil. 2:12–13).

> Therefore, my beloved brothers, be steadfast, immovable, always abounding in the *work* of the Lord, knowing that in the Lord your labor is not in vain (1 Cor. 15:58).

Among these good works are good works in our speech. We can become creative in speaking words that bring a blessing to those who hear:

Let no corrupting talk come out of your mouths, but only such as is good for building up, as fits the occasion, that it may give grace to those who hear. And do not grieve the Holy Spirit of God, by whom you were sealed for the day of redemption (Eph. 4:29–30).[7]

---

7. For other cases of creativity in human speech, see appendix J.

# Exploring Examples of Language

O you who dwell in the gardens,

with companions listening for your voice;

let me hear it.

—Song of Solomon 8:13

What does God's involvement with language look like? We can illustrate with a simple example.

## A Sample of Language

Suppose I say to my wife, "I am going to the store to get more bananas." She understands the word "going" and all the other words that I have used. Let us focus on the word "going." It is one of several grammatical forms of the word "go."[1] What does "go" mean? You can look it up in a dictionary: "1: to move on a course: PROCEED ... 2: to move out of or away from a place expressed or implied: LEAVE, DEPART <they *went* from school to the party> <she is *going* away for the summer> ...."[2]

"Go" is a common word, and everyone who knows English already knows what it means. We do not need to look it up. The dictionary makes explicit what native speakers know instinctively or implicitly. And it is important that speakers have

---

1. Technically, "going" consists of two "morphemes," namely, the root *go-* and the suffix *-ing*. But we will not get into the complexities just yet.

2. *Webster's Ninth New Collegiate Dictionary.*

this knowledge *in common*. If my wife and I did not have a common knowledge of "go," communication would not succeed.

We can look in a similar way at every other word in the sentence spoken to my wife: "I," "am," "to," "the," "store," and so on. Each one has a meaning, which a dictionary tries to summarize. Each one also has a sound, if spoken orally, and a spelling, if written down. The sounds of different words are distinct, so that my wife knows *which* word I have said. (Occasionally, different words, like "site" and "sight" and "cite," have the same sound. But the context usually enables us to tell them apart.)

Using language is so natural to us that we typically do not think about all the knowledge and all the kinds of organization in language on which we are relying. Once we look under the surface, however, we find astonishing complexity and astonishing detail in structure. This complexity has been established by God, as part of his overall plan for the universe and for our role in it.

## God's Involvement in Language

We have the word "go" in English. It has meaning and sound and spelling that God has given it. It also has a history behind it; it is part of the story of the English language and its development. And it has a history in my personal life. I had to learn English as I grew up. I learned the meaning and the sound of "go" through hearing it used by others. Thus human beings had a decisive role. Both my parents and my immediate friends, and those who preceded them through the centuries, were involved in transmitting this word "go" to me.

God sovereignly rules over and controls all these events in my past and the past of others who transmitted the word "go." It is important to say so. Otherwise, instead of thinking in terms of the God of the Bible, we will probably be thinking in terms of an absentee god, for example the god of deism. Deism says that a god created the world and set it going at the beginning. But after that he is distant and essentially uninvolved. The world goes on simply by itself, like a clock that has been wound up and can then keep on ticking. The god of deism would be involved in our present-day language only in a very indirect way, through his act of creating the world in the very distant past. The God of the Bible, by contrast, is intimately involved with the world at all times, including the present. As *primary cause* he is the one who has controlled the way in which I learned the word "go" from my parents, as well as its present meaning and sound.

God also gave me and other human beings the capacity to use the word "go." He gave me a mouth and a tongue, so that I can form the "g" sound. He gave me vocal chords and lungs, and the ability to hear vibrations in the air at the frequencies with which my vocal chords vibrate. He gave me a brain that can process the vocal sounds that I hear from others. We rely on all these stabilities every time we use the word "go."

God has charge not only of individual words like "go" but of entire utterances like "I am going to the store to get more bananas." The words fit together in a particular way, designed by God, in order to make a complete communication. And there are smaller pieces within the utterance that have an identifiable unity of their own, like the prepositional phrase "to the store," indicating the destination, the infinitive clause "to get more bananas," indicating the purpose, and the noun phrase "more bananas," indicating the object to be obtained.

Ordinarily we take for granted the existence and stability of these pieces. But they can be a source for praising God. God gives us this stability. "Thank you," we can say. God gives us the resources for communication, and the pleasures and accomplishments that come in communication. God is always there, always faithful, always wise, always supplying and sustaining both our bodies and our mental resources and our language resources. God is involved in the details. God gave me the useful word "go."

## Perspectives on Language: The Wave Perspective

We have been looking at language as composed of stable pieces. It is composed of words like "go" that have stable meanings ("proceed, leave, depart"), stable sounds, and stable spellings. It also has larger pieces, such as whole sentences. This way of looking at language as composed of stable pieces is a valid one, and is the most common one among people who are not trained in academic linguistics. The linguist Kenneth L. Pike has dubbed it the "particle view."[3] Within academic linguistics this perspective has its uses, but there are times when linguists may adopt other perspectives, specifically the "wave" perspective or the "field" perspective.[4] What do these perspectives do?

The *wave perspective* looks at language not *primarily* in terms of stable pieces but in terms of process. According to this approach, language is *dynamic*. I say to my wife, "I," followed by "am," followed by "going," and so on, in a process. The pieces are still there, but they can be decomposed. "am" decomposes into

---

3. "The normal, relaxed attitude of the human being in most of his actions treats life as if it were made of particles" (Kenneth L. Pike, *Linguistic Concepts: An Introduction to Tagmemics* [Lincoln and London: University of Nebraska Press, 1982], 19). Pike's approach to language and linguistics, though not as familiar as some other approaches, is congenial to my purposes. For one thing, it explicitly acknowledges the importance of multiple perspectives on language, and in so doing avoids reducing language to a single one of its dimensions. (See appendix F for a discussion of the trade-off between rigor and complexity.) I learned from personal conversations that Pike was also convinced that language contained reflections of the Trinitarian character of God, and the three perspectives that we introduce here are one instance of this pattern.

4. Ibid., 19–38.

a + m, either in sound or in writing. The "a" flows into the "m". The mouth is open in pronouncing "a," and then *gradually* closes at the lips until the lips are pressed together for the "m."

The processes flow. One sound often flows directly into one another in a continuous process. Sometimes words flow into one another, as when a person says "I'm" instead of "I am." And the hearer, my wife, gradually processes what she hears. She hears one sound after another, flowing into one another, and one meaning after another, flowing into one another. The meanings flow because she gradually constructs an impression of what I am intending to communicate. When she hears, "I am," she does not know whether the word "am" will function as part of a helping verb in a verb complex like "am going," or whether it will be a linking verb leading to an adjective: "I am sad." She has to be open for both, but she already knows that "I" is the subject and that "am" is either the whole verb or the beginning of a verbal complex. So she is in the *process* of preparing for the rest of the sentence.

A whole utterance is also part of a larger process. I tell my wife where I am going. I go out the door, go to the store, get the bananas, come back, and tell her, "Here are the bananas." She says, "Couldn't you get any ripe ones?" I say, "No, they only had these under-ripe ones." I put them on top of the refrigerator. They ripen. Eventually we eat them, one by one. Then she goes to the store to get more food. And so on. Processes continue on and on, for a whole lifetime. The verbal communications fit into life processes, and find useful functions within those life processes, which include many *nonverbal* actions and purposes.

The processes involving the bananas fit into one another in complex ways. My utterance before leaving for the store fits into what I do at the store. My explanation, "No, they only had these under-ripe ones," is not only an immediate response to my wife's query but also refers back to the time at the store, and indicates some of the circumstances that led to my less-than-ideal purchase. I nevertheless purchased the bananas, because, from the further past, I already knew something about bananas. I knew that they would ripen if left for a while. That already anticipates what happened after the bananas were set on top of the refrigerator. And of course all these small-scale actions fit the larger purposes that we have in life. I got the bananas because we need food to eat to sustain us, in order to carry on all kinds of activities in work, leisure, child rearing, and socializing. My particular utterance makes sense within a much larger, richer complex of human knowledge, intentions, and plans, and those in turn make sense within a world in which bananas ripen and are good for food.

God is in control of all these processes. God specifies the stabilities of the pieces, as we have seen with regard to the particle perspective. He also specifies the processes. He has designed the world so that one event flows into another, and so that actions have consequences. In fact, "control" is a process, in the usual way in which we think about it. God *acts* and *causes* things to happen in the world. He causes one thing, and then another thing, and then another, as the "primary cause." At the same time there are these secondary causes in human actions, and even in subhuman actions, as when one billiard ball hits another.

God controls the little actions, like my saying the word "am." He controls the bigger actions, like my going to the store. He controls still bigger sequences, namely, entire lifetimes: ". . . in your book were written, every one of them, the *days* that were formed for me, when as yet there were none of them" (Ps. 139:16). God knows all my days, including the days that are still future and unknown to me. By implication, he knows all the details in the days. He knows about each bite of food that I will eat, each time of distress or joy, each work of each cell in my intestines in the process of digestion, each work of each muscle cell in the beating of each heartbeat, each movement of my vocal chords, each movement of my tongue in making a speech. "Even before a word is on my tongue, behold, O LORD, you know it altogether" (Ps. 139:4). He knows the details, and controls them.

He also controls larger groupings, such as periods of human history:

For his dominion is an everlasting dominion, and his kingdom endures from generation to generation; all the inhabitants of the earth are accounted as nothing, and he does according to his will among the host of heaven and among the inhabitants of the earth; and none can stay his hand or say to him, "What have you done?" (Dan. 4:34–35).

The Most High rules the kingdom of men and gives it to whom he will (Dan. 4:32).

There is a God in heaven who reveals mysteries, and he has made known to King Nebuchadnezzar what will be in *the latter days* [concerning several successive kingdoms over a period of hundreds of years] (Dan. 2:28).

God knows the word "go" that I use. He controls not only my immediate memory of the word "go" and its uses but also the entire process of centuries of English-speaking culture that transmitted that word to me. I thank him for it.

To many people nowadays, it might seem that such thorough control from God is also thoroughly oppressive. But it is not. Human decision making, human choices, and human responsibility play a central role in this process. I decide to go to the store. I decide to tell my wife what I am going to do. In the process I am responsible to tell the truth. The language resources that God gave me through my past open up a large number of possibilities: to say nothing, to lie, to tell a joke, to talk about the weather, and so on. The process of speaking involves a large number of choices, each of which is linked to the preceding choices and to choices with respect to my overall plans.

## The Field Perspective

A third way of looking at language is the *field perspective*. We focus on the network or "field" of relations between various parts of language. This focus offers a *relational* perspective on language.

The relations are of many kinds. The word "go" is related in meaning to other words with similar meaning, like "proceed," "depart," "leave," and "move." It is related to verbs of motion like "walk," "run," "drive," and "travel." It is related to words with somewhat contrasting meaning, like "come" and "stop" and "stay" and "remain."

The word "go" also has grammatical relations with its various forms: "go," "going," "went," and "gone." And these relations fit into larger patterns. The relations among the forms of "go" show similarities to the relations that occur in other verbs: "sing," "singing," "sang," and "sung." We can begin to fill out a chart of verb forms (chart 7.1).

### Verb Forms

| Simple Present | Participle | Simple Past | Past Participle |
|---|---|---|---|
| go | going | went | gone |
| sing | singing | sang | sung |
| move | moving | moved | moved |
| wash | washing | washed | washed |
| introduce | introducing | introduced | introduced |
| see | seeing | saw | seen |
| hide | hiding | hid | hidden |
| ... | ... | ... | ... |

CHART 7.1

Each row contains a distinct verb. Each column represents a particular form of the verb: present tense ("go"), participle ("going"), past tense ("went"), and past participle ("has gone").

The chart shows a regular network of relations that involves not only forms of "go" but forms of many other verbs in English. Those who speak English know how to use the forms of the word "go." This knowledge is not simply an isolated piece of information but has a close relation to information about how to use forms of other verbs.

If you think about it, this is a very good thing. It would be burdensome, and in the end impossible, to master a distinct set of rules for "go," and another set of rules for "sing," and another set for "move," and so on. We depend on the regularities of language to save us from this tedium. In effect, we learn a single set of rules about when it is appropriate to use the simple present form of a verb—any verb—and when it is appropriate to use a participle ("going") or a simple past ("went"), or for that matter an infinitive ("to go"). Language depends on a network of relations that tie all the verbs together, through a single set of rules. And we could make a similar observation about nouns and adjectives and prepositions.

Of course there are also tantalizing variations that do not reduce completely to general rules. The past tense of "go" is "went." You could not have predicted that fact from the fairly general observation that *usually* the past tense of a verb is formed by adding "-ed": "wash" becomes in its past tense "washed." But even though "went" has a very different sound and spelling than "go," it still fits into the verb chart (chart 7.1). We depend on the regularities represented in the chart in the process of understanding how to use "went" and how its meaning and function differ from "go."

The verb "go" not only has a relation to other verbs; it also relates to what comes before it and after it in a sentence. The word "go" expects to have a subject, as in the sentences "I go" or "I am going." Optionally, it can have a prepositional phrase after it indicating the goal: "I am going to the store." Some verbs regularly have a direct object: "I hit the ball." But "go" is called an "intransitive" verb because it does not take a direct object. We do not hear people saying, "I am going the ball." All these are regularities about the word "go," and they are regularities that consist in *relations* between the word "go" and words and phrases that go with it or do not go with it.

God specifies all these relations. Just as he rules over the processes that are the focus of the wave perspective, so he rules over the relations of the field perspective. Likewise, all the pieces of language, the "particles," have a *relation* to God. They are what they are in relation to him. Since he is the origin of all meaning and all order, everything that exists is sustained in relation to him. Likewise, the processes are related to him as the giver of processes, and the relations between various pieces depend on him. All order in language derives from God's having given order. And so, relations to God are an indispensable aspect in accounting for any particular thing. When we study language, we are uncovering a display of the wisdom that God has in giving us this stable, complex, and flexible tool for our use. (Thank you, God!) We can praise God for his wisdom, and for his generosity and goodness in giving us language, one of the most valuable things that human beings can ever enjoy.

## Three Interlocking Perspectives

So we have three distinct perspectives on language, namely, the particle, wave, and field perspectives. These three perspectives are an image of the Trinity. The particle perspective is closely related to stability, which is established by the unchanging stability of the plan of the Father. The wave perspective is closely related to the controlling work of the Son, who brings about action in history: "he upholds the universe by the word of his power" (Heb. 1:3). The field perspective is closely related to the Spirit's presence. Whenever we relate two pieces of language to one another, we conceive of them as simultaneously present in mind, and often even as simultaneously present in space, as we lay them side by side in a pattern. The Spirit, as present to us, and indwelling us who are believers in Christ (Rom. 8:9–11), expresses God's *relation* to us. Accordingly, the three perspectives on language—particle, wave, and field—are coinherent.

Each of the three perspectives can be applied to any part of language. They are complementary to one another and interlocking. For example, the field perspective depends on the fact that there are distinct pieces of language, like "go" and "went," that enjoy a relation to one another. That is, the field perspective depends on the "particles," on the stable pieces. It depends also on the fact that, as analysts, we can move from one set of relations to another. This movement is itself a "wave" made by the analyst. We shift, for example, from considering the relation of "go" and "went" to considering the relation of "sing" and "sang."

Similarly, the particle perspective depends on the field perspective. Any one piece of language, like the word "go," is identified for what it is partly through its distinctive sound and spelling. It is "go" *rather than* "no" or "so." It is related to other words that are similar to it or that contrast with it. And knowing about "go" involves knowing how to use it in communication, which is a wave process. We depend on this process of communication for language learning.

The wave perspective likewise depends on the particle perspective. Movement from one sound to another or from one meaning to another becomes perceptible as movement precisely because there are stable endpoints. The endpoints can be identified as distinct wholes, as pieces. They are stable, that is, particles. And various wave movements are related to one another (field perspective) as instances of more general patterns. For example, the contraction "I'm" for "I am" is one of a number of contractions with "I" plus helping verbs: "I'll," "I'd," "I've," where the verb begins with a vowel or an open consonant ("w," "h").

## Dependence

The field perspective makes it evident that no one word exists in absolute isolation. It exists, to begin with, as part of a particular language. "Go" is a word of *English*. It would be meaningless in some other language, just as "chien," which is French for "dog," means nothing in English. In fact, the meaning of "go" depends not only on English as a whole but in a subtle way on things in its environment, and on the dynamics of its use.

For example, the present tense in English is distinctly a *present* tense partly by its being in contrast to the simple past tense. "I go" contrasts with "I went."

By itself, no tense is perfectly specific, because there are not an infinite number of tenses.

We find that the present tense is used in several kinds of ways. It may be used to describe something that is regularly true: "I *go* to the grocery store every Wednesday." It can describe something in the near future: "Tomorrow I *go* to school." Or it can describe an event in the past, within the context of a larger narrative:

> Let me tell you what happened yesterday. I was standing on the sidewalk, and I saw a beggar looking at me pleadingly. So I *go* to him and say, "I know what you are thinking . . ."

The exact significance of the present tense depends on the *context* in which it is used. Its meaning is not simply the meaning of the present tense in isolation, but in relation to a context. The context shows whether it is being used for a regular, repeated event, or for the near future, or in some other way.

Words are sometimes used in a metaphorical or figurative way. For example, Jesus says about Herod, "Go and tell *that fox,* . . ." (Luke 13:32). We know from the context that Jesus is referring to Herod, rather than to a literal fox. The context *in relation to* the word "fox" indicates that we have a metaphor. So, in such a context, is the meaning the old, original meaning, or a new meaning imparted by context? And could we not create still new metaphors and new contexts, indefinitely, and so destabilize an original "fixed" dictionary meaning?

If meanings depend on the context of language, are they a stable basis for knowledge? Or are they inherently unstable? A kind of stability comes from the interaction of two parts, namely, the sameness of an identifiable word and a relation to a particular context. Consider an example. My friend hears me say, "Tomorrow I go to school." From the word "go" he knows that I am talking about motion of some kind. That knowledge comes from the stable meaning of the word "go." But from the one word alone—without context—he cannot know whether I am talking about the present or the past or the future or a repeated event. But he also hears the word "tomorrow." He knows from the use of the word "tomorrow," and from the way that "tomorrow" is linked to "go" within the sentence, that I am talking about the future. By observing the *relation* of the word "go" to its context, he comes to a definite conclusion.

But does he really know? Maybe I am joking, and the context of our previous conversation, or the smile on my face, shows that I am joking. So my friend must look not only at one sentence, but must know something about discourse. And discourse occurs in the context of human culture. And human cultures are multiple. They arise in the context of the environment of the whole world, and the whole history of the world.

To determine the meaning of the word "go" in a particular context, we begin with what we already know about the stable meaning of the word. But we also look at its relations. We push out into the environment, both the environment of English as a language and the environment of speakers using words in waves of communication. The field of relations extends out indefinitely, from word to sentence to utterance to small acts of human behavior to whole human lifetimes. And the final environment is God. God is at the beginning of history as its creator, and at the end as its consummator. And he is in between as the sustainer of the entire environment of the universe. Knowing the meaning of the word "go" depends on knowing relations, which depends on God. We can thank God for all of this provision.

# The Rules of Language

Forever, O LORD, your word
is firmly fixed in the heavens.
Your faithfulness endures to all generations;
you have established the earth, and it stands fast.
By your appointment they stand this day,
for all things are your servants.

—Psalm 119:89–91

God sustains language partly by sustaining *regularities* about language. Even with a small piece of language, like the word "go," we meet an impressive number of regularities or rules. The word "go" has a stable meaning, and the dictionary gives a kind of rule or rules about what meanings it has. The dictionary also gives a description of how the word "go" is pronounced and how it is spelled, and those descriptions are rules. The word "go" also has distinct forms, like "went" and "gone." There are regularities describing how to use these forms, that is, how to use different verbal tenses in English.

We need to look at the character of language *rules*, because here also God shows his goodness and his control.

## The Rules

Each person who uses language relies on language rules. Many of the rules he knows tacitly, without having them explicitly taught in a classroom.[1] He may

---

1. On tacit knowledge, see especially Michael Polanyi, *The Tacit Dimension* (Garden City, NY: Anchor, 1967); and more expansively, Polanyi, *Personal Knowledge: Towards a Post-critical Philosophy* (Chicago: University of Chicago Press, 1964).

not be able to formulate what the rules are, but he shows that he knows them by his usage. For example, if he has begun to learn English, he knows that the word "banana" describes a certain kind of fruit. He knows that "moved" is the past tense form of the verb "move." He knows that in making a declaration, the subject precedes the verb: "The cat is on the mat." He knows that in a question, some form of helping verb or some question word precedes the subject: "Is the cat on the mat?" He knows that in a noun phrase with a definite article ("the"), the words occur in a certain, fixed order: "The three large cats" is acceptable, while "Large cats three the" is not. He knows these rules even if he uses language to deny that we can know anything, or to deny that we can know about language rules. The rules are indispensable.

So what are the rules? Linguists make careful study of some of them. There are grammatical rules, such as the rules about the order of words in the noun phrase, "the three large cats." There are rules concerning the sounds of words.[2] For written language there are spelling and punctuation rules. There are rules about speech acts, that is, rules about how various kinds of language usage function in the larger context of human action.[3]

We cannot hope fully to specify all of these rules. Each word in the dictionary has a meaning, or in some cases more than one meaning. The dictionary, by spelling out the meanings, gives us an idea of how and when it is appropriate to use the word. Each dictionary definition is thus a cluster of rules about how to use that particular word. But of course the dictionary definition is never exhaustive.[4] It gets us started. But we could never succeed in fully enumerating all possible felicitous or infelicitous *metaphorical* uses of a word, because such usages, though built on the dictionary meanings, employ the word in creative ways.

In each and every rule or regularity concerning language, we meet the power and presence of God. God has given language, and with language he has given us its order. It is God who specifies the rules. Linguists, when they do research, find rules that God has already put in place.

## Breaking Rules

It should also be clear that any one particular rule can be broken. Let me introduce a fictional character, "Rebel Bob." If you give Rebel Bob a rule about language, he

---

2. The technical term for rules about sound is "phonological rules."

3. Ludwig Wittgenstein and his successors in the study of speech acts have investigated such questions. So do the sociolinguists. See Kenneth L. Pike, *Language in Relation to a Unified Theory of the Structure of Human Behavior*, 2nd ed. (The Hague: Mouton, 1967). We discuss speech acts in appendix H.

4. On the partial character of most dictionary definitions, see William Croft and D. Alan Cruse, *Cognitive Linguistics* (Cambridge: Cambridge University Press, 2004), 30.

will show you that he can break it. He says, "Large cats three the." "There," he says, "I have broken the rule about the order of words within a noun phrase." Rebel Bob can also break rules of social behavior, if he so chooses. (But there may be painful consequences, if he commits a crime or betrays a trust.) The point to notice is not that the rules are unbreakable, but that, in the obvious cases, everyone is aware of the breakage. The rules are norms that specify what people normally do, and they also imply that deviations will stand out.[5] So a deviation or breakage itself serves to confirm the reality of the rule, the norm.

I should also add a technical qualification. Linguists have learned to distinguish *descriptive* linguistics from *prescriptive* grammar. In English, traditional school grammar taught earlier generations of students to say, "He and I are going to play ball," with "he" and "I" in the so-called "nominative case." This sentence was said to be "grammatically correct." The teacher formulated a *prescriptive* rule about how good speakers of English should talk. But on the playground, beyond the ear of the English teacher, you might hear some student say, "Me and him are going to play ball." The *descriptive* linguist would include the latter utterance within his data about how people *actually* talk, especially in colloquial English among the unlettered. He would also continue the analysis in order to discover rules for when the playground boy uses "me" and when he uses "I." There are such rules, descriptive grammatical rules. But they differ from the rules of the prescriptive grammar in the English teacher's classroom.

The rules of prescriptive grammar are genuine and real, but they are more like cultural rules prescribing cultural expectations for behavior in educated circles and in formal discourse, rather than being merely straightforward language rules. Educated people often notice when prescriptive rules are violated, but the violation is somewhat different from the breakage of a rule of descriptive grammar.

The example with "me and him" also shows that there can be dialectical differences between different speakers of English. There can be Boston English, Southern English, black English, Scottish English, and differences between uneducated and educated speakers in the same geographical location.[6] Linguists delight to study these differences, and formulate rules with respect to them. We could say that we have rules to describe the variations in rules among different dialects. Rules, rules, rules.

The more thorough the investigation, the more rules we find, and the more we find rules for accounting for the variations in the rules and the apparent and

---

5. On the possibility of deliberately "flouting" rules, see especially Mary Louise Pratt, *Toward a Speech Act Theory of Literary Discourse* (Bloomington: Indiana University Press, 1977).

6. Linguists have also spoken about an "idiolect," the special differences that belong to a single person's use of his language. An idiolect is a dialect specialized to one person. I grew up in central California, but I was influenced by my mother's Boston accent. So my own accent is not completely identical with the generic "California accent."

sometimes real breakage of an individual rule. We cannot escape the rules except by escaping into another language and another culture with its own set of rules, or else escaping into insanity. And of course psychopathology investigates regular patterns (rules) found in insanity!

Many linguists also recognize that the rules may "fade gradually" when we enter gray areas that are difficult to classify as either fully rule-obeying or overtly rule-disobeying. We may talk about some sentences being grammatical, and others being ungrammatical, that is, breaking the rules of grammar. But in between are some sentences that are doubtful. Native speakers may sometimes disagree with one another as to whether a particular sentence is grammatically acceptable. And sometimes it may depend on the context. Consider the following lines from a hymn:

> Lord, our Lord, thy glorious name
> all thy wondrous works proclaim;
> in the heav'ns with radiant signs
> evermore thy glory shines.
> Infant lips thou dost ordain
> wrath and vengeance to restrain;
> weakest means fulfil thy will,
> mighty enemies to still.[7]

As classic English hymnic poetry this is perfectly acceptable, but if similar grammatical constructions appeared in prose they would be awkward at best and sometimes grammatically unacceptable, because some of the word order is unusual, and the use of the words "thy" and "dost" is archaic.

This kind of situation regularly occurs in natural languages, and we can begin to formulate rules to describe it. So it should be seen as one aspect of the way that rules actually function in language rather than a failure of language to conform to rules. It all depends on how we conceive of the rules. If we formulate a simple rule about grammar, we may sometimes find exceptions, and the exceptions are "violations" of the rule. But the problem is that our formulation fails fully to capture the complexity of actual language. The actual rules are more complex than our formulation, and so of course we are going to be disappointed.

## God's Hand

God's hand is in the rules. By providing rules for each language, he gives a stable basis for communication.

---

7. "Lord, Our Lord, Thy Glorious Name," in *Trinity Hymnal* (Philadelphia: Great Commission, 1990), hymn 114; from Psalm 8, *The Psalter*, 1912.

# God's Rule

For his invisible attributes, namely, his eternal power and divine nature,

have been clearly perceived, ever since the creation of the world,

in the things that have been made.

—Romans 1:20

Let us now focus on the character of the rules of language. They reveal God in some striking ways.

## Omnipresence

First, the rules for English hold wherever English is spoken. For example, consider the rule that "moved" is the past tense of "move." That holds true for English everywhere. It holds not only where English is spoken but wherever English *could* be spoken, or else it would not be English.[1] That much seems undeniable. But then the rule about "moved" is truly universal; it is present everywhere. That

---

1. General linguistics at times tries to formulate fairly general rules that would hold with respect to any human language whatsoever (so-called "universal grammar"). But in the nature of the case we cannot be quite sure that there could never be an exception in some remote human language, or in a now-extinct language. That is, we cannot say that the human formulations of the rules completely capture the actual rules. In fact, that is also true for human formulations with respect to the rules of English. It is easier, in any case, to think of the particular rules of some particular language such as English. One of the rules of general linguistics would be that each

is, it is omnipresent. Spoken English, and human knowledge of English, are not omnipresent. But the rules are.

## Eternality

The presence of a rule at different places extends easily to embrace its presence at different times. The rule about "moved" applies whenever English is spoken, either past or future.

But now we must make a qualification. English or any other human language changes over time. In middle English the word "move" was "moven," which in turn comes from middle French, "movoir," which comes from Latin "movēre." We can see differences when we compare modern English with Shakespearian English or Chaucerian English. There are subtle and sometimes major changes in the meaning of some particular words. There are changes in pronunciation, and changes in grammar. There are changes in the surrounding cultures within which the use of language makes sense. So the rules change.

But we might just as well say that the changed rules to which we point are rules with respect to a somewhat different form of English, or a different dialect of English. If we are talking not about the whole history of English (how far back would we go?) but about contemporary English, we come back down to earth. Even here we must talk about a variety of dialects for English. But that variety, properly understood, is part of the rules, rules describing dialects and their differences. What is essential is that we not simply confuse our own English with Chaucerian English or older Anglo-Saxon, because if we did, we would make everything unclear. There is no lingual communication without a stable language within the bounds of which to communicate. If the rules we are talking about are merely the rules for any language whatsoever, that is little help. We must have particular rules for a particular language at a particular stage. These rules are applicable wherever that particular language is the medium of communication.

And so, yes, "moved" would be the past tense of "move" if, thirty centuries from now, some group of learned scholars of English were to revive English as a living language. More likely, they would create a language like our English but also subtly different, and so the rules for them would differ from ours at some points.

The rules are always to be understood as the rules for a particular language. Those rules hold anytime that particular language is used. And so the rules, though not the living use of the language, are eternal.

---

particular language has particular rules, partly unique to itself, concerning grammar, sounds, and meanings.

It may seem strange to talk about the rules of a language being eternal, since languages themselves change. But a similar principle holds with respect to any truth about the world. The world changes. But the truths about events in the world always hold, once we make the qualification that they are truths about an event at a particular time and place. Christ was crucified under Pontius Pilate. That truth concerning a particular event can be affirmed now, or in the future, just as much as at the time it happened.[2]

## Immutability

It follows also that the rules are immutable. The rule about "moved" does not change (with respect to English as it now exists), and indeed it cannot change, because a new rule would hold with respect to a new state of development of a historical language, rather than holding with respect to English as it now exists.

We should also say that there are rules to describe language change. Introductions of new meanings, or introductions of new pronunciations, take place in various regular ways. Regularities like this can be captured to some extent by rules.

## The Role of God

We have already spoken about the rules of language as omnipresent, eternal, and immutable. It is not an accident that we are seeing here some of the attributes of God. According to the Bible, God by his word governs the whole of the world:

> And God *said*, "Let there be light," and there was light (Gen. 1:3).

> By the *word* of the LORD the heavens were made,
>     and by the *breath* of his mouth all their host (Ps. 33:6).

> Who has *spoken* and it came to pass, unless the Lord has *commanded* it?
>     Is it not from the *mouth* of the Most High that good and bad come?
> (Lam. 3:37–38).

In particular, God governs the physical and biological world through his word. Scientists in studying scientific law are actually looking into the word of God that governs the world. A similar situation holds when linguists study rules about language.

We can summarize the situation with respect to scientific law as follows:

---

2. See the discussion about the divine attributes of truth in Vern S. Poythress, *Redeeming Science: A God-Centered Approach* (Wheaton, IL: Crossway, 2006), chapter 14.

According to the Bible, he [God] is involved in those areas where science does best, namely areas involving regular and predictable events, repeating patterns, and sometimes exact mathematical descriptions. In Genesis 8:22 God promises,

> While the earth remains, seedtime and harvest, cold and heat, summer and winter, day and night, shall not cease.

This general promise concerning earthly regularities is supplemented by many particular examples:

> You make darkness, and it is night,
>     when all the beasts of the forest creep about (Ps. 104:20).

> You cause the grass to grow for the livestock
>     and plants for man to cultivate,
> that he may bring forth food from the earth (Ps. 104:14).

> He sends out his command to the earth;
>     his word runs swiftly.
> He gives snow like wool;
>     he scatters hoarfrost like ashes.
> He hurls down his crystals of ice like crumbs;
>     who can stand before his cold?
> He sends out his word, and melts them;
>     he makes his wind blow and the waters flow (Ps. 147:15–18).

The regularities that scientists describe are the regularities of God's own commitments and his actions. By his word to Noah, he commits himself to govern the seasons. By his word he governs snow, frost, and hail. Scientists describe the regularities in God's word governing the world. So-called natural law is really the law of God or word of God, imperfectly and approximately described by human investigators.

Now, the work of science depends constantly on the fact that there are regularities in the world. Without the regularities, there would ultimately be nothing to study. Scientists depend not only on regularities with which they are already familiar, such as the regular behavior of measuring apparatus, but also on the postulate that still more regularities are to be found in the areas that they will investigate. Scientists must maintain hope of finding further regularities, or they would give up their newest explorations.[3]

Similar observations hold when it comes to considering human beings. God in governing the world of human beings governs language as well. The rule about "moved" is a rule from God himself, as he acts in governing language.

---

3. Poythress, *Redeeming Science*, 14–15.

We need to add a further complexity. God's laws or rules with respect to the physical world are never violated or broken. Miracles are surprising to us, because they "violate" *our expectations* concerning laws, but they are in conformity with God's plan and his word, which is the real law. On the other hand, God's rules with respect to a particular language, like English, can be broken. They are broken when we make an ungrammatical expression like "large cats three the." In that respect the rules of language are more like God's *moral* law.

God says, "Do not steal." Rebel Bob can go ahead and steal, if he wants, just to show that he can break God's law. He does indeed break God's law. But God's law, as a moral standard, remains unchanged. Rebel Bob does not succeed in changing it, but only in violating it. And his violation also fits within God's rules, in several senses. For one thing, his acts are still within the scope of God's decrees, God's words that specify the whole course of the history of the world.[4] For another, Bob is accountable for his violation. There are consequences, both on earth and after death. God's rules also specify these consequences.

Now let us return to consider the breaking of a grammatical rule. A violation of a grammatical rule is not the same as a moral violation. Within a social context where we are discussing the nature of language, we can playfully break a grammatical rule, if we want, and sometimes achieve a morally positive goal. But rules concerning the interpretation of language and rules concerning social interaction govern such unusual moves in language as well as the more usual ones that faithfully observe grammatical rules. So this is not an exception that takes us away from rules. Moreover, even if we break a rule, we need the rule to remain stable and unchanged in order effectively to break it.

With this understanding, let us proceed to explore further, and to ask whether the rules of language display other attributes of God. For convenience, I will follow the order of discussion I used in the book *Redeeming Science* to discuss scientific law.[5] Many of the observations remain the same when we focus on laws (rules) concerning language.

## Invisibility

Rules concerning language are at bottom ideational in character. We do not literally see *the rule* that "moved" is the past tense of "move." We see and hear only the effects of the rule on our use of language. The rule is essentially immaterial and invisible, but is known through its effects, like the occurrence of the word "moved." Likewise, God is essentially immaterial and invisible, but is known through his acts in the world.

---

4. On God's decrees, see the discussion in Poythress, *Redeeming Science*; and discussion of God's decrees within Reformed theology, e.g., John M. Frame, *The Doctrine of God* (Phillipsburg, NJ: Presbyterian & Reformed, 2002), 313–339.

5. Poythress, *Redeeming Science*, chapter 1.

## Truthfulness

Real rules, as opposed to linguists' approximations of them, are also absolutely, infallibly true. Truthfulness is also an attribute of God.

## The Power of Rules

Next consider the attribute of power. Linguists formulate rules as *descriptions* of regularities that they observe. They say that "moved" is the past tense of "move." But that was already true before the rule about it was formulated. The label "past tense" was invented by students of language. But the thing they described with the label was already there. The human scientific formulation follows the facts, and is dependent on them. A law or regularity must already hold for "moved." The linguist cannot force the issue by inventing a rule that the past tense of "move" will be "mowd" and then making the language to conform to it. Language rather conforms to rules already there, rules that are discovered rather than invented.

The rules must already be there, and they must actually hold. They must "have teeth." Even if Rebel Bob deliberately breaks the rule by saying "mowd," the rule remains what it was and remains true. No language event escapes the "hold" or dominion of the rules. Even Rebel Bob, when he breaks the rule, is still subject to the rule in the sense that everyone can see that he is breaking the rule. The power of these real laws is absolute—in fact, infinite. In classical language, a rule of language is omnipotent ("all powerful").

If the rule about "moved" is omnipotent and universal, there are truly no exceptions. Do we, then, conclude that violations of grammar are impossible, because they are violations of a rule? No, our example with Rebel Bob shows that the universality of a rule for language is of a different kind than with physical laws like the law of gravity. The rule remains in place as a *standard*, a norm, to which Rebel Bob is subject, even when he breaks it. In addition, the violations of a rule are within the purpose of God for language. They take place in accordance with his predictive and decretive word. So the power of any one rule about "moved" is to be understood in the context of other rules, including rules describing the possibility of breaking the one rule.

Initially, a linguist may have formulated a rule in a very simple manner in order to describe a regularity that he has observed. But the real rules of God encompass not only the ordinary regularity that the linguist has observed but also the irregularities that he has not yet accounted for. God's rule, as distinct from the linguist's rule, encompasses the very possibility of breaking the linguist's rule. Similarly the Ten Commandments, as given by God, include within their context indications from God that he knows that the Israelites may violate them. That is one of the reasons he issues the commandments in the first place. The violations do not take God by surprise, but are in fact encompassed by the commandments, some of which include consequences for disobedience as well as blessings for obedience (Ex. 20:5–7).

## Transcendence and Immanence

The rules are both transcendent and immanent. The rule about "moved" transcends particular instances of "moved," and it transcends particular human beings by exercising power over them, conforming them to its dictates. The rule is immanent in that it touches and holds in its dominion the particular occurrences of "move" in the past tense.[6] Transcendence and immanence are characteristics of God.

## Are the Rules Personal or Impersonal?

Many agnostics and atheists by this time will be looking for a way of escape. It seems that the key concept of rules of language is beginning to look suspiciously like the biblical idea of God. The most obvious escape, and the one that has rescued many from spiritual discomfort, is to deny that rules of language are personal. They are just there as an impersonal something. It just "happens to be the case" that "moved" is the past tense of "move."

Throughout the ages people have tried such routes. They have constructed idols, substitutes for God. In ancient times, the idols often had the form of statues representing a god—Poseidon, the god of the sea; or Mars, the god of war. Nowadays in the Western world we are more sophisticated. Idols now take the form of mental constructions of a god or a God-substitute. Money and pleasure can become idols. So can "humanity" or "nature" when it receives a person's ultimate allegiance. "Scientific law," when viewed as impersonal, becomes another God-substitute. But in both ancient times and today, idols conform to the imagination of the person who makes them. Idols have enough similarities to the true God to be plausible, but differ so as to allow us comfort and the satisfaction of manipulating the substitutes that we construct.

## Rule-giving, Rationality, and Language-like Character

In fact, a close look at rules of language shows that this escape route is not really plausible. Rules imply a rule-giver. What gives power to the rule about "moved"? Someone must think the rule and enforce it, if it is to be effective. But if some people resist this direct move to personality, we may proceed more indirectly.

Linguists in practice believe passionately in the rationality of the rules of language. We are not dealing with irrationality, totally unaccountable and unanalyzable, but with lawfulness that in some sense is accessible to human understanding. Rationality is a sine qua non for scientific investigation of any kind, including the social-scientific investigation undertaken by linguists. Moreover, the ordinary

---

6. On the biblical view of transcendence and immanence, see John M. Frame, *The Doctrine of the Knowledge of God* (Phillipsburg, NJ: Presbyterian & Reformed, 1987), especially 13–15; and *Doctrine of God*, especially 107–115.

person as well as the linguist must assume that the rules of language are fundamentally rational. Otherwise, his own usage of language has no rational bottom, and his own utterances are all irrational.

Now if the rules are rational, they are also personal, because rationality belongs to persons. Persons have rational capacities, but not rocks, trees, and subpersonal creatures. If the rules are rational, which linguists assume they are, then they are also personal. God shows his personhood in making the rule for "moved," which is a rational rule, intelligible to persons.

Linguists also assume that rules can be articulated, expressed, communicated, and understood through human language. Scientific work includes not only rational thought but also symbolic communication. Now, the original, the rule "out there," is not known to be written or uttered in a human language. But it must be expressible in language in our secondary description of it. We can say, in English, that "'moved' is the past tense of 'move.'" And this rule must be translatable into not only one but many human languages. In the new language, we may have to explain what a "past tense" is, if that is an unfamiliar concept with respect to the new language. We may represent restrictions, qualifications, definitions, and contexts for rules through clauses, phrases, explanatory paragraphs, and contextual explanations in human language.

The rules concerning language are clearly like human utterances in their ability to be grammatically articulated, paraphrased, translated, and illustrated. A rule is utterance-like, language-like. And the complexity of utterances that we find among linguists, as well as among human beings in general, is not duplicated in the animal world.[7] Language is one of the defining characteristics that separates man from animals. Language, like rationality, belongs to persons. The rules of language, being themselves language-like, are therefore in essence personal.

## An Objection from Evolutionary Naturalism

But now we must consider an objection that could be raised using the philosophy of evolutionary naturalism.[8] Evolutionary naturalism postulates that a process of Darwinian evolution, without any personal purposes, has produced the human race and its language abilities.[9] According to this scenario, the rules of language

---

7. Animal calls and signals do mimic certain limited aspects of human language. And chimpanzees can be taught to respond to symbols with meaning. But this is still a long way from the complex grammar and meaning of human language. See, e.g., Stephen R. Anderson, *Doctor Dolittle's Delusion: Animals and the Uniqueness of Human Language* (New Haven, CT: Yale University Press, 2004).

8. Concerning evolutionary naturalism, see Poythress, *Redeeming Science*, chapters 5 and 19.

9. This view must be distinguished from "theistic evolution," which says that God used an evolutionary process and controlled the process by which he created the various kinds of living

would have originated in the end from the biological structures of the human brain, and would be reducible to the brain. The apparent rationality and language-like character of the rules with respect to language is somehow a projection or effect of the more basic rationality and language-like features originating in the structure of the human brain.

But this move simply postpones the question by pushing the rules back from being rules of language to being rules of biology and rules for brains and rules for evolution. It so happens that those rules, those scientific laws, are also rational and language-like and personal, as I argued in *Redeeming Science*.[10] No, we will not escape God that way.

Finally, we might be troubled by the plurality of rules for language, and more broadly about the plurality of scientific laws. Are there many gods, or one? There is only one God, as the unity and harmony of all the laws testify. But he has plurality in himself, the plurality of three persons in one God. The plurality of laws and language rules is no more an accident than their harmony.

## Incomprehensibility of Law

In addition, rules for language are both knowable and incomprehensible in the theological sense. That is, we know truths about language, but in the midst of this knowledge there remain unfathomed depths and unanswered questions about the very areas where we know the most. Why is there a past tense in English? The rules never succeed in making transparent why there is language at all, and why it is rational in the way that it is, and so on.

The knowability of rules is closely related to their rationality and their immanence, displayed in the accessibility of effects. We experience incomprehensibility in the fact that the increase in understanding only leads to ever deeper questions, "How can this be?" and "Why *this* rule rather than many other ways that the human mind can imagine?" The profundity and mystery in language can only produce awe—yes, worship—if we have not blunted our perception with hubris (Isa. 6:9–10).

## Are We Divinizing Nature?

We must consider another objection. By claiming that rules for language have divine attributes, are we divinizing nature? That is, are we taking something out of the created world, and falsely claiming that it is divine? Are not rules for lan-

---

things. And of course it is even more obviously distinct from various creationist views. On the various alternatives, see ibid., 252–258.

10. Ibid., chapter 1, pp. 19–20.

guage a part of the created world? Should we not classify them as creature rather than Creator?[11]

I suspect that the specificity of the rule about "moved," and its obvious reference to the created world of human speech using "moved," has become the occasion for many of us to infer that this rule and others are a *part* of the created world. But such an inference is clearly invalid. The speech describing a butterfly is not itself a butterfly or a part of a butterfly. Speech *referring* to the created world is not necessarily an ontological *part* of the world to which it refers.

In addition, let us remember that we are speaking of real rules, not merely our human guesses and approximations. The real rules are in fact the word of God, specifying how the world of creatures and the world of language are to function. So-called "rules" are simply God speaking, God acting, God manifesting himself in time and space. The real mistake here is not a matter of divinizing nature but of refusing to recognize that the rules are the law of God, nothing less than God speaking.

The key idea that the law is divine is not only older than the rise of modern science; it is older than the rise of Christianity. Even before the coming of Christ, people noticed profound regularity in the government of the world and wrestled with the meaning of this regularity. Both the Greeks (especially the Stoics) and the Jews (especially Philo) developed speculations about the *logos*, the divine "word" or "reason" behind what is observed.[12] In addition, the Jews had the Old Testament, which reveals the role of the word of God in creation and providence. Against this background John 1:1 proclaims, "In the beginning was the Word, and the Word was with God, and the Word was God." John responds to the speculations of his time with a striking revelation: that the Word (*logos*) that created and sustains the universe is not only a divine person "with God," but the very One who became incarnate: "the Word became flesh" (1:14).

God said, "Let there be light" (Gen. 1:3). He referred to light as a part of the created world. But precisely in this reference, his word has divine power to bring creation into being. The effect in creation took place at a particular time. But the plan for creation, as exhibited in God's word, is eternal. Likewise, God's speech to us in the Bible refers to various parts of the created world, but the speech (in distinction to the things to which it refers) is divine in power, authority, majesty, righteousness, eternity, and truth.[13]

---

11. The Bible (especially Genesis 1) shows that God and the created world are distinct. God is not to be identified with the creation or any part of it, nor is the creation a "part" of God. The Bible repudiates all forms of pantheism and panentheism (see, e.g., Ex. 20:4–6; Acts 14:15; 17:24–26).

12. See "Word" in *The International Standard Bible Encyclopedia*, ed. Geoffrey W. Bromiley et al., rev. ed. (Grand Rapids, MI: Eerdmans, 1988), 4:1103–1107, and the associated literature.

13. On the divine character of God's word, see Vern S. Poythress, *God-Centered Biblical Interpretation* (Phillipsburg, NJ: Presbyterian & Reformed, 1999), 32–36.

The analogy with the incarnation should give us our clue. The second person of the Trinity, the eternal Word of God, became man in the incarnation but did not therefore cease to be God. Likewise, when God speaks and says what is to be the case in this world, his words do not cease to have the divine power and unchangeability that belong to him. Rather, they remain divine, and in addition have the power to specify the situation with respect to creaturely affairs. God's word remains divine when it becomes law, a specific directive with respect to this created world.

## The Goodness of Rules

Are the rules of language good? Ah, here we run into struggles. Many people say that the evils in the world are the greatest obstacle to believing in God.[14] Usually they are troubled by the suffering that takes place in the world at large. How can there be so much evil in the world if God rules over it? Since we are focusing on language, we may also observe that people can be troubled by the evils that take place through language. Language not only enables noble accomplishments but can be used for evil. People may lie, deceive, manipulate, and propagandize. And if we were to be immersed in a society filled with propaganda, as Nazi Germany once was, or as North Korea more recently has been, we would find it difficult as individuals to escape its clutches. The United States and Europe are not free from such baneful influences, if modern advertising has contributed to materialism and consumerism. How can God be good, and how can his rules for language be good, if the result contains evil?

But it is not simple to escape the presence of God in these struggles. We may appeal to a standard of good in order to judge that an existing situation is evil. In doing so, we appeal to a standard beyond the confines of the empirical world. We appeal to a standard, a law. To give up the idea of moral law is to give up the very basis on which criticism of evil depends. Moral law is thus indispensable to an atheist's argument, but at the same time it presupposes an absolute. And this absolute, in order to obligate us and hold us accountable, must be personal. The Bible's answer alone gives clarity here. God's character is the ultimate source of moral law. Man, made in the image of God, is aware of this law but has rebelled against it (Rom. 1:32). The existing evils are a consequence of that rebellion. Do not cast moral blame on God, but on man.

With respect to language, we may say the same thing. When people lie or deceive, do not cast blame on the rules of language but on the people who lie and deceive. The ninth of the Ten Commandments says, "You shall not bear

---

14. Edward J. Larson and Larry Witham, "Scientists and Religion in America," *Scientific American* 281/3 (September 1999): 90–91.

false witness against your neighbor" (Ex. 20:16). It leaves the door open to the possibility that someone may in fact bear false witness. It anticipates it; why else would it be issued as a command, if not to warn against violations? But God and the rule of God do not become less good if someone bears false witness. Likewise, the rules concerning language open the possibility for lying, and even anticipate it. But the rules themselves are good.

The goodness of God is displayed most clearly in the *moral* law of God. But that is not our focus. Do the rules of language show God's goodness?

Subtle indications of the goodness of God can be seen in the rules for language. Language is indeed a gift, a benefit, even if we ourselves misuse the gift. It allows fellowship with one another, encouraging one another, passing on knowledge to one another, expressing affection for one another, appealing to another for help. It provides a tool for increasing mastery of the world. To crown all, it serves to convey the very voice of God to us, in order that we may be forgiven and reconciled to him, and receive his blessing.

## The Beauty of the Rules

To linguists, at least, the study of language reveals many beauties. The average person takes for granted his own native tongue. If he tries to learn a second language, the complexities of the language may begin to overwhelm him, and he feels frustration over strange differences between the new language and his old one. For many, it is not fun. But linguists find strange, hidden harmonies in the sound system of a language, in the way in which it is designed to make clear certain key distinctions, necessary for communication, without overtaxing our speech apparatus with tongue-twisting. There are clever means in the grammar and in the meanings that speakers may use to construct incredibly complex and multilayered communication, which a poet instinctively knows how to use. For example, in English it is convenient that for most verbs the past tense is formed by adding -d or -ed to the end. The regularity makes it easy to learn and remember the rule.

But to the ordinary user, the proof is mostly in the eating, in the enjoyment of the fruits of language. Language allows beauty in communication, both in poetry and in elegant prose. It serves as a key instrument through which we see the beauty of other human beings. It is wonderful, a blessing, and in this sense a beauty in the world.

The beauty of language shows the beauty of God himself. Though beauty has not been a favorite topic in classical expositions of the doctrine of God, the Bible reveals a God who is profoundly beautiful. He manifests himself in beauty in the design of the tabernacle, the poetry of the Psalms, and the elegance of Christ's parables, as well as the moral beauty of the life of Christ.

The beauty of God himself is reflected in what he has made. We are more accustomed to seeing beauty in particular objects within creation, such as a butterfly or a lofty mountain or a flower-covered meadow. But beauty is also displayed in the wisdom and profundity of the rules for language, which allow the expression and transmission of such beauty. Why should such elegant rules even exist?

## The Rectitude of Rules

Another attribute of God is righteousness. God's righteousness is displayed preeminently in the moral law and in the moral rectitude of his judgments, that is, his rewards and punishments based on moral law. Does God's rectitude appear in the rules of language as well?

The traces are somewhat less obvious, but still present. People can try to disobey physical laws, and when they do they often suffer for it. If a person attempts to defy the law of gravity by jumping off a tall building, he will suffer consequences. There is a kind of built-in righteousness in the way in which laws lead to consequences. Similarly, if a person tries systematically to violate rules of language, he will suffer for it, when other people fail to understand him or even feel that they have been betrayed.

In addition, the rectitude of God is closely related to the fitness of his acts. It fits the character of who God is that we should worship him alone (Ex. 20:3). It fits the character of human beings made in the image of God that they should imitate God by speaking and by exercising dominion over the world (Gen. 1:28–30). Human actions fitly correspond to the actions of God.

Likewise, punishments must be fitting. It is fitting that a thief should pay back double for what he has stolen (Ex. 22:9). "As you have done, it shall be done to you; your deeds shall return on your own head" (Obadiah 15). The punishment fits the crime. There is a symmetrical match between the nature of the crime and the punishment that fits it.[15]

In the arena of rules for language we do not deal with crimes and punishments. But rectitude expresses itself in the fitness of language for our tasks. Language is indeed suited to us, fitted to us. It is what we need. This "fitness" is perhaps closely related to beauty. God's attributes are involved in one another and imply one another, so beauty and righteousness are closely related. It is the same with the area of rules for language. The rules are both beautiful and "fitting," demonstrating rectitude.

---

15. See the extended discussion of just punishment in Vern S. Poythress, *The Shadow of Christ in the Law of Moses* (Phillipsburg, NJ: Presbyterian & Reformed, 1995), 119–249.

## Rules as Trinitarian

Do the rules for language specifically reflect the *Trinitarian* character of God? Philosophers have sometimes maintained that we can infer the existence of God, but not the Trinitarian character of God, on the basis of the world around us. Romans 1:18–21 indicates that unbelievers know God, but how much do they know? I am not addressing this difficult question,[16] but rather reflecting on what we can discern about the world once we have absorbed biblical teaching about God.

Rules for language are a form of the word of God. So they reflect the Trinitarian statement in John 1:1, which identifies the second person of the Trinity as the eternal Word. In addition, as we saw in chapter 2, all three persons of the Trinity are present in distinct ways when God speaks his Word.

Man is made in the image of God, and so his language is in the image of God. And so his language reflects the Trinitarian pattern. For example, human speech involves a speaker, a speech, and breath carrying the speech. These correspond to the roles of the Father, the Son, and the Holy Spirit in divine speech. The rules of language specify, among other things, that language is Trinitarian. Human language also displays a coinherence, which reflects the archetypal coinherence in the Trinity.[17]

---

16. But see the later discussion, where we at least deal with some of the related issues on the situation for human beings in rebellion against God.

17. See chapter 4.

# Responding to God's Government

> ... they did not honor him as God or give thanks to him.
>
> —Romans 1:21

Everyone who uses language relies on the rules of language. Since the rules are from God, everyone is relying on God. And everyone who uses language relies on the coinherence of speakers, speeches, and media of communication bringing the speeches to the accomplishment of their purposes. People rely on the coinherence of the Trinity.

### But Do They Believe?

Do these language users therefore believe in God? They do and they do not. The situation has already been described in the Bible:

> For what can be known about God is plain to them, because God has shown it to them. For his invisible attributes, namely, his eternal power and divine nature, have been clearly perceived, ever since the creation of the world, in the things that have been made. So they are without excuse (Rom. 1:19–20).

They know God. They rely on him. But because this knowledge is morally and spiritually painful, they also suppress and distort it:

> For although they knew God, they did not honor him as God or give thanks to him, but they became futile in their thinking, and their foolish hearts were darkened. Claiming to be wise, they became fools, and exchanged the glory of the immortal

God for images resembling mortal man and birds and animals and creeping things (Rom. 1:21–23).

Modern people may no longer make idols in the form of physical images, but tacitly, in their ideas about the rules of language, they idolatrously twist their knowledge of God. They conceal from themselves the fact that God's rules are personal and that they are responsible to *him*. Or they may substitute the term "human nature," and they talk glowingly about the wonderful character of human nature, which gives us the power to talk. They evade what they know of the transcendence of God over nature.

Even in their rebellion, people continue to depend on God being there. They show *in action* that they continue to believe in God. Cornelius Van Til compares it to an incident he saw on a train, where a small girl sitting on her grandfather's lap slapped him in the face.[1] The rebel must depend on God, and must be "sitting on his lap," even to be able to engage in rebellion.

## Do We Christians Believe?

The fault, I suspect, is not entirely on the side of unbelievers. The fault also occurs among Christians. Christians have sometimes adopted an unbiblical concept of God that moves him one step out of the way of our ordinary affairs. We ourselves may think of either "scientific laws" or "rules of language" or "laws of human nature" as a kind of impersonal cosmic mechanism or constraint that runs the world most of the time, while God is on vacation. God comes and acts only rarely, through miracle. But this is not biblical:

> Even before a word is on my tongue,
> > behold, O LORD, you know it altogether.
> You hem me in, behind and before,
> > and lay your hand upon me.
> Such knowledge is too wonderful for me;
> > it is high; I cannot attain it.
> Where shall I go from your Spirit?
> > Or where shall I flee from your presence?
> If I ascend to heaven, you are there!
> > If I make my bed in Sheol, you are there!
> If I take the wings of the morning
> > and dwell in the uttermost parts of the sea,

---

1. I do not know the location of this story in print. For rebels' dependence on God, see Cornelius Van Til, *The Defense of the Faith*, 2nd ed. (Philadelphia: Presbyterian & Reformed, 1963); and the exposition by John M. Frame, *Apologetics to the Glory of God: An Introduction* (Phillipsburg, NJ: Presbyterian & Reformed, 1994).

> even there your hand shall lead me,
>     and your right hand shall hold me (Ps. 139:4–10).

Let us not forget it. If we ourselves recovered a robust doctrine of God's involvement in daily caring for us *in detail*, we would find ourselves in a much better position to dialogue with skeptics who rely on that same care.

## Principles for Witness

In order for those of us who believe in God to use this situation as a starting point for witness, we need to bear in mind several principles.

First, the observation that God underlies the rules of language does not have the same shape as the traditional theistic proofs—at least as they are often understood. We are not trying to lead people to come to know a God who is completely new to them. Rather, we show that people *already know* God as an aspect of their human experience in language and communication. This places the focus not on intellectual debate but on being a full human being within the context of life.[2]

Second, people deny God within the very same context in which they depend on him. The denial of God springs ultimately not from intellectual flaws or from failure to see all the way to the conclusion of a chain of syllogistic reasoning, but from spiritual failure. We are rebels against God, and we will not serve him. Consequently, we suffer under his wrath (Rom. 1:18), which has intellectual as well as spiritual and moral effects. Those who rebel against God are "fools," according to Romans 1:22.

Third, it is humiliating to intellectuals to be exposed as fools, and it is further humiliating, even psychologically unbearable, to be exposed as guilty of rebellion against the goodness of God. We can expect our hearers to fight with a tremendous outpouring of intellectual and spiritual energy against so unbearable an outcome.

Fourth, the gospel itself, with its message of forgiveness and reconciliation through Christ, offers the only remedy that can truly end this fight against God. But it brings with it the ultimate humiliation: that my restoration comes entirely from God, from outside me—in spite of, rather than because of, my vaunted abilities. To climax it all, so wicked was I that it took the price of the death of the Son of God to accomplish my rescue.

Fifth, approaching people in this way constitutes spiritual warfare. Unbelievers and idolaters are captives to Satanic deceit (1 Cor. 10:20; Eph. 4:17–24; 2 Thess. 2:9–12; 2 Tim. 2:25–26; Rev. 12:9). They do not get free from Satan's captivity

---

2. Much valuable insight into the foundations of apologetics is to be found in the tradition of transcendental apologetics founded by Cornelius Van Til. See Van Til, *Defense of the Faith*; Frame, *Apologetics to the Glory of God*.

unless God gives them release (2 Tim. 2:25–26). We must pray to God and rely on God's power rather than the ingenuity of human argument and eloquence of persuasion (1 Cor. 2:1–5; 2 Cor. 10:3–5).

Sixth, we come into this encounter as fellow sinners. Christians too have become massively guilty by being captive to the idolatry in which language is regarded as self-sufficient rather than dependent on God. Within this captivity we take for granted the benefits and beauties of language for which we should be filled with gratitude and praise to God.

Does an approach to witnessing based on these principles work itself out differently from many of the approaches that attempt to address intellectuals? To me it appears so.

# PART 2

# From Big to Small: Language in the Context of History

# Small Pieces of Language within the Big Pieces

*. . . he does according to his will among the host of heaven*
*and among the inhabitants of the earth.*

—Daniel 4:35

"Are not two sparrows sold for a penny? And not one of them will fall to the ground apart from your Father. But even the hairs of your head are all numbered."

—Matthew 10:29–30

Now we consider some of the ways in which language occurs in bigger-sized and smaller-sized pieces, and how those pieces are designed by God to function in communication.

Consider the sample sentence, "I am going to the store to get more bananas." This sentence is composed of words, namely, "I," "am," "going," and so on. The sentence as a whole is a larger-sized piece, and the words within it are smaller-sized pieces. Sentences are composed of words, and that makes them a different *kind* of piece than the words within them. Linguists may sometimes say that sentences belong to a higher "level." The sentence level consists of structures composed of words, which are at a lower level. So the larger "size" of sentences in this sense does not mean physical length. A long word, such as "disambiguation," can be physically longer than a short sentence, such as "I went." But the sentence still belongs to its own, higher level.

Speakers do not just throw words together at random to make a sentence. If we start with the words from our sample sentence, and then rearrange them, we can produce a random list: "get am bananas I to more the to store going." The result is just a list, not a sentence. A real sentence has a particular grammatical structure, according to which the words fit together in a regular way. There are grammatical rules governing how to form sentences. The rules are rules from God.

Actually, when linguists analyze a sentence, they may point out that there are pieces intermediate in size between the sentence and the words within it. Words fit together into phrases, such as "am going," "to the store," "to get," and "more bananas." The phrases fit together into clauses: "I am going to the store" and "to get more bananas." The clauses fit together into a sentence. So there are several levels. Each level is formed from pieces belonging to lower levels.

We can extend this analysis to pieces that are even smaller or bigger than what we have discussed so far. For instance, we can sometimes break up a word into even smaller pieces. The word "going" can be broken up into two smaller bits, namely, "go" and the suffix "-ing." We can also look at larger pieces of language. A sentence may occur within the larger context of a paragraph, and a paragraph within a section of a larger discourse. *Hierarchy* is a name given to denote this arrangement of pieces within pieces, at successively higher levels.[1]

## Meaning and Context

This kind of grouping of pieces within pieces occurs not only within human language but also in the broader realm of general human action, both short-range and long-range. Monologues, that is, whole discourses, occur in the context of dialogues and conversation. And conversation occurs within the context of other activities that go before and after it.

Is the *context* of human action significant? Yes, it is. Earlier we observed that the total meaning and function of a piece of language depend on the stability of its pieces (the particle perspective). They also depend on how the pieces flow together in time (the wave perspective). And they depend on the relationship that the pieces sustain in various ways to other pieces in language and in the world (the field perspective).[2]

---

1. Kenneth L. Pike, *Linguistic Concepts: An Introduction to Tagmemics* (Lincoln and London: University of Nebraska Press, 1982), 13–15. More technical discussion can distinguish three distinct subsystems that are manifested in hierarchy. See the later discussion of subsystems of language in chapter 32; and Vern S. Poythress, "A Framework for Discourse Analysis: The Components of a Discourse, from a Tagmemic Viewpoint," *Semiotica* 38/3–4 (1982): 277–298; and Poythress, "Hierarchy in Discourse Analysis: A Revision of Tagmemics," *Semiotica* 40/1–2: (1982): 107–137.

2. See chapter 7.

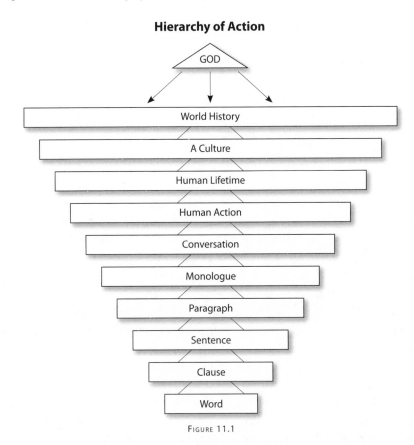

FIGURE 11.1

When we pay attention to the patterning of pieces within pieces, we are using the wave perspective to see what goes before and after a particular piece of language. Typically, other pieces of language sit alongside a single piece. And then there are also other activities, other human beings who are speaking and working and playing and conversing. Using the field perspective, we could focus on the relation of one human activity to its social and physical environment. Other human activities give us a human background for understanding the particular piece of language on which we focus. To obtain a full understanding of the meaning of any one piece, we have to look at the relations. We look at context, the pieces around the one piece of language with which we start.

Conversation takes place in the context of human daily living, and human daily living fits into the context of whole cultures and human lifetimes, and lifetimes into the whole history of the world. And the whole history of the world begins with God, who surpasses history (see fig. 11.1). God began history by creation (Gen. 1:1) and consummates history in a glorious fulfillment (Rev. 21:1–22:5). Thus, the meaning of any one piece, however small, ultimately depends on God.[3] God is the final context, both at the beginning of history and at the end.

But God is present all along the path of history, not just at the beginning and the end. All these relationships of pieces within pieces exist according to the plan of God, according to the will of God. He specifies them; he rules over them. And rules describe the ways in which smaller pieces combine into bigger ones.

## Complex Embedding

In language, the pattern of pieces-within-pieces is quite complex. The most obvious patterns involve instances when one level, such as the paragraph, is built out of the pieces from the next lower level, such as sentences. Similarly, sentences are built out of clauses (see fig. 11.1). But other patterns occur as well. You can skip a level or two, as when you build a sentence out of one word: "Go!" Or you can plug a piece from one level back into the *same* level.[4] For example, phrases can be repeatedly embedded in phrases: "the gnat on the fly on the wart on the frog on the log at the top of the hill in the range of mountains." Or you can plug a piece from a higher level back into a lower level.[5] Consider the expression, "the man who is working in the garden." The expression "the man" is a phrase. To this phrase is attached a relative clause, "who is working in the garden." The clause, which is a higher level, is thereby embedded in the phrase, "the man," which is a lower level.

As another example, consider the practice of quoting someone. When we quote someone else's speech, we are using a form of embedding. We may quote a whole sentence or even a whole monologue consisting of several paragraphs. All of this speech is then embedded in what we ourselves say. We may start a sentence with "he said . . ." and then what follows is a whole speech. So someone else's speech has become embedded in a single sentence, namely, "He said . . ." This kind of embedding of a higher level in a lower level has been called "backlooping."[6]

Quotation is a particularly powerful use of language, because we use language to talk about a second piece of language. But we can do other things besides produce an actual quote of someone's speech. We can quote a hypothetical speech, or a fictional speech. We can quote a fragment of language, such as in this instance: "I am talking about the phrase 'across the street.'"

The ability to quote enables us to do linguistics, where we use the technical language of linguistics to talk about ordinary language. But of course the technical language of linguistics is embedded in real acts of language communication among

---

3. See Robert E. Longacre, *The Grammar of Discourse* (New York/London: Plenum, 1983), 337–356.

4. Ibid., 279–280. The technical term for such embedding is "recursion."

5. Ibid., 280–289.

6. Ibid., 280.

the linguists. Linguists' talk about language is part of the actual use of language among linguists. And so there can be "metalinguistics," which can be defined as the study of what linguists do in their talk, and the study of the relation of linguistics to its object of study. And in theory there could be meta-metalinguistics, which talks about metalinguistics. There is no end to the possibilities of standing back and talking about the process of talking.

This phenomenon called "backlooping" is easiest to illustrate by the embedding of one *grammatical* piece within another. In quotation, a whole sentence or monologue becomes grammatically the object of a verb like "said." But this kind of *grammatical* embedding is closely related to an embedding of meaningful *content*. For example, the expression "the lecture" can be used to summarize or encapsulate a large amount of content found in the lecture in question. Various kinds of summary expressions, such as "the lecture," "the theory," "the history," and "the nation," can encapsulate a large whole in a small language package.

Consider the expression, "the entirety of history." It is a relatively small expression, from a grammatical point of view. It is a phrase. We condense into a single phrase a very broad viewpoint. Or consider the word "universe." Language provides capabilities for discussing a large whole, not merely through grammatical backlooping but through meanings. Meanings of single phrases or single words may be used to refer to complex wholes. We might call that a kind of backlooping in meaning. Or, more simply, we could just say that it shows the capability of human thought and of language.

These moves involve the use of capabilities that are built into natural language. But they also indicate something about human beings who have this kind of capability. Human beings have the ability to stand back from their immediate situation and look at larger wholes. They can even think about the whole of history. In this ability, they imitate God, who has complete knowledge of himself and of all of history. So our ability in thought and language reflects the fact that we are made in the image of God.

We can put it in another way. We can in a sense "transcend" the immediacy of our local situation and our small-scale use of language. In our minds we can imagine the whole of our situation as it might look "from above." This ability for "transcendence" imitates and reflects the greater transcendence that belongs to God. God transcends the entire created world. We are creatures, so we do not. But in our thinking and in our language we can achieve a kind of imitation of God's transcendence.

In both thought and language we "package" wholes and so in a sense stand above them enough to consider them as wholes. In a sense we "transcend" them. And of course there can be packages within packages within packages. Our understanding of the universe is today enormously enriched by astronomy and the growth of the sciences. We may observe that the semantic sense of the word "universe" is similar to "world" or "whole world" and does not magically contain within it all the available information. A child can use the word "universe" correctly without knowing the whole of astronomy. But when used in various contexts of human communication, the word "universe" easily evokes massive information among those recipients who know such information. The word "universe" is used to refer to the universe, and the universe itself, in our modern conceptualization, evokes packages within packages within packages of knowledge. So it has rich associations in that sense. The organization of human knowledge shows the human capacity for transcendence, for standing back and encapsulating a large whole.

# Imaging

"And let them make me a sanctuary, that I may dwell in their midst."
—Exodus 25:8

God made man in his own image (Gen. 1:26–27). That is the origin for our human capacity to transcend our immediate situation, and to use language to describe large wholes.

We can obtain further insight by considering broader occurrences of the theme of imaging in the Bible. Naturally, imaging is associated in a number of passages either with human beings as they were created or with human beings as redeemed and recreated "after the likeness of God" (Eph. 4:24; see Col. 3:10). But the theme occurs in broader ways. According to Colossians 1:15, Christ is the original "image of the invisible God." And, strikingly, the tabernacle and the Solomonic temple are copies of a heavenly reality, and so in that respect they "image" that reality (Ex. 25:9; Heb. 8:5–6; 9:1–28; 1 Kings 8:12–13, 27–30).[1]

## Imaging in the Tabernacle and the Temple

Let us begin with the tabernacle and the temple as images. Both the tabernacle and the temple symbolize God's dwelling with his people. The New Testament indicates that God comes to dwell with us in final form through Christ. John 1:14 says, "And the Word [God the Son, the second person of the Trinity] became flesh and *dwelt* among us, and we have seen his glory, glory as of the only Son from

---

1. See, for example, the extended discussion of imaging in Meredith G. Kline, *Images of the Spirit* (Grand Rapids, MI: Baker, 1980).

### Spaces in the Tabernacle

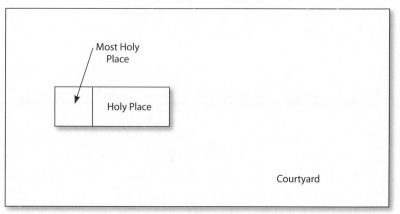

FIGURE 12.1

the Father, full of grace and truth." The word "dwelt" suggests that his dwelling among us fulfills the Old Testament tabernacle and temple dwellings.

But the connection is actually stronger than that. The Greek word for "dwelt" is *eskēnōsen*, an unusual word for "dwelling." It is related to the Greek word *skēnē* for tent, and so evokes the memory of the tabernacle of Moses, which was a tent. The mention of *glory* in the same verse alludes to the cloud of the glory that filled the tabernacle and the temple of Solomon after they were completed (Ex. 40:34–38; 1 Kings 8:10–11; 2 Chron. 5:13–14; 7:1–3). The cloud signified the presence of God, and anticipated the glorious presence of God in Christ's incarnation. Thus the tabernacle and the temple were forward-pointing symbols anticipating the coming of Christ. They were shadows or copies or images not only of the heavenly dwelling of God but of the dwelling of God in Christ.[2]

The tabernacle and the temple also show some *internal* structure that expresses the theme of imaging (fig. 12.1). They both have three distinct spaces, with increasing degrees of holiness. The outermost of these is the courtyard, where there is an altar for burnt offerings (the bronze altar). The individual Israelite worshiper could come into this space and present his offering. The offering would be received by one of the priests, the sons of Aaron. They alone were permitted to approach the bronze altar, where a portion or all of the offering was to be burned.

A higher degree of holiness belonged to the "Holy Place," the outer of the two rooms of the tabernacle. It was a tent structure positioned on the far side of the bronze altar. Only the priests were permitted to enter this room. Beyond this room was a second room, "the Most Holy Place," with the greatest degree of holiness

---

2. Hebrews 8:5; 10:1; see also Vern S. Poythress, *The Shadow of Christ in the Law of Moses* (Phillipsburg, NJ: Presbyterian & Reformed, 1995), 9–40.

(Heb. 9:1–10). Only the *high* priest was permitted to enter this room, and only once a year, on the day of atonement (Heb. 9:7; Leviticus 16).

The two outer spaces are in some ways images or shadows of the Most Holy Place, and the Most Holy Place is in turn an image of God's heavenly dwelling. And God's heavenly dwelling still points forward to the dwelling of God with man through Christ. In addition, the priests in the Old Testament point forward to Christ the final high priest (Heb. 7:1–8:13). In this respect they are "images" of Christ.[3]

The tabernacle and the temple, when considered as wholes, are images pointing to Christ. But there is also imaging within them. So we can say that we have images like the Most Holy Place that themselves produce *other* images, namely, the Holy Place. Such multiple imaging crops up in a number of places, and is quite understandable.

### Imaging in Mankind

Christ is the original image, "the image of the invisible God" (Col. 1:15). He is himself God, so he is a *divine* image. Adam was made in the image of God, and so is a *created* image. We can say more precisely that he is in the image of Christ, so he is in a sense an image of an image. In addition, there is imaging beyond Adam. Adam "fathered a son in his own likeness, after his image, and named him Seth" (Gen. 5:3). Seth, then, is an image of Adam.

Imaging is a *dynamic* structure, expressing the life and activity of God. Imaging among created things is itself an image of the living activity of God, who from eternity fathers the Son (or in the older language of theology, "begets" the Son).[4] Likewise, in the tabernacle, the Most Holy Place is not only an image of God's heavenly dwelling but produces another image, the Holy Place, which produces a third image, the courtyard of the tabernacle. And the holiness within the tabernacle is imitated or "imaged" by the holiness of Israel as an entire nation.

### The Activity of Imaging

The tabernacle shows the activity of imaging, and shows the fecundity or productivity of imaging. Holiness is productive, and reproduces itself. Adam, as a father, is productive, and reproduces his image in his son Seth, who in turn has a son, leading to successive generations of children.

Language has its own productivity and fecundity. We can produce new utterances using old words. We can string together longer and longer phrases: "the gnat

---

3. Poythress, *Shadow of Christ in the Law of Moses*, 9–68; Kline, *Images of the Spirit*; Vern S. Poythress, *Redeeming Science: A God-Centered Approach* (Wheaton, IL: Crossway, 2006), 228–231, 285–292.

4. See Poythress, *Redeeming Science*, 239–240.

on the fly on the wart on the frog . . ." We can produce packages within packages within packages of meaning. We can stand back from our immediate situation, and then stand back to analyze the process of standing back, and so on. The process of repeatedly standing back is itself a form of imaging. So it also reflects God's original image of himself in his Son, who is *the* Image (Col. 1:15).

### Transcendence and Immanence Represented through Imaging

We have already said that the human ability to stand back and analyze imitates the transcendence of God. We can re-express this theme through imaging.

Let us begin with the tabernacle, which is an image of God's heavenly dwelling. The tabernacle shows that God is *present* with the Israelites and their earthly dwellings. In the instructions for the tabernacle, God says, "And let them make me a sanctuary, that I may dwell *in their midst*" (Ex. 25:8). God draws near to his people, anticipating the time when he would draw near to them in Christ, who is "Immanuel," that is "God *with us*" (Matt. 1:23).

By contrast, God's heavenly dwelling more prominently depicts his transcendence. He *transcends* the limitations of creatures dwelling on earth. If a king has his throne placed above the level of the commoners, that exalted position of the throne connotes his authority and his rule over the commoners. When God's throne is depicted as exalted to heaven itself, it depicts his control over the entire universe. In sum, we can say that God's transcendence is represented by the upper dwelling in heaven, while his immanence is represented by the earthly copy of that dwelling.

But that is not the complete story. Both the tabernacle and its heavenly original accurately express God's character. They express both his control (transcendence) and his presence (immanence). These two aspects of God coinhere. His presence may be more obviously expressed in the earthly copy. But it implies his control. God's instructions for building the tabernacle indirectly indicate God's control, because the tabernacle is in fact built according to those instructions (Exodus 36–39). God controls its structure.

God's control is also expressed after the tabernacle is built. The tabernacle becomes a source of blessing from God, or of curse from God, depending on whether the people observe its regulations.

Nevertheless, it is convenient to think of control as being associated with the upper dwelling, and presence with the lower dwelling.

This same pattern is then reflected (imaged) in the inner and outer rooms of the tabernacle. So, from this point of view, the inner room, the Most Holy Place, represents transcendence, and the outer room, the Holy Place, represents immanence. We then can produce a diagram to indicate this representation (fig. 12.2).[5]

---

5. See further discussion of transcendence and immanence in appendix C.

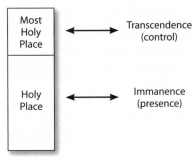

FIGURE 12.2

Since man is made in the image of God, human beings reflect God's control and presence by their own finite control and presence. Their control comes from within them, through the plans and will of their minds and hearts. Their control is made manifest through the activities of their bodies, which express their presence on earth. Thus we can have a diagram that indicates human derivative control and presence (fig. 12.3).

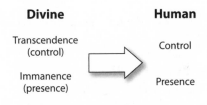

FIGURE 12.3

Man is of course subordinate to God's rule and control. And when man is obedient to God, he represents God's rule among the creatures. In his own person and presence he expresses a special presence of God. And so we can shift the diagram to represent both man's subordination to God's control and his ability to represent God's presence on earth, as in the next diagram (fig. 12.4).

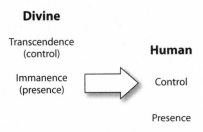

FIGURE 12.4

A human being is a creature, not the Creator. But he is capable of exercising a kind of derivative creativity, as when he makes up a story or makes a manufactured object like a table. When he makes up a story, he creates a fictional world.[6] So we could represent human creativity by adding a further level, for fictional creation (fig. 12.5).

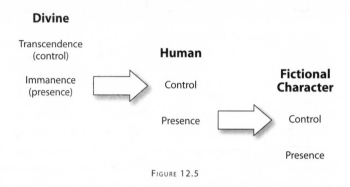

FIGURE 12.5

A fictional character within a story can become a writer and write his own story in turn. So we can see the potential for an indefinite series of images.

## Selecting Some Big and Small Pieces

Within language, the process of imaging is reflected in the process of embedding. Packages occur within packages within packages. One instance of packaging occurs when an author writes a book, a language "package," in which is a fictional character. If the fictional character writes an essay, this essay is itself a package. And the essay may refer to still other characters who engage in writing packages.

So we propose to look in more detail at our ability to use big and small packages within language. That is, we will look at some of the distinct levels, like monologues and sentences and words.

For the sake of brevity, we will in subsequent chapters be selective in our focus. We will not focus on everything that professional linguists take as their interests. Instead, we can begin with God and the whole of history, and then narrow down. We will travel down from the biggest groupings of history, to daily human action, and then to monologue, to sentence, and to word.

It is important that we begin with the larger vistas of human action, because even small pieces of language function to talk about human action and the world that God made.

---

6. See Dorothy L. Sayers, *The Mind of the Maker* (New York: Harcourt, Brace, 1941), on artistic creativity as imitative of God's creativity.

# World History

> "It is done! I am the Alpha and the Omega, the beginning
> and the end. To the thirsty I will give from the spring
> of the water of life without payment."
>
> —Revelation 21:6

We now focus on the widest vista of personal action: the whole history of the world. This history is governed by God's word, his language: "he [Christ] upholds the universe by the *word* of his power" (Heb. 1:3). But history is wider than any one human description. Human language has meaning within this larger context, which only God fully masters. So it is important that we think about history, and not simply isolate language from history. But of course for our purpose we will need eventually to bring our observations about history back around to yield insights about language.

The world did not always exist. Rather, it began when God created it (Gen. 1:1–31). The world therefore exists in a more ultimate context, the context of God and his actions. God exists eternally. The Father loves the Son and the Son loves the Father forever, in the unity of the Holy Spirit.

God in his eternal being and his eternal activity is the source and foundation for activity in creation. God exists. Creatures exist in a derivative manner, dependent on God's existence. God himself acts. And creatures act in a way that analogically reflects his action.

## Plan and Goal

God is also at the center in the goal of creation, namely, the consummation depicted in Revelation 21:1–22:5. The goal of history is to "unite all things in him [Christ]" (Eph. 1:10). God had a plan from the beginning (Eph. 1:11). He created the world as the first stage in the execution of his plan. The plan will reach its fulfillment when God is "all in all" (1 Cor. 15:28). God's glory will be displayed in the whole of the new heaven and the new earth (Rev. 21:1, 22–27). Both the plan and its execution involve all three persons of the Trinity: the Father (1 Cor. 8:6), the Son (the Word, John 1:1–3), and the Holy Spirit (Gen. 1:2).

In particular, the work of God in creation involved the Father saying, "Let there be light" (Gen. 1:3) and other words of command. These commands originated in the fullness of God's word, that is, the Word, the second person of the Trinity (John 1:1). The world reaches its goal in a glorification that takes place in a way that is patterned after Christ's glorification. How is this so?

We can begin with Romans 8:18–25:

[18] For I consider that the sufferings of this present time are not worth comparing with the glory that is to be revealed to us. [19] For the creation waits with eager longing for the revealing of the sons of God. [20] For the creation was subjected to futility, not willingly, but because of him who subjected it, in hope [21] that the creation itself will be set free from its bondage to corruption and obtain the freedom of the glory of the children of God. [22] For we know that the whole creation has been groaning together in the pains of childbirth until now. [23] And not only the creation, but we ourselves, who have the firstfruits of the Spirit, groan inwardly as we wait eagerly for adoption as sons, the redemption of our bodies. [24] For in this hope we were saved. Now hope that is seen is not hope. For who hopes for what he sees? [25] But if we hope for what we do not see, we wait for it with patience.

The creation has "longing," "futility," "bondage," and "groaning" in waiting for final deliverance. Its situation is patterned after the situation of the sons of God, who "groan inwardly as we wait eagerly for adoption as sons, the redemption of our bodies" (verse 23). The redemption of our bodies is after the pattern of Christ's resurrection, according to 1 Corinthians 15:42–49. The pattern of Christ's suffering and glory is also reflected in Romans 8:18, which speaks of believers' suffering and glory: "For I consider that the sufferings of this present time are not worth comparing with the glory that is to be revealed to us."[1] Thus Christ is the pattern for believers, and believers for the whole of creation.

---

1. I owe this insight to William Dennison, who drew my attention to the pattern of suffering and glory in Romans 8:18–25.

We can find a similar point being made in Revelation 21. We can see in the center of the new heaven and the new earth the glory of God in Christ: "And the city has no need of sun or moon to shine on it, for the glory of God gives it light, and its lamp is the Lamb" (Rev. 21:23). The glory of God is the glory revealed supremely in Jesus Christ: "And the Word became flesh and dwelt among us, and we have seen his glory, glory as of the only Son from the Father, full of grace and truth" (John 1:14). The glory of God was displayed during Christ's whole earthly life. But it is climactically displayed in the crucifixion, resurrection, and ascension:

> Now is the Son of Man glorified, and God is glorified in him. If God is glorified in him, God will also glorify him in himself, and glorify him at once (John 13:31–32).

> I [Jesus] glorified you on earth, having accomplished the work that you gave me to do. And now, Father, glorify me in your own presence with the glory that I had with you before the world existed (John 17:4–5).

> Father, I desire that they also, whom you have given me, may be with me where I am, to see my glory that you have given me because you loved me before the foundation of the world (John 17:24).

In the new Jerusalem of Revelation 21:1–22:5, this glory is displayed centrally in God and the Lamb, but the whole city has the glory of God: "he . . . showed me the holy city Jerusalem coming down out of heaven from God, having *the glory of God,* . . ." (Rev. 21:10–11). Thus the pattern of Christ's glory extends to the fullness of the new creation.

Christ's resurrection is the "firstfruits" for the resurrection of believers:

> But in fact Christ has been raised from the dead, the firstfruits of those who have fallen asleep. For as by a man [Adam] came death, by a man [Christ] has come also the resurrection of the dead. For as in Adam all die, so also in Christ shall all be made alive. But each in his own order: Christ the firstfruits, then at his coming those who belong to Christ (1 Cor. 15:20–23).

The "firstfruits" is not only first in time, but is the pattern for the rest. Christ's resurrection body already belongs to the order of the new creation. It is the firstfruits, the first "piece," the foundation piece, for the whole.

Christ's resurrection also points to his ascension and rule. The latter two are implications of the resurrection:

And being found in human form, he humbled himself by becoming obedient to the point of death, even death on a cross. *Therefore God has highly exalted him* and bestowed on him the name that is above every name, so that at the name of Jesus every knee should bow, in heaven and on earth and under the earth, . . . (Phil. 2:8–10).

We see stages in divine action in the life of Christ. At the beginning, there is the initiative of God, both in the incarnation and in the commission of the Son by the Father. In the middle, the Son accomplishes the work of the Father. In the end, God rewards him in exaltation. These three stages involve the life of one person, the Son. But they also have *cosmic* significance. The Son, as 1 Corinthians 15:45 and 15:22 indicate, is the "last Adam," the representative for the new humanity. So we can stand back and see stages with respect to the whole of history.

## Stages

At the beginning of human history, God created man in his image, which corresponds to the Son's being in the image of God (Col. 1:15; Heb. 1:3). God commissioned Adam to the work of dominion (Gen. 1:28–30), corresponding to the commissioning of the Son (Gal. 4:4; John 17:4). Adam was then supposed to carry out his work in obedience to God, but he failed and disobeyed. Hence Christ, the last Adam, intervened. Christ as the last Adam achieved his goal of dominion in the ascension:

> . . . he [God] worked in Christ when he raised him from the dead and seated him at his right hand in the heavenly places, far above all rule and authority and power and dominion, and above every name that is named, not only in this age but also in the one to come. And he put all things under his feet and gave him as head over all things . . . (Eph. 1:20–22).

Thus, for the whole of history, we have a pattern of commission, work, and reward. These three stages should have been followed by Adam. They are achieved by Christ as the Last Adam.

These three stages reflect in a way the three persons of the Trinity. All three persons are involved in all three stages. But the commission can be particularly associated with God the Father. The work is preeminently the work of the Son, who is, as it were, the "executor" of the Father's will. And glorification takes place through being filled with the Spirit. The Spirit is "the Spirit of glory" (1 Pet. 4:14).[2] The diversity in the stages of the work of God reflect the diversity within

---

2. See, in particular, Meredith M. Kline, "The Holy Spirit as Covenant Witness," Th.M. thesis, Westminster Theological Seminary, 1972.

God himself. God is not a creature, and is not subject to time; he is not limited by temporal development. But, in view of the activities of God in time, we can also say that time, development, and climax are not out of step with the character of God. He acts in time in a manner reflective of his character, and his entire plan from beginning to end is in thorough accord with his Trinitarian nature.

We can also see distinctive modes of action that are characteristic of the three phases. In the first phase, in commissioning, the Father speaks and the Son hears. The action is verbal. In the second phase, in the accomplishing of the work, the Father and the Son are both acting in *power*: "the Father who dwells in me does his *works*" (John 14:10). In the third phase, the Father blesses and crowns the work with reward. And the heart of the reward is the presence of God himself, who is the fountain of all blessing. So the three phases could be summarized as involving first speaking, then powerful working, then blessing.

The characteristic feature in each phase is not entirely absent from the other phases. Rather, each phase shows all the features, but not with the same prominence. For example, the speaking of God can empower people and can be a source of blessing (or sometimes curse). Speaking coheres with power and blessing. So God speaks in all three phases. Likewise, the exertion of God's power is meaningful, and all God's works can be described as being accomplished by speaking: "Is it not from the *mouth* of the Most High that good and bad come?" (Lam. 3:38). Works can be a blessing, and blessing can take the form of a work.

In fact, these three characteristic features correspond in some ways to the three aspects of God's lordship: meaning, control, and presence. *Meaning* corresponds to God's speech and commission, which lays out beforehand the meaning of the program to be accomplished. The work of accomplishment shows *control*. And the blessing is a blessing of God's *presence*. These three—meaning, control, and presence—are aspects that are present in all of God's lordship. They are perspectives on the whole.

Finally, we can also see a relation of the three phases to the three "offices" of Christ as prophet, king, and priest.[3] The role of the prophet is primarily to speak on behalf of God, and so is related to the function of speaking and meaning. The role of the king is primarily to rule on behalf of God, and so is related to the function of power and control. The role of the priest is primarily to mediate in the communion of God with man, particularly communion with his presence— presence in blessing. And so the priest is related to the function of blessing and presence. The three offices are generally distinct from one another in the Old Testament, though some figures like Moses perform all three roles. In Christ

---

3. See the *Westminster Shorter Catechism*, answer 23: "Christ, as our Redeemer, executeth the offices of a prophet, of a priest, and of a king, both in his estate of humiliation and exaltation."

the roles come together. They are aspects of his work rather than being strictly separable.

The result of all this is that God's actions in *speaking* are closely tied with a whole variety of actions, which together constitute the whole history of the world. Human action, and human speaking, are to be understood within the larger context formed by God's speech and actions.

# The Fall into Sin

And the great dragon was thrown down, that ancient serpent,

who is called the devil and Satan, the deceiver of the whole world.

—Revelation 12:9

We have taken a very broad viewpoint by looking at world history as a whole. Now we should look at two crucial events within history, events that have radically changed the situation for the whole of the rest of history. First we look at the fall of mankind. In the next chapter we look at the redemption accomplished by Christ.

According to the Bible, humanity today is in a state of rebellion against God. That has implications for our thinking about language. We are not neutral observers. We no longer readily and joyfully acknowledge the gift of language by giving thanks to God. We are morally and spiritually sick, in fact, spiritually dead (Eph. 2:1). And this spiritual death has corrupted the use of language as well. Human beings today sometimes deceive and manipulate others through language.

How did this come about? Human beings did not retain the original harmonious communion with God that they enjoyed in the beginning. They rebelled. Genesis 3 tells the story. The rebellion involved two individuals, Adam and Eve, but it was not confined to them. Not only did Adam suffer the penalty of death (Gen. 3:19; 5:5), but his descendants did too (Gen. 5:1–31). Sin multiplied in the lives of Cain and his descendants (Gen. 4:1–24), leading to increasing corruption (Gen. 6:5–7).

Adam was the head and representative of the whole human race, and when he fell, he plunged the race as a whole into sin and rebellion (see Rom. 5:12–21;

1 Cor. 15:21–22, 45–49). Ever since, we have come into the world already in a state of alienation from God.

So the story in Genesis 3 has two sides. On the one hand, it is the historical record of the original fall of the first man and the first woman. On the other hand, it shows the character and meaning of the fall, and in this respect has implications for understanding our present condition. We ourselves are infected from birth with sin and rebellion against God. We find growing up in our own hearts, like a poisonous weed, the same plant that Adam and Eve grew in their hearts. That poisonous weed infects our use of language as well as other areas of life.

## Deception and Confusion

The events leading to the fall did not really begin with Adam and Eve, but with the serpent. The serpent said to the woman, "Did God actually say, 'You shall not eat of any tree in the garden?'" (Gen. 3:1). The fall began with language. It began with an insidious question, framed in language that the woman understood. Language played a central role in the fall, and we may suspect that it continues to play a central role in the ongoing effects of the fall.

Serpents do not normally talk. Among God's earthly creatures, human beings alone have the capacity for complex, fully articulate language. Yet this particular serpent did talk. He began with a question that concealed its spirit of attack underneath a seemingly innocent request for clarification. But his next utterance unveiled his bold opposition to God: "You will not surely die."

Clearly this was no ordinary serpent. Adam and Eve themselves could have seen that, even without any further information. It should be no surprise, then, that the Bible later on lifts the veil a little more to indicate that behind the literal snake stood a more crafty, bold, and determined opponent, namely, Satan, a powerful spirit, a fallen, rebellious archangel, who is denominated "that ancient serpent" (Rev. 12:9; 20:2; see Isa. 27:1). He is "the deceiver of the whole world" (Rev. 12:9). His deceit began in the garden. But, as the book of Revelation indicates, it continues to this day. So it is worthwhile to think about the deceitful use of language in this one case, in order to have a framework for understanding the deceitful use of language throughout history.

Satan already attempted to deceive Eve in his first question, "Did God actually say, 'You shall not eat of any tree in the garden?'" (Gen. 3:1). He insinuated that God could withhold from Eve what was good. The deceit then escalated when Satan directly contradicted God's earlier statement by saying, "You will not surely die" (Gen. 3:4; contradicting 2:17).

Rebellion against God involves the use of language, and the use of the mind, to undermine and obscure knowledge of key truths about humanity, about the world (the tree), and also about God. The denial concerning the effect of eating from the tree is a denial about future events in the world. But it is also indirectly a denial concerning God. The serpent seems to concede that Eve is correct about what God said, but insists that God is lying. The serpent implies that either God does not have the power or he does not have the willingness to bring the penalty of death. Probably, suggests the serpent, God never intended to execute the death penalty in the first place, but is merely producing a vain threat in order jealously to keep some benefits for himself alone, and to keep Eve from enjoying them. Maybe the serpent's speech is all the more effective because he does not directly blurt out all his conclusions and all his ideas about God, but allows Eve to follow the trail of insinuations herself, and to arrive at her own conclusions.

To arrive at her own conclusions—is not that the point? "You will be like God, knowing good and evil" (Gen. 3:5). In effect, the serpent suggests, "You will make up your own mind about good and evil, by looking at the fruit, and by exercising your own independent judgment as to what seems right. This is God-like autonomy in morality, as opposed to the 'babyhood' of meekly submitting to whatever God says." Within our fallen race, we should not be surprised to find some later thinkers reacting to the Genesis story of the fall by claiming that it was a fall "upward," from moral babyhood into moral maturity. For them, autonomy is equated with moral maturity.

We could reply to this idea by pointing out that, indeed, Adam and Eve did start out in a situation where their knowledge and their experience were just beginning to grow. But God had his own plans for maturity, as he indicates in the cultural mandate to "fill the earth and subdue it" (Gen. 1:28). Adam and Eve could have chosen to mature by following the way of obedience rather than the way of disobedience.[1]

One decisive way in which Adam and Eve could have matured would have been by *resisting* the serpent's temptation. If they had resisted, they would have experienced in themselves a growing knowledge of good, in the very process of doing what is good. And they would have experienced a growing knowledge of evil, in the process of resisting evil. Through resisting they would have seen evil more deeply for what it is. The joint effects of these experiences would have given them a growing "knowledge of good and evil." But it would have taken place in the way of obedience rather than disobedience.

Unfortunately, such reasoning tends to be lost on rebels. They may turn God's morality upside down by claiming that the fall went morally upward rather than downward. We should not be surprised that they do so, because they are following the same path of deceit that the serpent laid down for Adam and Eve. They are being seduced by the very same Satanic arguments. By their captivity to deceit they

---

1. Jesus Christ, as the last Adam, followed the way of obedience perfectly, and so undid for us the effects of Adam's rebellion (Heb. 2:10–15; 5:7–10). See the next chapter.

confirm in their own lives that, even to this day, the serpent's strategy is indeed crafty and alluring. The processes in their own minds confirm the truthfulness of the biblical account.


## Religious Commitment

Now we may begin to draw out several implications from this account of the fall. First, language challenges us concerning *religious commitment*. Will you trust God, or will you refuse to trust him? Will you serve God, or will you refuse to serve him? Will you pursue fellowship with God, or will you run away from him into would-be autonomy?

The challenge confronts us in each of the three aspects of God's lordship: meaning, control, and presence. First, the challenge to trust God is a challenge about *meaning*. Is God's meaning clear? Is he forbidding you from taking from *any* tree whatsoever? Has he said that you shall not touch the tree? And will you trust that he is telling you the truth? ("You shall not surely die," says the serpent.)

The challenge confronts us not only when we deal with the speech of God, but when we deal with the speech of the serpent. What is the serpent's meaning? Is it clear? What does the serpent mean by his initial question, "Did God actually say, 'You shall not eat of any tree in the garden'?" How does he know as much as he knows about what God did say? And if he knows what God did say, why does he misrepresent it? And if he has gotten confused, what does it matter to him anyway? What is in it for him? Why does he seem to be insinuating that God would withhold something good? Why is this serpent speaking anyway? Is he claiming to be Eve's equal or superior?

Can I trust the serpent? And if, in the end, I do think that I can trust the serpent, will my trust in him tacitly involve an abandonment of trust in God? And if it does, am I giving to the serpent the kind of allegiance due only to God, and so committing myself to an alien god and an alien worship and an alien religion?

Second, we have here a challenge either to serve God or to refuse to serve. That is a challenge concerning *control*. Will we continue to have God control our lives, through his commandments, or will we usurp control for ourselves? If God says, "you shall not eat," is that enough for us? Or do we insist on "making up our own minds"? Or—watch out—will we end up *being controlled* by our own sin and by the manipulative, deceitful rhetoric of the serpent? Listening to the serpent also raises the same issues of control.

Third, we have a challenge to mature in fellowship with God, or to walk away from that fellowship into would-be autonomy. That is a challenge concerning *presence*. Will we continue to enjoy God's presence? Will we continue in fellowship with him, when he "walks in the garden" (Gen. 3:8) in a special expression of his presence? Will we also continue in fellowship when he is present with us through his word, which continues to sit in our mind and our memory all day? Will his instruction, "You shall not eat," be a continuing spiritual nourishment as we rejoice in communion with his mind, and rejoice in the goodness and wisdom that his word expresses? Or will we break free from that nourishment in the hope of nourishing ourselves, by ourselves, through an autonomous, independent exploration of the moral world?

And then, when we hear the voice of the serpent, into what sort of personal communion does that voice invite us? Who is this serpent, and what does he represent, and can he and his words really afford us an entrance into a presence that would displace and overpower and supersede the former presence of God?

In all three aspects—meaning, control, and presence—we confront the same basic issue: will we commit ourselves to God, or not? And the decision *not* to commit ourselves to God is just as religious as the decision to commit ourselves to God. Rebellion against God is a religious move, even if it is a negative one. Moreover, it is not wholly negative. We are incurably religious. If we do not serve God, we will end up serving something, whether that is one of the false gods in ancient Israel, or the god of material success, or human pride, or simply autonomy. G. K. Chesterton said, "If people do not believe in God, it is not that they believe in nothing. Rather, they believe in anything."[2] Adam's decision not to serve God is simultaneously a decision to commit himself to autonomy—"You will be like God"—and a decision to serve the word of Satan, as a substitute and usurper of the proper place of God's word. Adam decided to become a subject within the "domain of darkness," the kingdom of Satan (Col. 1:13; cf. Heb. 2:14–15; 1 John 5:19).

## Broad Relevance

Someone may be thinking, "All this was long ago, back in the Garden of Eden." Yes. But the fundamental religious issues are the same, all the way through history. The book of Revelation depicts the principles of spiritual war, a war between God and his agents on the one side, and Satan and his agents on the other. Revelation may be focusing to some degree on one particular period in history, such as the period of the Roman empire in which it was originally written, or the period of the final crisis just before the second coming. But the principles for spiritual war remain the same, and so it has broad relevance.[3] In this spiritual warfare, you are either for God or against him. People from time to time may change sides (as

---

2. These words are widely attributed to Chesterton, though their exact source is unknown. See http://chesterton.org/qmeister2/any-everything.htm.

3. See Vern S. Poythress, "Counterfeiting in the Book of Revelation as a Perspective on Non-Christian Culture," *Journal of the Evangelical Theological Society* 40/3 (1997): 411–418; Poythress, *The Returning King* (Phillipsburg, NJ: Presbyterian & Reformed, 2000), especially 16–25.

when someone is converted to faith in Christ). But there is no neutral ground. Whether you like it or not, your life involves religious commitment to one or the other side of the war.

Adam heard God's commandment concerning the tree (Gen. 2:17). Eve heard Satan's tempting words of deceit (Gen. 3:1, 4–5). But we do not hear such direct speeches now, do we? What about those alive today, who are just hearing the voices of other human beings?

Though the circumstances in the Garden of Eden were unique, there is still permanent relevance. For one thing, God did not utterly abandon mankind when Adam rejected fellowship with God. God continued to speak. He confronted Adam with his sin (Gen. 3:9–13). More than that, he gave a promise of redemption from sin (Gen. 3:15). He continued to expand on his promises, and the Bible is his word in permanent form. God continues to confront us with his claims through the Bible, and then indirectly through human beings who bring the message of the Bible to others. Thus, people today continue to hear the voice of God.

Even those who have never heard of God from the Bible do not escape. To this day, rebellious human beings, though they may flee from God's presence with enormous vigor, never escape his presence. Romans 1:18–21 is worth looking at again:

> For the wrath of God is revealed from heaven against all ungodliness and unrigh-teousness of men, who by their unrighteousness suppress the truth. For what can be known about God is plain to them, because God has shown it to them. For his invisible attributes, namely, his eternal power and divine nature, have been clearly perceived, ever since the creation of the world, in the things that have been made. So they are without excuse. For although they knew God, they did not honor him as God or give thanks to him, but they became futile in their thinking, and their foolish hearts were darkened (Rom. 1:18–21).

God's voice does not come to everyone as an immediate, audible voice. Nor has it come to everyone through reading the Bible, because not everyone has read the Bible. But God has a message about himself through creation, and through the very constitution of human beings, and no one escapes that message.

The message is present in the very rules of language itself, because those rules are a manifestation of the character of God who gives language and governs it through his word.[4] The message may not be formulated explicitly in particular words of a particular human language, but it is still there, it is still known, and it still demands the response: will you trust God or not? Will you serve him or not? Will you have fellowship with him or not? At this level, everyone continually confronts temptations that are the same in essence as the temptation of Adam and

---

4. See chapters 8–9.

Eve. The gloomy picture in Romans 1:18–21 says not only this, but that everyone succumbs to the temptation. We continue to rebel against God unless, through the gospel of Christ, God himself comes to rescue us (Rom. 1:16–17!).

God speaks to everyone through creation. Does Satan also speak? Modern snakes do not speak in audible voices. Eden was unique in that respect. But Satan is "the deceiver of the whole world" (Rev. 12:9). Deceiving involves language or something analogically akin to language. According to the Bible, when we rebel against God, we end up in "the domain of darkness" (Col. 1:13), under the kingdom of Satan:

> And you were dead in the trespasses and sins in which you once walked, following the course of this world, following *the prince of the power of the air, the spirit* that is now at work in the sons of disobedience—among whom we all once lived in the passions of our flesh, carrying out the desires of the body and the mind, and were by nature children of wrath, like the rest of mankind (Eph. 2:1–3).

It seems natural that people who have become captive in the kingdom of Satan, and whose minds have been deceived by his deceit, would often spew out that deceit from their own mouths. They become mouthpieces for Satan. In one particular illustrious case the apostle Paul specifically identifies one of Satan's mouthpieces:

> But Elymas the magician (for that is the meaning of his name) opposed them, seeking to turn the proconsul away from the faith. But Saul, who was also called Paul, filled with the Holy Spirit, looked intently at him and said, "You son of *the devil*, you enemy of all righteousness, full of all *deceit and villainy*, will you not stop making crooked the straight paths of the Lord?" (Acts 13:8–10).

Think about it. In our present cultural circumstances, why should Satan go to the trouble of speaking through a serpent, with all the suspicion and fear and creepiness that it might create, when he can so much more easily and inconspicuously speak through his own human agents? Several people, including C. S. Lewis in *The Screwtape Letters*,[5] have observed that in a modernist culture given to materialism and disbelief, it may be against Satan's own interests and strategy to make the existence of a spiritual world of demons conspicuous.[6]

Of course the people within Satan's domain of darkness still cannot escape God. In spite of themselves, when they use language they depend on God who

---

5. C. S. Lewis, *The Screwtape Letters* (New York: Macmillan, 1943).

6. But the Western world of the twenty-first century is seeing growing interest in "spirituality" of a vague sort. That interest or hunger may lead to a search for relationships to departed spirits or nature spirits or other forms of contact with the preternatural realm. So the secularism and materialism of the twentieth century may have been only a temporary phase.

gives and maintains the rules of language. In spite of themselves, they use logic and reason, which depend on Christ the Word of God, who is the original logic and reason behind the entire universe.[7]

What such people say is usually not going to be pure error, or pure truth, or pure deceit, but a complex mixture. A mixture can sometimes be more alluring to our own rebellious hearts than a blatant lie. A bald lie would too easily unmask its true character. When unmasked it would cease to be useful, either to Satan in his desire to lure us into evil, or to us in our desire to conceal from ourselves our baser motives. For maximum contentment in deceit, we do not need the blatant lie, but we need a whole culture that has corporately drifted and led itself along through a whole series of half-truths into a situation of self-deceit. Then it can be content, because everyone is deceived in the same way, and each assures his neighbor that all is well.

### The Power of Language for Evil

Culture does have enormous power to mold us. And maybe, just maybe, it has molded us in some evil ways as well as good. In fact, the Bible assures us that the "maybe" is not just "maybe" but a certainty.[8]

Through propaganda, Nazism in Germany succeeded in drawing many of the German people into delusions about themselves and their enemies. Militant Islam has succeeded in drawing its adherents into its delusions. Language has helped to captivate people so that they see the world and their own duties in a distorted way. The power of language—originally a good gift from God—becomes twisted to evil.

Unlike totalitarian countries, in the United States and in Europe we have the protection of freedom of speech, so we may think we are immune to propaganda. But we may still experience molding in more insidious ways. What about the power of advertising and the pressure of conformity?

---

7. See Vern S. Poythress, *Redeeming Science: A God-Centered Approach* (Wheaton, IL: Crossway, 2006), chapter 1.

8. Among many passages, we may cite the following:

> For although they knew God, they did not honor him as God or give thanks to him, but they became futile in their thinking, and their foolish hearts were darkened (Rom. 1:21).

> Now this I say and testify in the Lord, that you must no longer walk as the Gentiles do, in the futility of their minds. They are darkened in their understanding, alienated from the life of God because of the ignorance that is in them, due to their hardness of heart (Eph. 4:17–18).

> . . . Satan, the deceiver of the whole world (Rev. 12:9).

Yes, advertising helps to make us aware of some new product that would be useful. But it can also tempt us to be selfish in always wanting more. We become aware of not being stylish if we fail to keep up with the latest fashions of friends and neighbors. The major media and the major educational institutions may still follow like sheep mostly in one direction, and dissenting voices may be marginalized.

## Challenge from the Different Voices

So what we hear in our modern environment includes a complex mix of truth and half-truth and deceit. It includes the voice of God and the voice of Satan, mixed together. Each voice calls us to religious commitment. That is true not only when the voices are talking about "religion" in a narrow sense. It is true whenever anyone is speaking at all. The meanings in that person's voice are meanings that are ultimately rooted in God's meanings, and God's meanings are aspects of the plans and thoughts that he has not only with respect to himself but with respect to the whole course of history. Meaning, therefore, demands religious commitment.[9]

With respect to any meaning that we receive, the question may be raised whether we receive this meaning within a framework in which we acknowledge and rejoice in God as the supplier of meaning. Or do we propose to treat it by ourselves, in ourselves, without reference to any thanks to God or acknowledgment of his presence? And so we are continually making or confirming religious commitments as we process meanings. This is more obviously true when the meanings directly speak about religious commitment or some aspect of it. But it is also true with any meaning whatsoever.

## Antithesis

Satan hates God.[10] He is antithetical to God, and antithetical to God's word, because God's word faithfully represents God. So one of his goals is to tear down God's word. This he does by contradicting it. "You will not surely die," he says (Gen. 3:4).

---

9. "If, so the argument seems to run, we push meaning back far enough, even beyond the practical everyday dictates of reason, science or law, we encounter only Humean scepticism or metaphysics—in other words, God. If, as both Stein and Hart seem to concur, meaning is ultimately guaranteed by God, we do not need that theologians' holy grail, a 'proof' of God. The concept of 'proof' itself is meaningless without God" (Stephen Prickett, *Narrative, Religion, and Science: Fundamentalism versus Irony, 1700–1999* [Cambridge: Cambridge University Press, 2002], 220).

10. The opposition is vividly depicted in symbolic, pictorial form in the book of Revelation. See Poythress, *Returning King*, especially 16–25.

He not only openly contradicts a specific statement from God but also attacks God's word at a general level by undermining confidence with respect to meaning, control, and presence. When he makes the direct contradiction, "You will not surely die," he implies that God's *meanings* are not truthful and not to be trusted. But indirectly he also undermines the other aspects. He denies that God's word *controls* what will happen, by denying that death will ensue. And by denying that God can be trusted, he denies that God presents himself as he truly is. Satan implies that God is not *present* in his word, but rather is presenting in his word a deceitful substitute for himself.

Such is the case with Satan's initial attack on Eve. But, as usual, such will *always* be the case in Satan's strategy, because his hatred of God leaves him no other choice. He will always be antithetical to God.

## Counterfeiting

This antithesis to God is not, however, the only striking feature in Satan's attack. The attack also has subtlety and craftiness to it ("Now the serpent was more *crafty* than any other beast of the field . . ." [Gen. 3:1]). The craftiness first peeks out in the initial question, "Did God actually say, 'You shall not eat of any tree in the garden?'" (Gen. 3:1). The answer is no. The serpent is already introducing distortion. But there is some grain of truth. God did forbid one tree. Moreover, the serpent's speech has the form of a question, and so conceals his intent later to openly contradict God.

The craftiness comes out even more strikingly in the serpent's next speech:

"You will not surely die. For God knows that when you eat of it your eyes will be opened, and you will be like God, knowing good and evil" (Gen. 3:4–5).

What Satan says is actually uncannily close to the truth. Consider what actually happens in Genesis 3. Eve (and Adam as well) does eat the fruit (Gen. 3:6). But she does not die physically, at least not right away. Nor does Adam. In Genesis 2:17 God said, "in the *day* that you eat of it you shall surely die." But apparently this does not happen. Rather, what Satan said would happen is what actually happens. What is going on?

We have to ask about the meaning of both "life" and "death." Real life, life with meaning, life with joy and growth and fruitfulness, is life in communion with God. To be cut off from God means spiritual death (see Eph. 2:1). And spiritual death is actually more significant than physical, bodily death. Hardened rebels against God will experience bodily resurrection, according to John 5:28–29. But that does them no good at all. They experience spiritual death forever, the "second death" (Rev. 20:14). This second death is the real death, the death most to be dreaded

(Matt. 10:28). In comparison with it, bodily death is only a pinprick, an emblem, a shadow of the real thing to come. So God was right to say that Adam and Eve would die, and Satan was wrong. But Satan was not wrong if what he meant was physical death. He concealed his meaning. He gave them a half-truth.

Similarly Satan says, "when you eat of it your eyes will be opened" (Gen. 3:5). And what actually happens in the sequel? "Then the eyes of both were opened, and they knew that they were naked" (Gen. 3:7). Satan was right. Or was he? The opening of the eyes to more knowledge sounds like a good thing, an attractive thing. But it turns out not to be. Adam and Eve have their eyes opened only to feel shame. They have been tricked by Satan. And yet what he said was true, after a fashion. That is the kind of trickery we confront when dealing with the schemes of Satan. He offers something close to the truth, but it is a counterfeit. Like a counterfeit twenty-dollar bill, it has to look genuine in order to trick people. But a careful inspection discloses that it is fake.

Finally, Satan says, as his climactic promise, ". . . and you will be like God, knowing good and evil." That promise also comes true, after a fashion. In Genesis 3:22 God himself says, "Behold, the man has become like one of us in knowing good and evil." Some people see the statement in Genesis 3:22 as purely an ironic echo of Genesis 3:5. It is ironic, to be sure. But it is also true that man has come to "know good and evil" in a deeper way. That is, man has come to know good and evil experientially, in a way that he did not know before the test. He has experienced evil firsthand, in the deception of the serpent. He has also experienced it in his own succumbing to temptation. He has experienced it in the consequences of shame and flight and excuse-making. He has also experienced *good* firsthand, in the goodness of God promising redemption (Gen. 3:15) and mitigating the punishment of death. He has also experienced good secondhand, as an alternative that he rejected in his disobedience. He has come to know both good and evil at a new and deeper level. But if he has at all repented, he has also come, to some degree, to see that all this experience has a deep bitterness that could totally have been avoided by an experience of good and evil in the way of obedience. He could have "known" good by doing good, and "known" evil by seeing it for what it is and resisting it.

So has Adam become "like one of us" in the sense of Genesis 3:22? Has he become like God? In a sense he has, and so this aspect also of Satan's alluring promise has come true. Adam aspired to be "like God" in autonomously deciding about good and evil, and autonomously making his own path in the world. God alone has true autonomy, true and absolute control over his own moral judgments and over his future. Adam could never have that. But he has achieved a kind of pseudo-autonomy by separating himself from fellowship with God. Even in that separation, he cannot cease to be in the image of God, and therefore to imitate

God. But now he imitates God by aspiring to be autonomous rather than in the legitimate way that God appointed.

And what does it mean to be "like one of us"? Does it mean that Adam has become "like God"? In some sense yes, but also in some sense no. He has tried to be autonomous, as God is autonomous. But he has become an imitator of Satan's own rebellion and distrust, and not merely an imitator of God. And his would-be autonomy is a failure. He is still dependent on God, and he suffers the consequences of sin (Gen. 3:17–19).

So Satan, in all three aspects of the promise that he makes in Genesis 3:4–5, is using half-truths. He is counterfeiting. We can be the more confident about this theme of counterfeiting because it is clearly present in Revelation, when Revelation sums up the spiritual war between God and Satan. For example, Satan counterfeits God the Father, who is the planner. The Beast (described in Rev. 13:1–10) counterfeits Christ, who is the executor of the Father's will. And the False Prophet (described in Rev. 13:11–18 and mentioned later by name in Rev. 16:13; 19:20; and 20:10) counterfeits the Holy Spirit, who draws people to worship Christ.[11] A counterfeit that is close to truth seduces people more effectively than a blatant falsehood.

## The Challenge of Sorting Good and Bad Ideas

Satan seduced Eve, and Adam went along with her. But that was only the beginning. Satan is still operating today, according to 1 Peter 5:8: "Your adversary the *devil* prowls around like a roaring lion, seeking someone to devour." He may sometimes do so through subordinate evil agents, namely, evil spirits (1 Tim. 4:1). These agents may have access to people's minds. But because the effects of the fall continue in Adam's descendants, the seduction and counterfeiting crop up not only in demonic voices but also in the voices of human beings who are subjects in Satan's kingdom (see John 8:44; Col. 1:13; Eph. 2:1–3). Human beings speak a mixture of truth and error. The fragments of truth mixed in with error make the error more seductive.

This mixed situation makes human communication problematic. We ourselves must undertake to sort out truth and error. And the most dangerous error is not innocent error but desire for autonomy manifesting itself in distorted views of God, of humanity, and of the world. When we look at the products of counterfeiting, we simultaneously confront truth and error, truth and the antithesis of truth.

The writings of Cornelius Van Til are pertinent to the sorting process.[12] Van Til uses two terms, *antithesis* and *common grace*. *Antithesis* designates the radical

---

11. Ibid., 16–22.

12. See especially Cornelius Van Til, *The Defense of the Faith*, 2nd ed. (Philadelphia: Presbyterian & Reformed, 1963).

difference in allegiance between those who serve God and those who are in rebellion against him. This difference in allegiance influences thought and language, so that human communication regularly contains the challenge of whether we will serve God or a substitute god—God or self. The antithesis between servants of God and enemies of God, or between Christians and non-Christians, manifests itself in differences in worldview, differences in conceptions of humanity, and differences in conceptions of the mind, rationality, and language.

Van Til's second expression, *common grace*, expresses the fact that non-Christians are not as bad as they could be. They hold to fragments of truth, and they sometimes perform acts in external conformity with God's moral law. *Common grace* is closely related to what we have said about counterfeiting. Truth remains among human beings, in spite of the fall. And this remaining truth can be evaluated positively, as a gift from God. The gift remains among all people, not just those who consciously give their allegiance to God. But unfortunately the remaining truth can also function negatively, because fragments of truth, or half-truths, can be used to captivate people in the service of false gods and false allegiances.

# Redemption through Christ

For the word of the cross is folly to those who are perishing,
but to us who are being saved it is the power of God. For it is written,

"I will destroy the wisdom of the wise,
and the discernment of the discerning I will thwart."
—1 Corinthians 1:18–19

How can we escape from the effects of the fall? In particular, how can we sort through the mixture of truth and error left by the effects of counterfeiting? We need real wisdom to do so. Where do we get wisdom? God is the ultimate source of wisdom. But the fall alienated us from him. How do we return?

The Bible directs us beyond the fall to a second crucial event within world history, the coming of Christ. Christ came to rescue us from the fall and from its effects—not only sin, but the confusions of half-truths in propaganda and in counterfeiting. Christ provides wisdom: "And because of him [God] you are in Christ Jesus, who became to us *wisdom* from God, righteousness and sanctification and redemption" (1 Cor. 1:30).

The fall had many effects. Naturally in this book we concentrate on the effects on language. But the effects have penetrated every area of human life. The immediate effect of the fall into sin was alienation from God and spiritual death. That effect remains to this day, unless Christ rescues people from their alienation. But effects multiply: physical death among human beings, disease, war, hatred, murder, oppression, sins of many kinds. In addition, the threat of judgment looms over us, because God is a just and holy God, and we have behaved unjustly both toward him and toward our fellow human beings.

Christ undertook to redeem people from both sin and its effects. The redemption that he accomplished is comprehensive, touching on every area infected by the fall. We cannot explore every aspect of the implications of redemption. We will concentrate on its effects on language and on human thinking, because thinking is closely related to language.

How do we receive the kind of wisdom that will straighten out the confusions in human society?[1] The answer comes in several stages.

Christ ascended to heaven, and from there poured out the Holy Spirit:

> "Being therefore exalted at the right hand of God, and having received from the Father the promise of the Holy Spirit, he has poured out this that you yourselves are seeing and hearing" (Acts 2:33).

The Holy Spirit unites us to Christ:

> You, however, are not in the flesh but in the Spirit, if in fact the Spirit of God dwells in you. Anyone who does not have the Spirit of Christ does not belong to him. But if Christ is in you, although the body is dead because of sin, the Spirit is life because of righteousness (Rom. 8:9–10).

Through the instruction of the Holy Spirit we receive wisdom from God:

> Now we have received not the spirit of the world, but the Spirit who is from God, that we might understand the things freely given us by God (1 Cor. 2:12)

But Christ's ascension and his gift of the Holy Spirit are only part of his work. We should also consider the role of his crucifixion and his resurrection.

## Substitutionary Exchange

First, the crucifixion and the resurrection of Christ accomplished a substitutionary exchange. This exchange is expounded in the classic Protestant doctrines of penal atonement and justification. Christ bore the punishment for our sins on the cross (1 Pet. 2:24; Isa. 53:5–6), in order that the penalty for our sins might be paid and in order that we might be qualified with the righteousness of Christ, which makes us fit to stand in the presence of God the holy One, and to receive the blessing of the eternal inheritance in Christ (2 Cor. 5:21; Rom. 5:21). "Justification," in the

---

1. On the Old Testament theme of the quest for wisdom, see Vern. S. Poythress, "The Quest for Wisdom," in *Resurrection and Eschatology: Theology in Service of the Church: Essays in Honor of Richard B. Gaffin, Jr.*, ed. Lane G. Tipton and Jeffrey C. Waddington (Phillipsburg, NJ: Presbyterian & Reformed, 2008), 86–114.

technical sense of the word, includes both forgiveness of sins and the positive pronouncement from God as judge that we are accounted righteous on the basis of the righteousness of Christ.

Justification is defined in juridical terms, against the background of God as judge and the righteousness of God as the standard for judgment. But it has potential implications for other areas, in particular for knowledge and for language. To sort out good and bad ideas, we need wisdom from God. And such wisdom comes from fellowship with God. But by nature we are alienated from God. Justification is required in order to qualify for receiving wisdom from God. Christ as our representative has qualified. And then we qualify in him. His righteousness is reckoned to us, and that qualifies us. Justification is thus also a prerequisite for knowledge about the nature of language. By contrast, sinfulness disqualifies us from communion with God, the source of wisdom. It makes us liable to the punishment of cognitive darkness, of being stripped of the blessings of wisdom received in communion with God.

In the crucifixion Christ bore the punishment for sins. Ultimately the work of his atonement is mysterious. But we can infer that it included a cognitive dimension as well. Bearing the wrath of God, and being separated from communion with God, included being separated from communion with God's wisdom, and so would have included cognitive darkness. This darkness culminated in death, which is loss of knowledge in its normal dimensions. As one aspect of his suffering, Christ suffered cognitive darkness in order that we might receive cognitive light.

We receive the benefit of cognitive light because Christ in his ascension has first received it for us. His ascension gives him access to God's own wisdom. And because in his ascension he represents those who belong to him, he gives us access to God's wisdom.

## Common Grace

Wisdom is a benefit of Christ's atonement. So how can a non-Christian have any knowledge or wisdom at all? In fact, we can press the issue even further. If sin makes people liable to death and hell, why do not the sins of non-Christians lead to their immediate deaths?

The doctrine of "common grace" addresses such questions. "Common grace" is an undeserved benefit from God given to a non-Christian.[2] It is in contrast with "special grace." Special grace means undeserved benefits given to people who are in union with Christ, and who are saved by him. And sometimes the term "special grace" is extended to include those who are chosen in Christ before the

---

2. See chapter 14.

foundation of the world (Eph. 1:4), but who have not yet come to saving faith in Christ. These are people who *will* become Christians but who are not yet Christians. Because they are already chosen in Christ, we can understand how they might receive benefits that they personally do not deserve but that Christ has deserved and has obtained on their behalf. But what about common grace, to those who will never become Christians?

Genesis 8:20–22 can help. In Genesis 8 God makes a promise to Noah:

> "Neither will I ever again strike down every living creature as I have done. While the earth remains, seedtime and harvest, cold and heat, summer and winter, day and night, shall not cease" (Gen. 8:21–22).

In Genesis 9 God goes on to bless Noah and his sons and gives a dominion mandate very like that given to Adam (Gen. 1:28–30). These promises apply to Noah and his descendants, and so they include all human beings now on earth. God promises blessings even to those who are not included in his special holy people. They are thus blessings of common grace.

The blessings and promises were given immediately after "the LORD smelled the pleasing aroma" of Noah's burnt offerings (Gen. 8:21). These burnt offerings, like all the other sacrificial offerings by God's people in the Old Testament, prefigure the self-offering of Christ (Heb. 10:1–14). God is pleased with Noah's offerings, not as merely animal sacrifices but as prefigures of the work of Christ. We may conclude, then, that the work of Christ is the ultimate basis for God's blessings to Noah. And if so, it is the ultimate basis for the blessings of common grace given to Noah's descendants. Christ's work accomplished the salvation of the elect, the ones chosen in Christ from the beginning. But it *also* gave a basis for lesser benefits, the benefits of common grace that come to unbelievers. As sinners against God, we all deserve to die immediately. But we still receive life and food and sunshine and other benefits:

> "For he [God] makes his sun rise on the evil and on the good, and sends rain on the just and on the unjust" (Matt. 5:45).

> "Yet he [God] did not leave himself without witness, for he did good by giving you rains from heaven and fruitful seasons, satisfying your hearts with food and gladness" (Acts 14:17).

These are among the benefits of common grace.

Now we may apply these truths to the situation with respect to the knowledge possessed by unbelievers. Such knowledge is a benefit that they do not deserve in and of themselves. It comes as one of the benefits of Christ. Christ has not only obtained special saving wisdom for his chosen ones but has also obtained the blessing of "common grace" knowledge given here and there to unbelievers.

In particular, human knowledge concerning language derives from Christ's work. And Christ's work sustains human ability to sort through and distinguish good and bad ideas. This is so despite the fact that many of the beneficiaries do not know Christ, and might even be offended at the suggestion that he had anything to do with their having this knowledge.

## Dying and Rising with Christ

The work of Christ results not only in justification but also in sanctification. That is, we who are united to Christ not only enjoy freedom to stand before God on the basis of Christ's perfect righteousness (justification); we also experience progressive transformation into conformity with the image of Christ (2 Cor. 3:18). More and more, we obey and serve God in thought, word, and deed.

This process of sanctification takes place through fellowship with the dying and rising of Christ. We are identified with the dying and rising of Christ once and for all at the beginning of the Christian life, as symbolized by baptism:

> We were buried therefore with him by baptism into death, in order that, just as Christ was raised from the dead by the glory of the Father, we too might walk in newness of life (Rom. 6:4).

> We know that our old self was crucified with him in order that the body of sin might be brought to nothing, so that we would no longer be enslaved to sin (Rom. 6:6).

> For the death he died he died to sin, once for all, but the life he lives he lives to God. So you also must consider yourselves dead to sin and alive to God in Christ Jesus (Rom. 6:10–11).

We also experience fellowship with the death and resurrection of Jesus day by day:

> . . . that I may know him and the power of his resurrection, and may share his sufferings, becoming like him in his death (Phil. 3:10).

> . . . always carrying in the body the death of Jesus, so that the life of Jesus may also be manifested in our bodies. For we who live are always being given over to death for Jesus' sake, so that the life of Jesus also may be manifested in our mortal flesh. So death is at work in us, but life in you (2 Cor. 4:10–12).

Dying and rising with Christ includes *intellectual* transformation:

I appeal to you therefore, brothers, by the mercies of God, to present your bodies as a living sacrifice, holy and acceptable to God, which is your spiritual worship. Do not be conformed to this world, but be *transformed* by the renewal of your *mind*, that by testing you may discern what is the will of God, what is good and acceptable and perfect" (Rom. 12:1–2).

Today Christian people are talking about developing a Christian "worldview." They want to grow in appreciating a distinctive Christian view of the world, and in using that worldview in approaching modern issues. The terminology concerning a Christian worldview may be fairly recent, but in essence the idea is not. Being a disciple of Christ involves following him in every area of life, including intellectual areas. We strive to "take every thought captive to obey Christ" (2 Cor. 10:5).

The intellectual change does not happen without intellectual pain, without a figurative kind of death and resurrection in the intellectual realm. The Christian life of submission to Christ, including intellectual submission to his word in Scripture, is fundamentally at odds with the former life, where each person tried to use his mind in an independent way and judged God rather than being judged by him. A person becoming a Christian may then have an intellectual dimension to the crisis that he experiences in going from one allegiance to another.

Intellectual change also takes place progressively after becoming a Christian. When we come to consider issues about language, the same principle applies. In principle, in accordance with 2 Corinthians 10:5, we are committed to taking "every thought captive" in the area of thinking about language. We have already seen a number of ways in which Christians may think differently about language. They acknowledge God as the source of the gift of language, and God as the primary user of language. They acknowledge their own spiritual poverty and the need for Christ to renew both their persons and their language and their thinking about language. And so on. Giving up former ways of thinking may be painful, because we must not simply give something up but must sort through truth and error, in the midst of temptations to cling to the error, or temptations to give up some bits of truth because we want to avoid the hard work of assimilating them into a Christian worldview. Giving up the old ways of thinking is a kind of intellectual crucifixion and death. And receiving a new way of thinking is a resurrection, an intellectual form of experiencing new life.

One of the greater intellectual challenges is simply to have humility. Pride, pride in self, including pride in intellectual ability, is among the root sins that infect us most deeply. In fact, we can say that Adam's fall was a matter of pride, in thinking that he could manage a course independent of God. Intellectual pride is only one form, but it is perhaps the common failing of intellectuals. To submit to God, not just in one area but in every area, involves a crucifixion of self: "If anyone comes to me and does not hate his own father and mother and wife and children and brothers and sisters, yes, and even his own life, he cannot be my disciple. Whoever does not bear his own cross and come after me cannot be my disciple" (Luke 14:25–27). From fellowship with Christ (Phil. 2:3–11) we must have humility, and repeatedly learn more deeply from God how to look at language as well as every other area.

## Defeating Satan

A third benefit of the work of Christ is the defeat of Satan. The book of Hebrews indicates that Christ defeated Satan in his crucifixion and resurrection: "Since therefore the children share in flesh and blood, he himself likewise partook of the same things, that through death he might *destroy* the one who has the power of death, that is, the devil, and deliver all those who through fear of death were subject to lifelong slavery" (Heb. 2:14–15). "He has *delivered* us from the domain of darkness and transferred us to the kingdom of his beloved Son" (Col. 1:13). Deliverance includes deliverance from the intellectual darkness of Satanic deceit:

> And even if our gospel is veiled, it is veiled only to those who are perishing. In their case the god of this world has blinded the minds of the unbelievers, to keep them from seeing the light of the gospel of the glory of Christ, who is the image of God (2 Cor. 4:3–4).

> So Jesus said to the Jews who had believed in him, "If you abide in my word, you are truly my disciples, and you will know the truth, and the truth will set you free" (John 8:31–32).

> "You are of your father the devil, and your will is to do your father's desires. He was a murderer from the beginning, and has nothing to do with the truth, because there is no truth in him. When he lies, he speaks out of his own character, for he is a liar and the father of lies. But because I tell the truth, you do not believe me" (John 8:44–45)

Jesus won a victory against Satan in the resurrection, and that victory is fruitful in delivering people from the kingdom of Satan. The deliverance takes place at the beginning of the Christian life, when we first believe the gospel. And the deliverance is also progressive, as we come to know the truth more deeply and cast off deception more thoroughly. The deliverance includes deliverance in thought, as our thinking moves from deceit to truth. It is also deliverance in language, because language and thought go together. We hear and speak the truth in language. Receiving the truth from Christ also helps us to be discerning when we hear deceitful language; we become more adept at filtering it.

This intellectual change affects our view of language itself. In practice, we become more aware both of the positive power of language, to express truth, and of the negative power of language, to cause deceit. Language is not neutral, but is a battleground in a spiritual war concerning truth. And one key instrument in this battleground is the word of God coming to us in language:

> Stand therefore, having fastened on the belt of *truth*, and having put on the breastplate of righteousness, and, as shoes for your feet, having put on the readiness given by the *gospel* of peace. In all circumstances take up the shield of faith, with which you can extinguish all the flaming darts of the evil one; and take the helmet of salvation, and the sword of the Spirit, which is *the word of God*, *praying* at all times in the Spirit, . . . (Eph. 6:14–18).

# Peoples, Cultures, and Languages

"Worthy are you to take the scroll and to open its seals, for you were
slain, and by your blood you ransomed people for God from every tribe
and language and people and nation, and you have made them a kingdom and priests to our God, and they shall reign on the earth."

—Revelation 5:9–10

We have considered two great turning points within history, the fall and
Christ's work of redemption. Now we need to begin to look within world
history at progressively smaller scales. We look at the packages within world history.
Since language continues to be our focus, we need to think about the *diversity* of
languages. This diversity goes together with diversity in peoples and in cultures.

## Peoples

One of God's principal goals for world history is the salvation of many *peoples*
through the work of Christ:

> "Worthy are you [Christ] to take the scroll
>    and to open its seals,
> for you were slain, and by your blood you ransomed people for God
>    *from every tribe and language and people and nation,*
> and you have made them a kingdom and priests to our God,
>    and they shall reign on the earth" (Rev. 5:9–10).

> After this I looked, and behold, a great multitude that no one could number, *from every nation, from all tribes and peoples and languages*, standing before the throne and before the Lamb, . . . (Rev. 7:9).

In the ancient world as well as in the modern world, political empires have sometimes governed a large area including many "people groups," that is, ethnic groups with distinct languages and customs. The book of Revelation invites us to think not simply about the largest political empires but about these distinct ethnic groups as well. The issue of diversity in languages arises at this point, in close connection with the diversity of cultures. In the consummation, peoples with different languages will be integrated into a society and city of peace—the new Jerusalem (Rev. 21:2, 10). This is an appropriate context in which to consider the multiplicity of languages, and the prejudices and separations and tensions that may arise from language differences.

## Babel

The diversity of languages in the world originated at Babel:

> Now the whole earth had one language and the same words. And as people migrated from the east, they found a plain in the land of Shinar and settled there. And they said to one another, "Come, let us make bricks, and burn them thoroughly." And they had brick for stone, and bitumen for mortar. Then they said, "Come, let us build ourselves a city and a tower with its top in the heavens, and let us make a name for ourselves, lest we be dispersed over the face of the whole earth." And the LORD came down to see the city and the tower, which the children of man had built. And the LORD said, "Behold, they are one people, and they have all *one language*, and this is only the beginning of what they will do. And nothing that they propose to do will now be impossible for them. Come, let us go down and there confuse their *language*, so that they may not understand one another's speech." So the LORD dispersed them from there over the face of all the earth, and they left off building the city. Therefore its name was called Babel, because there the LORD confused the *language* of all the earth. And from there the LORD dispersed them over the face of all the earth (Gen. 11:1–9).

The multiplication of languages went together with people being "dispersed." They were separated by language, by geography, and by culture. As a result they ceased to be able to cooperate in doing evil. But they also ceased to be able to cooperate in doing good. Redemption, then, includes a plan from God for overcoming the barriers that grew up as a result of Babel.

## God's Promises to Integrate the Various Peoples

We see a beginning of the promise of redemption in Genesis 12:3. God says to Abram, "I will bless those who bless you, and him who dishonors you I will curse, and in you *all the families of the earth* shall be blessed." The mention of all the families of the earth reflects back on the division into people groups that took place at Babel and was cataloged in Genesis 10:1–32. All these "families" or groups, and not just Abram, will be able to receive God's blessing in connection with Abram.

Later parts of the Old Testament explain more about God's purposes for the different peoples:

> May all kings fall down before him,
>      all *nations* serve him! (Ps. 72:11).

> Praise the LORD, all *nations*!
>      Extol him, all *peoples*! (Ps. 117:1; see Rom. 15:11).

> It shall come to pass in the latter days
>      that the mountain of the house of the LORD
> shall be established as the highest of the mountains,
>      and it shall be lifted up above the hills;
> and *peoples* shall flow to it,
>      and *many nations* shall come, and say:
> "Come, let us go up to the mountain of the LORD,
>      to the house of the God of Jacob,
> that he may teach us his ways
>      and that we may walk in his paths."
> For out of Zion shall go forth the law,
>      and the word of the LORD from Jerusalem (Mic. 4:1–2).

In particular, the final lines in Micah 4:2 indicate that the nations will be instructed by God's word; and that implies the coming of his word in the various languages of the nations. The result of submission to God will be universal peace: "*nation* shall not lift up sword against *nation*, neither shall they learn war anymore; but they shall sit every man under his vine and under his fig tree, and no one shall make them afraid" (Mic. 4:3–4).

## Pentecost and Acts

Thus, in the Old Testament God gives promises about a future time when the nations will be blessed through Abraham. The New Testament indicates that the time has now come. The book of Acts describes the beginning of a process of bringing peace to the nations. In Acts 1:8 Jesus commissions the disciples to "be my witnesses in Jerusalem and in all Judea and Samaria, and to the end of the earth" (see also Luke 24:47). The commission begins to be fulfilled in Acts 2, when "the mighty works of God" (Acts 2:11) are proclaimed in the various languages of the Roman empire (Acts 2:8–9). The Holy Spirit miraculously enables the apostles to overcome the language barriers. God through the disciples speaks his message of salvation to the language groups and people groups. Acts 2 thus offers a picture of a kind of reversal of Babel. People from different languages are able to understand one another. This picture in Acts 2 is not complete, because the language groups still consist exclusively of "Jews" (Acts 2:5). But it anticipates the gathering of Gentiles as well.

The rest of Acts records further expansions. Cornelius the God-fearing centurion comes to faith in Christ in Acts 10.[1] Cornelius and his friends are Gentiles, not Jews, as the subsequent narrative makes clear (10:28, 45; 11:3, 18). Cornelius, like other Gentiles who were called "God-fearers," has already come to acknowledge the God of Israel as the one true God (10:2). Later, the gospel comes to pagan polytheists as well, in Acts 14:8–18 and 17:22–34.

Acts 2 describes the miraculous operation of the Holy Spirit's power. After Acts 2 the Holy Spirit continues to spread the gospel, but does so more by non-miraculous means, involving bilingualism and translation.

We can follow the message of the gospel through many stages. It begins with God the Father, whose purpose is to bring peace to all nations. Jesus Christ receives the Holy Spirit from the Father (Acts 2:33) and pours out the Spirit on the disciples, so that they proclaim his message and Christ speaks through them (Eph. 2:17). By the authority of Christ (Rom. 1:1; 2 Pet. 3:16) the New Testament canon is written, which transmits the gospel in written form. Through copying, preaching, and translating, the message spreads to the end of the earth (Acts 1:8). See fig. 16.1.

The spread of the gospel brings peace with God, because it announces reconciliation between God and man through Christ:

> Therefore, since we have been justified by faith, we have *peace with God* through our Lord Jesus Christ. Through him we have also obtained access by faith into this grace in which we stand, and we rejoice in hope of the glory of God (Rom. 5:1–2).

> All this is from God, who through Christ *reconciled us to himself* and gave us the ministry of reconciliation; that is, in Christ God was reconciling the world to

---

1. We may add here the Ethiopian eunuch, who seems to have been a God-fearer (Acts 8:26–40). There were also Gentile converts in Old Testament times, such as Rahab, Naaman, and the Queen of Sheba. But Cornelius represents the beginning of an era when larger numbers come to faith in the true God, through the gospel of Christ.

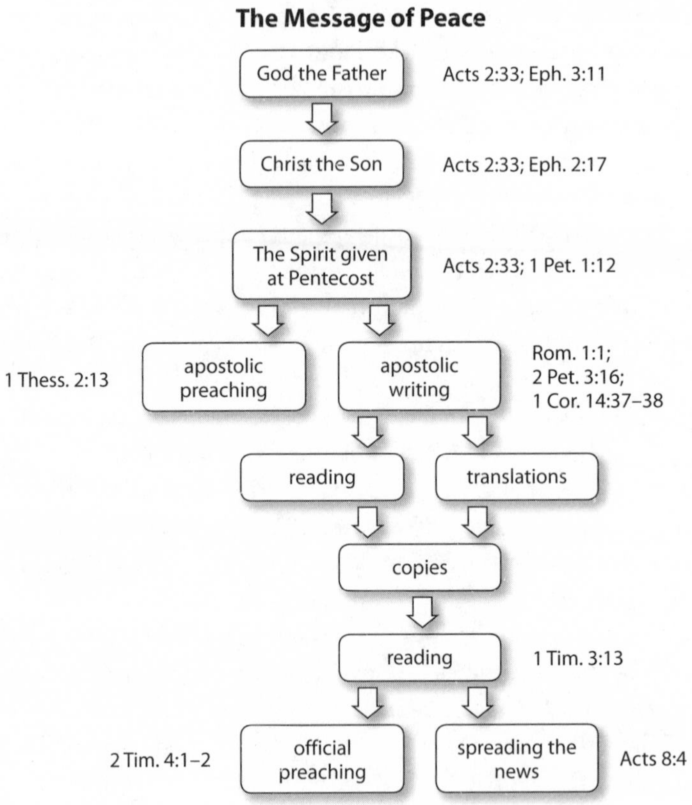

## The Message of Peace

| | | |
|---|---|---|
| God the Father | | Acts 2:33; Eph. 3:11 |
| Christ the Son | | Acts 2:33; Eph. 2:17 |
| The Spirit given at Pentecost | | Acts 2:33; 1 Pet. 1:12 |

1 Thess. 2:13 — apostolic preaching   apostolic writing — Rom. 1:1; 2 Pet. 3:16; 1 Cor. 14:37–38

reading   translations

copies

reading — 1 Tim. 3:13

2 Tim. 4:1–2 — official preaching   spreading the news — Acts 8:4

FIGURE 16.1

himself, not counting their trespasses against them, and entrusting to us the message of reconciliation. Therefore, we are ambassadors for Christ, God making his appeal through us. We implore you on behalf of Christ, be reconciled to God (2 Cor. 5:18–20).

Peace with God leads also to peace with one another:

For he himself is *our peace*, who has made us both [Jews and Gentiles] one and has broken down in his flesh the dividing wall of *hostility* (Eph. 2:14).

Peace between Jew and Gentile has fundamentally been achieved through the reconciling work of Christ. But it remains to be worked out in practice. The New Testament has numerous indications that struggles occurred. To work out peace with one another, the people in the church had to receive both spiritual power through the Spirit of Christ and good theology concerning the implications of the work of Christ.

## Jew and Gentile

The distinction between Jew and Gentile is the most fundamental cultural division, because it is not merely cultural, and not merely "religious" in the sense that pagan religions might differ from one another. A boundary was put in place by God himself, "the law of commandments expressed in ordinances" (Eph. 2:15), which separated the people of Israel from all the other peoples of the world, to be a unique people. At the time of the exodus from Egypt, God distinguished the people of Israel from all the other peoples:

"Now therefore, if you will indeed obey my voice and keep my covenant, you shall be my treasured possession among all peoples, for all the earth is mine; and you shall be to me a kingdom of priests and a holy nation" (Ex. 19:5–6).

When Christ came, he removed this separation:

For he himself [Christ] is our peace, who has made us both one and has broken down in his flesh the dividing wall of hostility by abolishing the law of commandments expressed in ordinances, that he might create in himself one new man in place of the two, so making peace, and might reconcile us both to God in one body through the cross, thereby killing the hostility (Eph. 2:14–16).

Thus the removal of the boundary described in Ephesians 2:14–16 is a unique step. But the reconciliation between Jew and Gentile also illustrates in specific form the broader reconciliation between nations of which Micah 4:3 speaks: "nation shall not lift up sword against nation, neither shall they learn war anymore."

In the case of Jew and Gentile in the church, peace does not require that Gentiles become Jews. Cornelius and his Gentile friends are uncircumcised, that is, non-Jews. They are baptized with the Holy Spirit, and then baptized with water signifying their incorporation into the church (Acts 10:44–48; 11:15–18).

The apostle Peter appeals to this divinely ordained precedent when the Jerusalem council discusses the issue of Gentile converts (Acts 15). In Acts 15, the apostles and elders give a ruling that lays some requirements on Gentile believers (Acts 15:20, 28–29). Significantly, the ruling does *not* require the Gentiles to be circumcised and thus to become Jews—even though some people initially argued for such a rule (Acts 15:1, 5). Likewise, Jews are not required to become Gentiles or give up their customs (Acts 21:20–26). But neither are the customs sacrosanct. Compromises with respect to custom are sometimes appropriate in order to express and maintain the unity of the *one people* of God in Christ (Gal. 2:11–14).

The unity in the body of Christ is a unity in diversity. There is one body, but many members, and the members have different functions (1 Corinthians 12). This unity and diversity applies not only to differences in gifts but to differences in culture as well. Each individual and each culture makes a contribution to the body of Christ.

The biggest divisions among human beings are the divisions of language and culture. But even those who share a common culture can sometimes be divided by hatred and by marked differences in personality. Each individual is different from any other. At an intermediate level, there can be divisions and misunderstandings among different subgroups within a larger culture. Thus, in the modern United States, we can single out various youth subcultures, rural subcultures, medical subcultures, prison subcultures, theater subcultures, arts subcultures, immigrant subcultures, young-urban-professional subcultures, and so on. The picture of unity and diversity in the body of Christ, developed in 1 Corinthians 12, addresses in principle all these kinds of division.

# Principles for Cultural Reconciliation

And he came and preached peace to you who were far off
and peace to those who were near.
For through him we both have access in one Spirit to the Father.
—Ephesians 2:17–18

Peace among nations and peoples and languages has already been achieved through the one sacrifice of Christ, who reconciles us to God and to one another. The peace and reconciliation of the gospel will be fully manifested in the new heaven and the new earth. Within this life, peace is to be progressively worked out in the context of the unity and diversity in the church, the body of Christ (Eph. 4:7–16; 1 Cor. 12).

Within the body of Christ, each people group retains its distinctiveness in language, customs, and culture, just as Jewish and Gentile Christians did. At the same time, each people group grows by interacting within the body of Christ. Growth requires the abandonment of some practices from the past. A people group must give up anything that is sinful itself, whether in language practices like lying, or in cultural practices like prostitution or false worship, or in mistreatment or hostility or prejudice toward other cultures. In addition, in building relations with other groups, especially within the church, the people in various groups must practice loving their neighbors. This will involve cultural compromises in cases that involve cross-cultural friction (think, for example, of Jewish food laws, which were a source of friction in Gal. 2:11–14).

## Crossing Barriers in Language and Culture

It is never easy to build a bridge between two distinct cultures. Frictions arise partly because of human pride and greed but also because of misunderstandings, frustrations, and the challenges of adjusting to what is initially strange and uncomfortable.[1] The Christian who attempts to cross a cultural barrier out of love for others finds inevitably that it involves a painful dying to self. He dies as he surrenders the pride that he may have had in his native culture. And he experiences a kind of emotional "death" in the pain of repeatedly submitting to what is strange, and, in some cases, in the humiliations of finding himself inferior to children who are growing up in the new culture and therefore know more about that culture than he does.

The difficulties may prove particularly intense as a Christian attempts to learn a new language. He strains his mind and his memory in trying to adjust to its strangeness. For example, for a native speaker of English it seems natural to call light "light." Someone raised in a completely monolingual environment might be astonished at any suggestion to the contrary. "What else would you call it?" he asks. Then he finds out that Hebrew calls it "or." "No," he objects, "that is perverse. 'Or' means 'or,' as in 'either-or.' Perhaps it means an 'oar,' a blade for paddling through the water. It already means that. Why in the world would you confuse things by making it mean something else?" As he goes on, it becomes worse. The feminine pronoun for "she" in Hebrew is "he."[2] The pronoun for "he" in Hebrew is "hu," pronounced like the English word "who." The language learner not only has to force his memory to learn new words; he also fights against the memory of what intuitively he feels things should be like according to his native tongue.

Moreover, natives within the new culture can at times be quite pitiless: they may laugh at an adult who makes stupid, childlike mistakes with their language. The Christian finds here one instance where he experiences fellowship with the suffering and crucifixion of Christ. Christ crossed the biggest barrier of all, the barrier between God and man. Christians are called on to cross the subordinate barriers between cultures and languages.

In a previous chapter we considered several aspects of Christ's work. He died and rose again for us. He also accomplished a substitutionary exchange, in that he bore the penalty of our sins and gave his righteousness to us. His substitution is unique. But a faint echo of that unique exchange can nevertheless be found in acts of mercy that Christians do. A Christian may choose to undergo pain or inconvenience for someone else's benefit. In the case of learning another language, a Christian dies to the comfort and familiarity of his own native language

---

1. We cannot here enter into a detailed analysis of all the kinds of adjustments and their challenges. We only begin to touch on them in this and the following chapter.

2. Graphically, it is transliterated *hy'* or *hiy'*, pronounced *hee*.

in order that the benefit of hearing the gospel may come to people who speak another language.[3]

Crossing language barriers with the gospel also leads to a defeat of Satan. Satan as lord of the "domain of darkness" (Col. 1:13) held the nations captive, through bondage not only to guilt but to the worship of idols and spirits. The gospel, in coming to a new language, opens the door to the people of that language to receive deliverance.

## Cultural Change

Deliverance in the long run includes change on many levels. A particular culture or a particular language is not an unchangeable monolith. Cultures can and do develop and change (we have only to think of the impact of modernity on many traditional cultures). The question is how and in what direction? Do they develop under the power of the gospel, in a manner bringing progressive purification, light, peace, and blessing? For example, do marriages change over the decades as husbands and wives and children are empowered by the Spirit to obey God's pattern in Ephesians 5:22–6:4? Do governments change as Christians take a place in government and move it away from corruption and favoritism? Or does a culture develop or even disintegrate in a merely reactive manner, as has sometimes been the case when traditional cultures have clashed with modernity?

The possibilities for diverse cultures suggest by analogy possibilities for diverse languages. In small ways changes in culture automatically produce some changes in language meanings, because language is used to refer to cultural practices. For example, the words for "family" and for "government" no longer mean quite the same thing, if the shape of families and of government changes because of industrialization or secularization. Families and governmental practices within a people group can also change if a culture is being transformed by the gospel and the working of the Holy Spirit. The coming of the Christian faith to a particular culture changes people, and the people begin to change the larger culture.[4]

God has a universal plan that includes the spread of the gospel to all peoples and languages. That means that the gospel can in fact be translated into any human language on the face of the earth. But there are sometimes obstacles. The obstacles

---

3. For the theme of death and resurrection with Christ, see Philippians 3:10; 2 Corinthians 4:7–18. Of course non-Christians who learn a new language have to go through a similar struggle. In this struggle they benefit from common grace, which is ultimately a blessing from Christ (chapter 15).

4. On Christ and culture, and the issues of Christians as agents of cultural change, see John M. Frame, *The Doctrine of the Christian Life* (Phillipsburg, NJ: Presbyterian & Reformed, 2008), 853–908.

occur in the heart of the individual, when that individual through spiritual blindness resists the gospel:

> And even if our gospel is veiled, it is veiled only to those who are perishing. In their case the god of this world has blinded the minds of the unbelievers, to keep them from seeing the light of the gospel of the glory of Christ, who is the image of God (2 Cor. 4:3–4).

In addition, sometimes whole cultures have a pattern of thinking that poses an obstacle. For example, Greek philosophy and most of Greek religion were not receptive to the idea of resurrection from the dead, and so many Greeks balked when it appeared as a central part of the message of the apostle Paul in Acts 17:30–32.

## Challenges in Languages

The obstacles can also occur within language itself. For example, consider a difficulty with respect to the word for "God." In the Greek language of the first century A.D., the main word for "God" was *theos*. Unfortunately, to a Greek pagan that word did not mean "God" in the sense that the Bible describes him.[5] The word occurred often in the plural, "gods," and it designated the plurality of gods of the Greek and Roman pantheon, that is, all the gods that they worshiped. Moreover, the Greek language made no distinction between a capitalized word "God" for monotheism and a lowercase word "god" for polytheistic gods.

Paul had to deal with the problem when he spoke to pagans at Lystra (Acts 14:11–18). After seeing Paul perform a miracle of healing, the people said, "The *gods* have come down to us in the likeness of men!" Acts then records, "Barnabas they called Zeus, and Paul, Hermes" (Acts 14:12), where both "Zeus" and "Hermes" were names of Greek gods.

Paul continued to speak to these people. But he could not expect to be understood if he merely used the word for "god" without explaining it. So he proceeded to explain the biblical teaching of monotheism. One all-powerful God (*theos*) created the whole world and continues to sustain it (Acts 14:15–17). By this teaching Paul proceeded to redefine the meaning of the word "god" (*theos*) within the context of his teaching. Fortunately, human language has this flexibility. The Greek language in Lystra, as understood by the people of Lystra, was not an ideal vehicle for expressing the truths that Paul had been commissioned to proclaim. It was contaminated by the false thinking of the people. Fortunately, however, the language was an *adequate* vehicle. Given time for explanation, Paul could

---

5. The Greek world did have some philosophers, such as the Stoics, who spoke about one "god." But most Greeks and Romans in the first century thought in terms of many "gods."

use enough words to work his way through the mistaken assumptions normally associated with the Greek word *theos*.

The same thing happened again at Athens, when Paul preached to pagans. Again he had to explain about the true God, as the background for proclaiming Christ's resurrection (Acts 17:22–34). A similar thing happened with the Septuagint, the ancient Greek translation of the Old Testament. The Septuagint translators had to find a Greek word to translate the Hebrew word for God. They chose *theos* ("god").[6] Because the Septuagint was a translation, it did not have space for an extended explanation such as what Paul gave in Lystra and in Athens. But anyone reading the Septuagint would read Genesis 1 and other passages that make it clear from the total context that the God here spoken of is different from the many gods of Greek religion. The total context enables readers to adjust their thinking—to adjust, that is, if their ears are spiritually open.

In extended discourse, such as the Old Testament as a whole gives us, communication in language has the capability through the Holy Spirit to adjust thinking, even quite radically. People who have lived in spiritual darkness for their whole life, and in a culture of spiritual darkness, can come to the light, and the coming of the light can sometimes be quite sudden:

> For God, who said, "Let light shine out of darkness," has shone in our hearts to give the light of the knowledge of the glory of God in the face of Jesus Christ (2 Cor. 4:6).

The Greek word for "god" is a particularly dramatic case where God's message, the gospel, calls for adjustment. But there are other, less dramatic cases. Previous to contact with the gospel, a language may not have within its vocabulary a word for "sin." In English, because of the preceding centuries of exposure to the gospel and to the contents of the Bible, we have developed an idea of "sin" that has theology built into it. Sin means falling short of God's righteousness, falling short of his moral standards. Without the idea of God, who is one universal God and who is holy and righteous, "sin" would not mean quite the same thing as it does in a Christian context, which has been informed by the Bible.

In some languages we may even have trouble translating the word "human" or "humanity." A tribal culture with little exposure to the outside world may think of

---

6. The situation is more complicated, because the Septuagint (LXX) was produced primarily for Jews, not for the pagan public. Prior to the production of the LXX, Greek-speaking Jews would have already made the adjustment of using *theos* in a monotheistic sense. See James Barr, *Semantics of Biblical Language* (London: Oxford University Press, 1961), 266–267.

others outside its group as effectively subhuman. The tribe may not be prepared to think in terms of a basic commonality that they share with the outsiders.[7]

Why do such difficulties arise? They are direct or indirect effects of sin on whole cultures. To put it another way, they are barriers, erected by sin and ultimately by Satan, to keep people in bondage and darkness. "In their case the god of this world [Satan] has blinded the minds of the unbelievers, to keep them from seeing the light of the gospel of the glory of Christ, who is the image of God" (2 Cor. 4:4). But even in these cases God exercises sovereign control. According to his own purposes, he has not created each individual human being in total independence of his surroundings, but has made him part of a family and a culture. And his connections with family and culture can have bad as well as good effects. God himself indicates a family connection with respect to the effects of sin:

> ". . . a God merciful and gracious, . . . keeping steadfast love for thousands, forgiving iniquity and transgression and sin, but who will by no means clear the guilty, visiting the iniquity of the fathers on the children and children's children, to the third and fourth generation" (Ex. 34:6–7).

The effect on future generations is specifically tied to idolatry:

> "You shall not make for yourself a carved image, or any likeness of anything that is in heaven above, or that is in the earth beneath, or that is in the water under the earth. You shall not bow down to them or serve them, for I the LORD your God am a jealous God, visiting the iniquity of the fathers on the children to the third and the fourth generation of those who hate me, but showing steadfast love to thousands of those who love me and keep my commandments" (Ex. 20:4–6).

Spiritual darkness is not only a natural effect of continuing in sin, but a judgment from God. We may conclude that one of the effects of idolatrous practices within a culture is to corrupt the thinking of that culture, to introduce confusion about the nature of the spirit world, and in the long run to corrupt the language as well.

Suppose that a whole culture ceases to worship the true God and makes for itself idols (Rom. 1:18–25). It frequently talks about these idols, as if they were gods; it stops talking about the true God. Then, over a period of generations, the language of that culture still has a word "god," but that word has been corrupted by being customarily used to refer to the "gods." In new generations, people grow up without conscious awareness of an earlier meaning, when the word referred to the true God. And so the language itself becomes corrupted.

---

7. Paul had to make a point about the unity of mankind in a Greek context where the Greeks thought of themselves as superior to "barbarians": "And he [God] made from one man every nation of mankind to live on all the face of the earth, having determined allotted periods and the boundaries of their dwelling place, . . ." (Acts 17:26).

In sum, after the fall of Adam, and after the division of languages at Babel, we cannot assume that language is simply a neutral package in which we can neatly place the gospel and expect to have it carried to its destination. Many times missionaries and translators must do some hard thinking. But the Bible still guarantees a basic commonality among human beings. All are made in the image of God, and no one escapes knowing God (Rom. 1:18–25). We also have the guarantee that God will save people from all nations. Through the power of the Holy Spirit, the gospel can overcome the barriers, and be received with faith among all the peoples and languages.

# Good and Bad Kinds of Diversity

... that there may be no division in the body,
but that the members may have the same care for one another.
—1 Corinthians 12:25

Now you are the body of Christ and individually members of it.
—1 Corinthians 12:27

Languages and cultures do differ, sometimes in striking and in serious ways. Languages differ from one another not only in their vocabulary stocks, but in the way in which grammar fits together smaller pieces into bigger ones in order to form whole discourses.[1] But when the barriers of human sin are overcome, and people come to Christ, they are united in one body. The unity does not dissolve the diversity. The diversity of languages and cultures remains. But people are united in "one faith" and "one hope" as well as "one Lord" and "one God" (Eph. 4:4–6). The "one faith" indicates commonality in belief and in knowledge.

## Kind of Diversity

We have already at several points introduced multiple perspectives on the same subject matter.[2] When multiple perspectives are legitimate, they are intrinsically

---

1. See, e.g., Robert E. Longacre, *The Grammar of Discourse* (New York/London: Plenum, 1983); Kenneth L. Pike and Evelyn G. Pike, *Grammatical Analysis* (Dallas: Summer Institute of Linguistics, 1977).

2. More about perspectives can be found in Vern S. Poythress, *Symphonic Theology: The Validity of Multiple Perspectives in Theology* (Grand Rapids, MI: Zondervan, 1987; reprinted, Phillipsburg,

harmonizable, because there is only one God, and one world that God has made. The diversity of languages and diversity of cultures are like perspectives through which people understand God and the world. The differences in language and culture are not merely to be homogenized, as if they were trivial. But neither are they in tension, at least if all the people involved are in contact with the truth. This kind of diversity enriches the body of Christ.

What kind of diversity are we talking about? Within the body of Christ diversity does not mean a shallow "tolerance" of all kinds of differences. That is, we do not follow those postmodernists who have given up because they think that no one can know the truth.[3] Rather, because God has blessed us through Christ, and has given us his word and his Spirit, we do know truth, including truth about God and about his moral standards. At the same time, we can grow by adding more truths to what we know, and by knowing truth more deeply. We grow partly through learning from others, as is described in Ephesians 4:11–16:

> And he [Christ] gave the apostles, the prophets, the evangelists, the shepherds and teachers, to equip the saints for the work of ministry, for building up the body of Christ, until we all attain to the unity of the faith and of the knowledge of the Son of God, to mature manhood, to the measure of the stature of the fullness of Christ, so that we may no longer be children, tossed to and fro by the waves and carried about by every wind of doctrine, by human cunning, by craftiness in deceitful schemes. Rather, speaking the truth in love, we are to grow up in every way into him who is the head, into Christ, from whom the whole body, joined and held together by every joint with which it is equipped, when each part is working properly, makes the body grow so that it builds itself up in love.

In addition, we grow in the truth partly through repudiating false teaching:

> Now the Spirit expressly says that in later times some will depart from the faith by devoting themselves to deceitful spirits and *teachings of demons*, through the insincerity of liars whose consciences are seared, who forbid marriage and require abstinence from foods that God created to be received with thanksgiving by those who believe and know the truth. . . .
>
> If you put these things before the brothers, you will be a good servant of Christ Jesus, being trained in the words of the faith and of the *good doctrine* that you have followed. Have nothing to do with *irreverent, silly myths*. Rather train yourself for godliness; . . . (1 Tim. 4:1–7).

---

NJ: Presbyterian & Reformed, 2001); John M. Frame, *Perspectives on the Word of God: An Introduction to Christian Ethics* (Phillipsburg, NJ: Presbyterian & Reformed, 1990); and the triad for lordship in Frame, *The Doctrine of the Knowledge of God* (Phillipsburg, NJ: Presbyterian & Reformed, 1987).

3. On postmodernism, see appendices A and B.

Love is one of the bonds that creates enjoyment of diversity and unifies us in the midst of diversity. If we love, we exercise patience in listening to others and trying to understand them, and then we learn more of the truth that they have grasped. On the other hand, genuine love also implies being willing to protect others from false teaching, which corrupts people's minds and lives. In this process the Bible guides us, just as Paul gave inspired guidance to Timothy and expected that he would be able to tell the difference between true and false teaching.

The love in the body of Christ ultimately reflects the love between God the Father and God the Son.[4] Hence, the unity in diversity in the body of Christ reflects Trinitarian unity in diversity. The enrichment of the body of Christ through the diversity of languages is a positive reflection of the Trinitarian diversity of persons.

## Diversity in Expressions of Truth in Languages

We can put the same point in another way. Consider first the principle of unity. The Father knows all things in his "language," who is the Word, expressed in the "breath" of the Spirit. God's unified knowledge is his eternal vision of truth. God reveals his knowledge to us in Christ, and in the Bible, so that we come to a unified understanding of the truth. All the members of the body of Christ share in one faith, and in "the unity of the Spirit in the bond of peace" (Eph. 4:3), thereby expressing their unity. In the new heaven and the new earth, each of us will "know fully," "face to face" (1 Cor. 13:12); we will see God's face (Rev. 22:4). Human beings will enjoy profound unity, and a depth of satisfaction that we cannot imagine. All ethnic groups with their different languages come to share in this unity.

Next, consider the principle of diversity. On the divine level there are three divine perspectives on knowledge, the perspectives of the Father, of the Son, and of the Holy Spirit.[5] Within the Bible, there are four Gospels, which offer four perspectives on the life and work of Christ. The four Gospels are a good example of the positive value of the right kind of diversity. Matthew emphasizes that Jesus fulfills the Old Testament promises about the coming Messiah in the line of David. John emphasizes that Jesus reveals God the Father. Since each Gospel is what God says, and God speaks truly, there is no contradiction between the different Gospels. They are all in harmony.[6] At the same time, they offer differences in emphasis and differences in what they choose to include.

---

4. This love is expressed in the Holy Spirit (John 3:34–35), so that all three persons of the Trinity are involved.

5. See Poythress, *Symphonic Theology*, 47–51.

6. But it may sometimes be hard for us as human readers to figure out just how they harmonize. See ibid.

On the human level, within this world, there are many vocabularies, and many languages. The gospel is spreading and is being translated into each language. As it spreads, the truth is being manifested in *each* language. Behind the human communicators of the gospel is God, who empowers them. Through the gospel God himself addresses the hearers: "Therefore, we [bearers of the gospel] are ambassadors for Christ, *God* making his appeal through us. We implore you on behalf of Christ, be reconciled to God" (2 Cor. 5:20). In this way God is a speaker in each language community, and makes himself known in each language. The diversity of languages and cultures, like other forms of diversity in the body of Christ, enriches the body. Each person grows in the truth through receiving truth from those with different perspectives, including different languages and vocabularies.

Since the church has multiple languages and multiple ethnic groups, human beings do not now have on earth one "final vocabulary" or final language. Unity does not arrive through a final vision of truth *in a unitarian way* that eliminates all diversity.[7] Rather, the unity of one faith is compatible with the diversity of languages in which God communicates the truth to each ethnic group. That is analogous to the fact that the unity of *one* work of Christ is compatible with the diversity of the accounts in the four Gospels.

## Language as Barrier or Benefit?

Language is not a permanent barrier, blocking access to truth and to reality, but rather is a means that provides such access. God created human beings in his image, and that commonality guarantees that the languages of the world can all serve as a means to truth.

But that optimism about language is qualified by what we have already observed about the corruptions that originate from the fall. Human language has split apart into many languages as a result of sin. Can the barriers between languages be bridged? And what about corruptions within a particular language? False religion, in particular, corrupts both culture and language. Culture is corrupted by false worship, superstitious practices, and various kinds of immorality. Language, more subtly, is corrupted by false assumptions that people attach to key words like "god" or "human."

---

7. The unity and diversity among different people in the church is analogous to the archetypal unity and diversity among the persons of the Trinity. Within the church, a single monolithic vision of the truth, without diversity, would be analogous to unitarianism, which believes in one God but no diversity in God (unitarianism denies that there are three persons in God). The opposite extreme would be diversity without real unity: each person would have a distinct conception of truth, and the different conceptions would never be reconciled. That kind of diversity corresponds to polytheism. True unity in diversity within the church reflects the true unity and diversity in the Trinity. See appendix D.

Fortunately, both culture and language are capable of redemptive transformation. People can hear God speaking as the gospel comes even to the darkest dungeons of human depravity. Christ came to save sinners, not the righteous: "I have not come to call the righteous but sinners to repentance" (Luke 5:32; see Matt. 9:13).

Thus, even though the fall has had its effects, the universality of the reach of the gospel confirms that we will still find "language universals," universal capability throughout all languages that make the gospel expressible in each language.[8] The Bible can be translated into each—and has been translated into many languages, more than any other book. Because the Bible is breathed out by God (2 Tim. 3:16) to address all nations (Luke 24:47), it is true and pertinent to every culture. God so designed it. We know it is universal in its reach, not by intellectual insight that has given us a godlike superiority, but simply because God has told us so, and we trust him. But that universal reach is not worked out in practice without missionaries and translators having to confront surprising knots, complexities, resistances, and rich perspectival diversities.

The Bible is not acultural. It does not owe its universality to rising above cultures into thin, disembodied universal philosophical platitudes (which would actually falsify its very specific message). In the Bible God addresses immediate issues in the first century and in the Hebraic cultures of Old Testament times. Through the apostle Paul God warns the Corinthian church about divisions; he warns the Galatian churches to rely on Christ and not on circumcision. God also speaks universally, by indicating to all nations how he accomplished worldwide salvation precisely in the once-for-all, culturally and historically specific events concerning the descendants of Abraham leading up to Christ. As part of its universal scope, the Bible also contains many general, universal statements: "All have sinned and fall short of the glory of God" (Rom. 3:23). "The LORD is one" (Deut. 6:4). "Righteous are you, O LORD, and right are your rules" (Ps. 119:137). God expects us to believe his universal claims, and not to evaporate them by artificially restricting them to one culture.

The missiologist does not need to "make" the Bible universal. It is already that (Acts 1:8).[9] Rather he needs to help people in each culture take their place as

---

8. Longacre, *Grammar of Discourse*, notes some of these universals that are manifested in language structure. All of these universals are due to the commonality of human nature, made in the image of God. The spread of the gospel does not create the universals but rather relies on their already being there. At the same time, God's design for saving the nations reassures us that no language of the world has become so corrupt that it has permanently lost fundamental structures that would be necessary for communicating the gospel.

9. Thus the idea of distilling a "supracultural" core to the Bible is reductionistic. We can of course summarize the gospel in a few words (e.g., 1 Cor. 15:1–4; Acts 10:36–43; Rom. 10:9–10; 1:2–6)—but the summaries are many and each points to the larger whole. The whole Bible is both culturally specific and "supracultural" in that God speaks it to all nations. The two sides are

disciples in the Bible's universal world history. The disciple of Christ does not slavishly duplicate the details of the wilderness wandering or the Davidic monarchy or the Corinthian church, but grows in understanding how God addresses both David and Corinth, each in his context, and how through them God also addresses a Manila grocer. The Manila grocer can grow, and needs to grow, in understanding the cultures of Bible times, in order for him to see the cross-cultural span of the Bible's vision and lose his cultural parochialism. (The same goes, of course, for American or Spanish parochialism.) The missionary anthropologist can be a facilitator, but he needs to beware of becoming a new intermediary, a new priest. The Manila grocer, in fellowship with a Manilan church, can understand the Bible in his language.

## Counterfeits to Cross-cultural Integration

Because of the magnitude of differences in culture and in language, achieving peace between different people groups is not easy. It can come through the power of Christ and his gospel. But it comes at a price. The price is the shedding of "the precious blood of Christ" (1 Pet. 1:19). Followers of Christ also pay a price in their own way, because each one must give up his pride. On top of the challenges of translation comes the challenge of dealing with human pride in one's own culture. God created human diversity, and so there can be a proper way in which people may rejoice in the blessings and the human community that they have received through their native language and culture. But since sin has come in and contaminated human relations, human pride distorts our attitude toward our native language and culture. We have a protective pride, and with that comes a disdain or hatred for what is different. This is a sin, for which the gospel is the remedy.

Because all people are made in God's image, all have desires to overcome the pain in the differences in language and culture. For some people, the desire to overcome pain may take hideous form. They are tempted by hatred to wipe out another ethnic group, or forcibly to convert them to their own way of life. That is a counterfeit remedy for cultural pain.

Among sophisticated Westerners, counterfeits come in more genteel forms. For example, counterfeit solutions to cultural differences appear in philosophy. Philosophy in many of its forms has claimed to arrive at godlike knowledge that would rise above the limitations of any one culture or any one language.

Within the twentieth century, in particular, ordinary language philosophy has attempted through the analysis of natural language to arrive at universal truths.

---

perspectivally related. See the discussion of contrast (universality) and variation (particularity) in chapter 19, and the discussion of perspectives in chapter 34 and in Poythress, *Symphonic Theology*.

But how does it know, from working only in one language, or working only in a small number of European languages, that its insights are truly universal? How does philosophy respond to the challenge of postmodernism, which claims that your language limits your access to truth? In fact, ordinary language philosophy tends to assume that language gives access to truth, if only we could think clearly enough. But how does it know this? In particular, how does it know without having a thorough knowledge of many other cultures and languages outside the tradition of Western philosophy? Too often, it appears that the answer is fundamentally to assume that all is well with its own vision—and that involves both human pride and overlooking the corruption of language from Babel onward.

Postmodernism, in contrast to much of Western philosophy, wants to treat with utmost seriousness the diversity of languages and cultures. But that diversity threatens the peace and unity of mankind. How do we deal with this threat?

One form of postmodernism offers a reconciliation and a peace based on the principle of tolerance. Postmodernism might say that traditional religions have a place. According to its viewpoint, they are one colorful aspect of culture. We learn to "tolerate" them by seeing them as expressing the commitments and customs belonging to their own particular culture. This kind of approach provides a place for religion. But it forbids religion from "getting out of hand" by making a universal or intolerant claim that would apply to *other cultures*. Religions are thereby tamed. But they can be tamed only by a strong claim, namely, that religions are merely cultural preferences, since no one can know religious truth. That claim is itself a kind of religious claim, since it claims to see deeper than the adherents to any one religion. It is a godlike claim to godlike insight.

So the postmodernist recipe for cultural peace is a counterfeit for the peace and reconciliation offered in the Christian gospel. Both postmodernism and Christian faith want to promote reconciliation among diverse cultures. One, the Christian form, finds reconciliation through the work of God in Christ, and the spiritual power to love and to crucify pride. The other, the postmodern form, finds reconciliation in a self-achieved godlike vision of the nature of religion and language and knowledge (see chart 18.1).[10]

Unity and diversity can take both good and bad forms. The difference between good and bad comes out when we consider the missionary challenge of contextualization. How do we communicate the gospel in a clear and winsome way to a new culture? The term "contextualization" means a process in which a missionary adapts the gospel to a new cultural context. Is this a good or a bad thing?

A rigid, monolithic emphasis on unity might insist that contextual thinking is not necessary or important. Some nineteenth-century missions made the mistake of thinking that the task of missionary work was to "civilize the heathen" and make

---

10. On postmodernism, see appendices A and B.

them Europeans; Christianizing was part of the total package of civilizing. That extreme view obviously does not respect the diversity of cultures, and makes a mistake analogous to requiring Gentiles to become Jews.

### Reconciliation among Cultures and Languages

| Feature | Christian | Rationalist Western Philosophy | Postmodernism |
|---------|-----------|-------------------------------|---------------|
| unity among human beings | man made in the image of God | common rationality | universal limitations in language and culture |
| problem | sin | ignorance, tradition | limitations of language and culture |
| solution to human hatred | transformation through the Holy Spirit toward Christlike love | insight into universal truths | insight into limitations |
| key message | the gospel concerning Christ | teaching how to analyze rationally | message about the effects of language and culture |
| savior | Christ | your mind | a self committed to tolerance |
| goal | unity and diversity in the body of Christ | uniformity | celebrating diversity |

CHART 18.1

Less dramatically, a missionary may mistakenly think that issues from within one culture can be transported *without any adaptation* into all other cultures. Let us consider an example. Broadly speaking, the Reformation was concerned to address the universal problem of human guilt and the universal human tendency to seek salvation by works, accompanied by pride in human achievement. The human tendency to pride can take subtle as well as blatant forms. The blatant form is to base salvation directly on human achievement. One subtle form is to introduce pride into a framework where people give token acknowledgment to God's grace.[11]

These problems, though universal, take different particular forms in different cultures. In the time of the Reformation the issue came to focus in the practice of indulgences. The Roman Catholic Church did affirm that salvation came partly through grace offered in Christ. But the church's offer of an "indulgence" alleged that a monetary payment—a work—could buy someone's way out of purgatory. That practice based salvation partly on human work.

In the first-century church, reliance on human work cropped up in the issue of circumcising the Gentiles. In an animist culture, reliance on human work may come to focus in the demand to propitiate the spirits in order to protect crops. In Hindu religion, reliance on work is expressed in the idea of karma, which says that you must

---

11. See, e.g., John Piper, *The Future of Justification: A Response to N. T. Wright* (Wheaton, IL: Crossway, 2006).

pay for your misdeeds in future reincarnations. The particular temptations within a particular culture, and not just the general principle, need to be addressed.

The opposite mistake in contextualization is the "postmodern" mistake, that is, the mistake of uncritically celebrating every kind of diversity. In the name of contextualization, a missionary can make his version of the "gospel" fit in so well with the target culture that it is indistinguishable from the culture and does not challenge it at a fundamental level.

The mistake also occurs in less obvious forms. People can talk about developing African or Latin American theologies as if these theologies had to start all over again in order to be authentic to their own cultures. But the truths that the Reformation uncovered in the Bible are indeed truths, and so they are true and applicable to all cultures everywhere. Thinking through implications for a new context is quite different from despising the insights of the Reformation. Such despising of the fruits of Western theology is itself a kind of reverse ethnocentrism, in that it runs the danger of endorsing a false pride and isolation in Third World Christians. The unity in the body of Christ implies not isolation of various indigenous theologies but cross-cultural appropriation, Europe to Africa, Africa to Asia, Asia to Europe, and so on. Otherwise, we are denying the unity of the one faith (Eph. 4:5). Each truth found in each context, if it is indeed the truth at all, is universal truth.[12]

What does proper Christian unity look like? We can only begin to sketch it. In a culture that is in bondage to the fear of evil spirits, a missionary may easily start with announcing Christ's victory over Satan and over the evil spirits under him (Luke 10:18–19; Col. 2:15; Heb. 2:14–15). But deliverance from Satan must include deliverance from his *accusations* (Rev. 12:10), and therefore deliverance from guilt. That thought leads to acknowledging the importance of Christ's substitutionary atonement and justification from guilt.

Conversely, suppose the missionary confronts a culture that is beset by guilt. He first proclaims Christ as the substitute who bears the penalty for guilt and wins justification for us. But one aspect of guilt is guilt for having abandoned service to God and given allegiance to false gods, behind which stand Satan and his demons (1 Cor. 10:20). So deliverance from guilt must include deliverance from demonic bondage. Each culture should, over time, grow in realizing that Christ's deliverance is deeper and richer than what they first imagined they needed.

Because of the dominant influence of the West in industry, trade, entertainment, and ideas, it may often seem to the struggling contextualizer that he has only two black-and-white choices: to accept the West or to repudiate it. In the first alternative, he accepts Westernization, including the Westernization of his theological thinking. Then he unilaterally imposes on every culture all the particularities that

---

12. On truth, see Vern S. Poythress, *Redeeming Science: A God-Centered Approach* (Wheaton, IL: Crossway, 2006), chapter 14.

belong to the issues in their Western form. He paralyzes his ability to adapt to a non-Western culture.

Or he chooses the second alternative. He rejects Westernization, ignores the Reformation, and starts fresh with so-called indigenous theology, constructed from the ground up.

But both routes are deeply wrong. In practice, they deny the unity and universality of the truth. And both avoid the cross of Christ, by refusing the challenge to suffer in order to bring together diverse cultures at a deep level.

We must work not merely to appropriate truth from other Christians in other cultures, but to appropriate critically, testing truth claims in the light of Scripture, and warning fellow Christians when we see dangers of syncretism and cultural compromise. Someone who is foreign to a particular culture runs the danger of premature, harsh judgment against cultural practices that he does not understand. But, conversely, the foreigner may sometimes be able to discern sins when the native is unaware, because the native's culture has hardened his conscience to some areas of sin.[13]

## The Challenge to Christians

The challenge of cross-cultural reconciliation for Christians is not *primarily* intellectual. We who are Christians must avoid falling into the trap of seeking merely an intellectual solution, such as others have sometimes offered. The Bible offers an answer that does indeed address human intellectual capacities and that does give satisfaction in the long run. Christ has given us a Bible that includes within it not only spiritual nourishment but intellectual instruction, and a worldview in which cultural differences have a positive place. But the Bible's answer centers on Christ and on his suffering. And Christians must suffer in serving him.

Culture-crossing and language-learning and translating the gospel are hard. Loving and reaching out to people who may be hostile to the gospel are hard jobs. To love, we have to suffer and thereby follow the pattern of the suffering of Christ. We are to strive through the gospel to bring genuine reconciliation to people

---

13. Consider an example. In 2008, African Anglican bishops called on American Episcopalian clergy to repent of their abandonment of biblical authority and their endorsement of homosexual practice. This movement of theology and exhortation goes from Africa to the United States. Unfortunately, the Americans, when they are ethnocentrically confident about their own allegedly "progressive" culture, are not likely to listen. Their culture tempts them to harden their conscience and excuse their sin. Postmodernism does not help. It naturally wants to favor multicultural "tolerance," according to which each church and religion within a culture would develop in its own way, in harmony with its culture. Almost automatically it sides against the Africans for trying to "impose" their patterns on Americans. But in so doing, it shows its European-American ethnocentricity: it is prejudiced against the belief found in other cultures—and above all within the Bible itself—that universal truth exists and matters.

groups through cultural unity in diversity and diversity in unity. We replicate in human beings the glory of the unity and diversity in the Godhead.

This unity in diversity offers an answer that differs from other common answers abroad today. Our answer differs from forced uniformity, which some people think they can attain through autonomous reason. That hope for uniformity is the answer associated with what has been called "modernism." Our answer also differs from "postmodernism," which in its common form celebrates diversity but gives up on universal truth (see chart 18.1).

# Human Action

"All things have been handed over to me by my Father, and no one knows
the Son except the Father, and no one knows the Father except the Son
and anyone to whom the Son chooses to reveal him."
—Matthew 11:27

Language use by human beings always occurs in a context of surrounding
circumstances and cultures. And the context can have a decided influence
on the meaning of language. So let us now consider human action in general,
with the purpose of eventually narrowing to verbal communication as a specific
kind of human action.[1]

Human action includes interaction between different cultures. Such interaction, as we saw in the previous chapters, can be both a great struggle and a challenge for reconciliation. It takes a very significant role in God's plan for drawing
all nations to himself. But most human action takes place within the context of
some particular culture. Divine action superintends all of history. But God also
interacts with each particular culture. So we now take another step in narrowing
our focus. We focus not on world history and its many cultures, but on smaller-
scale actions within a particular culture.

---

1. See Mary Louise Pratt, *Toward a Speech Act Theory of Literary Discourse* (Bloomington: Indiana
University Press, 1977), 113: "any discussion of *speaker*/Audience relations will ultimately have
to find its place in a more general account of *performer*/Audience relations, which will in turn be
defined in relation to turn-taking relations." Thus verbal communication makes sense within the
context of expectations arising in more general human relations.

## Insiders and Outsiders

Meaning is always meaning in context.[2] The same physical action may not have the same cultural meaning when seen within the context of two distinct cultures. That difference can generate misunderstanding, anger, and pain. For example, an American may cross his legs when as a guest he is enjoying a conversation in his host's living room. In traditional Chinese culture, showing the sole of your shoe to another person is a way of insulting the person. So people keep their feet on the floor and do not lift up their feet to cross legs. The person who travels from one culture to another may not be aware of the differences, and may as a result generate misunderstanding.

In addition, a particular culture may have ceremonies and customs with no real equivalent outside the culture. The people have special dances, or festivals, or architectural styles, or gestures, or a regular order for meals. All these have meaning within that culture, but they may be difficult for the foreigner to decipher. The same is true even more strikingly with language. The language has meanings that a foreigner may spend years in learning.

## Insiders' and Outsiders' Perspectives

The native and the foreigner have different *perspectives* on a culture. The native grasps the inside meaning. The foreigner starts with only vague ideas or possibilities for meaning. Consider a particular example. Within any one language, some differences in sound are regularly used to distinguish words. In English, "sale" and "shale" differ only in the initial sound. (The initial sound in "shale" is represented in writing by a series of two letters, "s" and "h," but if you listen carefully, you can see that it is really *one* sound to the ear.) The analyst therefore says that the two sounds, of "s" and "sh," are distinct elements of sound within the system of the English language. Linguists say that they are two distinct *phonemes*. The native speaker pays attention to the difference between the two.

On the other hand, unlike English, koine Greek uses no distinctive "sh" sound to distinguish different words. When Greek borrows a name from Hebrew, which does have an "sh" sound, the "sh" in Hebrew is usually represented in Greek merely as an ess sound. Two distinct sounds become one in Greek, because Greek never makes a systematic distinction between the two. Greek has only one sound element in this particular case, while English has two. The insider who uses English is aware of the important distinction between the two sounds, while the outsider who speaks another language may not be. The two points of view differ.

Consider another case. German has two words, "Back" and "Bach," which differ only in the final sound. "Back" ends in a sound almost exactly like the English

---

2. See especially chapter 7.

"k." By contrast, "Bach" ends in a sound that has no equivalent in English, but is similar to making a "k" without completely closing off the stream of air. Air seeps through between the back of the tongue and the velum, making a continuous frictional sound. German has two distinct sound elements, while English has only one (the "k" sound).

This difference can be generalized. An insider and an outsider differ not only in their awareness of sound, but in their awareness of all kinds of other elements that belong to language and to culture.[3]

Actually, there are two distinct kinds of outsiders. The first kind is the foreigner trying to learn a particular language or culture for the first time. He has the learner's perspective. The second is the theorist who tries to generalize about many languages or cultures, and who classifies the phenomena of one language into a larger taxonomy. He has the classifier's perspective. Both are "outsiders" in a sense. But the latter may in fact also be an insider, who is temporarily standing back from his involvement in one culture, in order to conduct multicultural analysis.

This existence of inside and outside perspectives derives from the diversity among human beings, which also makes its way into the diversity of the body of Christ. The diversity is designed by God. It does not make any of the perspectives "unreal." In particular, the insider is experiencing exactly what God designed him to experience. It is all real, including the sound elements in his language and the cultural meanings that attach to the festivals and the meals and the gestures. These are all specified by God, who has the mastery over every culture in every detail. The classifier's outsider perspective can open the door to the temptation to think that only an outsider's universal, "scientific," "objective" analysis shows what is real. But that would be to reduce to one perspective the fullness of what God creates and sustains.[4] The classifier's perspective, insightful though it may be in certain respects, does not dissolve the realities of other perspectives.

The reality of the insider's perspective is particularly worth emphasizing because some postmodernists have claimed that a culture or language group "con-

---

3. In technical terms, the insider's perspective is called "emic," while the outsider's perspective is called "etic." These terms need explanation. The study of the sounds used in languages is called *phonetics*. Phonetics takes an outsider's or foreigner's point of view. It studies the sounds as a machine might record them. Linguists can also study sound from the insider's point of view, by asking which sounds are perceived as making a difference. This study is called *phonemics*. Kenneth L. Pike (*Language in Relation to a Unified Theory of the Structure of Human Behavior* [The Hague/Paris: Mouton, 1967], 37–72) generalized and codified this difference with a pair of distinctive terms, "emic" and "etic," which apply to language analysis and cultural analysis in their broadest forms.

4. For an analogous problem that crops up in the natural sciences, see the discussion in Vern S. Poythress, *Redeeming Science: A God-Centered Approach* (Wheaton, IL: Crossway, 2006), chapter 16.

structs" the world of human meaning. There is a grain of truth in this claim. It is true that any one human being can have innovative thoughts and speeches, and in that sense introduce a new idea into his culture. Even such innovations, of course, do not take God by surprise but are eternally known by him and are under his control. But in addition, cultures and languages are passed on to the next generation. No generation literally "constructs" its culture from scratch. More important, no generation ceases to live in the presence of God, under the control of God, with meanings specified by God. By contrast to this situation involving God, the word "construct" can tend to suggest autonomy in human action. And it can suggest that the cultural meaning is illusory, because it is "mere" construction rather than a reality appreciated by God even if every human being should disappear or forget.

## Behavioremes

We now turn to consider the insider's perspective. Insiders have a perspective not only on language but on culture in general. Kenneth L. Pike invented a general term to describe any unified human action within a particular culture: the *behavioreme*. A behavioreme is a unit of human action that has human purpose and is recognized as a meaningful unified whole within the culture in which it occurs.[5] It is recognized by *insiders*.

A behavioreme may consist in the unified action of a *single* human being: in America, brushing one's teeth is a behavioreme. But other behavioremes may consist in a whole series of actions by a number of human beings acting in a coordinated way. A party, a workday at a business, a basketball game, a family breakfast, and a church service are all behavioremes.

The insider recognizes the action as a whole, and he shares that recognition with others within his culture. His perspective on the action may differ markedly from that of an outsider. The outsider sees the human action but does not know its cultural significance.

Behavioremes include acts of verbal communication; verbal utterances are one kind of behavioreme. But the term applies more broadly. It applies to any

---

5. Pike, *Language*, 73–149. Technically, "A BEHAVIOREME is an emic segment or component of purposive human activity, hierarchically and trimodally structured, having closure signalled by overt objective cultural clues within the verbal or nonverbal behavior of the domestic participants or domestic observers, and occurring thorugh [sic; through] its free or conditioned, simple or complex variants within a behavioral system (or composite of systems) and a physical setting which are also emically, hierarchically and trimodally structured" (ibid., 121). The "trimodal" structuring is closely related to the interlocking of (1) contrastive-identificational features, (2) variation, and (3) distribution, as discussed below. The ending "-eme" indicates that we are treating the unity of behavior as perceived by an insider. The insider's perspective is called an "emic" perspective (cf. note 3, above).

culturally significant activity. So it is an important bridge between human speech and the larger sphere of human action.

A behavioreme is characterized both by particular instances and by a general, somewhat regular pattern common to its instances. Any particular basketball game is a behavioreme. But we may also think in general terms of *the* basketball behavioreme, the common pattern apparent in many such individual games.[6]

Why does this matter? Pieces of language have meaning in the context of larger pieces. Behavioremes include large-scale pieces. They may include within them language activity with a larger context of human action (and divine action). For example, a basketball behavioreme includes language communication by the ref-

---

6. Philosophers and students of language have spoken of the "type-token" distinction. A "token" is any particular instance—any one basketball game, or any one occurrence of the English ess sound. A "type" is the generality—the class of all basketball games or the class of all instances of the English ess sound. Kenneth Pike's theory differs subtly from many analyses at this point, because it acknowledges that, in practice, type and token, though distinguishable in principle, are never isolated from one another. We grasp the general class through its instances, and we grasp the instances as instances of one or more classes. The classes are closely related to the contrastive-identificational features; the instances are variations in the class (see below). Both occur in ways qualified by context. See Pike's discussion of the related issue of form-meaning composites (Pike, *Language*, 62–63), and coinherent modes (ibid., 84–94; Kenneth L. Pike, *Linguistic Concepts: An Introduction to Tagmemics* [Lincoln and London: University of Nebraska Press, 1982], 41–65). Thus there are no "pure" universals that we know apart from particulars, and no "pure" particulars known apart from universals. This coinherence of universal and particular is ultimately founded in the unity and diversity in the persons of the Trinity in their coinherence.

The interlocking of universals and particulars also shows a limitation in Ferdinand de Saussure's distinction between language system (*langue*) and speech (*parole*), to be discussed in appendix E. The language system (which is like a universal) is learned and known through particular speeches, and speeches through the language system. The two cannot be isolated, except by an artificial idealization or abstraction. Thus:

[O]ne can extend to the system of signs in general what Saussure says about language: "Language [the linguistic system, *langue*] is necessary for speech [*parole*] to be intelligible and to produce all its effects; but speech is necessary for language [the system] to be established; historically, the fact of speech always comes first." There is a circle here, for if one rigorously distinguishes language [*langue*] and speech [*parole*], code and message, schema and usage, etc., and if one is to do justice to the two postulates thus enunciated, one does not know where to begin, nor how something can begin in general, be it language or speech. Therefore, one has to admit, before any dissociation of language and speech, code and message, etc. (and everything that goes along with such a dissociation), a systematic production of differences, the *production* of a system of differences—a *différance*—within whose effects one eventually, by abstraction and according to determined motivations, will be able to demarcate a linguistics of language [*langue*] and a linguistics of speech [*parole*] (Jacques Derrida, *Positions* [Chicago: University of Chicago Press, 1981], 28; quoted in Jonathan Culler, *On Deconstruction: Theory and Criticism after Structuralism* [Ithaca, NY: Cornell University Press, 1982], 96–97).

erees, by the players, and by the fans. But it also includes nonverbal actions such as dribbling, passing the ball, and making a basket. The language used between players makes sense only when you understand what game they are playing. That is, you have to understand the context of human action—playing basketball—in order to understand the verbal pieces embedded within the action. Language will ultimately be evaporated of meaning if it is not related to human and divine action.

## Interlocking Aspects: Contrast, Variation, and Context ("Distribution")

We can now briefly explore some of the characteristics belonging to behavioremes in general. As we do so, we are preparing the way to use the results when we later focus specifically on verbal communication.

Behavioremes can be described in terms of three interlocking aspects, which are related to three perspectives: the particle, wave, and field perspectives.[7] Look at a basketball game from the standpoint of the particle perspective. It is a distinct whole. It is not a baseball game, or a game of hopscotch, or a family breakfast. It is identifiable by a distinct structure of human interaction and a distinct set of rules. It has an identity, and it contrasts with other kinds of behavioremes. This first aspect may be called *contrastive-identificational features.*[8]

Second, we use the wave perspective. The game takes place in time and is spread out in time. But this by itself is not what we are going to focus on. The awareness of development is closely connected to awareness of the specificness of this particular game. This game in the details of its unfolding is not quite like any other basketball game. In other words, it is a particular instance, never to be repeated. Other games at other times and places will show considerable variation, without ceasing to be instances of the basketball behavioreme. A game of basketball remains fundamentally the same kind of game, even though each instance is different. Each instance is part of the *variation* possible for this behavioreme. The second aspect is therefore called *variation.*[9]

For the sake of simplicity, analysts of culture often treat a particular culture as uniform. But a more refined analysis always shows up variations among subcultures. Each individual is never exhaustively assimilated into a particular culture or subculture but remains unique and different. He is still able to interact with

---

7. See chapter 7.

8. In Pike, *Language,* this aspect is closely associated with the "feature mode." See also Pike, *Linguistic Concepts,* 42–51.

9. In Pike, *Language,* this aspect is closely associated with the "manifestation mode." See also Pike, *Linguistic Concepts,* 52–59.

those around him, and to share in commonly identified behavioremes, because the behavioremes allow variation in subcultures and in individuals.

Third, we use the field perspective. From this perspective we see the basketball behavioreme as embedded in a larger human context. A particular game belongs to a whole season of games in which various teams play one another in an organized pattern. Each team probably belongs to a league. And the fans as well as the players integrate their participation in games into the larger whole, which includes times spent at the school or in the organization that the team represents. They participate within a community that feels some loyalty to the team, and within a pattern of basketball seasons, year by year, where the team may have its ups and downs. The basketball behavioreme occurs within particular human contexts, and in Kenneth Pike's terminology we say that we are then describing the *distribution* of the behavioreme in its larger contexts. This third aspect is called *distribution*. Why not just call it "context"? The word "distribution" is intended to be a little more specific. For a basketball behavioreme, we are not just interested in any context whatsoever. We focus on the characteristic patterns that belong to just those contexts in which a basketball game is expected to occur. The patterns that characterize the typical contexts of basketball games help to define what a basketball game is within the culture. Basketball games are "distributed" in various places in the culture.[10]

---

10. See Pike, *Language*, 85–86; Pike, *Linguistic Concepts*, 60–65. A more fine-grained analysis of distribution can distinguish three dimensions or aspects to distribution. The first dimension is distribution "as a member of a substitution class." Here is Kenneth Pike's explanation:

> A unit, whether a person or word, is in part characterized by its membership in a class of replaceable units which may appropriately occur in the same place(s) in a particular kind of structure. The set comprises a distribution class of units. For example, kitten, dog, bicycle are members of a (sub)class of nouns which can appropriately substitute one for another as head of a noun phrase; compare the phrase *a large kitten* with *a large dog*, *a large train*, *a large bicycle* (ibid., 62).

A basketball behavioreme is a member of the "distribution class" of team sports games that occur in certain relatively fixed roles within high school and college and professional sports seasons.

The second dimension of distribution is distribution "as part of a structural sequence." Pike explains:

> . . . a unit is in part defined by the constructions in which it occurs, in addition to the class of items of which it is an appropriate substitute member within such structured sequences. The nouns just listed are in part recognized by the fact that they can occur in a noun phrase, preceded in that phrase by an article (*the kitten*), or an adjective (*the lovely kitten*), or followed by a modifying phrase (*the kitten I used to own*) (ibid.).

For an organized school team, the basketball behavioreme occurs within a sequence of activities of the school, spread throughout the day. In addition, it occurs within a sequence of "season games" that determine the final standing of the team.

## Coinherence in Aspects of Behavioremes

All behavioremes are characterized by contrast-identity, by variation, and by context ("distribution"). And these interlock. They are "coinherent." For example, one of the features that makes a basketball game a game is not merely human movements that look like they might be part of an actual game,[11] but an understanding on the part of the players, an understanding that comes from context, where they have already agreed to play a game. Thus the contrastive features identifying the game cohere with actions before the game, that is, actions in context ("distribution"). And when the fans come to watch the game and root for their team, they too have a cultural context in which they come to a certain place already with the idea that there will be a game there for *their* team. Thus their participation has as one of its features coherence with the distributional context involving their knowledge of the players, the history of their team, and the existence of other teams for other schools. Moreover, for both the players and the fans, part of the meaning of the game in many cases has to do with its role in a season. Is it a practice game, or a preseason game, or a postseason semifinal elimination round? These are distributional aspects that belong to the game.

There can be variations *in* the distributional aspects. Some games are part of a season, while others may be "pickup" games that are not part of an organized sequence of games. The variations also help to define in the average person's mind what a basketball game actually is. Variations in tempo, variations in the number of scores, and variations in the fervor of the fans do not make one particular instance of basketball anything other than basketball. But some variations would: for example, if we permitted a player with the ball to keep moving without dribbling ("traveling"), or if we permitted eight or more players playing at a time on the same team.[12]

---

The third dimension of distribution is distribution "as a point in a system." Pike explains:

> One can in part define a unit by the place it fills in a matrix of units (an n-dimensional system of units) (ibid., 65).

A basketball behavioreme fits into a multidimensional classification of various types of individual, team, and group behavior.

These three aspects of distribution correspond to particle, wave, and field perspectives on distribution, respectively. These perspectives are rooted in the Trinity (chapter 7). The character of distribution shows one area where Trinitarian coinherence is reflected in more microscopic as well as a macroscopic analysis.

11. It should be said that "shooting hoops" or practicing for a game is a behavioreme of its own, related to but distinct from the basketball-game behavioreme.

12. Such an increase of players might on occasion be tolerated in an informal context of a pickup game. Then we can imagine arguments as to whether it is still a "real" basketball game, because the boundaries of a behavioreme are in fact fuzzy at the edges. As we observed that lan-

Behavioremes also involve God's action in an inextricable way. God is always involved as primary cause in addition to the secondary causes in human action. God *specifies the meanings* expressed in behavioremes; he *controls* the action and development in behavioremes; he is *present* in the entire development, and present with each individual in the action. These three aspects of God's lordship are expressed in the three perspectives, particle, wave, and field. To put it another way, God specifies the contrastive-identificational features, he controls the variations, and he is present both in the action itself and in its distributional context.

God's intention, and with it his meaning, is the foundation for human meaning and human intentionality in the individual and corporate action. God's power, and with it his control, is the foundation for human power to influence the course of action. God's goal, and with it his presence in blessing at the end of history, is the foundation for the goals involved in human action. Winning the game is a little echo of the winning of the eternal reward toward which the whole of history travels.[13]

To put it another way, human action is purposeful. Human beings have plans and hopes that animate their actions, though sometimes these hopes are inchoate. Human beings work at a project, using the powers of action and control that God through creation has given to them. Human beings arrive at some goal, either the hoped-for goal or something else, that gives them satisfaction or disappointment as the fruit of their action. That fruit depends for meaning on its beginning, when the participants had hopes that are now compared with the result.

Behavioremes are unified wholes at least partly because they are meaningful in terms of an intention (beginning), a work (middle), and a culmination (end), the last of which is tied to the originating intention. Human action has built into it both imitation of and empowering by divine action.

The Holy Spirit brings to us the power of God animating human action. He gives life, not only at the supernatural level of regeneration, but at the natural level of human action, as we can see by comparing the following verses:

> "*The Spirit of God* has made me,
>> and the breath of the Almighty gives me life" (Job 33:4) (natural human action).

> "As long as my breath is in me,
>> and *the spirit of God* is in my nostrils, . . ." (Job 27:3) (natural human action).

---

guages and cultures change over time, so here the perceptions of a group as to what is a basketball behavioreme might change.

13. See J. R. R. Tolkien, "On Fairy-Stories," *Essays Presented to Charles Williams*, ed. C. S. Lewis (reprint; Grand Rapids, MI: Eerdmans, 1966), on "eucatastrophe," 82–84.

"If he should set his heart to it
   and gather to himself *his spirit* and his breath,
all flesh would perish together,
   and man would return to dust" (Job 34:14–15) (natural human
   action).

"Truly, truly, I say to you, unless one is born of water and *the Spirit*, he cannot enter the kingdom of God" (John 3:5) (supernaturally renewed, eternal life).

"It is *the Spirit* who gives life; the flesh is no help at all" (John 6:63) (supernaturally renewed, eternal life).

Some of the passages about natural human action may have in mind partly the role of a person's human spirit within him. But even these suggest that God's Spirit is the ultimate source and sustainer of the life of the human spirit.

## Communicative Action in Language

All behavioremes have meaning in a broad sense. Members of the culture identify them as distinct (contrastive-identificational aspect) and as having a purpose and "fit" within the culture (distribution). In a broad sense, all behavioremes "communicate" something both to those participating in them and to those who are part of the larger culture. The principle applies then in particular to behavioremes involving language as well as other communicative media like music, painting, sculpture, and film (including silent film).

Conversations are behavioremes where language is dominant. They may also include gestures, facial expressions, and postures that serve the communication. We are not disembodied, and communication in language occurs in context (distribution). Conversations include monologues, speeches by individuals. And of course monologues occur in other situations, such as political speeches, sermons, and public lectures, all of which are behavioremes.[14]

Behavioremes, in fact, occur in many different sizes. Smaller pieces are embedded in larger ones. A sermon is a behavioreme that is one piece of the larger behavioreme, the church worship service. And this behavioreme may be included in a still larger behavioreme, the Sunday morning program, which includes two worship services with Sunday school sessions sandwiched between, and maybe space for coffee drinking and casual conversation. The sermon contains within it paragraphs, sentences, and words, all of which are themselves embedded behavioremes.

---

14. Monologues can also be termed "utteremes." See Pike, *Language*, 121, 133–149, on the "uttereme" and utteretics; and see appendix H on speech-act theory.

Verbal behavioremes come in many types and sizes, corresponding to the richness of language uses and the ways in which language occurs in interaction with human action of other types:

> It is probably misleading to think of language as embedded in simple fashion within the still broader context of human behavior. Verbal activity does not embed in nonverbal activity like an egg in a paper bag. Rather, to a large degree man's verbal activity informs, interprets, and structures his non-verbal activity. Patterns of human activity are very complex and language can not [sic] be left out of account at any turn. At any event, however, any given stretch of verbal activity must be considered to be part of broader situational and behavioral patterns which are not exclusively and often not even primarily verbal.[15]

As we have already seen, a small piece of language can refer in summary fashion to a large behavioreme.[16] And the context of description, explanation, and evaluation in language is one distributional context that enables inhabitants in a culture to see a particular behavioreme as a meaningful, unified whole.

Because human purposes are complex and richly structured, there are many kinds of behavioremes, including verbal behavioremes.[17] We will not examine them all equally, but in the following chapters concentrate on cases of particular interest.

---

15. Robert E. Longacre, *The Grammar of Discourse* (New York/London: Plenum, 1983), 337.
16. See chapter 11.
17. See Pike, *Language*, 135–139, on the task of classification of verbal behavioremes ("utteremes").

# PART 3

# Discourse

# Speaking and Writing

All the ways of a man are pure in his own eyes,

but the LORD weighs the spirit.

—Proverbs 16:2

The heart of the wise makes his speech judicious

and adds persuasiveness to his lips.

—Proverbs 16:23

A dishonest man spreads strife,

and a whisperer separates close friends.

—Proverbs 16:28

Verbal utterances are one kind of human action. Since we are interested in language, we can focus specifically on verbal utterances amid the many other kinds of action that surround them. We include both speaking and writing.

Whole utterances have a unity that an insider can recognize. That unity is related to human purposes. Speakers and writers have intentions in what they do. One way of defining meaning is to say that the meaning is the speaker's intention or the author's intention.[1]

---

1. On the possibility of other definitions of "meaning" and other foci for interpretation, see the next chapter.

## Unified Meaning

It is natural in many ways to assume that we will find a *unified* meaning. Consider again my statement to my wife, "I am going to the store to get more bananas." That has a definite meaning that I expect my wife to grasp. But sometimes I may be sloppy. I say "bananas," but maybe I am looking for plantains, and don't realize that there is a different word to designate them. I say, "I am going," but maybe I don't go right out the door; I leave only five hours later. Maybe I am going to an open-air market rather than a conventional store. And maybe I already have in mind that I might make more fruit purchases, and not just stop with bananas. So my purpose in going to the store is broader than just "to get more bananas."

With published writing we expect more, because we know that more care goes into published work, and people check and recheck the product. The author has organized his thoughts, and we keep working with his text in order to see the meaning of any one piece in harmony with the rest. Yes, that makes sense up to a point. But there are complexities.

For one thing, some authors may not be as organized as we could wish. Maybe they hold views on various subjects that in fact contradict one another, but they are unaware of the contradiction. Maybe the problem is not outright contradiction but a lesser tension in an author's text. Nevertheless, the interpreter keeps working toward harmony for a long while, in order to make sure that he has not missed something. In the end, he may sometimes conclude that there is tension or contradiction.

Good authors do better. But even here we must reckon with the effects of the fall. Human beings contaminated by sin are never in perfect harmony with themselves. On the one hand, they are made in the image of God, with the built-in impulse to be in fellowship with God and to worship God. On the other hand, they are in rebellion. They are not only in rebellion against God but in a sense in rebellion against themselves, against what they were created to be. The result is double-mindedness. At a deep level, they are not of one mind. And so they cannot have one, perfectly unified intention in producing a text.

We may illustrate with the example from Acts 17:28, "In him we live and move and have our being." The apostle Paul here quotes from a Greek poet, probably Epimenides of Crete. There is some uncertainty about the poet's views, but he probably meant the sentence in a pantheistic sense. That is, he meant that we are a part of god or identical with god. This view misrepresents our relation to God. But it also distorts a more original knowledge of God that we cannot escape. On the one hand, in opposition to the true knowledge of God, the poet affirms pantheism. On the other hand, in harmony with true knowledge of God, he affirms the presence of God and his dependence on God. The poet is in conflict between two possible meanings of God's immanence, namely, a Christian and a non-Christian view.[2] This instance is only one possible way in which a person may be in conflict with himself.

When a person comes to faith in Christ, he is renewed and transformed. He has a renewed mind: "Do not lie to one another, seeing that you have put off the old self with its practices and have put on the new self, which is being renewed in knowledge after the image of its creator" (Col. 3:9–10; see 1 Cor. 2:16). But the renewal is progressive (Rom. 12:1–2). Consequently, insofar as the believer is not yet perfected in his mind, he too is double-minded. As a result, no text of merely human origin represents fully unified meaning.

The same is true even of a simple utterance like "I am going to the store to get more bananas." My purpose is not completely unified, but at a deep level includes double-mindedness. I am going to the store partly to serve my wife and my family. But, in addition, I am going partly in order to appear to be good and helpful, and selfishly to get the benefit of the appearance. Neither the good nor the bad intention gets directly expressed. One of my intentions in the utterance is not only to give my wife information but to reinforce our personal relationship by keeping her informed. And that contains within it the possibility of a double intention, one side of which is godly and the other side of which is not. In many cases I am not conscious of being double-minded. I seem to be sane, and to have a coherent idea about what I am going to do. But my intentions are still divided.

The difficulties occur with readers as well. The same double-mindedness presents itself when a reader reads a text. He may read it with love for the author, genuinely wanting to understand. At the same time, he may read with imperfect love, and in selfishness may also want to twist the text for his own benefit. He obtains a result that is a mixture of good and bad.

We once again confront the importance of redemption and of receiving wisdom from God. The same observations that we made earlier concerning the work of Christ apply in the sphere of language as well as every other area of life.[3]

### God's Meanings

God himself is holy, pure, and unified in his own mind. There is complete harmony. And so he produces harmonious communication. When Christ became incarnate as man, he spoke with complete truthfulness, and with harmony not only with respect to his divine nature but with respect to his human nature. But there is disharmony in the confrontation between God's holiness and the human

---

2. See the discussion of Christian and non-Christian views of immanence in John M. Frame, *The Doctrine of the Knowledge of God* (Phillipsburg, NJ: Presbyterian & Reformed, 1987), 13–15; and appendix C.

3. See Vern S. Poythress, "Christ the Only Savior of Interpretation," *Westminster Theological Journal* 50/2 (Fall 1988): 161–173.

unholiness of sin. Christ had severe words to say concerning the seriousness of sin. These words, as well as the Bible as a whole, present not only the unity of the divine mind but also instruction and divine power to renew us, to pull us out of the mire of sin, and to give us unity of mind.

But we should note one other truth. The unity of the mind of God is a unity of one God, with one plan. It is also the unity of the Father, the Son, and the Holy Spirit, in the diversity of persons. Unity of meaning within God himself is not unitarian, but Trinitarian. Each person in the Trinity knows all truth and all meaning in knowing the other persons.

Among the persons of the Trinity, each person's knowledge is unique to that person, as well as in total harmony with the knowledge of the other persons. God's unity is the model or archetype for the unity in diversity that is to be achieved by many cultures and many peoples coming together in the body of Christ.

But this analogy is limited. God is infinite, and we are finite. And as long as we are in this life, our minds are not entirely free from sin. So within the church we have to sort good from bad. Scripture, by contrast, is perfectly pure (Ps. 12:6; Prov. 30:5).

## Diversity within Unity

We can look at several instances of diversity within unity. Consider first what happens with inspired speech in the Bible. A person who speaks in the power of the Holy Spirit is speaking not just his own mind but also the mind of the Spirit. The Spirit as well as the human person speaks. The Spirit knows his meaning perfectly. The speech through the human author has perfect purity, because he is guided by the Spirit. The human being agrees with the Spirit, and so there is unity of meaning. But the human author remains finite and does not plumb all the depths of the implications of what he says. And so his understanding is not exactly the same as the understanding by the Holy Spirit. This is a diversity in understanding. And so there is both unity and diversity in meaning when a human being speaks by the power of the Spirit. This is true for the writings of Old Testament prophets and New Testament apostles and other divinely authorized spokesmen for God.[4]

Now consider noninspired speech by human beings. In such cases the human beings are fallible. But they may sometimes speak the truth. The Bible says, "Let the word of Christ dwell in you richly, teaching and admonishing one another in all wisdom, singing psalms and hymns and spiritual songs, with thankfulness in your hearts to God" (Col. 3:16) Christians can be filled with the Spirit, and the

---

4. See Vern S. Poythress, "Divine Meaning of Scripture," *Westminster Theological Journal* 48 (1986): 241–279; and appendix J.

Spirit can use what they say, even though it is not infallible or absolutely pure. So the Holy Spirit has his intentions even in this kind of case. In this case also there is a unity between the Spirit's meaning and the human speaker's meaning. But there is also diversity, because the Holy Spirit understands more, and understands more deeply, than the human speaker. And what the Holy Spirit means is completely pure, while what the human speaker intends may be contaminated by his remaining sinfulness.

The goal of human communication, the goal that will be climactically fulfilled in the new heaven and the new earth, is not autonomous, independent speech on the part of human beings, but speaking out of a mind in deep fellowship with God and empowered by the Spirit of God. Such speech has both unity and diversity in meaning. It is not human speech in isolation from God, but speech that makes manifest the wisdom of God and the power of God, speech that surpasses the capacity of "independent" humanity. We aim for harmony in fellowship with God. We aim to express God's meanings along with our own.

## Meaning Under Control

Let us continue to reflect on some of the limitations in noninspired speech. Even if an author could enjoy full unity as an individual, he would still experience limitations in his expression. For example, I may not know that there is a word for "plantain," and so I say, "banana," which is the nearest word I can find. I show my limited mastery of English vocabulary.

Because authors are made in the image of God, they do have powers of speech. They have dominion and control. But they are not God, and so their control is not exhaustive. As illustrated in fig. 20.1, they do not completely master the language they use; they do not exhaustively control the meanings of its words or its constructions; they do not know their own thoughts perfectly; they do not plan completely what they write; when writing a longer work they do not remain completely the same over the time during which they are writing; they are not conscious of all the implications that they may want readers to draw from what they write. When the content of the communication is simple, these limitations may not make much difference. But with more complex communication they have their effects.

We can see some of these limitations more clearly when we consider a small child learning language, or an adult learning a second language. Neither is master of the language. So when does a child become master? At ten years of age, or fifteen, or twenty, or fifty? In fact, through conversation and reading and practice in writing, or through formal instruction, people can always develop greater skill in writing. No one is a perfect master.

## Partial Mastery of Language

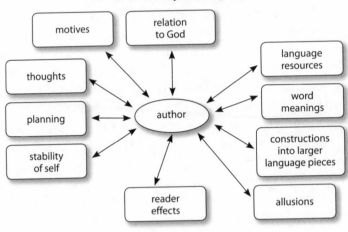

Figure 20:1

Moreover, because of the presence of variation in meanings and in words and in sentences and in authors' contexts, meaning is not fixed with infinite precision. There are different varieties of banana. The word "banana" does not distinguish among them. There are different kinds of store. The word "store" does not distinguish among them.

Authors do not have the God-like control to attain infinite precision. They have only partial control, both in their thoughts and in their previous mastery of language and in their expressive products. They may express things about themselves that they hoped to conceal; they may fail to express some aspects of what they wanted to express. My tone of voice may tell my wife that I resent having to go to the store, even though I didn't want that information to be shown.

Moreover, even in their own minds authors do not define with perfect precision what they intend. I say that I am going to get more bananas. But I may not have decided one way or the other whether I intend to shop for more kinds of fruit as well. The statement that I am going to get bananas may nevertheless tend to imply that I will limit my goal to the bananas. Thus the ideal of perfectly precise authorial intention is indeed an ideal, and a dangerous ideal as well, since it could appear to give to man the kind of control that only God possesses.

## Reader Limitations

Similar limitations affect readers. Readers do not perfectly master their language; they do not exhaustively control the meanings of words and sentences that they receive; they do not know their own thoughts perfectly as they go through the experience of reading; they do not remain completely the same as they go through the process of reading; they do not plumb all the implications of what they read. A reader who grasps an author's meaning does "control" it in some sense. But for human beings the grasp of meaning is partial, and the control is partial. Each reader is different from each author and from every other reader, and even subtle differences are instances of variation that affect understanding in subtle ways.

## Effective Communication

We have been focusing on limitations. But many times communication still succeeds. We rightly pay attention to speakers and authors because we assume that they have something to say and that they are capable of saying it. We assume that they give us a stable intended meaning because in many easy cases we can discern what their intention is, and we can re-express their meaning in paraphrases. We have real understanding, understanding that is sufficient and effective for practical goals. For example, when the photographer says, "Stand roughly there," you know what to do, even though the communication is not as precise as it could be.[5] So with communication in general. The presence of imprecision, and the presence of the possibility of variation, does not destroy all stability.[6] Stability is still there, and we express that stability when we give paraphrases. We rightly talk about two expressions having the same meaning or two speakers meaning the same thing.

---

5. I owe this example to John Frame.

6. Stability is the focus of contrastive-identificational features, which express the unity of meaning. Stability is enhanced, rather than destroyed, by recognition that the meaning of a particular utterance depends also on distributional context. See the previous chapter for discussion of contrastive-identification features, variation, and distribution.

# Analysis and Verbal Interpretation

It is the glory of God to conceal things,
but the glory of kings is to search things out.
—Proverbs 25:2

Human action includes instances where human beings undertake me-thodical analysis of human action. Human beings study themselves, and that shows our ability to stand back and "transcend" the immediacy of our situation.[1]

## Analysis as Human Action

In the West, especially, we have developed a complex tradition of "scientific" analysis that includes not only natural sciences but social sciences as well. The social sciences in one sense have an advantage over the natural sciences, in that the subject of study is always close at hand. We are studying ourselves, human beings, or at least some aspect of human beings. But the advantage is also a disadvantage, because our own preconceptions about ourselves and others threaten to have an influential role in the actual work. The problem is the problem of transcendence. How do we obtain a grasp of a whole of which we ourselves are a part?

In fact, as one aspect of being made in the image of God, human beings can "stand back" from their involvement in some sense. This standing back can take place with great self-conscious attention to establishing and maintaining meth-odological controls, often in imitation of the natural sciences. Some investigators

---

1. On backlooping and human imitation of God's transcendence, see chapters 11–12.

want the rigor that comes from quantifying and statistically analyzing data. But quantification is itself a choice to leave out aspects that are not easily captured by quantity. There are many ways of "standing back" and thinking about what we are doing or have done.

Each of these many ways has its own unity of human purpose. We have the purpose of focusing on and understanding consciously a particular aspect or form of human action. Accordingly, the unity of analytical purpose is a purposeful unity, recognized in Western culture.[2] It is recognized by insiders. It has an *identity* distinct from other kinds of human action. *Variation* permits us to say that there are many subtypes, some more "scientific" and some less. Various kinds of analysis are more or less extensive in length, and may be focused in more than one direction—sociological, anthropological, linguistic, psychological, cognitive, logical, and so on.

The writing of this book is one instance of this kind of analysis. And so is the reading of this book. Linguistics is built up by linguists who engage in analysis focusing on language. Analysis can bring to our attention many interesting facts and interesting structures in human behavior. But the very nature of analysis is to be selective. We focus on one thing or one aspect while simultaneously leaving others in the background. Finite consciousness does not focus simultaneously on everything. As a result, we can always ask what is being left out.[3]

## Verbal Interpretation

The process of interpreting verbal communication deserves special attention. It is a particular kind of purposeful human action.[4] We are especially interested in looking at it because interpretation is closely related to meaning, which has been a principal theme for us all along. And one special instance of interpretation is biblical interpretation, which is integral to Christian living and discipleship.

## Interpretation as Reflective

Some discussions of interpretation like to say that almost all human interaction is interpretation. We "interpret" the meaning of a green light or a stop sign. We may even "interpret" the beauty of a sunset.

---

2. To make plain that this analysis constitutes a behavioreme (see chapter 19), we can even give it a name: "the analytical behavioreme."

3. See appendices E–H for discussions about what may be left out in various kinds of analysis relating to language.

4. In the terminology of chapter 19, it is a behavioreme, which we might name "the interpretation behavioreme."

This kind of description has a reasonable basis. We bring to our current experience the fund of knowledge, attitudes, and expectations from our previous experience, as well as the uniqueness of our own personalities. How one person reacts to a sunset may be different from another. In this sense everyone "interprets" the Bible when he reads it.

The illustration with the green light is even more pertinent, because the meaning of the green light depends on a system of signification within a given culture. In the context of modern traffic, the green light *signifies* that traffic can go forward. A person coming from another culture, with no knowledge of vehicles and traffic, would not know that the green light means "go." Its meaning must be *interpreted* to him. Similarly, the Bible originated in ancient cultures, and presents certain challenges for readers unfamiliar with those cultures.

But in many common situations people do not talk about "interpreting" the green light. They react automatically to a light. They do not have to pause to think it out. Nor would people commonly talk about "interpreting" their spouse's casual comments about work or dinner, or "interpreting" a TV news report. Why not? They do not usually stand back and reflect on what has been said. They do not need to. They already understand what was said—automatically, as it were. They just go on to the next thing. Of course the process of understanding has become automatic only because a long record of experiences, language learning, and enculturation preceded their reception of a particular utterance. But in the end it *does* become automatic.

Similarly, in many situations reading the Bible, or listening to oral reading, results in automatic understanding, at least of the main point.

Ordinary conversation does sometimes pose problems. One person fails to understand well. If he recognizes his failure, he still can decide just to ignore it and go on. Or he asks the other person to repeat or explain what was said. This process is still not usually called "interpretation," but rather merely a process of clearing something up. But a third person present in the conversation may try to explain, in which case he "interprets" the speaker's utterance.

Interpreting the Bible, or interpreting other written works, can be similar. The person who understands better explains the work to someone else. But with more challenging works, the interpreter has often first engaged in study himself. He has reflected on the work, perhaps extensively. He has learned from still other interpreters before him.

## Goals of Interpretation

So what is the goal for this kind of reflective study and interpretation? There might be many goals. If the interpreter is interpreting for the benefit of someone else, it depends on what the inquirer's difficulties are, and what his interests are.

Study can focus on the author, on the text, on the intended readers, or on real or hypothetical modern readers. The text can be used as a resource for historical research into the culture in which the author lived, rather than primarily as a source concerning the author's ideas. Or it could be used primarily as a source for modern entertainment.

Using the earlier categories of presence, meaning, and control,[5] we can distinguish three foci for interpretation. We can focus on what the speaker or author expresses about himself (presence); we can focus on discourse content, including information, commands, and wishes expressed (meaning); we can focus on the purposes and possible effects on readers (control). As usual, these three categories interlock.[6]

Reflective interpretation involves standing back and consciously analyzing, rather than just immersing oneself in the process of communication. Often, the analysis takes place on behalf of other potential readers, in which case the interpreter stands between the author and the readers. Analysis may interrupt or put to one side the author's self-expression and its effects on readers. The analysis then focuses almost wholly on meaning in the sense of stable propositional content. Thus many traditional forms of interpretation naturally focus on content. That is one possible choice, but only one.

E. D. Hirsch and others have argued that the goal is or ought to be the recovery of the author's intended meaning.[7] This goal offers one way of focusing on discourse content. The goal is a worthy one, from the standpoint of biblical ethical standards. The Bible proclaims, "You shall love your neighbor as yourself" (Gal. 5:14; Lev. 19:18). A living author is my neighbor; so out of love I should respect the author and try to understand what he means. But there are complexities even here. Are we required to love dead authors? We can no longer do anything for them personally. Yet even dead authors were made in the image of God, and so we infer that they deserve respect as fellow human beings. In addition, even when an author is dead, *interpreters* of the author are still alive. Out of love for them, as well as for the sake of the truth, we do not want to misrepresent a dead author's meaning. Yes, paying attention to authors' intentions is an implication of biblical ethics.

Just *how* we ought to pay attention depends on the situation and the purposes of a particular communication. If the particular communication is a promise, or a command, or a formal contract, or technical architectural specifications for

---

5. See chapter 3.

6. As usual, the triad for human speech analogically reflects the triad for God's speech. See chapter 4 and the further discussion of the expressive (speaker-focused), informational (discourse focused), and productive (audience focused) perspectives in Vern S. Poythress, *God-Centered Biblical Interpretation* (Phillipsburg, NJ: Presbyterian & Reformed, 1999), 102–103.

7. E. D. Hirsch, *Validity in Interpretation* (New Haven, CT: Yale University Press, 1967).

a building project, the human purpose in the situation may require very close attention to an author's purpose. If unclarity remains, the people involved work in dialogue until all the significant sources of unclarity are eliminated. In other situations, an author has as a main purpose stimulating the thought and creativity of readers. Then it is not so important to try to clear up all imprecision. In fact, the author may use imprecision in order to leave open to readers a spectrum of opportunities for creativity.

Authorial intention is supremely important if we are dealing with the Bible and with God as its author. Then, if we are to submit to God, we must listen to him and avoid imposing our own ideas on the text. We must find out his *meanings*. But we also *meet* God; we experience his presence. Meaning coheres with presence. And God's meanings cohere with control. God transforms us by what he says: "... you have been born again, not of perishable seed but of imperishable, through the living and abiding word of God" (1 Pet. 1:23).

For written works in general, we can say similar things. Understanding the author is still a worthy goal, but not the only possible goal. The word *meaning* can be used in contexts where people are interested in other things. For instance, we can ask what the text *meant* to this or that reader. Then we have reader orientation. Or we can ask what a legal contract *means* or implies even in a case where the author who drew up the contract is trying to escape its implications. Then we have a textual orientation.[8]

In sum, there are various goals that we can have in practice. Because in these days there is confusion about goals for interpretation, it is valuable to make clear the choices.

## Limits to Pursuing Understanding

We should be aware of several other aspects of the situation. First, any one person's time and energy are limited. If other matters are calling for his attention, he may legitimately *stop* worrying about an author's meaning in order to go on to those other things. It depends on the calling of the interpreter. Is he a student to whom the teacher has given an assignment to understand the author? Or is he just an ordinary reader looking for entertainment or stimulating ideas?

Going on to other things may mean just putting the book down for good. But it may also mean asking whether we can get good ideas by interacting with the book in ways that the author probably did not intend. For example, someone may choose to use an author's work merely as the springboard for his imagination. Is that all right?

---

8. In general, as we indicated in chapters 2 and 4, we find a measure of coinherence among the three foci, on author, on text, and on reader. But the three never collapse into one.

It depends on the situation. If we have a specific obligation to an author, to obey a command, or to keep a promise, or to uphold a contract, or to explain his ideas accurately to someone else, we need to meet our obligation. We must not twist the author's meaning to escape. On the other hand, if we are merely reading a book that an author offers to the general public, our choices open up. We may exercise our imagination.

Christ has set us free, to be free to love others in many ways (John 8:32). "You were bought with a price; do not become slaves of men" (1 Cor. 7:23). Freedom in the imagination is one dimension of freedom, and it is important to exercise this freedom in order that through discoveries of the imagination we may bless other people, as well as praise God more deeply.

## Corrupt Content

Second, we must reckon with the fall as well as creation in the image of God. Authors are fallen, and readers are fallen. And that contaminates communication, and introduces Satanic ideas into human communication. Listeners and readers cannot always trust speakers and authors. Sometimes the listener should filter what is said. Sometimes the reader should just put the book down, because it is garbage. True love does not mean accepting anything whatsoever. In fact, loving another person includes being hardy enough to resist the evil in what he is saying, and to figure out something of what is wrong. Depending on the opportunity, it may include rebuking the speaker or writer.

"Understanding" the other person or deciphering his meaning is not an absolute ethical requirement, from a biblical point of view. In a sense we are not supposed to "understand" morally evil thoughts and arguments, but reject them. The counsel of the apostle Paul is relevant:

> Finally, brothers, whatever is true, whatever is honorable, whatever is just, whatever is pure, whatever is lovely, whatever is commendable, if there is any excellence, if there is anything worthy of praise, think about these things (Phil. 4:8).

> I want you to be wise as to what is good and innocent as to what is evil (Rom. 16:19).

Love involves listening to another person long enough and with enough sympathy to be able to try to communicate a helping word in an apt way. Even when we are listening to someone who is wrong, we may sometimes obtain useful insights, by virtue of common grace.[9] Or we may find that our own ideas need to be corrected. We are to listen respectfully to the rebukes and criticisms of others,

---

9. On common grace, see chapter 14.

as well as to their positive ideas: "Whoever heeds instruction is on the path to life, but he who rejects *reproof* leads others astray" (Prov. 10:17).

But there are limits to listening. Some Christians, according to their callings, will have greater ability to interact without moral compromise with anti-Christian thinking. Others will have lesser ability in this area, and they must accordingly draw back from ideas that corrupt their minds. Both types of people are always to respect the limits indicated in God's own biblical instructions about moral purity. When a neighbor is engaging in moral evil, we must out of love for the neighbor search for ways of helping him out of the evil. But the help of another human being is always limited. Only God has unlimited ability to bring people out of evil. We must believe that he can do so even when we find that we ourselves can do nothing except pray. Engaging in moral compromise in the hopes that it will help others never really does good within God's world.

It is worthwhile for academics, in particular, to reflect on this principle. We along with all other human beings are flesh and blood, subject to temptation, and obligated to moral purity, including purity of *thought* and *imagination*. Some types of reading are not good for us, because they are too tempting or too deceitful. The world of scholarship can sometimes generate the pretension that purity can be ignored, and that we have an infinite and absolute obligation to pursue objective authorial meaning or "understanding." But that claim too is a Satanic distortion—and a prideful one—of the real obligation of love.

"But," says the exploring mind, "how can I know which ideas are true, without first looking at all of them?" Well, as time and calling allow, we do look at some of them; we look at the most promising ideas. No one has the time to read all the books ever written. When we do look, we must still respect the fact that God's way of wisdom for mankind is to be nourished and purified spiritually through one pure source, his own word, in order effectively to sort through the pretended wisdom from other sources. Once we have learned from God's word, we have spiritual solidity, and we are then able more and more to discern in other areas.[10]

---

10. To the world, particularly to the postmodern world, such confidence based on God's word looks like "dogmatism." The world detests such dogmatism. This disapproval of dogmatism does have some good motives behind it. People are looking at the damage done by fanatics with their false claims of certainty and their lack of sympathy for others (see appendix A). Fanaticism of a dangerous kind can arise within Christian circles as well as elsewhere. Those who have come to know the truth through the Bible's instruction may still pridefully overestimate the depth and thoroughness of their grasp of truth. They may ungraciously attack those who disagree and are a threat to their pride. They may deceive themselves about their motives by labeling their attitude "righteous zeal." And then through their pride they bring disgrace on the name of Christ.

Nevertheless, people who humbly devote themselves to hearing God's speech in the Bible can legitimately have confidence about what God has shown them. The world is skeptical about such confidence. But why? Can we for a moment be skeptical about the skeptics? Modernism dogmatically thinks that in its autonomous rationalism it is superior to the humble Christian.

## Crossing into Another Person's Viewpoint

Suppose, then, that in a particular case we are morally able to pursue the quest for an author's intended meaning. Can we understand? The author is a different person. His thoughts are not necessarily the same as ours. It is easy for a reader to impose his own meaning, too quickly assimilating an author to his own viewpoint. The challenges are especially great when the author belongs to a different culture. We could easily repeat here what we have already observed about the diversity of cultures, and the challenge that Christians face in crossing cultural barriers.

Even when the author belongs to the same larger culture, there remain differences in subcultures, and differences in individuals. In a broad sense, deeply understanding another person always requires a step analogous to culture-crossing. No mechanical recipe automatically makes the crossing succeed. We need Christian love. We need willingness to sacrifice our own selfish interests for the sake of respect for another:

> Let each of you look not only to his own interests, but also to the interests of others. Have this mind among yourselves, which is yours in Christ Jesus, . . . (Phil. 2:4–5).

Trying to understand another person and his meanings is a form of love. Loving another person deeply comes through the power of Christ, and takes place in imitation of Christ, as Philippians 2:4–11 indicates. "We love because he first loved us" (1 John 4:19). In this respect as well, crossing into another person's ideas is like a small version of crossing into another culture or another language. When done rightly, it includes, figuratively speaking, a pattern of death and resurrection. The reader surrenders the security of his own ideas and his own desire to enforce his ideas on the other person. He thereby dies to himself and his pride and his selfishness. In reaching out, he grows in love, and thereby enriches his life. That enrichment is a figurative resurrection. It is an enrichment even if, in the end, he fails to understand the other person. At least he has tried. The Lord sees that and rewards it.

Love also involves a kind of substitutionary exchange. The reader gives up the exclusive concentration on his own ideas, in order that another person's ideas may prosper and momentarily have preeminence in the reader's mind.

Finally, love includes victory over Satan. It is always a victory over Satan to resist the temptation to selfishness and to treat another person respectfully. So it is a victory when it takes place in the area of interpretation. Increased understanding of truth is a victory over the lies and confusion in Satan's dominion (John 8:44).

---

Postmodernism dogmatically claims that God cannot speak clearly to us. Both reject confidence in God's instruction because they have a counterfeit conception of God.

## Three Perspectives on Interpretation

Let us now use the particle, wave, and field perspectives to look at interpretation. In the particle perspective, we naturally focus on the stability of meaning. God is stable, and faithful to himself. And so all his utterances have stability of meaning. Human beings, created in the image of God, also produce utterances with stable meaning. In this area, as in others, the fall and sin lead to corruption but do not completely destroy human ability to produce meaning. We can paraphrase either an utterance of God or an utterance of man. The paraphrase expresses roughly the same meaning as the original utterance. We can go on with an indefinite number of paraphrases, by different people in different cultures, and so exhibit the stability of meaning and truth across cultural boundaries.

We may also use the wave perspective. Utterances by God or by human beings are meant to go somewhere. Utterances have intentions that go beyond the moment. Conversations in particular show real *dynamic* development of intentionality. Any particular utterance within a conversation is not meant (note the intention!) to be a complete expression of the speaker's views, but is to be taken in the context of his preceding remarks.

Suppose two people in conversation are both endeavoring to reach greater clarity and understanding about some difficulty, an ethical difficulty perhaps, or a physics problem. The conversation is moving toward clarity, and must be understood in the light of a goal that may never be fully achieved, even after many conversations. Then the meaning of any one utterance is to be understood in the light of the goal. If the goal is achieved, then they may look back and say that such-and-such a stage in the process was not very helpful, and that earlier remarks were confused and misleading, or that the moment of insight came at one particular point.

Even a literary work can function in this way. Do scholars discuss the literary work *only* in order to try to recover authorial intent? Perhaps some do. But for others there is interest in the whole train of secondary thoughts and writings that have sprung up in the wake of an important work. Do students of Platonic philosophy want only to recover Plato's original ideas? Or do some of them want to develop Platonic philosophy, even to the point where perhaps they could improve on their master? In the latter case, the dynamism of their goal goes beyond the authorial intent.

In fact, different groups, and different persons within a group, grow in slightly different ways as they interact with a particular text or discourse. The author of the discourse may even have intended that a text have many diverse benefits for many diverse people. Remember the model of the unity and diversity in the body of Christ. There is health, not merely danger, in diversity.

For each of us human beings, our understanding is finite and human, not divine. It is not absolutely comprehensive. So also, our re-expressions of meaning in paraphrase are not comprehensive. Good paraphrases do share many of the contrastive-identificational features in the meaning they express. They do all express one meaning. But they express it with *variation*. They show differences as well as common features.

In a wave perspective, meaning is not quite the easy thing that either modernist or postmodernist thinking may take it to be.[11] Modernist thinking is prone to want unity without diversity, through the complete domination of pure, autonomous reason. In modernist thinking, meaning is what it is, namely, a pure, isolated essence, and we must all submit to it by wiping out, suppressing, and destroying all differences.

By contrast, postmodernist thinking is prone to want diversity without unity. Each person in his diversity produces whatever meaning is right in his own eyes. Since most postmodernism believes that God is nonexistent or inaccessible, there is no way to adjudicate among interpretations, and no confidence that the Holy Spirit will bring the humility and love that lead to genuine understanding of the Bible—or of any author, for that matter. So, for the sake of peace, postmodernism celebrates diversity of all kinds, including error and aberration.[12]

We may also use a field perspective on meaning. Especially in ordinary conversation, people understand the *relations* of what they are saying to a larger social interaction. At office parties an employee may be expected to converse with others not merely for the sake of particular information but for general socialization. He cements the social atmosphere of the office. The speech-making at a political rally is one focal point within a total experience that is intended to promote the morale, the dedication, and the fund-raising for the political cause. The total experience is important, and the "meaning" of a political speech is found not merely in its obvious content but in its social contribution *in relation to* the rally as a whole. To focus in isolation on the speech as informational content, or as persuasion, would be possible, but it would miss other dimensions, because meaning in a broad sense belongs to the relations of the speech to the whole rally.

Similarly, the "meaning" of any particular human utterance is integrally related to other meanings, including not only meanings in other verbal utterances but also the cultural meanings in the surrounding cultural contexts. We would subtly falsify the richness of human communication if we pretended that meaning could be precisely cordoned off, delineated with infinite precision, and confined to a text, now treated in isolation.

---

11. On modernism and postmodernism, see appendix A.

12. How we deal with unity and diversity on earth among human beings tends to reflect what we believe about unity and diversity in God. Postmodernists tend to promote diversity without enough unity, which is akin to polytheism (many gods, with little or no unity). Modernism, by contrast, is like unitarianism, which affirms one God, but not three persons in the Godhead.

# Interpreting the Bible

And he gave the apostles, the prophets, the evangelists, the shepherds and teachers, to equip the saints for the work of ministry, for building up the body of Christ, until we all attain to the unity of the faith and of the knowledge of the Son of God, to mature manhood, to the measure of the stature of the fullness of Christ.

—Ephesians 4:11–13

The three perspectives—particle, wave, and field—can also be applied to the interpretation of the Bible. With the Bible we confront added richness, because we are dealing both with the divine author, God himself, and various human authors of individual books. Dual authorship has been discussed elsewhere[1]; here let us concentrate on insights that can come from using the three perspectives.

## A Particle Perspective on Biblical Interpretation

First, let us apply the particle perspective to biblical interpretation. If we focus on the divine author, we can say that he knows beforehand all of the ways in which he desires people to appropriate individual passages in the Bible, and to appropriate the Bible as a whole. His knowledge encompasses all the uses of the

---

1. See Vern S. Poythress, "Divine Meaning of Scripture," *Westminster Theological Journal* 48 (1986): 241–279; Poythress, "The Presence of God Qualifying Our Notions of Grammatical-Historical Interpretation: Genesis 3:15 as a Test Case," *Journal of the Evangelical Theological Society* 50/1 (2007): 87–103; see also appendix J.

Bible throughout history. All the approved uses are part of his intention. Even uses that God does not approve of are still within his sovereign control.

In fact, in a larger sense God's intention for the Bible would include hypothetical approved uses that do not happen to occur in the actual historical process. God knows the possibilities, as well as the actualities (see, e.g., 1 Sam. 23:9–12). The knowledge of God is complete and does not change. So his total intention for the Bible does not change with time. In the particle perspective, we would focus on this unchanging total intention. If we equate God's meaning with his intention, we can say that the meaning is unchanging. "Heaven and earth will pass away, but my words will not pass away," Jesus says (Matt. 24:35). Not only the utterance but its meaning remains for all time.

## A Wave Perspective on Biblical Interpretation

Now let us consider the wave perspective on interpretation. Individuals and communities grow gradually in the knowledge of Scripture and its implications. Growth is a wave; it is a process. Within this life it does not come to an end.

The process includes moments of careful, exacting analysis of word meanings, grammatical constructions, and ancient cultural contexts. The careful, exacting analysis has come to be associated with the label "grammatical-historical interpretation." Bible scholars in particular endeavor to discipline themselves, so as not merely to read in what they want. They try to see what God was saying to people back in the remote past, as a check on the sinful tendency to make the Bible say something that leaves the present reader comfortable with his sin. This is a valuable contribution to the body of Christ, particularly because whole groups of Christians may collectively develop a subculture and a tradition that finds ways to "tame" the message of the Bible. The tradition distorts the Bible in order to avoid the pain of confronting the community's corporate sins. The scholarly investigation is a process, but its goal is stable meaning, in particular meaning that would have been in the human author's mind or would be perceptible to the original readers.[2]

But the total process of interpretation also includes creative insights. The creativity can take the form of envisioning a new way of construing human authorial meaning. Or it could be insight into an application to the reader's circumstances or to the life of a friend who needs counsel. Or it could be a sense that God is speaking these words to me here and now, in a way that may not derive from my best discernment of the meaning of the human author. Or it may be a thought,

---

2. I have written elsewhere concerning the benefits and limitations of this mode of interpretation. See Vern S. Poythress, *God-Centered Biblical Interpretation* (Phillipsburg, NJ: Presbyterian & Reformed, 1999), especially chapters 9–10; Poythress, "Presence of God."

seemingly out of nowhere, only loosely associated with the words of the text, but which seems to be a thought given by God's blessing.

Not all such thoughts and not all such meanings are approved by God. We need to remember that the devil *tempted* Christ by quoting Scripture and giving it his own spin, his own evil application:

> Then the devil took him to the holy city and set him on the pinnacle of the temple and said to him, "If you are the Son of God, throw yourself down, for it is written,
>
> > "'He will command his angels concerning you,'
>
> and
>
> > "'On their hands they will bear you up,
> >     lest you strike your foot against a stone.'"
>
> Jesus said to him, "Again it is written, 'You shall not put the Lord your God to the test'" (Matt. 4:5–7).

So how do we distinguish between creative ideas that are a positive gift from God, and ideas that ought to be rejected? As the Reformers recognized, what is clear in Scripture interprets what is unclear.[3]

Creativity that gets into tension with what is clear is out of bounds. But creativity in harmony with Scripture is in bounds. Even creative thoughts "out of nowhere" can sometimes be valuable gifts from God. But we must avoid confusing them with the central, clear meanings from the Bible. In addition, we need to do what is normal for Christians in the body of Christ: test new ideas in the light of Scripture, and talk to other Christians to see what they think. In particular, we must not pressure other Christians to receive an idea that is not clearly supported by particular texts in the Bible.

God is the sole creator of the world. But human beings made in his image are derivatively creative, in analogy with his archetypal creativity. Those in fellowship with God should find that their creativity is stimulated and sharpened over time, rather

---

3. Some postmodernists delight in showing that no meaning is "clear," because we can always see it in a new context. Yes, contexts vary, and rebellious people often cleverly invent new contexts that suit them. But God controls all contexts. He calls on us to trust him, and to believe that through the work of the Holy Spirit he moves those who trust in him more and more into righteous paths, which provide the contexts for clarity:

> But the path of the righteous is like the light of dawn,
>     which shines brighter and brighter until full day.
> The way of the wicked is like deep darkness;
>     they do not know over what they stumble (Prov. 4:18–19).

than stifled. Many rebels have imagined that the Bible, because it gives definite moral boundaries, and definite boundaries for our thinking about God (no false gods), must stifle creativity. But God is the source of all fruitful human creativity. Knowing him richly expands our minds, expands our horizons, and lets the light in.

Modernism wants a firm, final, clear answer to textual meaning through mechanical application of the right method. That squelches creativity and personal fellowship. Postmodernist relativism wants creativity, but without God's presence creativity degenerates into arbitrariness, which is next door to meaninglessness. God's answer is different from both. We grow, as God has designed us to grow, in the body of Christ; we grow both in unity and in diversity, in stability and in creativity. Rightly used, creativity contributes to stability, because creative ideas from one believer can later be checked out more methodically and rationally by another believer. If they do check out, they add to stable knowledge. Conversely, stability contributes to creativity, because stability from one member of the body provides direction for another member's creativity: it points the way to the most promising new avenues that the creative member explores. When the church is functioning in the way in which it was designed, the Holy Spirit is present among the members, and the Spirit himself empowers them to serve one another within the body of Christ (1 Corinthians 12).

In science, the creative scientist does new explorations in Antarctica or in the Andes. The stable scientist provides a body of knowledge that instructs the creative scientist as to what kind of questions might be most fruitful when he travels to the Andes. So likewise in the body of Christ.

## A Field Perspective on Biblical Interpretation

In view of God's design for the body of Christ, individual interpreters of the Bible need to interact with other members of the body. This interaction includes interaction with Bible interpreters of previous generations who have left commentaries and theological writings. The principle of diversity in the body of Christ extends to biblical interpretation. Different members may notice different things, and their observations then supplement one another. They may also correct one another. Growth comes not only through the sharing of different observations about the positive message of Scriptures and its implications, but from correction and rebuke, when someone begins to distort the Bible.

Teaching gifts have a central role to play in the growth of the body:

And he [Christ] gave *the apostles, the prophets, the evangelists, the shepherds and teachers,* to equip the saints for the work of ministry, for building up the body of Christ, . . . (Eph. 4:11–12).

Now you are the body of Christ and individually members of it. And God has appointed in the church *first apostles, second prophets, third teachers*, then miracles, then gifts of healing, helping, administrating, and various kinds of tongues. Are all *apostles*? Are all *prophets*? Are all *teachers*? Do all work miracles? Do all possess gifts of healing? Do all speak with tongues? Do all interpret? But earnestly desire the higher gifts (1 Cor. 12:27–31).

Pursue love, and earnestly desire the spiritual gifts, especially that you may *prophesy* (1 Cor. 14:1).

All Scripture is breathed out by God and profitable for *teaching, for reproof, for correction, and for training in righteousness*, that the man of God may be competent, equipped for every good work (2 Tim. 3:16–17).

Reformed theology has spoken of "special office" and "general office" in teaching. Christ is our supreme teacher and prophet. Out of his fullness (Eph. 4:7) he has given teaching gifts to the church. "Special office" describes those who are officially recognized as elders and ministers of the word of God (Eph. 4:11; 2 Tim. 4:1–2; 2 Tim. 2:2; 1 Tim. 3:1–7). "General office" describes the privilege given to every member of the body to speak words of encouragement and rebuke, as the Holy Spirit empowers and enlightens him:

Let *the word of Christ* dwell in you richly, *teaching and admonishing* one another in all wisdom, singing psalms and hymns and spiritual songs, with thankfulness in your hearts to God (Col. 3:16).

I myself am satisfied about you, my brothers, that you yourselves are full of goodness, filled with all knowledge and able to *instruct one another* (Rom. 15:14).

Thus any one person's work in interpreting the Bible has a complex interaction with the body of Christ. No one person on earth has already arrived at a comprehension of all the implications of the Bible. One person supplements another, and corrects the other when the other is astray.

In addition, the Bible as "special revelation" from God enjoys a relation to "general revelation." All the world bears witness to God who made it (Rom. 1:18–25; Ps. 19:1–6). In particular, James tells us to "be doers of the word, and not hearers only, deceiving yourselves" (James 1:22). Being doers means applying the word to ourselves and to our situations. It means thinking about ourselves and about the world in the light of God's word. John Frame has developed the three perspectives on ethics—normative, existential, and situational—to highlight this very process of application.[4] The normative perspective focuses on the norms for ethics. These

---

4. John M. Frame, *Perspectives on the Word of God: An Introduction to Christian Ethics* (Phillipsburg, NJ: Presbyterian & Reformed, 1990).

norms are known in our conscience, according to Romans 1:32. But in a fallen, sinful world the conscience can become hardened. The norms are most clearly and fully set out in the Bible. So that leads us to biblical interpretation.

The second perspective is the existential perspective, also called the personal perspective. It focuses on the person. Look at yourself, and apply the Bible to your own mind, your own desires, your own conscience, and your own feelings. That means exploring the *relations* between the Bible and yourself.

The third perspective is the situational perspective. We are to look at the entire world around us. God has made the world. We are to see the hand of God in it. And we are to see our various obligations toward it: to understand and praise God, to care for his creatures, to exercise dominion, to use the subhuman environment in the service of love toward other human beings, and so on. In other words, we are to explore a multitude of *relations* between the Bible and our world. These relations include the relations in which we try to apply to the world a direct command of God given in the Bible. But they also include relations between the history told in the Bible—Abraham, Isaac, and Jacob—and the whole history of the world. When we explore the relations, we can consider everything that we know about the peoples of the world—about science,[5] about sociology, about language. We can try to bring all these areas into relation to what the Bible says, in order to be faithful to what we already know that the Bible says, and also to engage in creative discovery in the world. So paying attention to relationships can also foster the creativity that we discussed under the heading of the wave perspective.

In particular, I intend in this book to exercise creativity in thinking about language. Of course we must first pay attention to the clear and direct things that the Bible has to say about God's speech, about man's creation, about Satan, and about redemption. But then we also go out and look at language. We use the insights from those who have studied language intensively. We endeavor to sift through good and bad, and creatively to relate the Bible's more explicit teaching to what we are learning about language. I invite others to go beyond what I say, and to explore further. That is part of the wave perspective, which acknowledges continuing creativity.

We have now looked at particle, wave, and field perspectives on interpreting the Bible. We can apply each of these perspectives in interpreting any one passage of the Bible, or even any one sentence.

---

5. See Vern S. Poythress, *Redeeming Science: A God-Centered Approach* (Wheaton, IL: Crossway, 2006).

# Genre

Now these things happened to them as an example,
but they were written down for our instruction,
on whom the end of the ages has come.

—1 Corinthians 10:11

The different kinds of purposes that human beings have in their utterances have a relation to differences in genre. In the written medium we find detective stories, grocery lists, letters, novels, proverbs, newspaper reports, songs, and so on. With some thought, the different kinds of verbal behavioremes and speech acts can be transformed into a list of different genres.

But the two are not quite the same. The same genre, such as a letter, could be used for more than one purpose: to prepare for a visit, to thank someone, to solicit information, to provide information, to express love. A single letter may have more than one purpose. It looks as if Paul's letter to the Romans both expounds his understanding of the gospel for the benefit of the church in Rome (Rom. 1:16–17), and prepares for his visit to Rome (Rom. 15:22–33).

## What Is a Genre?

A genre may be defined as "a category of artistic, musical, or literary composition characterized by a particular style, form, or content."[1] We are here focusing on *verbal* rather than artistic or musical composition. We may expand the definition

---

1. *Webster's Ninth New Collegiate Dictionary.*

beyond the limits of "literary composition" into more ordinary compositions like personal letters, grocery lists, newspaper advertisements, and class notes.

Usually when people are talking about a genre they are speaking from an insider's point of view. A genre is identifiable by people within a particular culture. God as creator and sustainer has brought into being all the genres within each culture. He is able to speak using the genres, if he wishes. And as an all-competent speaker, he will use each genre in accord with its distinctive capabilities.

The principle of meaning in relationships implies that the meaning of any particular piece within a genre will be colored by the genre in which it occurs. The differences may be subtle, or they may be dramatic—as when one person thinks that a particular writing is satire and another thinks that it is a straight-faced communication. One person may take a particular writing as fiction, another as nonfiction.

Genre, then, has its effects. But those effects occur within a multitude of contexts. Those who concentrate on genre alone may therefore miss something or overestimate the significance of what they are perceiving.

## Other Influences

First, all genres arise in languages and cultures that God controls. Every aspect of meaning ultimately derives from him. So all the genres in all the cultures are what he designed them to be.

Second, a particular genre has contrastive-identificational, variational, and contextual (distributional) characteristics.[2] The contrastive-identificational features distinguish it from other genres. But within a particular genre, each instance is a *variation* on the genre as a general class. Each instance is unique. For example, each psalm within the book of Psalms belongs to the genre "Hebrew poetic song." But each is also unique. Each has its own content and style, which is not simply to be ignored or assimilated wholly into the generality of the class. The significance of a writing depends on what that particular writing says.

Third, genres may be large or small groups of writings. Poetry is a very broad category. Lyric poetry is a subcategory. Love poetry is a subcategory of lyric poetry. Love sonnet is a subcategory of love poetry. Each of these are genres. But broad genres tell us less.

Fourth, classifications by genre may cut across one another. For example, Psalm 104 is a Hebrew poetic song. Genesis 1 is a historical narrative, showing attention to organizational grouping of events. It also includes key formulaic repetitions: "And God said"; "And God saw that it was good"; "and there was

---

2. See chapter 19.

evening and there was morning." Our descriptions of Psalm 104 and Genesis 1 pay attention to stylistic features and "form." But if we pay attention to content, both can be classified under the common label, "statements about what God did in creating the world." The one kind of attention, concerning style and form, does not dispense with the other. Both naturally come into play when readers read the two pieces. And the two pieces invite reflection on the relations between them, partly because Psalm 104 expects readers to have in mind the history in Genesis 1.

Because genres allow variation, a writer is free creatively to adapt a genre for new purposes. For example, the parables of Jesus show some similarities to stories that other people have told. They belong to the broad genre of "story." But Jesus has a unique purpose, namely, to use these stories to tell people about the kingdom of God and to make statements about his own ministry. He also challenges people's preconceptions about the coming of the Messiah and the way in which God would fulfill his promises in the Old Testament. In these ways, Jesus' parables are not quite like anything before them; they are creative.

A writer may even create fused or crossover genres that show characteristics from more than one established genre. For example, the book of Revelation shows features that allow us to classify it either as a prophecy (Rev. 1:3; 22:7) or as "apocalyptic literature" (like Daniel and Zechariah), or as a first-century Greek letter (compare Rev. 1:4–5 with the beginning of other letters in the New Testament, such as Phil. 1:1–2).

Fifth, genres occur in the context of human action. As we already observed, the same broad genre, such as a letter, can be used for many distinct human purposes. The contexts of human purposes, that is, the distributional contexts, always color the significance of any particular instance of any genre. Fortunately, many pieces contain sufficient evidence internally to allow readers of later generations to infer human purposes with reasonable confidence. But this is not always so. It depends on the particular case. Writings to broad audiences or to "posterity" are more likely to make it easier for subsequent distant readers.

Finally, each author or speaker produces discourses that are *his*. They express his views and his purposes, not another's. So we can classify works not only by style or form, but by authorship. This classification cuts across other kinds of classification by genre, and so it is all the more important that we do not forget it. It makes a difference *who* is writing or speaking. We naturally interpret what he says within the context of what we know about him.

This principle becomes particularly important when the author is God. Each book in the Bible had a human writer (though the writer does not always identify himself). All the books have God as divine author. And that makes the Bible a unique genre, unlike books of merely human authorship. We should take into account who God is whenever we read any book in the Bible.

## Focus on Presence, Meaning, and Control

All genres express the presence, meanings, and control of their authors in inter-locking fashion. But in some genres or in some particular works within a par-ticular genre, one of these three tends to be more prominent. For example, many of the psalms, when considered as independent works, prominently express the thoughts and feelings of the human author; the presence of the author's struggles is notable. When they are included in the book of Psalms, God indicates that he means them to be sung, and then the aspect of controlling or transforming read-ers predominates. The singers and those who listen to the singing are supposed to identify with the words and absorb their lessons. Nathan's parable to David (2 Samuel 12) and Jesus' parables are predominantly transformative (control). In expository sections of Romans informational meaning predominates, though ethical implications and their transformative force are never far away.

Second Timothy 3:16 indicates that "All Scripture is breathed out by God and profitable for teaching, for reproof, for correction, and for training in righ-teousness." The word "profitable" indicates that all Scripture has transformative effect. God intends that we as readers should "profit" and be changed. At the same time, that change comes partly from "teaching," from the informative content of Scripture. The presence of God, as he speaks to us in the Bible, goes along with teaching content (meaning) and the power of God that transforms us (control). The three aspects—presence, meaning, and control—are complementary, and always go together. But sometimes one is more prominent.

Similar things are true, though on a different level, for speech from human authors. Genres expressive of the author as a person lend themselves to speaker-oriented analysis of the author's presence. Genres conveying information lend themselves to discourse-oriented analysis of discourse content (meaning). Genres that strongly affect readers lend themselves to reader-oriented analysis of transfor-mative effects (control). But all three dimensions operate in all genres. Authors express themselves through discourse to readers (presence); authors convey content through discourse to readers (meaning). Authors try through discourse to influence readers (control).

## Commonality

Because of the commonality among human beings across cultures, outsiders who observe ordinary human writings from a particular culture can often achieve a good approximation in their assessment of a particular piece of writing. The relative success of such outside observers does depend on which genre they confront, and the obviousness with which it can be associated with broader human purposes, in distinction from purposes that may be narrowly defined in the context of some culturally specific practice.

Now what about God's communication to us in the Bible? God makes the Bible available to generations to come. He has the purpose that the gospel, and the Bible as a permanent, canonical standard for understanding the gospel, would go out to the various peoples of the world. The Bible, then, is accessible in its meanings, even to those who do not have detailed knowledge of its ancient cultural settings. Not everything is perfectly understandable to everyone, and in some cases there are difficult details. We encounter either a word whose meaning is difficult to identify, or a sequence of words whose construction is difficult, or some uncertainty with respect to the genres at the time when the material was originally set to writing, or uncertainties with respect to the situation of the original readers. But, because God is in charge of all cultures, we can have confidence that the important meanings are accessible across cultures. God sends his Holy Spirit, and makes sure that those who approach him in humility are spiritually nourished.

In fact, God has designed language so that even ordinary human communication can succeed most of the time. We can use an everyday example. Suppose Barb tells Charlotte, "I am going to look for a new job in Syracuse." But Charlotte did not hear everything that Barb was saying, because someone else was talking in the background. But most likely Charlotte would still understand what Barb is saying, because she does not have to hear every sound and every syllable *exactly*. She can identify a sound such as an ess sound in "Syracuse" within reasonable limits, even without perfect hearing, because a unit of sound in language allows *variation* but still *contrasts* with other units of sound.[3] She can identify a word such as "look" even without hearing every sound exactly, for the same reason. And she can identify a sentence, even without hearing every word exactly. Even when she misses a few words, she can often make out the gist of what is said. Suppose she hears, "I . . . look for a new job in Syracuse," where the intervening words "am going to" were unintelligible because of noise. She can still make a good guess as to Barb's main point. The same is true if Charlotte misses a whole sentence somewhere in the middle of a longer speech.

All these instances confirm that human communication in language succeeds in situations involving noise. We may contrast this success with some forms of digital communication, such as computer programs, where the failure at a single point may sometimes produce a failure in the whole communication. The computer program may not work at all if, in object code, a single bit is lost or wrongly interpreted. Natural languages, by contrast, enable communication even when our knowledge is partial or incomplete.

---

3. In technical terms, we would say that a particular *phoneme*, like the sound "ess" in English, displays variation and contrast. It contrasts with the "sh" sound, the "zee" sound, and other phonemes in English. At the same time it allows variation: louder or softer, shorter or longer.

Communication in language contains what has been called "redundancy." Charlotte can guess the contents of a word or a sentence that she does not completely hear, because its contribution overlaps with the contributions of the portions that she does hear. We can see similar processes when we look at God's communication to us in the Bible. An obvious redundancy occurs when two different parts of the Bible teach the same thing. The two parts may use nearly the same words (1 Sam. 22 and Ps. 18; Ps. 14 and Ps. 53), but often use somewhat different words. The four Gospels, taken together, have much overlap or "redundancy" among them. A reader who misses the point made in one Gospel may nevertheless hear the same point later when he reads another Gospel.

The different genres of the Bible offer still other kinds of overlap. For example, much basic theology about God and man can be inferred from the Psalms. Or it can be inferred from more didactic portions of the Bible like the New Testament letters. The Psalms, because of their genre as songs, often affect us more in our emotions. The New Testament letters may sometimes affect us first of all in our mental beliefs. But the Psalms can also form our theological convictions and beliefs. God can work profound personal effects in helping us to absorb the truths on a deeper level. The reader absorbs knowledge of God not only from the didactic portions that have more overt teaching about God but also from the Psalms that drive home the personal effects. The two reinforce each other. The human reader does not need to know exhaustively either the genre or the content of the Psalms or the Letter to the Romans in order to use both to grow in knowing God.

Individual books of the Bible, and even individual sentences, also have overlap or "redundancies." If we were to delete or cover up a single word within a sentence, context would often allow a reasonable guess as to what the missing word is. That is because the rest of the sentence overlaps in function with the contribution of the single word.

"Redundancy" is not a terribly good label for this phenomenon, because it suggests that a good deal is superfluous, and this is far from true. The richness produced by reinforcements in meaning helps us in areas where we are dull, or slow to understand, or where we accidentally miss some detail, or where some detail of meaning is not easily available because of subtle changes in cultural context from then to now. God designed language to allow communication between himself and man, even in the situation where man is dull, or is resisting the truth. Having multiple means of communication is one way of overcoming dullness.

God made it so in order that we, in our finiteness, even when we are recovering from sin and rebellion, might have communion with him, in spirit and in truth. In this sense, the so-called "redundancies" are not redundant or superfluous, but a blessing according to God's design.

# PART 4

# Stories

# Storytelling

"Be fruitful and multiply and fill the earth and subdue it and have dominion over the fish of the sea and over the birds of the heavens and over every living thing that moves on the earth."

—Genesis 1:28

We will not hide them from their children,
but tell to the coming generation
the glorious deeds of the Lord, and his might,
and the wonders that he has done.

—Psalm 78:4

S torytelling is one particular genre, a common genre in many cultures.[1] There are many reasons for its popularity, and it is difficult to plumb them all. People enjoy stories, even made-up stories. They want information about what other people are doing or have done. They also identify with characters like themselves, and vicariously experience the disappointments or triumphs of these characters. They may enjoy imagining fantasy worlds, where the limits for personal action within the real world are stretched or bent, but in a way that may still indirectly

---

1. In fact, narrative discourse in a broad sense is a linguistic universal, characteristic of all human language. See Robert E. Longacre, *The Grammar of Discourse* (New York/London: Plenum, 1983), 3. But from the standpoint of an insider observer within a particular culture, there will be genres whose exact texture belongs with that particular culture and that language.

illumine their own personhood. They enjoy stories of the past, which may have instances of bravery or ignominy, and may help to explain the present.

Stories have some profound relations to God. We will take time to explore some of them.

Storytelling encapsulates a large amount of human action. The action may be spread across days or months or years. The story compresses this action into a few minutes or a few hours.[2] The story gives a view of human life, the life of personal action. In that respect, it offers a form of transcendence. Storytelling is for human beings made in the image of God. We can step back and look at ourselves, and reflect about ourselves, in a form of transcendence that images or reflects the transcendence of God. We talk about ourselves. We perform a verbal action that refers to other complex actions. We summarize, arrange, structure, and evaluate, elucidating the significance of human beings and their actions.

## Insiders' and Outsiders' Views in Stories

As a genre, storytelling will vary in some ways from language to language. There will also be subgenres, like novels, science fiction, historical reporting, epic stories, fairy tales, detective stories. But there are also commonalities to human nature, and commonalities also to human action in time.[3] It is on these that we will focus, since we cannot possibly exhaust the multiplicity of stories in the multiplicity of cultures.

The final context for human action is God's action. God has a "story," namely, world history. God has purposes from the beginning, and these are executed in time. At the center of world history God has the climactic history of redemption brought about in the life of Christ. Because human beings are made in the image of God, they have purposes, and they endeavor to bring about those purposes in time. So human stories are naturally analogous to God's world history. Human stories represent within language the nature of human action.

## Plot

God's story has a beginning, a middle, and an end. In the beginning God created the world. Shortly after the beginning of the human race, the fall disrupted

---

2. In the terminology of chapter 11, this encapsulation is a form of backlooping.

3. The particular genres in a particular culture are "emic" categories, in the terminology of chapter 19. The commonalities shared by different cultures are "etic." On "etic" and "emic," see Kenneth L. Pike, *Language in Relation to a Unified Theory of the Structure of Human Behavior*, 2nd ed. (The Hague: Mouton, 1967), 37–72.

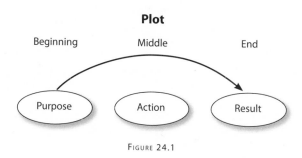

FIGURE 24.1

the original harmony. God then acts in the middle of history to redeem human beings. The end comes with the consummation, the new heaven and the new earth (Rev. 21:1).

God's actions exceed what human beings can do. And yet there are still similarities. We may re-label God's history as a story consisting in commission, work, and reward. Using this more general labeling, we can see similarities with human action. Human beings imitate God's purposes on smaller scales. Purposeful human action has an action "plan" of sorts; it has purposes. It also involves a concrete action and its result (fig. 24.1).

This pattern occurs both in real human actions in history and in fictional stories.

Story plots, as accounts of human action, therefore often show similar features. Stories may begin with a normal situation. But a problem or a disruption soon surfaces. Let me illustrate with a generic form of a fairy tale.

"Once upon a time, there was a good and faithful king who had a lovely daughter, the princess. But one day the princess was kidnapped by a dragon." The kidnapping represents a disruption of the normal situation. The disruption already suggests a task to undertake to remedy the disruption. The remedy will be a small-scale analogue of redemption. The princess must be rescued. That is the action plan; that is the purpose.

The introduction of tension and the resolution of tension lead to the possibility of drawing a "plot" of the tension at each point in the narrative. The tension goes up when difficulties increase; the tension goes down when the difficulties are resolved. The resulting plot has the shape consisting of a hump in the middle and valleys at the two ends. It is what has been called the "bell curve" for plotting tension in a narrative. The tension is introduced, rises to a climax, and then falls during the resolution and the period of reward (or failure, in a tragic plot). See fig. 24.2.

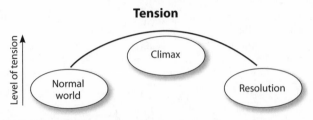

FIGURE 24.2

John Beekman,[4] building on the observations of many literary analysts, and based on experience with multiple languages, has produced a set of labels for the various main elements in a narrative episode, which are tied into the rise and fall of tension. We paraphrase Beekman's work in the following summary (see also fig. 24.3).

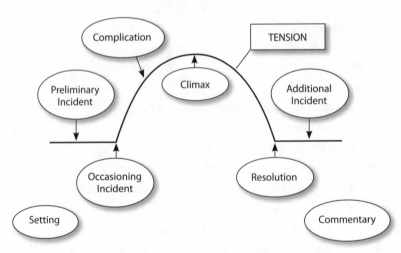

FIGURE 24.3

## Pieces of a Narrative Episode

*Setting* is composed of statements about static facts, location, time, circumstances, or movement in location. Usually such information comes at the very beginning of a new episode.

---

4. John Beekman, "Toward an Understanding of Narrative Structure" (Dallas: Summer Institute of Linguistics, 1978), 7–8. In what follows, I have introduced additional clarifications.

*Preliminary incidents* are events (not descriptions of static states of affairs) relevant to what follows, but before the problem or tension has been introduced into the episode.

The *occasioning incident* is the event that introduces notable conflict or tension. In the nature of the case, there is seldom more than one such incident.

*Complication* is an event increasing tension, making a solution (apparently) more difficult. There can be more than one paragraph devoted to complications of various kinds. (Unlike the "occasioning incident," "complication" can and often does occur more than once in a single episode.)

*Climax* is the incident of maximum conflict or tension. It is where, in a melodrama, we would expect the music to play the loudest.

*Resolution* is the event or events that solve the problem, release the tension, and unravel the tangles—or at least they contribute toward the solution.

*Additional incidents* are further events that are consequences of the climax or resolution, but are not significant parts of the climax or resolution itself.

A *commentary* contains the narrator's comments on, evaluation of, or moral for the story. Unlike "additional incidents," it does not contain events continuing the straight line of the narrative.

All of these elements except the first and the last—"setting" and "commentary"—represent an elaboration of the basic structure of human action consisting of three steps: (1) formulation of purpose; (2) action; and (3) result. The setting and the commentary are additional explanatory remarks that the narrator uses to situate the episode for the benefit of the reader.[5]

## Roles

The plot can be elaborated by the introduction of participants who execute particular phases in the plot. The king offers a reward for the rescue of the princess. This step is the beginning of the commissioning. The hero steps forward, and may be formally commissioned to execute the plan.

The hero then goes out, in the "work" phase of the plot. He may encounter various obstacles. There may be subplots in which he confronts obstacles along the

---

5. Commentary can also occur as an introduction to the story itself; it may supply reasons why the story is interesting.

way and overcomes them. The road is long. Finally, he confronts the dragon, the villain. The dragon, it may be noted, is the small-scale stand-in for the opponent of God's plan, namely, Satan (Rev. 12:9). Are we right in thinking so? Remember that man, made in the image of God, inevitably imitates God's action. So, yes, it makes sense that stories about human action should show analogies to the big story, the macrostory, concerning God's action.

But let us continue with our small, made-up story of the hero and the dragon. The hero defeats the dragon. That is the end of the "work" phase.

The king then rewards the hero by offering the princess in marriage. This is the blessing phase, or reward, and is an offer of communion with the source of blessing, the king, and subordinately with the princess. The princess, let it be noted, is the small-scale stand-in for the church, the bride of Christ, who is one part of Christ's reward for the accomplishment of his work. The macrocosmic hero is Christ, for which the fairy-tale hero is a small-scale stand-in.

## Actor Categories

In this stereotyped story there are certain important character roles: the hero, the villain, the sought-for person or object (in this case, the princess), the commissioner (the king), and the reward-giver. In this case the commissioner, the king, is the same person as the rewarder. And so it is with the macrocosmic story, with God the Father as both commissioner and rewarder. But the roles are distinguishable, and so in some human stories the roles may be occupied by distinct human beings. There may also be stories where there is confusion. The person who appears to be the hero, or sometimes the person who is the hero's helper, turns traitor, and must be replaced by another (in the story of the gospel, Judas is a traitor; and in a certain respect Adam became a traitor). There may also be subplots. In one subplot, a person who seems at first to be an opponent, or minor villain, turns out to be a helper.

There is a history to twentieth-century analysis of such stories. In 1928 Vladimir Propp published *Morphology of the Folktale* in Russian. It was translated into English in 1958, with a second edition dated 1968.[6] On the basis of analysis of a corpus of about a hundred Russian folktales, Propp found a regular structure both in the plot and in the roles of characters. Propp found eight roles: the "villain," the "donor" (who gives the hero a helpful object), the "helper" (who helps the hero on his quest), the "princess" (more generally, the sought-for person), "her father" (more generally, rewarder, punisher, tester), the "dispatcher" (who sends the hero

---

6. Vladimir Propp, *Morphology of the Folktale*, trans. Laurence Scott, 2nd ed. (Austin/London: University of Texas Press, 1968).

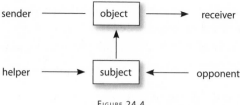

FIGURE 24.4

on his quest), the "hero," and the "false hero."[7] In his analysis Propp did not find a consistent distinction between the functions of the princess and her father. If those two roles are wrapped up together, there are only seven distinct roles.[8]

Propp applied his analysis to only one corpus of Russian folktales; he never claimed that it could be generalized. But Algirdas J. Greimas in 1966 undertook to generalize the approach so that it would apply to narratives from many sources.[9] Greimas compared Propp's work with an analysis of dramatistic roles by Étienne Souriau.[10] In synthesizing the two approaches, Greimas recognized complexities but settled on a set of six roles that he claimed could usefully categorize "mytho-logical manifestations only."[11] The roles, which he termed "actantial categories," are "sender," "object," "receiver," "helper," "subject," and "opponent." He summed up the relationship between the six roles in the diagram shown here as fig. 24.4.[12]

The "subject" is a generalization based on Vladimir Propp's "hero." The "op-ponent" covers both Propp's "villain" and Propp's "false hero." The "object" cor-responds to Propp's princess or sought-for person. The "receiver" is Propp's "hero" in his role of receiving the princess as bride. (The hero can play more than one role at different points in the story.) The "sender" includes Propp's "dispatcher" and the princess's father in his role of giving the princess.

Greimas's approach differs from Propp. Propp attempted to develop "insider" categories that would match the perceptions of tellers and hearers of the specific body of Russian folklore. Greimas, on the other hand, was obviously striving for a general set of categories that would work cross-culturally; he necessarily offered an "outsider's" set of categories, that is, classifier's categories that would work across multiple cultures.[13] More than one set of categories might prove to have

7. Ibid., 79–80.

8. Ibid., 79.

9. Algirdas J. Greimas, *Structural Semantics: An Attempt at a Method* (Lincoln: University of Nebraska Press, 1984); translated from *Sémantique structurale: recherche de méthode* (Paris: Larousse, 1966).

10. Étienne Souriau, *Les deux cent milles situations dramatiques* (Paris: Flammarion, 1950).

11. Greimas, *Structural Semantics*, 207.

12. Ibid. It is not clear why the line connecting "sender" to "object" is not an arrow.

13. In technical terms, Propp offered "emic" categories; Greimas offered "etic" categories. See Pike, *Language*, 37–72.

some use. Why then this specific set? Greimas's own explanations in his book do not go very far. He has obviously melded together a set of seven (or eight) roles from Propp, and six roles from Souriau, but other roles can be imagined.[14]

## Actor Categories in the Light of God's Work

We can find some clearer motivation for Greimas's selection by returning to the nature of man as prophet, king, and priest. Human action includes verbal action and thinking action (prophet), action in power (king), and action in blessing and reward, curse and punishment (priest). In many stories, the beginning presents a challenge. In the middle, the challenge is worked through in a test. And in the end there is a recompense (reward or punishment). These three phases correspond to some extent to the three "offices," prophet, king, and priest.[15] The prophet's role in speaking corresponds to the challenge. The king's role in exercising power corresponds to the test. And the priest's role in blessing corresponds to the recompense.

In talking this way, I am using the terms "prophet," "king," and "priest" in a very general way. The terms are describing activities in which ordinary human beings engage, because human beings are made in the image of God. But the use of the terms in the Bible is much narrower and more special. In the Bible "prophet," "king," and "priest" designate special offices that God appointed for redemptive purposes, and imply special authority that goes with the office. It is important to appreciate their unique role. At the same time, it is possible to see analogies between the special offices and human actions in general.

The same goes when we compare the historical accounts in the Bible with stories outside the Bible. The events reported in the Bible really happened. And the reports in the Bible have a special role, because God instructs us concerning events related to his redemptive plan. These events have key, unrepeatable roles in God's purpose for the world. But because these are key events brought about by God, they are likely to be imitated by human beings in many other circumstances, because human beings are made in the image of God. So the uniqueness of what is recorded in the Bible is not in tension with the generalities that we can explore about stories all over the world.

So let us return to consider Greimas's set of categories. The bottom row of Greimas's list of "actantial categories," namely, "helper," "subject," and "opponent" (fig. 24.4), focuses on power relations. The helper brings in his power to help the subject, while the subject uses his power to fight against the opponent. The top

---

14. For further discussion of various "structural" approaches to narrative, see Robert Detweiler, *Story, Sign, and Self: Phenomenology and Structuralism as Literary-Critical Methods* (Philadelphia: Fortress; Missoula, MT: Scholars; 1978), 103–164.

15. See chapter 13.

row in Greimas's list focuses on reward or recompense relations. The sender gives the object to the receiver, as a benefit, as a reward. But Greimas includes Propp's role of "dispatcher" under the category of "sender," and "dispatcher" concerns a role with more prophetic associations, namely, verbal commissioning. Finally, the relation between subject and object is a relationship of desire that gives rise to the main human intention and to a human project. That intention is what makes the whole narrative go forward.[16] It is actually closely related to the sphere of thought and plan, which has verbal and therefore "prophetic" associations.

We can perhaps attempt to separate out a little more clearly various strands in the total plot. First, a simple plot, uncomplicated by subplots, will generally have a movement from purpose to action to result. The purpose is the purpose of a "subject" to obtain a result, that is, an "object." The subject may be a group of people as well as an individual; and the object may be either a reward such as a royal treasure, or a person such as the princess. The relation between purpose and result structures the whole episode lying in between the endpoints.

Second, a plot may have phases that include planning, work, and reward. To rephrase it, the phases are the challenge, in the "prophetic" sphere; the test, in the sphere of kingly power; and the recompense, in the priestly sphere. Within each of these phases we may anticipate interactions between characters, and in these interactions the characters will characteristically play certain roles. If we look carefully at these activities, we can make further distinctions beyond what Propp or Greimas have done.

Let us start with the phase of the challenge. Here we may anticipate interactions involving primarily verbal communication. Propp supplies the label "dispatcher" for the person who issues the challenge. But there must also be someone who is "dispatched," who receives the challenge. Typically in Propp's stories the person dispatched is the hero. But we can see that there can be variations. To remind ourselves that we are generalizing beyond what Propp did, we may introduce some new labels, namely, "challenger" (for Propp's "dispatcher") and "challengee." A typical interaction may involve any or all of the moves in a three-move sequence: (1) a situation or a formulation of desire impacts a challenger; (2) the challenger issues a mandate to a challengee; (3) the challengee accepts or refuses the challenger.

In the phase of the test, we may anticipate interactions involving primarily power relations. One person sets up a test, and another is being tested. In Propp's stories, the person who initiates the test may be an opponent, namely, the villain, or may be an aid, namely, a donor (the donor gives a gift after the testee proves his worthiness). The person being tested is typically the hero. Once again we can

---

16. God the Father's love, and Christ's love for the church, are the final motivation for God's history of redemption.

generalize, and speak about a "tester" (the person or the thing that is the problem) and a "testee." We can again anticipate a three-move sequence: (1) the tester confronts the testee; (2) the testee struggles against the tester or the situation formed by the tester; (3) the tester acknowledges victory or defeat, success or failure, on the part of the testee.

In the phase of the recompense, we may anticipate interactions involving primarily evaluation and the conveying of consequences. There will be two parties in the interaction—a "recompenser" and a "recompensee." The "recompenser" is a generalization from the role of the father in Propp's analysis. We have a possible three-move sequence: (1) the recompensee is evaluated by the recompenser; (2) the recompenser issues a recompense; (3) the recompensee accepts or repudiates the recompense.

Obviously we have anticipated the possibility of different roles than those that Propp or Souriau or Greimas have listed. That is all right, because our categories are general categories, "outsider" categories; they are not intended to match perfectly with any one culture or any one set of stories. They serve well if they clarify the characteristic kinds of actions. These kinds of actions are what they are because human beings are what they are. Human beings have characteristic purposes and characteristic desires and characteristic powers. And human beings are what they are because they are made in the image of God. God is the archetypal speaker, and therefore challenger; he is the archetypal controller, and therefore tester; he is the archetypal source of blessing, and therefore recompenser. Human action imitates divine action, even when it is twisted by the fall.

In many stories there are complexities. The categories that we have mentioned so far do not eliminate the complexities, but rather offer only a very general overview. Within a particular story, two or more different characters may play the same role at different points in the story. At an early point, the donor becomes a recompenser when he gives to the hero, that is, to the recompensee, a magical object that will help him find his way or fight the dragon. At a later point, the king is the recompenser when he gives his daughter in marriage. It should also be clear that the same character can play two distinct roles at two different points in the story: the king can be challenger when he tells the hero to go and rescue his daughter. He can be recompenser when he gives his daughter in marriage. And finally, a single character can play a combination role. The villain as tester may confront the hero as testee, and in the confrontation verbally *challenge* the hero to combat, thereby becoming a challenger.

We can see also the potential for embedding small narratives within larger ones. The confrontation between the villain and the hero can be an extended confrontation, which becomes a small story of its own. It may show the whole story pattern of commission, work, and reward. Each of the Gospels has smaller historical accounts within it: accounts of Jesus' healings, his casting out demons, and his feeding the 5,000. Each particular incident of healing has its own small "plot." At the same time, each incident fits into the larger account of the whole Gospel.

We can make further distinctions if we like. If a challenger intends morally to aid the challengee, we may call him a *dispatcher* (Propp's term). If he intends morally to hinder the challengee, we may call him a *tempter* or *deceiver*. Satan appears in the role of tempter when he tempts Jesus in the wilderness (Matt. 4:1–11). But Satan and Satan's agents also appear in the role of tester, as when Pharaoh pursues the Israelites at the Red Sea. A challenger may use mediating objects or persons in his relation to the challengee. The mediating object can be either a guarantee or a threat. Satan says, "All these I will give you, if you will fall down and worship me" (Matt. 4:9).

Testers may also be morally for or against the testee. The tester who is on the side of the testee is typically a donor, who intends to bless the testee at the end of the test. The opposite of this is the villain, who intends to destroy the testee. Villains may enlist mediating objects or persons, who will be *opponents*. The barrel thrown at the testee, or the lighted stick of dynamite, or the villain's sidekick, is an opponent. Donors may enlist *helpers*, either tools or persons (for example, the person who becomes sidekick to the hero). In the Old Testament God acted as a donor by providing helpers, often human heroes like David, when Israel was in distress.

Recompensers may recompense in two directions, reward or punishment. The recompense itself is a mediating object or person. (The princess given in marriage is the reward from the king, who is the rewarder.)

## Using the Categories

Any particular story has details that will not be captured by these very general categories. A story may have subplots, or distinct episodes, which show some of the features in miniature. A story may have an inconclusive ending, or no ending at all (see Luke 13:6–9). The categories serve their purpose if they alert us to some commonalities that belong to many stories, commonalities both in plot and in the functions of the characters. I have chosen the categories in a way that also helps to underline the relation of human action to divine action.[17]

---

17. For further indication as to how these roles fit into a larger linguistic framework, see Vern S. Poythress, "A Framework for Discourse Analysis: The Components of a Discourse, from a Tagmemic Viewpoint," *Semiotica* 38/3–4 (1982): 277–298; Poythress, "Hierarchy in Discourse Analysis: A Revision of Tagmemics," *Semiotica* 40/1–2: (1982): 107–137.

# The Story of Redemption

For I delivered to you as of first importance what I also received: that Christ died for our sins in accordance with the Scriptures, that he was buried, that he was raised on the third day in accordance with the Scriptures.

—1 Corinthians 15:3–4

R edemption by Christ is a story. It is a story of something that really happened in history, in space and time. Because it is at the heart of God's purposes for the world, it is *the* one central story. So, in the end, all the other stories about working out human purposes derive their meaning from being related to this central story. We should not be surprised that the categories for stories in general analogically reflect the character of redemption, that is, the one central story. Let us consider the story of redemption in terms of the typical three phases in a story: challenge, test, and recompense.

## Challenge: The Opening of the Story

First, Christ is the challengee who receives from God the Father the commission to save the world. A commission is implied when the Bible speaks of the Father *sending* the Son: "But when the fullness of time had come, God *sent forth* his Son, born of woman, born under the law, to redeem those who were under the law, so that we might receive adoption as sons" (Gal. 4:4–5). ". . . the Father has *sent* his Son to be the Savior of the world" (1 John 4:14).

According to Galatians 4:4, God sent his Son to be born, implying that the "sending" takes place even before birth. The sending is a preincarnate exchange between the Father and the Son. But the sending is also confirmed in time, particularly when Jesus is baptized by John the Baptist. The voice from heaven, the voice of God the Father, says, "This is my beloved Son, with whom I am well pleased" (Matt. 3:17). That pronouncement might on the surface appear to involve only a confirmation of the identity of the Son. But it alludes to Psalm 2:7 and Isaiah 42:1, Old Testament passages that, taken in their larger context, anticipate the coming of the messianic Son and servant of the Lord who will accomplish the climactic salvation and deliverance of God's people. So the "challenge" for the Son's work on earth is implicitly contained in the Father's voice.

### Test: The Middle of the Story

Second, Christ accomplishes his work. This work includes his entire earthly life. God the Father is the ultimate "tester," who sets out the situations in which the Son works. Christ is the "testee." The test concerns not only whether he will bless the people around him but whether he will remain faithful to the work to which God the Father has called him. The alternative, for Christ to seek his purposes in an illegitimate way, is set forth by Satan in the temptation just before the beginning of Christ's public ministry (Matt. 4:1–11).

The test climaxes with Christ's crucifixion and death. Here he is supremely obedient to the Father in the midst of supreme testing; he says, "My Father, if it be possible, let this cup pass from me; nevertheless, not as I will, but as you will" (Matt. 26:39). "Do you think that I cannot appeal to my Father, and he will at once send me more than twelve legions of angels? But how then should the Scriptures be fulfilled, that it must be so?" (Matt. 26:53). And a tempting voice continues, "If you are the Son of God, come down from the cross" (Matt. 27:40). The supreme paradox of the Christian gospel is that victory comes through apparent defeat: "but we preach Christ crucified, a stumbling block to Jews and folly to Gentiles" (1 Cor. 1:23).

The villain in the whole story is Satan. But Satan has his helpers, namely, Herod, Pontius Pilate, the soldiers, the religious leaders, and the crowd that shouts to have Jesus crucified (Matt. 27:21–23).

### Recompense: The End of the Story

Both the crucifixion and the resurrection are recompense, but in two distinct ways. The crucifixion and death of Christ are God's recompense for sins; Christ bore the penalty of sins:

> But he was wounded for our transgressions;
>     he was crushed for our iniquities;
> upon him was the chastisement that brought us peace,
>     and with his stripes we are healed.

> All we like sheep have gone astray;
>> we have turned—every one—to his own way;
> and the LORD has laid on him
>> the iniquity of us all (Isa. 53:5–6).

He himself bore our sins in his body on the tree, that we might die to sin and live to righteousness. By his wounds you have been healed (1 Pet. 2:24).

The resurrection and the ascension are God's recompense to Christ for his obedience:

> He was manifested in the flesh,
>> vindicated by the Spirit, . . . (1 Tim. 3:16).

And being found in human form, he humbled himself by becoming obedient to the point of death, even death on a cross. *Therefore* God has highly exalted him and bestowed on him the name that is above every name, so that at the name of Jesus every knee should bow, in heaven and on earth and under the earth, and every tongue confess that Jesus Christ is Lord, to the glory of God the Father (Phil. 2:8–11).

It [faith] will be counted to us who believe in him who raised from the dead Jesus our Lord, who was delivered up for our trespasses and raised for our justification (Rom. 4:24–25).

For our sake he [God] made him [Christ] to be sin who knew no sin, so that in him we might become the righteousness of God (2 Cor. 5:21).

Christ is the last Adam. He accomplished what Adam failed to accomplish. And Adam represented in himself the whole of humanity. Christ represents all those who belong to him. So Christ's work accomplished redemption with worldwide implications.

# Many Mini-redemptions

Then the LORD raised up judges,
who *saved* them out of the hand of those who plundered them.
—Judges 2:16

Let the redeemed of the LORD say so,
whom he has *redeemed* from trouble.
—Psalm 107:2

"Your faith has *saved* you; go in peace."
—Luke 7:50

In the Bible there are many small stories of small-scale "redemptions." Yet Christ's work needed to be done only once:

> But as it is, he has appeared *once for all* at the end of the ages to put away sin by the sacrifice of himself. And just as it is appointed for man to die once, and after that comes judgment, so Christ, having been offered *once* to bear the sins of many, will appear a second time, not to deal with sin but to save those who are eagerly waiting for him (Heb. 9:26–28).

Christ's work is effective not only for those who believed in him while he was on earth, but for all who are joined to him by faith, throughout the ages. Thus he is the *one mediator*:

For there is one God, and there is *one mediator* between God and men, the man Christ Jesus, who gave himself as a ransom for all, which is the testimony given at the proper time. For this I was appointed a preacher and an apostle . . . (1 Tim. 2:5–7).

## Mini-redemptions in the Gospels

What relation does Christ's one accomplishment of redemption have to the small stories of redemption in the Bible? When we read through the Gospels we find many small acts of "mini-redemption." Christ heals the sick, casts out demons, and pronounces forgiveness of sins. All of these actions result in reversing some effect of the fall. In that respect they are small pictures of the great redemption that reverses the fall comprehensively.

Consider the healing of the leper in Luke 5:12–16:

> While he was in one of the cities, there came a man full of leprosy. And when he saw Jesus, he fell on his face and begged him, "Lord, if you will, you can make me clean." And Jesus stretched out his hand and touched him, saying, "I will; be clean." And immediately the leprosy left him. And he charged him to tell no one, but "go and show yourself to the priest, and make an offering for your cleansing, as Moses commanded, for a proof to them." But now even more the report about him went abroad, and great crowds gathered to hear him and to be healed of their infirmities. But he would withdraw to desolate places and pray.

All human diseases are to be seen as part of the suffering that comes as a direct or indirect result of the fall. Healing of disease is therefore a small step in the direction of redemption from the fall. Any healing anticipates the great and permanent healing promised in the new heaven and the new earth: "He will wipe away every tear from their eyes, and death shall be no more, neither shall there be mourning, nor crying, nor pain anymore, for the former things have passed away" (Rev. 21:4).

Leprosy as a disease is not an exception. In fact, it is an especially appropriate example of disease, because in the Old Testament it makes a person ceremonially unclean. Uncleanness is an outward symbol for the contamination of sin (Leviticus 13–14).[1] Healing of leprosy therefore stands symbolically for healing from sin. The extra directions about doing "as Moses commanded" (Luke 5:14) serve not only to assure that there is an official religious record of the results ("for a proof to them") but also to remind readers of the symbolic associations of leprosy that are built into the Mosaic law.

---

1. The laws concerning uncleanness had several functions within their context in Israel. I am picking out one function that becomes particularly evident as we look back on the Old Testament in the light of its fulfillment.

Jesus then heals the leper as a small picture of the later "healing" from sin that he will accomplish on the cross. And how does he heal? It is in response to faith ("if you will"). This role for faith anticipates the role that faith in Christ plays in responding to the gospel (Rom. 10:9–10). Jesus touches the leper as well as declaring him healed. The touch, according to Mosaic law, would render the touching person unclean (Num. 19:22). Jesus by touching symbolically identifies with the leper. The symbolism suggests that Jesus himself would become unclean. Symbolically speaking, it is as if he took the uncleanness on himself and thereby healed the leper. This symbolism anticipates his identification with sins and bearing the sins of others on the cross. Thus the cleansing of the leper is indeed a small-scale picture analogous to Christ's work of redemption on the cross.

We may also see in this story of cleansing the three phases present in many stories. The leper issues a challenge to Jesus in saying, "Lord, if you will, you can make me clean." Jesus accepts the challenge. Then his power to heal is "tested" when he says, "I will; be clean." The "tester" in this case is the situation and the disease of leprosy in particular. When the text says, "And immediately the leprosy left him," we know that Jesus has succeeded. The reward phase of the story involves the official return of the leper to the status of clean. Interestingly, it is reward for the leper, not for Jesus. The text does indicate in a less direct way that there are effects on Jesus' ministry. The report spread, and great crowds gathered.

The smaller narrative episodes in the Gospels often have the typical narrative structure that we laid out in the previous chapter. Near the beginning of the episode a challenge appears in the form of a sick person or a person with a demon. Christ powerfully heals the person, and often the person or the bystanders praise God for what has happened. The endpoint is deliverance, redemption in a small but concrete form. The small episodes anticipate in their small way the great redemption that is coming at the end of Christ's earthly life. They are mirrors or pictures of redemption.

## Mini-redemptions in the Old Testament

What about stories of deliverance in the Old Testament? Figures like Moses and Joshua and David and Elijah bring small-scale deliverances. They are shadows anticipating the great mediatorial work of Christ. If indeed, as 1 Timothy 2:5 tells us, there is only one mediator, then the mediation symbolized by Moses and Joshua and others cannot ultimately depend merely on these individuals, or on their powers. No one deserves the blessings that God brings from time to time in the Old Testament. If nevertheless people receive the blessings, it must be on the basis of looking forward to the mediation of Christ, who takes away sins, including the sins of Old Testament saints.

So the redemptive stories of the Old Testament have a similar pattern to those in the Gospels.[2] Challenge, test, recompense. Distress, work of deliverance, and resulting blessing.[3]

## Application to Those Who Believe in Christ

According to Romans 6:1–11, those who believe in Christ undergo death and resurrection with him. The pattern for Christ's "story" is then reflected in them. This experience "with Christ" takes place when they are first united to him by faith. Galatians says that "those who belong to Christ Jesus have crucified the flesh with its passions and desires" (Gal. 5:24). Christians "have been raised with Christ" to new life (Col. 3:1). This application of Christ's death and resurrection to believers is symbolized by baptism:

> Do you not know that all of us who have been baptized into Christ Jesus were baptized into his death? We were buried therefore with him by baptism into death, in order that, just as Christ was raised from the dead by the glory of the Father, we too might walk in newness of life (Rom. 6:3–4).

But in another sense the pattern of dying and rising takes place again and again:

> For we who live are always being given over to death for Jesus' sake, so that the life of Jesus also may be manifested in our mortal flesh. So death is at work in us, but life in you (2 Cor. 4:11–12).

> ... that I may know him and the power of his resurrection, and may share his sufferings, becoming like him in his death, ... (Phil. 3:10).

Believers find in their lives small experiences of challenge, test, and recompense. By overcoming temptation, or helping others in distress, they achieve goals that God in his purposes has set for them. "For we are his [God's] workmanship, created in Christ Jesus for good works, which God prepared beforehand, that we should walk in them" (Eph. 2:10). Thus believers' lives contain many mini-instances of redemptive plots. Groups of people can also go through redemptive plots (Rev. 3:1–6).

---

2. For a fuller discussion of the relation of the Old Testament to Christ, see, e.g., Vern S. Poythress, *The Shadow of Christ in the Law of Moses* (Phillipsburg, NJ: Presbyterian & Reformed, 1995); Edmund P. Clowney, *Preaching and Biblical Theology* (Grand Rapids, MI: Eerdmans, 1961); Dennis E. Johnson, *Him We Proclaim: Preaching Christ from All the Scriptures* (Phillipsburg, NJ: Presbyterian & Reformed, 2007).

3. The book of Judges shows a pattern that also includes falling away and the consequent recompense in the form of suffering (cf. Judges 2:11–23; a tragic plot).

As we saw in chapter 24, plots typically have a "bell curve" showing the rise and fall of tension. The climax and events leading to the climax often involve not only tension but also suffering. The hero may nearly die. If the hero does not succeed in defeating the dragon, the dragon may kill him. Here we find a death-and-resurrection theme. Typically, of course, the hero does not literally die, but he does experience the threat of death, and, spiritually speaking, he must die to selfish desires for self-preservation. In that sense he lays down his life for the princess.

Paul calls on husbands to do the same. "Husbands, love your wives, *as Christ loved the church and gave himself up for her, . . .*" (Eph. 5:25). Husbands especially, but also Christians in general, must embody in their lives a pattern of suffering, a pattern of laying down one's life in order to receive it back again from God. That is the specific form that the redemptive story takes.

Christ's redemption includes substitutionary exchange. Dim shadows of that exchange occur in the lives of Christians as they imitate Christ. If a husband "gives himself up" for his wife, he renounces his selfish desires simply to work for his own individual benefit. He gives this up, and his wife receives the benefit. That is one exchange. It may sometimes have two aspects: a negative one in which he tries to bear some of her burdens, and a positive one in which he tries to bring her benefits.

Finally, Christ's work includes victory over Satan. Christians also achieve victory over Satan whenever God empowers them to resist sin or rescue others from sin and from Satan's clutches:

> The seventy-two returned with joy, saying, "Lord, even the demons are subject to us in your name!" And he said to them, "I saw Satan fall like lightning from heaven. Behold, I have given you authority to tread on serpents and scorpions, and over all the power of the enemy, and nothing shall hurt you" (Luke 10:17–19).

## Diverse Stories of Redemption with Diverse Purposes

In looking over these different stories we have emphasized what is common to them. This emphasis is legitimate, since all the redemptive acts of God come to a climax in the death and resurrection of Christ. But now let us emphasize the diversity in the stories. No small-scale story of redemption is merely a repetition of another. The details are different. As illustrated in fig. 26.1, they involve different people, with different needs, different responses to the needs, different routes to meeting the needs, and different outcomes.

Each Christian goes through many small-scale redemptive experiences in his life, as well as the initial experience of being born again. God tailors experiences to each Christian, at each time in life. God meets each person with an understanding

**Diversity in Redemption**

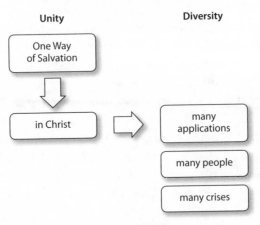

FIGURE 26.1

of that person's pains and struggles and sins and hopes and fears. The variations in people's stories are not merely random but express the wisdom of God, who knows how to apply the work of Christ to the particulars. The experiences also fit together in different ways into larger life stories. This variety is a manifestation of the *variation* in the general category of redemptive story. The contrastive-identificational features are the features of the general category, namely, the category of redemptive story; the particulars differ as variations within the general category. The variations show the meaning of the general pattern, as well as the general pattern showing the meaning of the variations. God's redemption is cosmic, when Christ works to redeem us; it is also particular, when Christ's work is applied to us and to the details in our lives.

We see variation also in the mini-stories within the Gospels. Jesus healed a number of people. He cast out demons a number of times. Each event involved particular people. God acted in Christ to care for those particular people, not just for an abstract idea of redemption. He loved Jairus and Bartimaeus and Lazarus, and Mary and Martha. We also see each small story in a context ("distribution"). For example, each small-scale particular story, from one day in the life of a Christian, belongs to larger stories spanning months and years. The stories in the Gospels fit together into the entire story told in one Gospel. The stories go somewhere. They tell of the announcement of the coming of God's saving rule by John the Baptist, of Jesus' public ministry, of growing opposition, of the arrest and crucifixion. We can see relations between the earlier and later parts, but never mere repetition.

If we emphasize variation, we emphasize the particularity. In fact, in the stories in the Gospels, there are more particularities not included in the record. In the events of Luke 5:12–16, did Jesus touch the leper with a finger, with a whole hand, or with an embrace? Did he touch him on the arm, or on the lobe of the right ear, or on the head? Which disciples were present to see the miracle? What effects did it have on them? We modern readers do not know, but God knows. He acts in redemption in massive, minute, even unfathomable particularity. Each of us has a longing for a redemptive answer to the minute particularities of his own soul and his own circumstances. God answers that longing in Christ through the Spirit.

## Existential and Normative Perspectives on Redemptive Stories

Redemption has rich implications. We can see the implications more extensively by using three perspectives originally developed by John Frame in his works on Christian ethics.[4] The first perspective, the *normative perspective*, looks at the norms, the commandments set out in the Bible. The *situational perspective* looks at the situation, and asks what will be a beneficial act of love toward others. The third perspective, the *personal perspective* or *existential perspective*, looks at the motives of the actor, particularly the motive of love. Within a biblical worldview, all three cohere in principle, because God specifies the norms, rules over the situation, and creates each human actor in his image.

We can use any of Frame's three perspectives when we look at redemptive stories. By focusing on *plots* in this chapter and the preceding one, we have given prominence to the situational aspect of redemption. Redemption—both Christ's act of redemption and its small-scale analogues—alters the *situation*. It rescues people from sin and death, or from captivity, famine, and war. But it has implications for the transformation of the people themselves, that is, existential transformation.

Existential transformation is one aspect of stories in general, not just the Bible's history of redemption. If we wish, we can focus on the existential perspective by following the development of *characters* as they travel through a particular story, rather than focusing on the plot. Naturally the two are intertwined. Characters develop through action, and action makes sense because it is action expressing the personalities of the characters. So the two are perspectives on one another. In Luke 5:12–16 the leper had faith in Christ and found his attitude as well as his body transformed. Christ as a man went through the process of suffering, death, and resurrection, and with respect to his human nature he experienced development and change:

> In the days of his flesh, Jesus offered up prayers and supplications, with loud cries and tears, to him who was able to save him from death, and he was heard because of his reverence. Although he was a son, he learned obedience through what he suffered. And being made perfect, he became the source of eternal salvation to all

4. John M. Frame, *Perspectives on the Word of God: An Introduction to Christian Ethics* (Phillipsburg, NJ: Presbyterian & Reformed, 1990); Frame, *The Doctrine of the Christian Life* (Phillipsburg, NJ: Presbyterian & Reformed, 2008), especially 33–35.

who obey him, being designated by God a high priest after the order of Melchizedek (Heb. 5:7–10).

We can also look at the biblical account of redemption from the normative perspective, and see expressed in it the norms of righteousness and sin, penalty and reward. These manifest the permanent character of God, and the aspects of his character that constrain the way of redemption. God's compassion is the source of redemption. His righteousness implies that sin must be punished. His holiness implies that sinners cannot stand in his presence. The way of redemption expresses both his righteousness and his love.

Similar principles apply to small-scale historical accounts within the Bible. We can look at these accounts from any of the three perspectives. Using the existential perspective, readers can identify with characters' attitudes, and may experience transformation in adopting new attitudes. For example, a reader of Luke 5:12–16 could identify with the leper's words, "Lord, if you will, you can make me clean," and be encouraged to have faith in Christ.

Using the situational perspective, readers can experience the operation of God on themselves in a manner analogous to the action of the story. In reading about the leper the reader may realize that Christ is able to stretch out his healing hand to cleanse the reader from sin. He experiences spiritual healing. Or a reader can be empowered to engage in redemptive action toward others in the name of Christ. The account motivates him to become an instrument for healing lepers, literally through medical care or figuratively through proclaiming Christ and exercising kindness toward spiritual lepers.

Using the normative perspective, readers can adopt the norms of particular characters, or receive insight into how to bring those norms to the aid of others. The norms of Christ himself are always a valid source for imitation. But apostles offer positive norms, and others, like Jesus' Pharisaical opponents, offer norms that are of mixed character, and that teach the reader what to avoid as well as what to follow (e.g., Matt. 23:2–3).

Readers can also experience transformation through adopting the attitudes (existential perspective) or norms that belong to God as the author of the story. Jesus' parables offer this possibility. For example, the parable of the lost sheep in Luke 15:3–6 is a picture of redemption that uses plot and its situational focus. But by using the existential perspective we also see Jesus' attitude. He used the parable in responding to the grumbling of the Pharisees and the scribes over his association with sinners (Luke 15:1–2). Readers may receive redemptive power through the Holy Spirit as the parable shows them Jesus' attitude. Some psalms, like Psalm 73, disclose a redemptive plot in which the human author goes through a struggle and comes to a resolution. The reader can identify with the transformation in attitude that the author experiences. The Holy Spirit may work in the reader to give him the attitudes expressed in a psalm. In this case, the personal development is not in the psalm but in the reader.

Readers can also experience a complex, combined effect of more than one of the routes, and may do so in many possible ways. God's redemption is rich. And the richness and many-sidedness of language gives us means of richly appropriating the history of redemption. In a variety of ways the Holy Spirit may enable readers to see the relation of "small" accounts of redemption to the central redemption that Christ has accomplished.[5] Readers will grow in faith in Christ and in appreciation for the wisdom and grace shown in Christ's work.

## Stories outside the Biblical Canon

Because of the Bible's overarching theme of redemption, it is not too surprising that we should find small analogues of redemption within the Bible. But can we also look at stories outside the Bible? Vladimir Propp started with a group of Russian folktales. Because Christianity has long had a place in Russian history, it is possible that these tales were influenced by the Christian story of redemption. Whether there was demonstrable influence or not, the plots do seem to suggest some analogies with the central story of redemption.

In fact, direct Christian influence is not necessary. The fall has introduced many kinds of disorder into the world, including not only the direct results of human sins but also disasters and disorders that make human beings aware of the unsatisfactory character of their present life. All is not well. And if all is not well, human beings have a built-in longing that it *would* be well, and that someone would set it right. The human desire leads to action.

From time to time in actual history, human heroes have acted and remedied a specific evil. Knights have rescued damsels in distress. That is, they have in their small way accomplished a victory over the effects of the fall. Indirectly, they have achieved a small victory over Satan. But the longing for well-being can also produce fictional stories that tell about the remedy for some evil, real or hypothetical. Those who strive to bring a remedy also find themselves opposed, either by beasts (the dragon being one form of opponent), by resistance from nature, or by resistance from evil human beings (the villain). Human beings know dimly that the righteous action sometimes meets opposition. They are dimly confronted with the works of the devil, though they may not have a clear understanding of the world of spiritual evil.

---

5. The concern for Christocentric preaching grows from understanding the centrality of Christ's *one* redemption. See Clowney, *Preaching and Biblical Theology*; Johnson, *Him We Proclaim*; Edmund P. Clowney, *The Unfolding Mystery: Discovering Christ in the Old Testament* (Colorado Springs: NavPress, 1988); Poythress, *Shadow of Christ*.

Even people who are in rebellion against God still know God, according to Romans 1:18–23. They can still have longings for redemption. So we can see how a redemptive-sounding plot can originate. We start with the nature of man, and the nature of possibilities for human action. The fall has corrupted human beings, but they still have a sense of right and wrong (Rom. 1:32). Common grace keeps them from being as bad as they could be. People still have desires for prosperity and elimination of trouble, and they dimly know that evil has corrupted the world. Together these elements in human knowledge and desire mix into some form of redemptive plot. The plot may be a simple story of healing a wound or repelling a thief or recovering a lost object. Or it may be elaborate, with subplots within plots, or episodes strung together into a long epic.

# Counterfeit Stories of Redemption

For the time is coming when people will not endure sound teaching, but having itching ears they will accumulate for themselves teachers to suit their own passions, and will turn away from listening to the truth and wander off into myths.

—2 Timothy 4:3–4

Human beings know that the troubles we experience are sometimes too great for the afflicted person to resolve. The princess cannot rescue herself from the dragon. Her plight is desperate. Another person must come and do it. That is, we need outside help. We need a substitute. We need God to save us. So we can expect that human beings long for a story of God's redemption. But in a fallen world, the stories are often twisted.

## "Myth"
Human beings know God, in the sense of Romans 1:18–25. But they suppress and distort that knowledge into idolatry. Whole cultures become confused about the spirit world and the nature of good and evil in that world. The superhuman dimensions of good and evil get confused. And so there may arise forms of stories that tell tales of superhuman heroes, tales of gods, tales of good and evil in the spirit world. Cultures tell myths, that is, made-up stories about gods or spirits or superhuman characters. The stories may concern either the origins of the troubles and evils in this world, or victories or defeats in combating evil, or means by which human beings may use spiritual power to their advantage. Even modern secular culture produces comic-book heroes with superhuman powers.

Human beings make up these stories. But when they do, they are still guided by religious ideas and hopes. On the one hand, they still know God, and they cannot completely escape him. So their stories will show some similarities to God's plan of redemption. On the other hand, people are in rebellion against God, and they replace God with idols (Rom. 1:18–23). They then distort the stories because of their idols.

## Deception and Counterfeiting
In fact, a person who gives himself to an idol is falling into deception and into the dominion of darkness. "The whole world lies in the power of the evil one" (1 John 5:19). Behind idols stand demons: "No, I imply that what pagans sacrifice they offer to demons and not to God. I do not want you to be participants with demons" (1 Cor. 10:20). Demons bring deception: "[the devil] has nothing to do with the truth, because there is no truth in him. When he lies, he speaks out of his own character, for he is a liar and the father of lies" (John 8:44). Even this deception is sovereignly controlled by God, and is used as a punishment on those who reject the truth:

> Therefore God sends them a strong delusion, so that they may believe what is false, in order that all may be condemned who did not believe the truth but had pleasure in unrighteousness (2 Thess. 2:11–12).

The Bible indicates that demons are real and have real power, immense super-natural power: "For we do not wrestle against flesh and blood, but against the rulers, against the authorities, against the cosmic powers over this present darkness, against the spiritual forces of evil in the heavenly places" (Eph. 6:12). False worshipers are "participants with demons" (1 Cor. 10:20). So it is not astonishing that they should make up stories that involve superhuman powers or human or animal manifestations of these powers. Demonic deceit overlays the whole, so that human beings can have the delicious feeling of penetrating into deep spiritual secrets when actually they are being entrapped into demonic deceit. That is why some of these stories—which to an outsider may look silly—can actually be believed, and can hold whole cultures in captivity. Myths are not only a human product; they are also a demonic product. And the demonic holds people captive through counterfeiting.

## A Classic Counterfeit of Redemption
Consider one such counterfeit. In the ancient world, the Babylonian story *Enuma Elish* said that one of the goddesses, Tiamat, waged war against the others. Tiamat's conflict symbolizes a disruption of normality. Tiamat plays the role of villain in her destructive rampage. Marduk, the patron god of Babylon, responds to the

challenge of disruption, fights against Tiamat, defeats her, and receives the rewards of victory. The story clearly has a "redemptive" theme in a broad sense. Marduk is the hero who defeats the villain and redeems the situation.

## The Enlightenment Myth

Even if people do not believe in gods and goddesses, they can have counterfeit stories of redemption. In the West the spirit of the Enlightenment tells a counterfeit story of redemption in which Reason the hero rescues the princess, Western civilization, from the villain Superstition, who appears in many guises: belief in witchcraft, belief in evil spirits, and belief in mystifying religion.

## Marxism

A number of people have recognized that classic Marxism has a redemptive plot that counterfeits Christian hope (see chart 27.1). Instead of sin, as understood within the context of Christian theology, Marxism has the oppression of the workers. Instead of Christ's triumph over sin, Marxism has the communist revolution. Instead of the gospel it has the call for workers to unite and cast off their chains. The communist party is the vanguard announcing the gospel and the nucleus of the new society, so it is analogous to the Christian church. And the coming communist society of prosperity and peace is the analogue of biblical hope for the new heaven and the new earth. Instead of God, the laws of history propel humanity toward its utopian goal. The climactic tipping point, the communist revolution, brings the death and resurrection of political and economic structures, through which the new world is inaugurated.

| Christian Redemption | Marxist Redemption |
| --- | --- |
| sin | economic oppression |
| redemption in the work of Christ | communist revolution |
| death of Christ | destruction of old economic order |
| resurrection of Christ | entrance of new order |
| church | communist party |
| gospel | call to workers |
| consummation in new heaven and new earth | communist society of prosperity and sharing |
| God's plan for redemption | laws of economic history |

CHART 27.1

## The Stories of Evolutionary Naturalism

Consider now evolutionary naturalism. Evolutionary naturalism uses the neo-Darwinian theory of evolution as a platform to propound a materialistic worldview.[1] This materialistic worldview contrasts not only with views in which God works miraculously to create some forms of life, but also with the view, often called theistic evolution, that God has worked out his purposes for various forms of life using the secondary means of evolutionary gradualism, means that he sovereignly controls. The contrast is between the work of a purposeful God on the one hand, and on the other hand the purposeless development of life in a situation in which God is absent or nonexistent. This contrast shows that evolutionary naturalism is not just a narrow scientific theory for explaining specific material phenomena; it is also a worldview with close ties to philosophy.[2] According to this worldview, the world consists primarily in matter and energy in interaction. There is no God or gods, and mind and consciousness have arisen without the influence or guidance of God or gods. All of life has arisen by gradualistic, chance processes that take place without any purpose directing them.

Evolutionary naturalism, as a worldview, offers answers to "big" questions. Who are we? Where did we come from? Who or what made us? Where are we going? What is our purpose? Which kinds of questions have answers? Naturalism, by offering answers to such questions, claims to offer a godlike point of view. But its answers differ from the answers in the Bible, and so it is a counterfeit.

Does evolutionary naturalism have a redemptive story? Actually it has at least two such stories. The first and larger one is the story of the development of the universe, the origin of life, and the evolution of life. These developments took place by chance, without purpose.

A story that lacks purpose is not very satisfying. Nor is it really redemptive. It runs the danger of collapsing into a mere list, one meaningless thing after another. So popular versions of the story often add an extra layer, which addresses the need that human beings feel to find purpose and to relate the story to themselves. The added human purpose is the development of human life. The story then becomes a story about a process leading toward complex forms of life, and then the rise of consciousness, reason, and the self-reflective knowledge of human beings. The story can be mildly redemptive: evolution itself is the hero, and we as human beings are helpers to the hero; we triumph over the intellectual weaknesses of our animal and cellular origins.

The second, smaller story in evolutionary naturalism is the story of how we have come to know what we allegedly know. The story includes the rise of modern science, the progressive independence of human thought from religions and superstition, and the rise of Darwinism. Darwinism is a key step, because it provides a satisfying causal explanation for the origin of life, which otherwise has

---

1. See Vern S. Poythress, *Redeeming Science: A God-Centered Approach* (Wheaton, IL: Crossway, 2006), 79–80.

2. See ibid., 79–81, 259–283.

the appearance of divine design. With Darwinism, atheism becomes easier. With atheism, man throws off the last remnants of superstition. Here is the climactic act of redemptive deliverance from intellectual chains.[3]

This story is really a story about the quest for wisdom.[4] Wisdom of the deepest kind includes the attainment of a godlike point of view, which gives us knowledge of ourselves and our role in the cosmos. The story told by evolutionary naturalism pictures mankind as acquiring wisdom by the end of the story. But it is obviously an alternative story to what the Bible tells, because the Bible stresses that God is the source of wisdom: "The fear of the LORD is the beginning of wisdom" (Ps. 111:10).

According to evolutionary naturalism, why was there superstition in the first place? Because man arises from the gradualistic improvements of random evolution. In his early history he still retains the limitations—the chains—of his imperfect animal origins. The animal origins are the unsatisfactory starting state that leads to the quest. At the end of the quest man has achieved not only knowledge of his world but knowledge of himself as well. The evolutionary naturalists have in one way already attained the endpoint for the human quest, though of course further development of scientific knowledge may always take place. The task of the naturalists now is to help deliver those who are still captive to superstition, by proclaiming the "true gospel," which includes both an account of the actual origin of their superstition and the means of deliverance, namely, rational enlightenment through an understanding of the evolutionist story.

The story is thoroughly redemptive, and thoroughly counterfeit. To see one angle of the counterfeiting, consider the issue of purpose. Purpose was introduced into the story merely to satisfy human longing. It is a "mythological" addition. According to the materialist's own point of view, there is no real purpose to history. The cosmos just "is," without any purposeful goal. If the materialist removes purpose from the story, "superstition" and so-called "knowledge" are both equally real[5] characteristics of human tribes and equally the product of purposelessness. So why should we prefer one to the other? What makes one a more desirable goal? A materialist would claim that evolution has trained us to fight for intellectual as well as physical survival of the fittest. Then both materialists and superstitionists will fight for their views. But, in a purposeless universe, it may be the case

---

3. C. S. Lewis offers a "funeral oration" on "the Evolutionary Myth" in "The Funeral of a Great Myth," *Christian Reflections* (Grand Rapids, MI: Eerdmans, 1967), 82–93.

4. On the quest for wisdom and its counterfeit forms, see Vern S. Poythress, "The Quest for Wisdom," in *Resurrection and Eschatology: Theology in Service of the Church*, ed. Lane G. Tipton and Jeffrey C. Waddington (Phillipsburg, NJ: Presbyterian & Reformed, 2008), 86–114.

5. Or unreal. According to radical materialism, both kinds of thinking are merely the result of neurons firing in the brain.

that superstition may prove to be more "fit" than materialism, because it offers purpose to people who crave it.

The materialists assume that "knowledge" is superior. That assumption is part of their small-scale human purposes. They have the purpose of gaining and spreading truth. So they tell themselves a story that has the spread of truth as its goal. But, when stripped of mythology, their *large-scale*, cosmic story has no purpose, and therefore it is illegitimate for them to project their small-scale purpose onto it. According to their cosmic story, the spread or survival of ideas among human tribes is in the end a matter of chance. It is random. Maybe an idea is more likely to survive if it indirectly promotes reproductive fitness. On the average, practical knowledge of hunting and food gathering promotes fitness, so practical knowledge may promote survival. That is all. And maybe on the average people who think in terms of purpose have more reproductive fitness, if they are less likely to commit suicide, less likely to have abortions, more likely to have clear goals for getting food and reproducing. According to the materialist's own viewpoint, no innate reproductive superiority necessarily belongs to the idea that there is no purpose. So what would make the purposeless materialist story innately superior to any other story? Its alleged "superiority" is part of the mythological illusion generated by projecting the evolutionists' private purposes onto the cosmos.

In fact, human beings made in the image of God know about purpose and need purpose. Evolutionary naturalists themselves, as human beings, cannot do without it. And so they will have their redemptive story, however ungrounded it may be.

## Postmodern Contextualism

Postmodern contextualism also has its redemptive stories. Among them we find stories of quests for wisdom. Typically, postmodernists tell stories that start back with religious superstition. They then travel up through modernism. The modernism of the Enlightenment thought that reason would be the hero to deliver us from darkness, religious strife, and hatred. And, according to some postmodernist stories, reason did do part of the job. It delivered us from tyrannical, mystifying priests—villains. But reason sometimes tyrannized over minorities by enforcing a monolithic majority view of what was reasonable. Reason became what those in power defined it to be for their own benefit.

So, according to postmodern thinking, the epic story of the search for wisdom had to have another cycle.[6] Reason, as the hero, had to apply itself to analyze the political failings of reason. In particular, reason through the social sciences applied itself to understanding the limitations of reason in the face of human diversity.

The latest climactic redemption has come through postmodern insight. We have seen our finiteness, our situatedness, and the limitations to claims about a

---

6. See Poythress, "Quest for Wisdom," 109–111.

universal, godlike philosophical vision of the Truth. We are chastened, humbled. Now we know about multiculturalism and we tolerate differences.

This story is a redemptive story. The villain is confidence in unlimited reason. The hero is postmodernist self-reflective insight. The visionary achievement of the hero, after he has climbed to the top of the mountains of hermeneutics and analysis, delivers us from delusions of grandeur. With that deliverance we become peaceable. We die to the pride of grandiose claims about reason. We rise again to a new life of sensitivity to others. According to this story, there is still much work to be done in propagating the "gospel" of postmodernism.

Postmodernism also, in its "humility," knows that its insights are not ultimate. Its story includes a dream for the future, a futuristic story, in which there will be an interminable series of mini-redemptions, a series of quests for new wisdom. But the postmodernist story says that in one sense the climactic triumph is behind us. We know that, in the nature of the case, there can be no final resting point, no unsurpassable philosophical vision, no definitive redemption. And, according to postmodernism, that insight has redeemed us from one of the most insidious bondages of all, the bondage of the desire to be god or to know God.[7]

Paradoxically, this one claim about the lack of an endpoint is itself still godlike. That is, the claim that there can be no final resting point is itself a transcendent claim about the character of human thinking, and in attaining this insight the postmodernist thinks he has achieved a godlike understanding of himself and his limitations. Desire for a god of some kind cannot be eliminated from human nature. According to the postmodern story, the best we can do is repeatedly to redeem ourselves from its latest forms, by repeatedly seeing the limitations and bondages present in earlier stages.

To understand the real significance of the postmodernist's story, we have to stand back from it. We can apply what we have learned from God's instruction in the Bible. In his rebellion, man desires to eliminate God. Or, to put it differently, he desires to eliminate transcendence. But he cannot fully succeed. The postmodernist's story is actually the story of man's flight from God, a flight both interminable and unsuccessful. The only plausible way of eliminating the desire for God is through a godlike act of tracking down and putting to death the traces of that desire. When a person has tracked down the desire, he creates a redemptive story about the heroic triumph of autonomy over desire. He then uses that story in

---

7. According to Jean-François Lyotard, one of the features of postmodernism is incredulity toward "metanarratives" (Jean-François Lyotard, *The Postmodern Condition: A Report on Knowledge* [Minneapolis: University of Minnesota Press, 1984], xxiv). A "metanarrative" is a big story accounting for our place in the world as a whole. Paradoxically, postmodernists have their own stories that look like metanarratives, namely, their central redemptive stories. But they tend to avoid making them completely explicit, and they would admit that the stories can always be retold in different ways.

order to motivate himself to redirect his desire in the direction of autonomy. But the story he uses is a counterfeit story, still dependent on his longing for redemption. It still shows his need for God. But now his desire becomes the desire to be a god. He must be his own hero and his own godlike savior. That too is a remnant of the original desire for God, the desire for infinitude, and so he must kill that too. The series of deaths is interminable and the suffering is interminable.[8]

It is a pitiful situation. Christians should pity postmodernists, and reach out to them, rather than primarily feeling angry toward them.[9]

## Creation Myths

If modern people would escape from God, they must tell themselves not only counterfeit stories of redemption but counterfeit stories of creation as well. Redemption, according to the Bible, is a kind of re-creation (2 Cor. 5:17; Rev. 21:1; Rom. 8:20). Sin disrupts not only us, but our relation to the rest of creation.

---

8. No one likes indefinitely prolonged suffering. The postmodernist Richard Rorty, in *Contingency, Irony, and Solidarity* (Cambridge: Cambridge University Press, 1989), indicates that what unites him with fellow humanists is the conviction that cruelty is the worst thing that humans can do. And yet the postmodernists are cruel to themselves. They are cruel in trying to deny themselves their deepest need, the need for God. For this reason also the postmodernists are right in thinking that they will be superseded by other movements that they cannot now anticipate. One danger is that by the time a human being tires of being cruel to himself, he may be so disoriented and upset that he will turn that cruelty toward others. Apart from the grace of God, the oppressed, when liberated, takes on the practice of the oppressor, from which he has not emotionally freed himself.

Regrettably, a form of spiritual cruelty to others has already begun: postmodern rhetoric, through its picture of the limits of languages and cultures, endeavors to lead others into the conviction that their thirst for God cannot be satisfied. It throws people into a prison of the mind, where they must live in spiritual thirst all their lives, consoled only by the conviction that their thirst is vain. They do have one drop of water, namely, the godlike feeling that they have mastered the problem of life by perceiving that there is no problem (Wittgenstein, *Tractatus*, 6.521). This water must be recycled interminably.

9. Atheistic evolutionary naturalists have analogous problems, though they are less aware of it. To motivate the overcoming of superstition, they need purpose and a redemptive story. They project purpose onto the cosmic story. But purpose in the cosmos means purpose coming from a personality, from a god. This idea of divine purpose must be killed, and so the materialist tells another purposeful story, with himself as hero, about killing the projected idol. This second story is also a redemptive story, which presupposes a large-scale purpose. And so on. The problem can be generalized. It is the problem of human beings seeking autonomy. The quest for autonomy is a quest, a redemptive story, and so presupposes divine meaning. A person must tell an interminable series of counterfeit redemptive stories, each with the purpose of overcoming the traces of dependence on God contained in the fact that the previous story is a counterfeit projection of the desire for infinite significance. With each successive story man transcends his dependence on a god, and at the end of each telling he has demonstrated his irrepressible desire for transcendence.

And because human beings have a key role in God's plan for creation as a whole, the disruption among human beings has larger consequences for the rest of the created order (Gen. 3:17–19). So, if human beings desire to be thoroughly free from God, they must try not only to redeem themselves but to create or re-create the entire world through their powers. Of course, that is not literally possible. But it is possible to use the rhetoric of creating in order to invest mankind with mystic, godlike powers.

We have already considered the *Enuma Elish*, an ancient Babylonian myth of redemption. *Enuma Elish* also has features of creation myth. After Marduk, the hero god, has defeated Tiamat, he divides up the carcass. One half becomes the sky, and the other half the earth. This story is a counterfeit for God creating the world.

Evolutionary naturalism tells a science-based story of the development of the universe. But it has difficulty with the very beginning, the Big Bang. Discussions under the label of the "anthropic principle" have made it increasingly clear that various fundamental physical constants in the universe have been carefully "tuned."[10] Even small variations would lead to a universe where life would be impossible.

Scientific investigation cannot travel back in time before the Big Bang to see how these physical constants might have come to be so carefully tuned. So speculative stories have to come in to help. There are stories of many universes, even though there is no way of checking these stories. And there are stories in which the anthropic principle becomes the ultimate explanation. The explanation runs, "we human beings are here, and so the universe had to be such that it was possible to have complex life." That too amounts to a story in which, at least at the level of explanation, man creates the universe.

Postmodern thought may talk about how human societies "construct" worlds through language and culture. The worlds so constructed are worlds where man has in a sense become god. It is *his* world, and any activity of a would-be old-fashioned god is far away and inaccessible to human thought. Human thought has already conformed the world to itself.

Human beings want to free themselves from what they see as a dangerous captivity to an outside god. They want freedom from the myths about gods that have held humanity captive. And the only way of doing this effectively is to replace the role of ancient "myths" with something that will give a more accurate account of our real situation. This account is the modern myth, the myth of man creating his worlds.

---

10. Among these constants are the speed of light, the gravitational constant that measures the strength of gravitational force, and the amount of electric charge on a single electron There are others as well, requiring more technical explanations.

# Modern Reinterpretations of Redemptive Stories

For we did not follow cleverly devised myths when we made known to

you the power and coming of our Lord Jesus Christ,

but we were eyewitnesses of his majesty.

—2 Peter 1:16

A nthropologists and analysts of culture have observed similarities between redemptive stories in the Bible and myths told in various cultures. Predictably, some of them have then argued that the Bible is full of myths. Or, if they admit that not everything in the Bible is fictional, they still claim that the central story, the story of Christ, is "myth." Christ's triumph over Satan, his resurrection, his ascent to heaven, his promise of redemption to his followers, and the promise of a new heaven and a new earth, are all alleged to be mythical.[1]

---

1. As an example, see Rudolf Bultmann, "New Testament and Mythology: The Mythological Element in the Message of the New Testament and the Problem of Its Re-interpretation," in *Kerygma and Myth: A Theological Debate*, ed. Hans Werner Bartsch (New York: Harper & Row, 1961), 1–44. Bultmann was preceded by David Friedrich Strauss, *The Life of Jesus, Critically Examined* (New York: Blanchard, 1856). We may find similar ideas among anthropologists and skeptics. Bultmann is striking because, while accepting the classification "myth," he still tried to redeem from the New Testament a positive message about authentic existential human existence, a message that modern man could accept without the alleged mythological "baggage."

## Underlying Assumptions

If we trace back this kind of analysis, we will find that it rests on a key assumption. The assumption is that religious ideas are generated by human nature *left to itself.* But in fact human nature is always in interaction with the God of the Bible (Rom. 1:18–25). And human nature in rebellion is disposed to suppress the knowledge of God and give itself to demons. By contrast, the purely "secular," horizontal analysis of "myth" within human nature assumes that God does not exist, that demons do not exist, and that religion is purely a human invention. Or, it may attempt to reinterpret myth as a product of "religious experience," perhaps of a panentheistic sort. Such secular analysis has never asked itself the fundamental question: are its own secularist assumptions correct? Does God exist, what kind of God exists, and is the world sustained by God rather than going along under its own independent power?

Thus, there are at least two accounts of myth, not just one. In the biblical account, myths are deviant stories of religious hope and frustration. They have similarities with the redemptive stories in the Bible in the same way that a counterfeit depends on the true. Man is made in the image of God, and even Satan in his counterfeiting must imitate God. So of course man and demons together will produce stories that show not only knowledge of the divine, but hopes for redemption as well.

Over against the biblical account, there is a second kind of account of myth. This second account assumes at the beginning that God is not present with humanity, or that he is not relevant. And so it develops an account of myth that makes it a merely human product, and necessarily fictional. Myth must be fictional, because the "enlightened" analyst already knows that gods and spirits are nonexistent. So, according to the kind of thinking that levels all religious phenomena into a common sociological analysis, the God of the Bible is alleged to be equally nonexistent.

In other words, modern concepts of "myth" can easily conceal within them an essential circularity in assumptions and arguments. The modern analyst assumes at the beginning a worldview that denies the presence of the God of the Bible. And so he arrives in the end with conclusions that reiterate that denial.

Such an analysis remains unaware that it can be read in reverse. Instead of reading stories in the Bible as a series of "myths" produced by the illusions of generic religious consciousness and experience, we can read the myths in various cultures as a product of distorted human longings for the archetype, the real account in the Bible. But the myths are distorted by demonic deceit.

C. S. Lewis grasped the point decades ago when he posed the question, "By what rule do you tell a copy from an original?"[2] The Bible presents God as he is, and redemption as it is. It is the original of which the polytheistic and spiritist myths are deviant copies. All the longings and hopes and groanings of humanity, and the stories generated by those longings, are deeply related to the Bible. But they are related not as just so many instances alongside one another. The redemption in Christ is the genuine, real fulfillment of these longings, insofar as they are valid longings. And it rescues and reorients and reinterprets and reforms these longings, insofar as they are deviant.

## Existentialist Transformation of the Redemptive Story

Rudolf Bultmann not only claimed that the redemptive story in the New Testament was cast in mythological form, but that it could be "demythologized."[3] The mythological clothing could be stripped off in order to recover the real core of the message, which was an existentialist call to authentic human existence. Many critics objected that Bultmann had remade the gospel rather than preserved it. I would agree. Unless Christ really rose from the dead, in time and space, we have no basis for the gospel, and no sound basis to argue that it will have beneficial transforming effects on the hearer:

> But if there is no resurrection of the dead, then not even Christ has been raised. And if Christ has not been raised, then our preaching is in vain and your faith is in vain. We are even found to be misrepresenting God, because we testified about God that he raised Christ, whom he did not raise if it is true that the dead are not raised. For if the dead are not raised, not even Christ has been raised. And if Christ has not been raised, your faith is futile and you are still in your sins. Then those also who have fallen asleep in Christ have perished. If in Christ we have hope in this life only, we are of all people most to be pitied (1 Cor. 15:13–19, esv mg.).

Yet Bultmann's idea appeared to some people to work. And that too has an explanation. The New Testament shows that benefits of Christ's work do come to those who are united with him. Their own small personal stories have analogies to the big story of Christ's redemption. So it is not surprising that someone could attempt just to take the stories in the lives of Christians, and to treat those stories as if they were themselves redemptive even when detached from the actual redemption that Christ accomplished.

---

2. C. S. Lewis, *The Pilgrim's Regress: An Allegorical Apology for Christianity, Reason, and Romanticism*, 3rd ed. (Grand Rapids, MI: Eerdmans, 1958), 64, 67–68; see also Lewis, *Christian Reflections* (Grand Rapids, MI: Eerdmans, 1967), 37–43.

3. Bultmann, "New Testament and Mythology," 1–44, and the surrounding discussion in the book.

We can also explain the plausibility of Bultmann's demythologization in another way. Bultmann's approach, though it does not agree with the biblical worldview, still has affinities to the personal/existential perspective on redemptive stories. It is true that each person must hear the biblical account of redemption, and must appropriate it to himself. Bultmann focuses on the nature of this appropriation. His approach is plausible precisely because we can temporarily focus on this one aspect. All the thoughts of my mind, and all my knowledge of the world, and all my attitudes toward God, world, and neighbor have to do with external realities, but they are also *mine*. We can concentrate on that me-ward aspect. That is akin to what Bultmann does.

Unfortunately, a distortion or reduction is easily introduced if we use *only* this perspective. It becomes all too easy to distort what we believe about the external realities. Within our modern cultural situation, some things, like modern science or a modern worldview or assumptions about miracle or assumptions about God, make vigorous claims about what is "real." If we let these latter beliefs govern our life, then the resurrection of Christ in time and space is pronounced unreal on the basis of an uncritically held modern worldview. Then that decision tends to determine what we think about the other things in our mind and consciousness, things like our personal commitment to Christ or our *belief* in Christ's resurrection. In comparison to the alleged "reality" of the modern worldview, these latter come to be seen as *merely* subjective.

In that case, we are making peace with modernity through cordoning off religious belief as "merely subjective," in contrast to beliefs about the reality of DNA, atom bombs, and the nonexistence of miracles. But that is merely arbitrary. *Beliefs* about DNA, as beliefs, are just as "subjective" as beliefs about the resurrection of Christ. But the existential perspective coheres with the situational perspective: beliefs, if they are real beliefs rather than psychological trickery, stake claims about the character of the world, that is, the situation. Christ did rise from the dead (the situational), and that is why we subjectively believe that he did (the existential). Accordingly, a modern worldview that claims that miracles are impossible must itself be subjected to critical scrutiny. Such a claim is a cultural *belief*. It is subjective. Do its claims actually harmonize with the world, or are they merely subjective?[4]

In short, Bultmann's program should be seen as a counterfeit form of redemption. It has plausibility only because it leans on insights from the redemptive account in the Bible, and because it harmonizes easily with some key assumptions uncritically accepted by many modern people.

---

4. On miracles, see Vern S. Poythress, *Redeeming Science: A God-Centered Approach* (Wheaton, IL: Crossway, 2006), 18–19, 179–180; C. John Collins, *The God of Miracles: An Exegetical Examination of God's Action in the World* (Wheaton, IL: Crossway, 2000); John M. Frame, *The Doctrine of God* (Phillipsburg, NJ: Presbyterian & Reformed, 2002), 241–273.

## Multiculturalist Transformation of the Redemptive Story

Multicultural treatments of redemptive stories[5] tend to follow a different route than Bultmann's, but we can give an analogous evaluation. Whereas Bultmann used the personal or existential perspective, analysts of culture may use predominantly what John Frame calls the "situational perspective."[6] They undertake to understand a particular story by looking at its context in culture, its "situation." How does the story function to unify the culture, to give it direction, to explain various tensions, to give hope? This perspective offers valuable insights, just as do the personal and the normative perspectives. Each perspective ideally can become a perspective through which we look out toward other perspectives and toward the world as a whole. Each deepens and enriches what we have seen from the other two perspectives.

Within a Christian worldview, the situational perspective will naturally include God as the most important person in the situation and in the culture. In looking at the situation, we would assess how the story encourages or helps or hinders reconciliation with God, and how it prepares people to think about their future death and resurrection and the last judgment, all of which are part of the extended situation.

On the other hand, a *secularized* analysis of culture may try to cut God out, and treat the "situation" as *merely* human. The members of a tribe who recount a tribal myth may think of it as referring to actual supernatural beings. But since, in the view of the analyst, these beings do not exist, the practical value of the myth can be interpreted in purely horizontal fashion: the myth functions as an integrating and explanatory force within human society. Even if an individual anthropologist is alert enough to acknowledge multiple dimensions in a myth, the modern listener is likely to ignore everything except the horizontal dimension. The story's meaning lies in its social function. Thus any story can be forced by modern assumptions to give up its right to mean anything more than what is "merely human" or "socially constructed." The modern listener may or may not be aware that he has ethnocentrically assumed the superiority of his modern context. His assumptions have already told him what the "real" meaning of stories must be.

---

5. For a beginning see Claude Lévi-Strauss, *Structural Anthropology* (New York: Basic, 1963); Lévi-Strauss, *The Raw and the Cooked: Introduction to a Science of Mythology* (New York: Harper & Row, 1970); Lévi-Strauss, *The Savage Mind* (Chicago: University of Chicago Press, 1966).

6. John M. Frame, *Perspectives on the Word of God: An Introduction to Christian Ethics* (Phillipsburg, NJ: Presbyterian & Reformed, 1990).

# Stories about Jesus

The beginning of the gospel of Jesus Christ, the Son of God.

—Mark 1:1

Inasmuch as many have undertaken to compile a narrative of the things that have been accomplished among us, just as those who from the beginning were eyewitnesses and ministers of the word have delivered them to us, it seemed good to me also, having followed all things closely for some time past, to write an orderly account for you, most excellent Theophilus, that you may have certainty concerning the things you have been taught.

—Luke 1:1–4

The temptation to tell counterfeit stories also arises when we try to understand the life of Jesus of Nazareth. The temptation is particularly strong here because of the central role of Jesus in redemption.[1] So we should expect that desires for human autonomy will set to work when people try to think through who Jesus was and what he did. People will try counterfeits. Over against the counterfeits is the Christian view. The Christian view of transcendence says that God has the right to tell us about Jesus; and the Christian view of immanence says that God can make himself clear.[2]

---

1. See Geerhardus Vos, *The Self-Disclosure of Jesus: The Modern Debate about the Messianic Consciousness* (reprint; Phillipsburg, NJ: Presbyterian & Reformed, 2002).

2. See Frame's square in John M. Frame, *The Doctrine of the Knowledge of God* (Phillipsburg, NJ: Presbyterian & Reformed, 1987), 14.

234

God himself has given us four historical accounts of Jesus' life, namely, the four Gospels of Matthew, Mark, Luke, and John. These accounts are God's word and have his authority. I cannot argue extensively here for their divine authority,[3] but it follows from the perception that the books of the New Testament are a continuation of the Old Testament, which has divine authority as the word of God. Jesus in his teaching confirms that the Old Testament is God's word (Matt. 5:17–20; John 10:35; Matt. 19:4–5; etc.). He commissions and empowers the apostles to be his witnesses (Acts 1:2, 8). It would be strange if God, having spoken with authority and clarity in the Old Testament, did not speak that way when it comes to the climactic acts of redemption.

Some people are troubled by the differences among the four Gospels. The four Gospels offer four perspectives.[4] They are in harmony in the mind of God—though we as finite creatures may not always immediately see how.

In the four Gospels God makes himself clear. Not everything is transparently clear, particularly to human minds corrupted by sin. But we learn about what Jesus did, how he died, and that he rose from the dead—all in fulfillment of the Old Testament Scriptures (Luke 24:44–47). The central points are clear.

Modern sinful people, like ancient people, do not want simply to accept the Gospels as God's own testimony. That would require abandoning their autonomy and following Christ. It would also require accepting the claim that Jesus rose from dead, and the claim, especially in the Gospel of John, that Jesus is God (John 1:1; 8:58; 20:28). Those claims are huge stumbling blocks to people who want to be autonomous. So they make up various stories that attempt to describe what they think "really" happened in Jesus' life, and why and in what ways the Gospels came to "distort" the story that the modern people now want to tell. Theirs are counterfeit stories that promise to "redeem" us modern people from the superstition and bondage that have allegedly been foisted on us by the Bible and by later Christians.

The counterfeit stories about Jesus are many. Some are naïve; some are very clever. The clever ones try to make serious contact with the four Gospels. But no one can make up a plausible story without having assumptions about the character of what is likely to happen in history. In other words, he has to relate his story coherently to the many other stories of what happened at various times and places

---

3. See Benjamin B. Warfield, *The Inspiration and Authority of the Bible* (reprint; Philadelphia: Presbyterian & Reformed, 1967); Herman N. Ridderbos, *Redemptive History and the New Testament Scriptures* (Phillipsburg, NJ: Presbyterian and Reformed, 1988).

4. See especially Vern S. Poythress, *Symphonic Theology: The Validity of Multiple Perspectives in Theology* (Grand Rapids, MI: Zondervan, 1987; reprinted, Phillipsburg, NJ: Presbyterian & Reformed, 2001), chapter 5. Through the centuries we have also accumulated a substantial body of explanation that discusses in detail the apparent discrepancies among the Gospels. John Calvin, *Commentary on a Harmony of the Evangelists, Matthew, Mark and Luke*, 3 vols. (Grand Rapids, MI: Eerdmans, n.d.), may be cited as one fruitful example.

in history (the field perspective). He has to deal with regularities among a huge number of stories. What he thinks is likely to happen depends on the regularities of this world, both regularities of the type that sciences explore, and regularities in human nature, and regularities in the histories that people live through. He has to reckon with the fact that ancient people had ideas and worries and fights and lived through histories that would fit in with their cultural environment but would also fit in with human nature in general.

To do all this, a person must have a conception of regularities. The regularities derive from God or from a substitute for God. For the substitute a person uses a non-Christian view of transcendence and immanence. He tells his story with non-Christian assumptions about the character of history. In the West, the usual assumptions among professional historians of this type are that there are no exceptions to impersonally conceived scientific law (no miracles), and that all events have meaning only through their immediate causes and immediate effects. In effect, they have told themselves stories about the nature of the universe and the nature of humanity within it. These macrostories form the background for constructing their mini-story about the life of Jesus.[5]

In God's plan, there are such things as secondary causes, that is, immediate causes and effects. The historians are right about that. But God is the primary cause. So our theology—our knowledge about God—shows us part of the meaning of history. And God also has an overall plan, so that events like the exodus from Egypt and David's fights against the Philistines are God's acts of redemption anticipating the coming climactic redemption in Christ. The earlier events can be described as "types" or symbols pointing to a greater fulfillment (1 Cor. 10:6, 11). The relation between earlier events and later events is described as "typological." Thus, correspondences in meaning over long periods of time are part of the meaning of history. Correspondences in meaning, including what we know as typological correspondences, are built into history by the purposes of God. They are not merely added to history by later human interpreters.

Historians with a substitute for God generally do not believe in this kind of relation, nor do they believe that theology shows the meaning of history. So they *systematically* and thoroughly distort the actual meaning. To oversimplify: they look at only one dimension, the dimension of immediate secondary causes. They suppress both the reality of God as primary cause, and the reality of long-range patterns (relations in meaning).[6] The long-range patterns include both patterns

---

5. The pervasiveness of the field perspective makes it impossible to tell a mini-story without a larger human context, which includes having a host of tacit assumptions about the world. For non-Christian assumptions, see appendix C.

6. In a history of actual events, the immediate secondary causes and effects come naturally into view with the wave perspective. The field perspective leads us to pay attention to the many relations with other histories and with roles like heroes, helpers, and recompenses. The particle

on a common level, such as different instances of healing, and patterns on two or more distinct levels, such as the relation between the healing of the leper, the spiritual healing from sin by substitutionary exchange on the cross, the healing of the whole body in the resurrection, and the spiritual and bodily healing of individuals at various other times in the history that God unfolds.

We can still learn something from secular historians, because of common grace. Looking at secondary causes is genuinely illuminating, because these also are part of God's purpose. And indeed such a focus may sometimes help to shake the church out of complacency, if the church has fallen into the pattern of remaking Christ into what it wants him to be, or thinking only of the deity of Christ, and not his humanity, or thinking only of the general principles of redemption, and not of the concrete way in which God accomplished it through Christ.

### Definitive Stories

But please note: the four Gospels already do the job that people are seeking to do over again in trying to tell a new story of Jesus' life.[7] Then why do they attempt it again? Mainly because they do not accept the job that God has already done for them.

To be sure, even people who believe the four Gospels can still profitably look into the relations of the Gospels with their historical environment. Human verbal action, and divine action as well, occurs within larger contexts. The meaning of an action depends partly on its relation to those contexts. This is an aspect of God's own design. Hence we can profit from a better understanding of Jewish life in Palestine within the first century A.D. Based on the evidence that we gather, we can give explanations that help to picture that ancient culture and the various opinions, hopes, fears, and struggles of those people. Jesus' words and deeds came in the context of that environment, and so the meaning relations with the environment can help refine our understanding.

People can also look at relations within the Gospels, and then they may give subsidiary accounts that help us better to understand the four main accounts in the Gospels. Of course that makes sense, as long as we remember that the four main accounts are God's accounts, and the human retellings do not displace the unique authority of the four main accounts.

People who believe the Gospels can also try to persuade people who do not believe them. They can help the unbelievers partly by trying to put together explanations through secondary causes, trying to show how the life of Jesus

---

perspective leads us to pay attention to a particular history in its unity and integrity. And then we ask what God means by that history, leading to a focus on God as primary cause.

7. Frame, *Doctrine of the Knowledge of God*, 79–85, makes the analogous point that systematic theology does not displace the primacy of Scripture.

makes sense within its cultural and historical environment. They can also try to persuade skeptics by taking up the skeptic's point of view, for the sake of argument, and trying to show him how different details in the life of Jesus make sense even with the skeptic's starting assumptions. Very well. But there are limits. The ultimate limit is the human desire for autonomy, which works like a cancer to fill all of human culture. It includes the making of substitutes for God within its conception of history, and substitutes for the real Jesus in the form of a purely human Jesus.[8]

## The Struggle over the Meaning of History

Even scholars who believe that Jesus was God in the flesh can fall partway into the trap of wrongly assessing the Gospels. They hold their beliefs in the back of their mind, in their "religious" moments and "religious" activities. But they may think that they cannot possibly bring those beliefs directly to bear on what they as scholars read in the Gospels, and what they study in history, because they think that the idea that God can do anything will annihilate the possibility of historical research.[9]

Actually, the omnipotence of God is the only possible foundation for historical research. God controls the regularities of history. And God, as we have seen, is the origin of every story, both the histories that people live through and the stories that they tell. If we do not acknowledge the true God, we have a counterfeit god. We come to know the true God rightly, and so come to have a purified basis for historical research, by coming to know him through Jesus who is God. We come to know the meaning of history through observing divine as well as human action in the Gospel accounts about Jesus.

But these scholars, who believe only far back in their minds, ignore these foundational truths about history when they turn to historical research. And they also think that they must turn truths into pretended ignorance for the sake of interacting meaningfully with other historians, who may not share their beliefs. In academic discussion, they think, they must talk only about immediate secondary causes and only about how to make sense of history on the basis of Jesus' human nature.

---

8. The opposite error is a purely divine Jesus: the heresy of *docetism* said that Jesus was divine but only *appeared* to be human. But nowadays, among scholars at least, the substitute consisting in a purely human Jesus, or a merely human Jesus who is somehow adopted to be God's special son, is far more common.

9. See Vern S. Poythress, "The Presence of God Qualifying Our Notions of Grammatical-Historical Interpretation: Genesis 3:15 as a Test Case," *Journal of the Evangelical Theological Society* 50/1 (2007): 87–103.

It does no good for a person who believes in the Bible to pretend that historical research can be properly conducted without believing in the Bible. It cannot, because then the person has counterfeit versions of history and stories and
redemption and god.[10] At the same time, those who believe must still be patient
with those who do not believe. Everyone lives his own life, and we should be
realistic about other people's views. It does no good to try to force a person along
a path that he is not ready to take.

Consider now one form of counterfeit: the idea of history as bare events.[11]
Some people would like to make a sharp distinction between history and a
narrative about history (or between history and "historiography"). For them,
"history" designates the events out in the world, while "narrative about history" designates what we say about the events. "History" is bare events, before
they have any interpretation. But God in Christ governs history by his word of
power (Heb. 1:3). God speaks, and it is so. God's speaking through his word of
power *is* history.[12] There is no other. It is a counterfeit illusion to imagine that
there is such a thing as "mere" events without God's word commanding them
and interpreting them. The effect of the counterfeit is to allow us to impose *our*
meaning on events that we allege were previously without meaning. We thereby
ignore God's meanings. We make ourselves into gods who create meaning out
of bare events.

Unbelieving people eventually have to come to grips with the fact that they
are counterfeiting for the sake of their autonomy. And to come to grips with it
honestly is impossible, because desire for autonomy corrupts honesty along with

---

10. On this point the postmodernists can claim to have seen deeper than the modernists.
They at least see that the counterfeit gods are pluralizing and fissiparous. And if someone wants
to write history, whether the story of Jesus or any nonfictional story, he cannot avoid prior commitments to gods—that is, to metanarratives, to global assumptions about the nature of historical
causation and meanings in events. Modernism thought that it could take its stand in science, and
in objective, rational investigation of the facts, which it assumed were secular, nonmiraculous, and
empty of gods. It worshiped its versions of the goddess Reason. "Critical realism" is chastened
enough to admit that it embarks with previous commitments in train, but it hopes by a spiral
process of criticism to make these commitments revisable. But is the methodology of the spiral
itself revisable? It is supposed to be. And through the grace of God individuals may in their own
personal histories gradually revise their views and come by many strange paths into a true Christian
view of the world. But somewhere along the path they, like the prodigal, will meet a crisis. Most
modern scholarly criticism still worships methodologically at the altar dedicated to autonomous
man, insofar as it has determined to exercise a godlike critical spirit in examining the testimony
of the four Gospels. From the spiral of autonomous criticism there is no autonomous escape. A
person must instead come to the end of his own resources. His pride must undergo crucifixion
before the presence of the Son of God.

11. Cornelius Van Til refers to the hypothetical bare events as "brute facts" (Cornelius Van Til,
*The Defense of the Faith*, 2nd ed. [Philadelphia: Presbyterian & Reformed, 1963], especially 137).

12. What God tells us in the Gospels is adapted to human reception, unlike his telling in the
sense of Hebrews 1:3. But all God's tellings cohere with one another.

everything else into a counterfeit.[13] Then who can be saved from the cancer of counterfeiting? God must do it: "What is impossible with men is possible with God" (Luke 18:27). And how does God deliver us? He uses many means. But among them are the four Gospels, which the world considers foolish:

> For since, in the wisdom of God, the world did not know God through wisdom, it pleased God through the folly of what we preach to save those who believe (1 Cor. 1:21).

---

13. John A. T. Robinson wrote the book *Honest to God* (Philadelphia: Westminster, 1963) thinking that he was being honest. But mere desire for honesty does not save us from sin at a deeper level.

# PART 5

# Smaller Packages in Language: Sentences and Words

# Sentences in Use:
# Foundations in Truth

"Your word is truth."

—John 17:17

Let us now consider a smaller-sized piece of language: the sentence. Most languages have a distinct grammatical "level" of sentence. The sentence is then a grammatical unit in the language, with a distinct unity and closure. But we will not focus as much on grammar as on what people *do* with grammar. What do they do with sentences?

## Sentence Types

A single sentence, or even a single word, can sometimes be the contents of an entire speech (a monologue). "Where did you go?" "Out." But sentences can also be pieces composing a much longer discourse, a whole speech with many paragraphs, or a whole book. Wherever they appear, their function depends not only on their unity but on their specific contents (variation) and on the context (distribution).[1] We cannot ignore context.

In English, sentences separate into three main types: questions, statements, and commands/requests.[2]

Question: "Are you going to the store?"

1. See the discussion of contrast, variation, and context (distribution) in chapter 19.
2. On exclamatory utterances, see Mary Louise Pratt, *Toward a Speech Act Theory of Literary Discourse* (Bloomington: Indiana University Press, 1977), 135–137. Most exclamations function

Statement: "You are going to the store."
Command: "Go to the store."

In one sense the sample question, statement, and command above all have a similar "core." All share a common subject matter. But the total communication does not simply boil down to information content. We have a context of human action, in which human beings seek information (the typical function of a question), or seek to communicate information and views and attitudes that they hold, or seek to get another person to act.

But it is not a simple division. A sentence with the grammatical form of a question can be used as a "rhetorical question," where no answer is really expected, but indirectly the speaker invites the audience to draw a conclusion (and so the question conveys information). "Are you going to the store? Then pick up some bananas while you are there." Or, in English, a sentence with the grammatical form of a statement can be turned into a question merely by a rising intonation at the end: "You are going to the *store*?" Sentences in the form of statements may be a soliloquy, where the object is not to convey information or views to another person, but to express and reflect on one's thoughts and feelings. In the end, sentences are used in the full context of the complex interplay of human intentions, both short-range and long-range. No simple summary will capture it all.

## Truth

Human action relies on truth. Human beings can sometimes be mistaken about the truth about God, or the truth about their situation, or the truth about themselves. But they rely on what seems to them to be the truth. Questions seek truth. And the formulation of a question already presupposes a good deal of truth. For example, "Are you going to the store?" presupposes that there is a store, a particular store that both speaker and hearer know about. If there is more than one store that might realistically be referred to, the question usually presupposes that there is some way from the immediate context that the hearer can reasonably infer which store the speaker has in mind. The question also presupposes that "you" is a person capable of hearing, digesting, and reacting to the question. In a typical case, it also presupposes that the person has easy access to the question. In cases of oral communication, the person is within hearing distance. And the person is capable of figuring out with reasonable confidence that the question is addressed to him rather than someone else in the vicinity. And so on. Human

---

in a manner similar to statements, but with stress on "tellability" or the striking nature of the matter at hand.

verbal communication takes place within a context of shared life and many shared assumptions. Shared truth is necessary for a question to work.[3]

We can make similar observations about statements. Statements formulate truth. Commands and requests seek to set in motion human actions that (a) rely on a background in which the participants have an understanding of the situation; (b) rely on values that humans desire, and assumptions about how people think they may achieve a desired result; and (c) rely on a conception of a possible future, in which the truth will include the fact that the action in question has been successfully completed. For example, consider the simple request, "Please help me wash the dishes." This request relies on a background. The participants understand what it means to wash dishes, with soap or detergent, in a sink or an automatic dishwasher, with the purpose of getting food bits and any bacteria off the dishes. So there are truths about how to wash, about the importance of soap or detergent, about the role of water, and so on. There are also values that humans desire, in this case clean dishes that can be used for the next meal. And there is a possible future in which it will then be true that the dishes have been washed. The practical use of sentences depends on truth.

## Truth as Accessible

But do we have access to truth? Mere human beings are never infallible. They are not God. And this lack of infallibility seems particularly troubling to many people who want to operate independently of God. For them, access to truth would seem to demand infallible, assured access. They must be a god. But no.

We live in God's world. God cares even for the sparrow (Luke 12:6, 24), and cares for unbelievers as well as believers: "Yet he did not leave himself without witness, for he did good by giving you rains from heaven and fruitful seasons, satisfying your hearts with food and gladness" (Acts 14:17). God does good to people not simply by supplying food, but by giving truth. People differ in what they know and believe. But most people know a lot of truth, both truth about God (Rom. 1:18–25) and truth about themselves and the world. Yes, the truth they know is mixed with some mistakes and inaccuracies. But without truth we would not long survive in this world. You need to know some truth to keep away from speeding trucks and high-voltage power lines.

The foundation for truth is in God. God knows all things. Truth, we might say, is what God knows.[4] God made himself known supremely in Jesus Christ, in order that we might be restored in knowing those truths that are most centrally

---

3. As discussed in appendix H, speech-act theory examines these matters at length.

4. See the discussion of truth in Vern S. Poythress, *Redeeming Science: A God-Centered Approach* (Wheaton, IL: Crossway, 2006), chapter 14.

important. Jesus said, "I am the way, and *the truth*, and the life. No one comes to the Father except through me" (John 14:6). During his earthly life Jesus gave us the central truth about God. But his earthly words and actions are confirmed, enriched, and supplemented by other words that he endorses. "Sanctify them [disciples] in the *truth*; your word is *truth*" (John 17:17). The source of this truth is God himself, God who is true (John 3:33).

Truth belongs first of all to God and to his word. The truth in God's mind is *divine* and has divine attributes.[5] But God also makes truth of many kinds accessible to human beings, as a gift. Many times the truth comes by means of other human beings. I tell my wife that I am going to the store, and in the telling I provide her with truth.

Truth has a character and structure such as is presented in the Bible. Individual truths in individual sentences appear in the context of paragraphs and discourses that color their meaning. Truths on various topics within the Bible cohere and originate in the all-comprehending mind of God. Truth involves relations to other truths—the field perspective—as well as integrity and stability in the meaning of any particular truth—the particle perspective. The truth "I am going to the store" has stability. And it is related to other truths about where the store is, why I am going, and so on.

The reality of the field perspective has been a source of worry for postmodernists. If indeed meanings are always related to other meanings, and these meanings to still others, how do we have stability? We find an answer in the mind of God, who is stable, and who knows all truths in relation to one another. The partial character of human knowledge need not be a threat, because God takes care of us. But rebels do not acknowledge this, and so they worry.

We can also view truth from a *wave* perspective. As human beings, we progressively come to know truths. And the wave perspective is closely related to *variation*. Sentences that express truth are one kind of behavioreme, and they have contrastive-identificational features, variation, and context (distribution).[6] As an example, the statement "I am going to store" has contrastive-identificational features, in that it is making a definite statement about me, about my physical movements, and about the fact that the store is the goal of my journey. The statement also has variation. It is compatible with my going to the store either in a car or on foot. I may spend a longer or shorter time going. The expression "the store" may have more than one possible referent, depending on the context.

Human beings who aspire to autonomous mastery of the truth often hope to achieve mastery through their power of reason. They hope to know truth infinitely with infinite precision. And then, for the sake of mastery, they end up

---

5. Ibid.
6. See chapter 19.

trying to reduce truth to a context-free abstraction, a proposition with contrastive-identificational features, but with no variation and no context (distribution).[7]

Against this picture postmodernism rebels, because it has become aware of variation. It has become aware of differences in how human beings grasp a particular utterance. The grasp of truth *varies* among different human beings. Postmodernists celebrate this diversity. But if there is diversity, can my statement about the store mean anything at all, anything that a hearer chooses to make it mean? For some postmodernists it may seem that there is no way to protect this diversity without giving up unity, which is related to the contrastive-identificational features.

In fact we have both unity and diversity. God has designed language in such a way that it has both aspects, through and through, both in large pieces (whole monologues) and small pieces (individual sentences). The coinherence of contrast and variation ultimately reflects the coinherence of the Trinity. If we may simplify, we may say that people grasp truth in the contrastive-identificational features, which they share with other human beings, and through which they have access to the truth in God's own mind. Simultaneously, each person grasps the truth in his unique variation, colored by his unique personality, his unique situation, and his unique background history of language, that is, the language learning that colors the associations he brings to words. The unity, expressed in contrastive-identificational features, coheres with the diversity, expressed in variation.

Non-Christians as well as Christians repeatedly depend on truth. Especially, they depend on truth as a background in the use of sentences. But non-Christians distort the relation of truth to God. And so, indirectly, they distort the meaning of language that they use. They do not acknowledge the source in God, and they do not acknowledge properly the relation of particular truths to the comprehensive truth in the knowledge of God.

## Small Truths

Included in the truth are truths about what has happened, and about what will happen. There are truths contained in true stories. And so we come back to story. Even fictional stories presuppose something about the nature of what *can* happen, and that pertains to truth. Stories are shaped according to the nature of purposeful personal action. They have structure. A story involves personal purpose at the beginning, and achievement or failure at the end. Moreover, the nature of language makes it possible to tell a story in elaborate detail, or to compress it into a single sentence or even a single clause. "The hero rescued the princess."

---

7. See Vern S. Poythress, "Reforming Ontology and Logic in the Light of the Trinity: An Application of Van Til's Idea of Analogy," *Westminster Theological Journal* 57/1 (1995): 187–219.

Such summaries may have more than one grammatical form. We can express things in many different ways (variation). But language does provide resources for summarizing action even within a single sentence or a single clause. We can then analyze the clauses using "case relations."[8] The word "case" is used to describe the grammatical cases in Latin and Greek. But what we have in mind here is not the grammar but the character of the action in the world. "The hero rescued the princess" has the same character roles and relations as does the grammatically different sentence, "The princess was rescued by the hero."

In this case there are three roles, normally designated *agent*, *action*, and *patient*.[9] The *agent* is the personal, purposeful source initiating the action. In our particular case, the agent is the hero. The *action* is the event itself, which in this case is the rescue. The *patient* is the recipient whom the agent hopes to affect by the action. That is the princess.

There are also other case relations.[10] The "experiencer" is an actor who receives a perception. In the sentence "I saw the princess," "I" is the "experiencer" and the princess is the "source." Note that in the sentence "the butter melted," "the butter" is actually the *patient*, even though grammatically it is the subject of the sentence. "He melted the butter in the microwave" has an agent ("he"), a patient ("the butter"), and a location ("in the microwave"). It also implies an *instrument* (heat from the microwave). A simple story usually involves some central goal and some personal purpose to achieve that goal. When a simple story is compressed into a single clause, we most typically find that an agent works out his plan of action for a patient or for a goal. He does so through an action (or series of actions). The structure involves the unity of agent, action, and patient (or goal).

## The Dependence of Clauses on God

As we might expect, this level of action is imitative of divine action. It must be, because man is made in the image of God. God works his big purposes, purposes for the whole history of the world, through the action of a single person, the Lord Jesus Christ. Human beings work their little purposes. God's achievement does

---

8. Robert E. Longacre, *The Grammar of Discourse* (New York/London: Plenum, 1983), 20: "I propose here that plot is the notional structure of narrative discourse in the same sense that case relations are the notional structure of the clause." By "notional" Longacre means conceptual as opposed to syntactical structure.

9. The concept of *action* as a "role" is not typical. Many times "case roles" are assigned only to the items that surround the action. But this is a matter of terminology.

10. Longacre (*Grammar of Discourse*, 154–167) offers the following inventory of nuclear cases: experiencer, patient, agent, range, measure, instrument, locative, source, goal, path. For each he provides an explanatory definition. This inventory is a classifier's "outsider" inventory, intended to be universal across languages. The insider within a particular language and culture will have his own point of view.

not dispense with the actions of other human beings. On the contrary, it is what forms the foundation for their meaning. This foundation is especially evident for the activity of Christians:

> Therefore, my beloved brothers, be steadfast, immovable, always abounding in the work of the Lord, knowing that *in the Lord* your labor is *not in vain* (1 Cor. 15:58).

> Therefore, my beloved, as you have always obeyed, so now, not only as in my presence but much more in my absence, *work out* your own salvation with fear and trembling, for it is God who *works in you*, both to will and to work for his good pleasure (Phil. 2:12–13).

Though unbelievers have no basis for expecting an ultimate fruitfulness in their work, yet their work too is significant as a blessing of common grace.

Let us take an example. "The boy hit the ball." "The boy" designates the agent; "hit" designates the action. "The ball" designates the patient. The boy's purposeful action takes place in imitation of God's purposeful action for the whole of history. In addition, the boy's action is empowered by God's purposeful action. God controls the events of the boy's action. We may say, "God brings about the whole event." At the level of primary cause, God is the agent, his control is the action (represented by the expression "brings about"), and the event on earth is the patient (represented by the expression "the whole event").

"Cause" is a very general label for control. We can express a cause using a single clause, as follows: "Christ's obedience led to his enthronement." The expression "led to" expresses a causal connection. But we can also spread it out, as it is expressed in Philippians 2:8–11:

> And being found in human form, he humbled himself by becoming obedient to the point of death, even death on a cross. *Therefore* God has highly exalted him and bestowed on him the name that is above every name, so that at the name of Jesus every knee should bow, in heaven and on earth and under the earth, and every tongue confess that Jesus Christ is Lord, to the glory of God the Father.

Relations between clauses within the same sentence, or sentences within the same paragraph, frequently express the reality of connections among truths. God ordains and specifies not only particular truths but also the relations between them. The crucifixion and the resurrection are connected according to God's design. This connection is absolutely central to the redemption of the world. But minor and noncentral connections are also ordained by God. God designs the world so that, in its details as well as its large-scale history, it is going somewhere.

Human actions have significant consequences, and both actions and consequences are ordained by God. The boy's intention to hit the ball had consequences.

A single clause structure can be used to describe either God's action or human action. "God created the world" has an agent, an action, and a patient. It not only identifies these roles but expresses how they relate to one another in a single whole. In these ways it is analogous to "the boy hit the ball." The analogical structure is founded in the fact that God made man in his image. But it is also the background for understanding the unique work of Christ. When we say, "Christ redeemed his people," the assertion is true both with respect to Christ's divine nature and with respect to his human nature. With respect to his divine nature, God redeemed his people by acting in the second person of the Trinity and in his actions during Jesus' earthly life. It is also true that Christ *as man* lived his life on earth as representative for us as human beings, and that his human living resulted in our redemption. There is unity of divine and human action in the one person, Christ Jesus, without destroying the distinction between divine and human nature.

Within language, God ordained clause structure so that it could perform these functions. Language is capable of talking about both divine and human action. When we use language in these two ways, we rely on an analogy rather than a pure identity between the two. Even when non-Christians use clause structure, they use it as something that has been given by God. They rely on its ability to function analogically, even though the conscious philosophy of some of them may deny it.

# Foundations for Meaning
# in Trinitarian Inter-personal Action

The Father has sent his Son to be the Savior of the world.

—1 John 4:14

So far we have looked for foundations for meaning that come from some of God's actions in governing the world. We can also look at activity among the persons of the Trinity.

## Activities within the Trinity

For action within the Trinity, consider John 3:33–36:

> [33] Whoever receives his [Christ's] testimony sets his seal to this, that God is true. [34] For he whom God has sent utters the words of God, for he gives the Spirit without measure. [35] The Father loves the Son and has given all things into his hand. [36] Whoever believes in the Son has eternal life; whoever does not obey the Son shall not see life, but the wrath of God remains on him.

The context of John 3 is focusing on the Son in his redemptive work, and on the Son as the one who reveals God (see John 1:18). The "giving" of all things into the Son's hands in verse 35 has as one of its purposes the provision of redemption. The next verse says, "Whoever believes in the Son has eternal life; . . ." Within the

scope of "all things" that are given to the Son is the power to give eternal life, and
to give freedom from the wrath of God. The "giving" of all things is also closely
related to the giving of the Spirit in verse 34. The Father "gives the Spirit without
measure." The reference here is to giving the Spirit to the Son. This giving is based
on the love that the Father has for the Son (verse 35). The giving of the Spirit
expresses the love between the Father and the Son.

All these actions have as their purpose the redemption of human beings. But
they have as their background relations among the persons of the Trinity. The
Father loves the Son (John 3:35). That love is expressed and demonstrated in
time by the interaction and joint work of the Father and the Son during the
earthly life of the Son.[1] But it obviously has roots that go beyond time. God acts
in time in harmony with who he is eternally. The Father loves the Son eternally.
And, we may then infer, the Father expresses his love for the Son by an *eternal*
giving of the Spirit.

Some people may doubt whether we can so easily make inferences with respect
to eternal intra-Trinitarian relations. But we know that the actions of the Spirit
within time are in harmony with those eternal personal relations. So even though
there is mystery about these relations, we can infer that the fact that the Father
gives the Spirit to the Son in time is consistent with the eternal intra-Trinitarian
relations. This consistency is already enough to indicate that the language used
with respect to time has an ultimate basis in divine personal relations.

The Father loves the Son. And love is an expression of the activity of the Spirit.
The Father is the agent. The Son is the patient. The Spirit is closely related to the
"action" or activity of loving. In the clause "The Father loves the Son," the structure of the clause expresses the eternal activity of the persons in relation to one
another. Language in this respect is rooted in God's eternal intra-Trinitarian relations. Specifically, the clause structure is related to God's eternal intra-Trinitarian
relations.

The truth that the Father loves the Son is the archetype. The truth that the
Father loves Paul or Mary or any of us is an ectype. That is, it is a derivative
truth, related by analogy to the foundation in who God is, God in himself. The
commandment to love your neighbor is an ectype. Love is love because it is an
imitation of the Spirit expressing the relation of the Father to the Son.

---

1. In addition, the Father sent the Holy Spirit at Jesus' baptism (Matt. 3:16–17). And the
giving of the Spirit to the church at Pentecost is the result of the Father first giving the Spirit to
the Son: "Being therefore exalted at the right hand of God, and having received from the Father
the promise of the Holy Spirit, he has poured out this that you yourselves are seeing and hearing"
(Acts 2:33).

## Expressions in Language

Now when we focus specifically on language, rather than on the truth expressed in language, the situation becomes more complicated. We have to reckon with the relation between the piece of language and the truth itself. Language *expresses* truth. The sentence "the Father loves the Son" expresses the truth that the Father loves the Son. We can make a distinction between the *sentence* on the one hand, and the *reality* on the other. But the reality is meaningful reality, a meaning deriving from the meaning in the mind of God. God expresses his mind in his Word. The Son is the Word, the expression of the Father. The Son is also the image of the Father (Col. 1:15; Heb. 1:3). As the Word expresses the Father, so a sentence that God utters expresses the truth that the sentence formulates. For example, we *do* understand and grasp the truth that the Father loves the Son, through the sentence that states, "the Father loves the Son." The utterance gives access to truth, in imitation of the Word giving access to the Father.

Why belabor this point? Especially because of the influence of postmodernism, people wonder about the adequacy of language. Can language give us truth? The answer is yes. Language does not work because of any mechanical power innate in something about language that is just "there," independent of whether God exists. Rather, it is because God is continually present in every bit of language. (This is implied by the general doctrine of God's omnipresence, Jer. 23:24.) And God through his intra-Trinitarian harmony and fellowship gives to language its power to reveal. God through common grace gives wisdom and truth even to rebels. When God speaks to us, his language opens truth for us. This process imitates the work of the Son, who is the image of the Father, who reveals the Father, and who gives access to the Father.

But now consider another complexity. We may within language choose to express truth in more than one way. There are a variety of languages into which the Bible can be translated. In each of them we can translate John 3:35. Each translation and each expression will be different in some ways from the others. Words for "love" will differ from language to language, and the nuances in meaning will not be exactly the same from one language to another. Maybe some translations will capture the fullness of meaning in the original Greek of John 3:35 more fully than will others.

But all the translations translate truth. They make the truth about the love of God accessible to people everywhere. They do so in connection with the gospel and the rest of the Bible, which God uses through the Spirit to reform individuals and groups within any one culture, leading them from darkness to light. They may only gradually come to understand what God's love is. But they do come to understand. They come because God is present with his Spirit in his word, and he makes known to Bible readers in any language or culture the meaning of John 3:35. Their cultural context undergoes reformation through the power of the Spirit.

When they have a new, reformed context, they hear and understand John 3:35 as God intended it to be understood. The sentence then gives access to the truth.

Even within one language there are various expressions of truth. Consider two expressions: "the Father loves the Son"; and "the Son is loved by the Father." The "case roles" remain the same in these two expressions. The Father is the agent and the Son is the patient. But the linear organization in grammatical structure differs. Is there a difference in meaning? There is a subtle difference. In the first sentence, the Father is the topic, the starting point for thinking. In the second the Son is the topic. We might exaggerate the difference a little by saying that in the first case the relation of love is viewed from the perspective that starts with the Father, while in the second the perspective starts with the Son.[2]

We have already discussed perspectives. The human ability to have multiple perspectives has its roots in the diversity of persons in the Trinity. The Father has a personal perspective in his knowledge of the Son. And so does the Son in his knowledge of the Father.[3] Each person has a distinct "perspective"—though we must also say that because we are talking about God in his infinity, we as human beings never comprehend the persons of the Trinity in an exhaustive way, nor do we fully comprehend their unity and diversity in relation to one another.

We know that the persons of the Trinity are distinct from one another. This archetypal distinction leads to ectypal, derivative distinctions in language that expresses and reveals the truth about the persons. Each language on earth has its own distinct expressions, not entirely identical with other languages. And within English, the two expressions with "the Father" as subject and "the Son" as subject are distinct. The possibility of two distinct foci in English reflects human ability to have multiple foci. And this ability reflects—ectypally, derivatively, analogically—the archetypal distinctions within the Trinity. The archetypal distinction in the Trinity is reflected in English in the difference between an "active" sentence ("The Father loves the Son") and a "passive" sentence ("The Son is loved by the Father"). *Built into English grammar* is a reflection of the Trinity.

Of course, the sentence "The Father loves the Son" is only one sentence. But it is a paradigm for many others. The mind of God is the mind of the Father, the Son, and the Holy Spirit. And this pattern in God's mind is reflected in all that God has made. It is reflected in the mind of man. It is reflected in language,

---

2. In addition, William Croft and D. Alan Cruse, *Cognitive Linguistics* (Cambridge: Cambridge University Press, 2004), 61, citing Susumu Kuno and Etsuko Kaburaki, "Empathy and Syntax," *Linguistic Inquiry* 8 (1977): 627–672, suggest that the speaker indicates "empathy" with the subject reference. Such capacity for empathy is also a result of being made in the image of God.

3. See Vern S. Poythress, *Symphonic Theology: The Validity of Multiple Perspectives in Theology* (Grand Rapids, MI: Zondervan, 1987; reprinted, Phillipsburg, NJ: Presbyterian & Reformed, 2001), 50–51.

because language originates from God, and God uses it in divine-divine as well as divine-human communication. And so every other sentence in English sustains a relation to these key sentences about the Father loving the Son. "The boy fed the dog" can become "The dog was fed by the boy." Active and passive sentences allow differences of perspective. We can start with either the boy or the dog. These perspectives in language are what they are because they reflect, on their humble level, the reality of multiple perspectives within the Trinity.

Of course the area of active and passive sentences is only one of indefinitely many illustrations. The richness of the mind of God is infinite. This richness is reflected in language.

Instead of focusing on the relation between the two kinds of sentence, active and passive, we can focus on all transitive clauses and their common pattern. The sentence "The Father loves the Son" illustrates the classical grammatical categories of subject, predicate, and object that make up the structure of a transitive clause. Subject, predicate, and object within this sentence express relations that are eternally true among the persons of the Trinity. And so, by implication, every transitive clause within English is analogically related to the relation of persons within the Trinity.

## Normality in Language and the Origin of Language

Some people may think that the comparisons between language for God and language for events in the world are suspect. They might say something like this:

> Language for God is a special case, and it is only one case. The same clause structures are used over and over again for all kinds of other things. So surely the hurly-burly of all the other things is the real "foundation." Use with respect to God is an extension from the ordinary use. And, for many modern people, it is a doubtful extension at that.

Yes, language describing God is a special case. But sometimes one case can be the foundation for everything else. For example, when God created man, he made him "in his own image" (Gen. 1:27). We know from later parts of the Bible that Christ existed eternally as the image of God (Col. 1:15; Heb. 1:3). So when man was created, there was *already* an image of God. And this first image, the eternal Son, was the prime image. The Son was always God (John 1:1), and so he "images" God in a more definitive way than can be the case for man. He is the archetypal image, while man is the ectypal, derivative image. So imaging relations in God's works in time have as their ultimate foundation an original that is eternal. This original, the eternal Son, is a "special case." But the special case is the foundation for all the other cases.

Now reflect again on the fact that the Son is also the Word, who is God (John 1:1). He is the original Word. All words, all discourses spoken in time, are derivative from this original. The Son is the *archetypal* Word. Moreover, when God gave the gift of language to mankind, it included the intention that God would participate as a speaker of language. And if he is a speaker, he is the *prime* speaker, whom we imitate because we are made in his image. Thus language as God uses it has a certain ontological primacy. And language used when God talks about himself has a primacy. The special case of God is the prime case.

So language as a whole derives from God. And if that is so, we are also invited to see how particular pieces within language owe their origin to God.

But the objector may point out that, when children learn language, they learn it by hearing their parents and other people speaking about all kinds of things. They hear, "The boy hit the ball." Their parents may never even mention the word "God," and some children may not ever hear the word until they are older. And then they would need to have it explained to them. Or, if they were to grow up in ancient pagan Greece, they would hear a word for "gods" but never hear about the true God of the Bible. So God cannot be relevant to them.

Yes, this reasoning makes sense if we have forgotten about God's presence in the world through general revelation. According to the Bible, everyone knows God inescapably (Rom. 1:18–25). The children who grow up in an atheist or pagan home know God. They suppress the knowledge, and their parents of course promote and aid that suppression. Within God's world, with minds made in the image of God, the children hear the sentence "The boy hit the ball." That sentence is possible, and the truth about which it speaks is possible, only because God is continually present. God created the boy with the ability to hit the ball. He gave the boy the ability to have purposes, and in particular to have the purpose of hitting the ball. He created the ball in such a way that it could be a patient for the hit. He ordained the structures of cause and effect, and he himself is continually at work as primary cause. He brings about language and its structures. He specifies the structures in such a way that they can be used to talk about the boy's action *in analogy with* God's action. Analogy, as well as the presence of God's action, comes with the parents' sentence. The child cannot escape God, and part of the reason why he cannot escape is that he cannot escape language. The child experiences the presence of God and the presence of God's action in each sentence. He does not merely receive a reference to the boy's action *in isolation from God.*

The Father expresses his love for the Son in making a world that imitates the intra-Trinitarian love. This imitation includes the humble relation between agent, action, and patient that God sustains in the boy's activity.

Consider the boy's action from the perspective of God's involvement. God empowers the boy with the ability to have purposes and to intend as an agent to hit the ball. Even in the process of having purposes and making plans, the boy imitates the fact that God has purposes and plans. The boy's planning illustrates the fact that the boy is made in the image of God.

God empowers the boy in the action of hitting, and God as primary cause brings about the hitting. The boy, of course, is active on his level, and that too is significant; he is the secondary cause. God empowers the relations of secondary causes and effects, so that the ball gets hit—it becomes a patient.

God's control goes together with his meanings and his presence; they are inseparable. In particular, God is *present* when the boy hits the ball. And God is present in the sentence that describes that fact. He also expresses his *meanings*. The boy's hitting the ball has meaning in relation to God's plan. And God's plan has meaning in relation to his character, which is preeminently expressed in God's loving his Son. The plan concerning the world is an expression of the Father's love. God makes the boy to imitate meaningfully his initiating purpose of love. God brings about the action of hitting as an expression of the meaning of his love for his Son. The ball receives the hitting because the Spirit as the Spirit of power brings about the effect, and this action of the Spirit reflects the Spirit's action in bringing the love of God *to* the Son. We can also say that the Son is present in the action; the action of God is the action of all three persons in the Godhead.

At the same time, we should underline the full particularity of the boy hitting the ball. The particularity and unrepeatability of events go together in harmony with their relations to universals, that is, to general patterns. We may feel a peculiarity in relating an event as specific as "The boy hit the ball" to the general truth that "the Father loves the Son" because this specific act by the boy is related in many other directions to many truths—truths about other boys who hit other objects, and about this boy doing other actions like jumping and eating and speaking. It is also related to many other things that we might say about God, about his speaking and judging and showing mercy and so on. We single out the one action of God, "The Father loves the Son," not to suggest that it stands alone, but rather because among many other statements about God it expresses his character. And God's character is expressed meaningfully in his presence in everything that he plans and executes and for which he brings recompenses.

Children who are learning language have before them in the sentence about the boy the manifestation of the meaning, control, and presence of God. The sentence cannot do anything other than reveal God, because it has meaning only in relation to the mind of God.

## Clause Types

We have been contemplating transitive clauses, and how they are related to an archetypal transitive clause, "The Father loves the Son." But in English there are other types of clauses.

What about bitransitive clauses like "The boy gave his sister a doll"? This clause is called "bitransitive" because there are two objects: the "direct object," namely, "a doll," and the "indirect object" or beneficiary, namely, "his sister." This clause is structurally and grammatically related to the clause in John 3:34, "for he gives the Spirit without measure." "He," that is, the Father, gives the Spirit, where "the Spirit" is the direct object. There is also implicit in the sentence an indirect object, since we expect an indirect object with the verb "give." The Father gives *to the Son*. Thus eternal Trinitarian relations are the archetypal ground for bitransitive clauses in English.

We could then go on to talk about descriptive clauses, such as "the book is red."[4] The archetype here is a clause like "God is true" (John 3:33). The structure of clauses has its roots in the character of God.

What about equative clauses such as "the boy is a soldier"? One archetype for these is the statement "the Word was God" (John 1:1). Intra-Trinitarian relations once again offer an ultimate foundation for a statement of classification. And the structure of language enables us to receive the truth about the relation of the Word to God, as well as statements about created things.

## Connections

Consider another sentence: "The boy hit the ball hard, and *so* he got a home run." The word "so" indicates a connection. The world is designed by God so that there is such a connection. And language is designed by God so that it can express the connection. The design of the world goes back to the plan of God, and also to the intra-Trinitarian activity of God, the divine activity of the Father with the Son and the Spirit. God's activity is the archetype for human creaturely activity. God's word, ruling the world, specifies that human beings can use language to express the meanings and purposes that they intend.

The design of language goes back to the plan of God. And it also expresses the intra-Trinitarian activity of God, in which the Father speaks to the Son in the "breath" of the Holy Spirit. God's speaking is the archetype for human speaking. Language coheres with the world, because both language and design for the world cohere in God. He is in harmony with himself. That harmony in God is the foundation for the faithful functioning of language, including the functioning of clauses. And that harmony is the ultimate source for all our satisfaction and our joy. The joy of using language, and contemplating truth, and understanding something about a boy hitting a ball—these are an echo of the joy that the Son has in the presence of the Father (Heb. 12:2; John 15:10–11; 17:24–26).

---

4. Robert E. Longacre, *The Grammar of Discourse* (New York/London: Plenum, 1983), 308.

# Subsystems of Language

Jesus said to them again, "Peace be with you. As the Father has sent me,
even so I am sending you." And when he had said this,
he *breathed* on them and said to them, "Receive the Holy Spirit."

—John 20:21–22

Sentences offer us a good starting point for looking at the interlocking of
subsystems of language. We have already indirectly touched on the topic
of subsystems in the previous chapter, where we distinguished the *grammar* of a
sentence from the organization of the actors and actions about which the sentence
speaks. Grammar is distinct from *reference*. The grammatical features of a language
make up a *subsystem* of language distinct from the subsystem for reference. It is
time to look at these subsystems.

When examined in detail, languages show complex, intricate systems that they
make available for use in communication. Ordinary people seldom concentrate
on these intricacies, because they want to get on with the task of communication.
But examining the intricacies can be like examining the intricacies of a human
cell. We should marvel at the wisdom of God displayed in the way he made each
cell. Equally, we should marvel at the wisdom of God displayed in the structure
of human language resources. Linguists who make such study their professional
goal should be encouraged to do their work in the presence of God, serving God
and his goodness rather than thinking that they are just looking at facts that "just
happen" to be there.

## Resources for Content

The first subsystem, the referential subsystem, is in some ways the easiest to understand for people who normally do not think about the inner workings of language. We are aware of the *content* of what we say. We are aware of our human purposes in what we say. We seldom slow down enough to pay specific attention to the *way* in which we say it. "Content" is what the referential subsystem provides. Consider the following two sentences:

Bill does well in class without studying.
My friend does not crack the books, but still succeeds in the course.

If "Bill" and "my friend" are referring to the same person, and the same situation, the two sentences have at least roughly the same meaning. There are some differences in nuance, of course. But we are all familiar with the experience of saying "the same thing" in different words. The two sentences say roughly the same thing (content). That is referential commonality. But the two have different sounds and different grammatical constructions. That shows that there is something, namely content, that can be held roughly constant even when sound and grammar vary. The content is the referential aspect of the sentence. We are here using "referential" in a broad way. It includes not merely the function of referring to a specific object in the world, but all kinds of ways in which we use language to interact with the world.[1]

The referential *subsystem* designates the resources that a particular language like English provides beforehand for our use in producing meaning content in our verbal interaction. The referential subsystem includes means for referring to my friend Bill, for describing studying or not studying, for describing success or failure, and for describing the situation of a classroom course.[2]

We should make one clarification. In actual communication, we never meet the referential subsystem *in isolation*. All three subsystems that we will discuss are always functioning together. But when we step back and analyze language, we can see that the fruitful functioning of language depends on the presence of a multitude of relations. These relations can be classified into subsystems. The referential subsystem consists in relations and patterns in *content*.

---

1. Thus, we would include speaker attitudes and purposes, rhetorical strategies for persuasion or for inciting action. But the specific implementation of such purposes in speech would of course use grammatical and phonological as well as referential resources.

2. See Kenneth L. Pike, *Linguistic Concepts: An Introduction to Tagmemics* (Lincoln and London: University of Nebraska Press, 1982), 97–106; Vern S. Poythress, "A Framework for Discourse Analysis: The Components of a Discourse, from a Tagmemic Viewpoint," *Semiotica* 38/3–4 (1982): 277–298; Poythress, "Hierarchy in Discourse Analysis: A Revision of Tagmemics," *Semiotica* 40/1–2: (1982): 107–137.

## Resources for a Medium of Communication (Sound)

The second subsystem in language is the *phonological* subsystem or subsystem for sound. The phonological subsystem is the system of pertinent sounds for a particular language.[3] Many languages, but not all, have been supplemented by a graphological system, usually in the form of an alphabet.[4] But we are concentrating on the oral form of language for the moment.

A language does not use all sounds in all combinations, but has particular sounds, called *phonemes*, that make a difference in meaning. Consider, for example, the following words in English: "bet," "pet," "vet," "debt," "set," "let," "met," "net," "get," "yet." They differ in sound only by the first consonant. So all the first consonants are distinct from the standpoint of the native speaker, the insider. That is, the sounds for "b," "p," "v," "d," "s," "l," "m," "n," "g," "y" are distinct sound units. We also know that the structure with consonant plus "e" plus "t" is regularly used to form a complete syllable and even a complete word.

Now consider the following made-up sound sequences in English: "fet," "ket," "slet," "spet," "spret," "glet." These are not real words of English, but they could be, because they conform to the rules for combining sounds to form a word.[5] Other sound sequences are not allowed at the beginning of a word: "pnet," "pset," "kset," "mnet," "shlet." But some of these sequences *are* allowed in other languages. In Greek, for example, a word can begin with "pn" or "ps." And in fact we have some words in English inherited from Greek: "pneumonia" and "psychology." "Pneumonia" and "psychology" are both spelled in a manner that imitates Greek spelling. But the pronunciation in English has dropped the initial "p" sound. Orally we do not pronounce the initial "p." The pronunciation has been forced

---

3. See Pike, *Linguistic Concepts*, 84–96. More specifically, phonology studies the distinct minimal units of sound, the *phonemes*, which are perceived as distinct units from an insider's point of view. It can also include the study of higher "levels" or groupings of sound, like syllables and stress groups, again from an insider's point of view. On insiders and outsiders ("emic" and "etic" viewpoints), see chapter 19.

4. Technically, the graphological subsystem contains not only the alphabet but also specifications for the ways in which alphabetic letters fit together to form written words, and written words to form written sentences with punctuation. English has many cases where written spelling does not match the sound. For example, the written word "write" has an extra "w" that is not pronounced orally. Multiple graphological systems are possible (written communication in English can use shorthand, braille, and text messaging as well as the conventional Roman alphabetic system; mathematics, chemistry, and computer science use distinct systems of technical notation). Cultures with writing systems develop distinct written genres and written behavioremes, so that the relation between oral and written communication is complex rather than merely one-sided. Jacques Derrida is undoubtedly right that Saussure's methodological confinement to spoken language constituted a reduction (Derrida, *Of Grammatology* [Baltimore/London: Johns Hopkins University Press, 1976], 30–44).

5. The technical name for such rules is "phonological rules."

into conformity with the normal regularities for sound patterns in English. The regularities in Greek are different.

Languages with writing systems have a subsystem for writing. In the case of alphabetic systems, the writing system is closely related to sound. But syllabic and pictographic systems (like written Chinese) are also possible—showing that the subsystem for writing is not necessarily just a reproduction of the subsystem for sound.

## Resources for Grammar

The third subsystem of language is the grammatical subsystem. We can see the grammatical subsystem in action if we look at a nonsense example from Lewis Carroll's poem, *The Jabberwocky*:

> 'Twas brillig, and the slithy toves
> Did gyre and gimble in the wabe:
> All mimsy were the borogoves,
> And the mome raths outgrabe.
> "Beware the Jabberwock, my son! . . ."[6]

The grammar is identifiably normal English grammar. "'Twas" is a poetic contraction of "It was." "Brillig" is an adjective. "The slithy toves" is a noun phrase with a plural noun "toves." And so on. But it is nonsense.

Actually, it is not complete nonsense. "Brillig," coming as it does after "'Twas," describes some weather condition, probably related to the word "brilliant." "Slithy" evokes the meanings of "slithery," "slimy," "slippery." "Gyre" is actually a word of English, meaning "to move in a circle or a spiral."[7] Though many people might not recognize this word, they would guess that it is associated with "gyration" and "gyroscope," and would associate it with circular motion. Thus a good many of the words have some secondary meaning associations. But the whole is nearly nonsense, and its nonsense would be virtually complete if we eliminated the secondary associations in meaning.

Such nonsense indicates clearly that grammar is independent of content (referential load). We can have normal grammar without content, and we could even have it without normal sounds, if we introduced some sounds or sound sequences that are not normal to English. Thus, a grammatical subsystem does exist. And it differs from language to language.[8]

---

6. Lewis Carroll, *Through the Looking Glass and What Alice Found There* (1871), chapter 1.
7. *Webster's Ninth New Collegiate Dictionary.*
8. Pike, *Linguistic Concepts*, 70–83; Poythress, "Framework."

## Interlocking Subsystems

In actual language the three subsystems—for content, for grammar, and for sound—interlock. They all appear together. It takes special effort, like Lewis Carroll's nonsense, to make one appear without the presence of another. The three subsystems are present at every point. If we take away all the sounds, nothing is left. If we take away all the referential functions in a normal sentence, we must take away all the words, and nothing is left. We can still invent a special nonnormal sentence, a nonsense sentence like the first sentence in Jabberwocky. It has made-up words like "toves," but even these have a kind of pretended referential function, namely, to refer to whatever in the fantasy world is a "tove." If all reference disappears, so does language in its normal use. We could still have sounds, but they would not be English or any other human language. Finally, suppose that we take away all the grammar. We must take away all the words, each of which has grammatical function, and again nothing is left. In one sense, any one of the subsystems covers the whole of language.

At the same time, one piece of language—a particular sentence, let us say—enjoys structuring that is related to all three subsystems. We can look at the same piece from any of three perspectives—referential, phonological, and grammatical. Moreover, the learning of any one subsystem by a child interacts with all three subsystems at once, and with the larger human environment as well.

And all this is really a good thing, though it may be frustrating to an analyst who is trying to separate cleanly one subsystem from another. The child, for the sake of learning, must learn both meaning and sound. He must learn both the meaning of the word "dog" and how the word sounds. How will he learn the meaning of a particular word or sentence unless he can identify distinct sounds that distinguish that word from all the other words and sentences with quite different meanings? The sound has to be there all the time to access meaning. And conversely, the meaning has to be there for the sound to make any difference. Otherwise it is just so much noise, noise that a child would eventually learn to ignore in order to go on to something meaningful. Language consists in "form-meaning composites."[9] It is never pure meaning or pure sound. The sound (or a

---

9. See the discussion of form and meaning in Kenneth L. Pike, *Language in Relation to a Unified Theory of the Structure of Human Behavior*, 2nd ed. (The Hague: Mouton, 1967), especially 62–63:

> ... in the present theory I am attempting to develop a point of view within which form and meaning must not be separated in theory; there are rather form-meaning composites...

> For convenience, one may on occasion discuss the form and meaning aspects *as if* they were separate, while taking pains to indicate that such an expedient is a distortion which must be corrected at proper intervals and in the relevant places in the discussion. ...

writing system or a sign language) must identify the meanings. And the meanings make the sounds significant.

The interdependence of the three subsystems is like a coinherence. Does this triadic structuring of language into three subsystems reflect the character of God? Yes, it does. As usual, God as creator is unique and cannot be placed on the same level as the world that he created. But we may find analogies.

## Language Systems and Utterances

To see the analogies, let us first think about the systematic character of a whole language like English. The systematic regularities of English are already there when people start communicating. For example, suppose that Amy uses English in a particular utterance, "This is my dog," to communicate some information. She uses words like "this," "my," and "dog" already available in English. The English language as a system supplies the resources.[10] Thus we have three aspects to Amy's communication: Amy with her purposes, the particular utterance "This is my dog," and the system of English. (See fig. 32.1.)

### Using a Language System

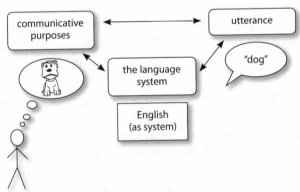

FIGURE 32.1

These three aspects of language correspond roughly to three perspectives—the particle, the wave, and the field perspectives.[11] Amy's particular communicative purposes are stable. We naturally focus on her when we use the particle perspective. The wave perspective naturally leads to focusing on the dynamics of communication: the specific utterance "This is my dog" travels out, dynamically produced by Amy's vocal apparatus and dynamically carried through sound waves. The field perspective focuses on the systematic relations among different utterances. That

---

10. Language as a *system* is close to what Saussure meant by *langue* (appendix E).

11. For an explanation of these perspectives, see chapter 7.

leads to awareness of the English language *system*, that is, the systematic patterns of relations among various utterances and speakers. The system of English includes patterns like the patterns for use of English tenses, or the patterns for sounds in English words, such as we saw earlier in this chapter.

Since man is made in the image of God, his speaking ability images God's speaking ability. When God speaks, there are three aspects similar to those with Amy: (1) God has his purposes, (2) he speaks a specific utterance, and (3) he has a system against the background of which he speaks.

Consider the example where God says, "Let there be light" (Gen. 1:3). "Let there be light" is the specific utterance. God's purpose is the creation of light. What language did he use? Later he had the utterance recorded in Hebrew (Gen. 1:3). But at the initial point at which he created light, God was not speaking to any human being, so the utterance would not necessarily be in any known human language. If God spoke in a particular human language, he would use the resources of that particular language system (a system that he himself fully controls). The system offers possibilities for many distinct utterances. But what God said still contrasts with many other things that he might have said. The deeper "system" behind all human languages is the system of God's wisdom, which he uses in creating the world (Prov. 8:22–31). He knows all the possibilities for what he might have created, and all the possibilities for what he might have said. Thus we have three aspects to God's speech: his purposes, his utterance, and the system of his wisdom. (See fig. 32.2.)

### God Speaking

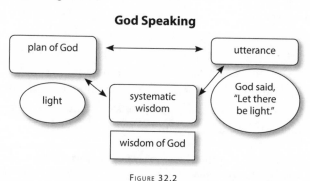

FIGURE 32.2

God's activity in speaking has its ultimate foundation in his Trinitarian character. The plan of God is the plan preeminently of the Father. The systematic wisdom of God is found in the Son: "in whom [Christ] are hidden all the treasures of *wisdom* and knowledge" (Col. 2:3; see 1 Cor. 1:30). And the Holy Spirit is like the breath of God that empowers his specific utterances. (See fig. 32.3.)

Thus the utterances of human beings display an image of the Trinitarian character of God.

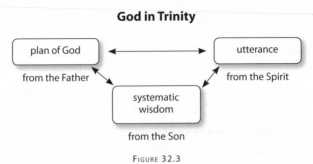

**God in Trinity**

FIGURE 32.3

## Three Subsystems

Now let us return to the situation of Amy saying, "This is my dog," using English. English as a system must have resources for enabling Amy to carry out her purposes through specific utterances.

In order to fulfill Amy's purposes, language has resources for talking about the world: for making statements, for issuing commands and requests, and for carrying out innumerable human purposes. These resources for talking about the world are the *referential* subsystem.

All languages also have resources for producing utterances using a *medium* of communication. Usually this medium is sound. The stable resources for this purpose are the system of sounds, that is, the *phonological* subsystem. Finally, languages offer resources for regular ways for building structures that combine both sounds and referential resources *together* in an internally consistent way. This internal structuring takes the form of the *grammatical* subsystem. (See figs. 32.4 and 32.5.)

Not all linguists have chosen to organize the thinking about these resources in exactly the same way.[12] There are different linguistic theories, partly because linguists may have differing interests and differing purposes.[13] But virtually all linguists would acknowledge at some point that human languages show structured organization in sound and in grammar, and that the languages are used in communication to accomplish tasks in the larger world.

---

12. My own approach is a variation on tagmemic theory. I use this particular theory partly because it has tended to be "antireductionistic," in comparison with other theories that have at times sacrificed something of the fullness of language for the sake of rigor (see appendix E). Tagmemic theory has also been "trimodal." Kenneth L. Pike, its main architect, suspected that the interlocking of three aspects dimly reflects the trimodal coinherence of persons of the Trinity (see Pike, *Language*; Pike, *Linguistic Concepts*). See also Poythress, "Framework," and Poythress, "Hierarchy," which expound the difference between referential, grammatical, and phonological aspects by speaking of subsystems. Standard tagmemic theory has preferred to talk in terms of three hierarchies. But hierarchy (wave perspective) and system (field perspective) interlock.

13. As an example, we may refer to the three perspectives—particle, wave, and field—all of which can be used by linguists. For a survey of structural linguistics, see appendix E and the literature cited there.

**Needed Resources**

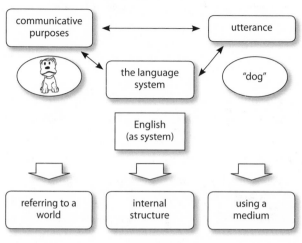

FIGURE 32.4

**Subsystems**

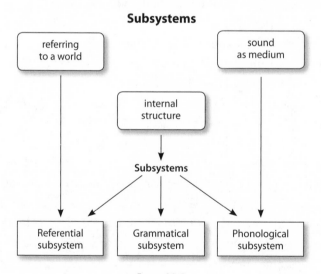

FIGURE 32.5

## Human Dependence

The three subsystems of language have their ultimate foundation in God's Trinitarian nature. Human purposes using the referential subsystem imitate God's purposes, and more specifically the purposes of God the Father. Human speaking with sound imitates God's utterances, which he utters through the power and "breath" of the Holy Spirit. Human speaking uses a language system, in imitation of God who uses the systematic wisdom of God the Son. The interlocking among reference, sound, and grammar reflects the coinherence among the persons of the Trinity. Human beings must rely on all three subsystems and on their interlocking whenever they use language. They are using a gift from the Trinitarian God.

## An Illustration

We can illustrate the interlocking of subsystems with the familiar sample sentence, "I am going to the store to get more bananas." Each word has a meaning, a content. And the sentence as a whole has a meaning, in which it says that I am going out for a particular purpose. So I am using the referential subsystem. When I do that, I am thinking and expressing myself in imitation of God the Father, who thinks and expresses his thoughts.

Second, the sentence has a grammatical structure. Each word can be classified as a noun, or a verb, or a preposition, and so on. The words fit together into a grammatical construction to make a whole sentence. I express myself with structure, in conformity with grammatical rules. In doing so, I imitate God, whose Son is the systematic wisdom of God.

Third, the sentence goes out from my mouth as a series of sounds. It has the force of my breath. I am using the phonological subsystem. In doing so, I imitate the Spirit, who breathes out the speech of God.

The thinking and speech of a human being do not create anything absolutely new. God knows all our thoughts beforehand (Ps. 139:4–6, 16). Human thinking means thinking God's thoughts and God's meanings after him. It means imitating the thinking of the Father. Human speaking is articulate speaking, relying on grammar. It relies on the systematic regularity specified by God's rules, which are the rules of the Word, the Son of God. And human speaking usually uses human breath, which is empowered by the breath of the Holy Spirit. Human speaking thus relies on the Trinitarian God, both his meanings, his power, and his presence in empowering human breath.

## Writing

In drawing the analogy with the Trinity we have focused on oral language, produced using human *breath*. But we could arrive at a similar conclusion with written language as our starting point. The Ten Commandments were written on two tablets of stone, "written with the finger of God" (Ex. 31:18). According to 2 Corinthians 3, this Old Testament writing is analogous to the writing of the law on the heart "with the Spirit of the living God":

And you show that you are a letter from Christ delivered by us, *written* not with ink but with the Spirit of the living God, not on *tablets of stone* but on tablets of human hearts (2 Cor. 3:3).

Now if the ministry of death, *carved* in letters on stone, came with such glory that the Israelites could not gaze at Moses' face because of its glory, which was being brought to an end, will not *the ministry of the Spirit* have even more glory? (2 Cor. 3:7–8).

The expression "finger of God" in Exodus 31:18 indicates the activity of God's power, and is closely associated with the Spirit of God. We can also compare Luke 11:20 with Matthew 12:28:

"But if it is by the *finger* of God that I cast out demons, then the kingdom of God has come upon you" (Luke 11:20).

"But if it is by the *Spirit* of God that I cast out demons, then the kingdom of God has come upon you" (Matt. 12:28).

The two passages together show that the Spirit is the ultimate "finger" of God. God's word in both oral and written form goes forth by the power of the Spirit, who is thus the archetypal source for both speaking and writing. When human speakers speak, they use breath, and by doing so they imitate the Holy Spirit, who is the "breath" of God. When human writers write, they use fingers, and by doing so they imitate the Holy Spirit, who functions as the "finger" of God.

Non-Christians rely on this gift of language, and on the wisdom of the Trinitarian God who gave it, even though they do not give thanks to him. "They did not honor him as God or give thanks to him" (Rom. 1:21).

# Words and Their Meanings

... and the name by which he is called is The Word of God.

—Revelation 19:13

W hat are words? We all know, because we use them all the time. A word is something like "dog" or "banana" or "going." For native speakers of a language, a large amount of this knowledge is *tacit*. We know how to use words, but seldom concentrate on them explicitly. When linguists do undertake to analyze words in detail, they find startling complexity.

### Multidimensional Relationships for Words

Words interact with all three of the subsystems of language that we examined in the previous chapter. First, words have *referential* relations, relations to meaning content. A word may have several distinct senses. For example, the word "dog" is used to designate the domestic dog (*Canis familiaris*). But "dog" is also used as a verb, as when we say that "John *dogged* his steps." And the word "dog" has another quite distinct sense, in which it designates an andiron or a mechanical device for gripping. It has still another meaning in the fixed expression "hot dog."

Let us focus on the most common sense of the word "dog," in which it designates the domestic dog. The word "dog" has multiple relationships. First, it is used to refer to dogs in the real world or imaginary worlds. The word has a relation to dogs in the world. Children typically learn the word "dog" by seeing it used either in connection with real dogs, or pictures of dogs. And the pictures of dogs have meaning in relation to dogs.

The word "dog" also has relationships with words that are near to it in meaning: "pooch," "puppy," "mutt," "bitch," "canine." It has contrastive relations with words that designate other members of the dog family (*Canidae*): "wolf," "fox," "coyote," "jackal," "dingo." It has relations to words that designate specific breeds of dogs: "terrier," "hound," "poodle," "collie," "retriever." It has relations also to words for other kinds of animals: "cat," "bear," "horse," "cow," "bird." All these relations are meaning relations within the referential subsystem.

Second, the word "dog" has relations in *sound* in the phonological subsystem, the system of sounds in English. It is similar in sound to "dot," "don," "daub," "dock," "doll," "doff," "dodge"; and it is similar to "bog," "cog," "fog," "hog," "jog," "log."[1] Within the subsystem of sounds we can analyze "dog" into smaller pieces. It is composed of three smaller sounds (*phonemes*), the sounds corresponding to the letters "d," "o," and "g." Because English has a writing system, the word "dog" also has relations in the system for writing, the *graphological* subsystem. It is a structure built up from three written letters, "d," "o," and "g," which have variant forms such as "DOG" or "*dog*."

Third, the word "dog" has relations in grammar, within the *grammatical* subsystem. It occurs in singular and plural, "dog" and "dogs." It is called a common "count" noun, because we can count a number of dogs. We can attach numbers to the word "dog": "one dog," "two dogs," etc. Like many other nouns it can function as the head of noun phrases like "the big dog." In short, it enters into grammatical constructions in a way that is parallel to many other nouns. It has relations, then, to all the other nouns that can function in the same way, and relations to the constructions like the noun phrase "the big dog."

A native speaker of English does not just know the word "dog" in total isolation. He tacitly understands this multitude of relations. The relations are an essential part of knowing how to use the word. The speaker has to know relations in meaning to other words and to the world in order aptly to choose the word "dog" instead of a more specific term like "collie" or a more general term like "animal" or "carnivore." In addition the speaker has to know the properties of the word in sound in order to pronounce it correctly. He has to know the properties in writing in order to write it correctly, and the grammatical properties of the word in order to use it in a grammatical construction.

For the native speaker the word "dog" enjoys all these relations in a *unity*. Take away the sounds, and the entire word disappears. Take away the meaning, and the word disappears. (We may still imagine the *sound* of the word "dog," but without the meaning it would be a nonsense sound, not a word at all.) Take away the grammar, which includes the word "dog" as an instance of the grammatical category "noun," and nothing remains. The three aspects of language interlock.

---

1. These similarities in sound hold true with my dialect of American English.

As we saw in the previous chapter, this interlocking reflects the coinherence of persons of the Trinity. God and his character are reflected even in a single common word like "dog."

An immense amount of learning goes into mastering a language. Children seem to do it effortlessly, because they are not conscious of the learning that is taking place. Adults who learn a second language find out to some extent how complicated it can be. But even they rely on their first language in order to make intelligent guesses and generalizations. They tacitly use general knowledge about how language works and how it fits into the contexts of human action. And of course they may make mistakes when they carry over some feature that characterizes their native language but not the language they are learning.

We owe all of this heritage to God. It is God who made us in his image.[2] And one implication is that we have the capacity to learn and use language—at least insofar as the capacity has not been damaged by physical effects such as brain damage. But it is not only a capacity, an innate ability. God in his providence also has put us in families and in environments where language is used, and day by day gives the opportunities to children that issue eventually in their mastery of language.[3] The immensity of richness of any particular human language is also the immensity of richness in a gift that God has given to us. The immensity understandably becomes the fascination of those who study languages professionally. Even those students who profess not to know God see his wisdom and his beauty and his order and his richness in the object of their study.

## Aspects of Language: Features, Variation, and Context (Distribution)

Let us now consider the word "dog" in terms of another triad of interlocking aspects of language: features, variation, and context (distribution). We introduced this triad in analyzing the behavioreme.[4] In fact, behavioremes are of many different sizes. An entire basketball game is a behavioreme. So is a single utterance, a single sentence within the utterance, or a single word within the sentence. A word, then, can be characterized by its contrastive-identificational features, its variation, and its context (distribution).

In discussing the word "dog" above, we have for the most part focused on contrastive-identificational features. But we have already said a few things about context (distribution). The word "dog" occurs in the *distributional* context of

---

2. It is God also who multiplied the languages at Babel (Gen. 11:1–9).

3. In this and in other ways we can find sad exceptions within a fallen world. On occasion children are abandoned, or grow up in dysfunctional families, or in conditions of famine or war, where their opportunities with respect to language are severely curtailed.

4. See chapter 19.

a noun phrase like "the big dog." Another kind of context (distribution) is its distribution in relation to other nouns that can substitute for it in a particular sentence. Its relations to words of similar meaning or similar sound is a kind of distribution.

Now consider variation. The word "dog" can vary slightly in pronunciation. It can be pronounced quickly or slowly, loudly or softly, and still remain the *same* word. It can be whispered. Those kinds of variation are variation in sound (phonological variation). But there is also grammatical variation, in the fact that the word can occur in singular and plural form,[5] and can occur in a variety of different kinds of sentences, to refer to a variety of dogs in the world. It can be used by many different people in many different situations. Each use is a particular instance of its variation.

Contrast, variation, and context (distribution) of the word "dog" interlock. Here is another reflection of coinherence.

## The Search for Pure Concepts

Words are complex in their structure of relations. To a native speaker it seems simple to use them. We do it without thinking about it. But there are challenges when it comes to seeking wisdom through the use of language or categories of thought. Thought largely takes place in connection with language, so the words we use have an influence on our thought.

From as early as ancient Greek philosophy, philosophers have reached out for wisdom about the fundamental character of the world. *Metaphysics* or *ontology* is the study of the fundamental kinds of things that there are. In thinking about the world, we use language. So it is easy to use particular key words in an attempt to delineate fundamental ontology. Plato developed a picture in which the fundamental nature of the world was closely related to "forms" or eternal ideas: the idea of goodness, justice, love, piety, etc. There would also be "forms" or ideas corresponding to particular kinds of things: the idea of dog, the idea of chair, the idea of horse, the idea of man. Any particular dog would be an embodiment derived by impressing the idea of dog or "dogness" onto previously unformed matter. The idea "formed" the matter into a particular dog.[6]

---

5. *Dog* and *dogs* can be considered as variational forms of one word. Technically, the plural *dogs* is a grammatical construction formed out of two "morphemes," which can be defined as minimal units in the hierarchy of grammatical units. In the word *dogs*, *dog* is a morpheme, and the pluralization symbol "-s" is a second morpheme. This pluralization morpheme has several variant *morphs*, including the final ess sound as in *hats*, the final zee sound in *dogs* (zee sound, even though it is spelled [graphologically!] with the letter "s"), and the -es as in *sashes*. There are also irregular variants as in *oxen*. Here we see some of the complexity of a language system in its detail.

6. On Platonism, see appendix D.

There is a good deal of truth here. God did make the world with particular "kinds" of creatures, as Genesis 1 indicates. Plants and trees are created "according to their own kinds" (Gen. 1:12). God's word and God's power ordered the world. God spoke, and each particular kind of creature, including dogs, came into existence as a product of his speech.[7]

But the order of the world is a multidimensional order, an expression of the richness of God's word and the richness of his plan. It expresses the richness of his language, if you will. God does not start with preformed "ideas" that are superior to him and to which his acts of creation must conform. The ideas are *his* ideas. And using the word "idea" is not apt in this context, because we are dealing with the infinite richness of God's mind, not with merely a list of terms—"dog," "chair," "horse," "man." The picture of pure heavenly ideas, independent of God, is an idealization.

We can sense, then, that the attempt to explain the nature of the world starting with abstract categories like the idea of dog is a half-truth. It is not altogether untrue, since God created the kinds of creatures. But it replaces the living God with an abstract set of ideas originating with man.

## Avoiding Reductions

In fact, words are not pure abstractions. They are form-meaning composites, with both meaning and form.[8] The *meaning* of the word "dog" has to do with its function in the referential subsystem, and its relation to the concept of dog. The *form* is the sound of d-o-g or the written form "dog." The word "dog" is not "pure" meaning with no form. A pure meaning could not be used, because we could not talk about it. We need form (sound or written words, or gestures in sign language) for communication. And even when words are in our minds, they have relational ties to their use through language, including the ties not only to sounds but to the things in the world that we have seen them used for (even if it sometimes is imaginary worlds with unicorns).

When we think, not all of us always use words. Some of our thinking may be wordless, or may be only loosely tied to language. We can sometimes reach

---

7. For a discussion of *how* God brought about the present kinds of animals, see Vern S. Poythress, *Redeeming Science: A God-Centered Approach* (Wheaton, IL: Crossway, 2006), chapters 5, 18, and 19.

8. See the previous chapter. The search for a pure meaning, detached from all form and from all bodily manifestation, represents an unreachable ideal. And at least in some cases it may be a distorted ideal. It may express a desire to escape our finite condition. And in some cases it may be a reduction of the richness of what God has given us. The ideal of "pure" meaning can sometimes take the route of trying to reduce the three aspects—the referential, the grammatical, and the phonological—into one alone, namely, the referential, in order to master it perfectly and completely. In that case, it may be a desire for unitarianism.

conclusions intuitively, without formulating everything in consciously formed sentences. And the presence of synonyms, like "dog" and "pooch," shows that we can have roughly the same cognitive content using different words. But all our thinking within this world takes place with the help of our brains and our bodily existence. We are not creatures of "pure" thought; we are not independent of our bodies or our environment.

## The One and the Many

Our body plays a role in learning about dogs. We learn about individual dogs and also about the class of dogs. There are many dogs, but one class. But in our bodily experience, the two are involved in one another. When we learn about individual dogs, we classify them as dogs in our mind, and thus use the general idea of "dog." Conversely, we learn the general idea of "dog" by experience of individual dogs. The relation of these two has been called the problem of the one and the many. The universal category of "dog" or "dogginess" is "the one." The particulars— many particular dogs—are "the many." How do they relate?

In medieval discussions, there were two parties. The "realists" said that the universal category, "dog" or "dogness" or "canine," was the starting point, and that individual dogs were embodiments of the prior, real idea. By contrast, the "nominalists" said that the particular dogs were the starting point, and that the general category was a convenient kind of grouping together of the particulars under one name, "dog."

Our examination of words suggests that neither of these accounts is completely right. The contrastive-identificational features of words, particularly those related to the referential subsystem, are the focus of the realists. Word meanings are stable, and that stability suggests to the realists that the generality, the totality of general features of meaning, is more ultimate than the particulars. The nominalists are closer to focusing on variation. And some forms of modern structuralism constitute a kind of third alternative that focuses on distributional context: everything boils down to relations. All three of these approaches are partly right. But they become wrong if they insist that they have the whole account. All three aspects are necessary, and all three interlock. All three are ordained by God in their relations to one another.

Real dogs show a unity among different instances. And the word "dog" shows a unity among different instances. The unity goes back to the unity of the plan of *one* God. The diversity among different instances of dog goes back to the diversity in the plan of God for a diversity of dogs. And that diversity in the plan of God has its foundation in a diversity in God himself, in that he is three persons. So creation itself is a reflection of God.

But suppose a person does not want to acknowledge the role of God as the source of unity and diversity. He may claim that the unity of dogginess, the unity in the general idea, is simply a unity that is just "there" without any further explanation. Then how can it come about that the idea of dog ever has a particular embodiment in a particular dog? How do the particulars come about, and how do they come to have a relation to the general idea? There is no explanation, if the "one" is the only ultimate, of how the many come about.

A converse difficulty arises if we start with the particulars. If the particulars are just irreducibly "there," without further explanation, how does it come about that we can unite them under the heading of one general idea? Extreme nominalism might say that the unity is simply a unity imposed by the human mind. But if so, it is ultimately illusory, in comparison with how the things themselves are related to one another. And how can it come about that different human minds could agree on the unities?[9] We need God as creator to form the unity among human beings, humans created in his image.

## God's Name

We can see the challenge in another way if we consider what the Bible indicates about God's name. In modern American culture, personal names often have little meaning. But in ancient Hebrew culture names often had meaning. For example, "The man called his wife's name Eve, because she was the mother of all living" (Gen. 3:20). In Hebrew "Eve" resembles the word for *living*. God says to Abram, "No longer shall your name be called Abram, but your name shall be Abraham, for I have made you the father of a multitude of nations" (Gen. 17:5). "Abraham" means "father of a multitude."

In the same way, the name of God has meaning. For example, after Hagar's experience of encountering the Lord, "She called the *name* of the Lord who spoke to her, 'You are a God of seeing,' for she said, 'Truly here I have seen him who looks after me'" (Gen. 16:13). Hagar spoke a name that expressed something about her previous experience with God. God in speaking to Moses reveals his name as "I am who I am" (Ex. 3:14), in contrast to the earlier name "God Almighty" (Hebrew *El Shaddai*). A name for God reveals something of his character. It is not just an arbitrary sound. So when God says concerning the "angel" (that is, the messenger) of the exodus that "my *name* is in him" (Ex. 23:21), it implies that God's character is in him, that is, that the messenger is himself divine.

---

9. Once again we can see a relation to some themes in postmodernism. Postmodernists, in order to protect the diversity, are tempted just to give up on unity—except that they want everyone to agree about giving up, and in doing so they still cling to a final unity, even if it is a second-order negative unity of giving up on unity concerning first-order human judgments.

In the end, a name for God designates the entirety of God, no matter which particular name or description we start with. The "name" of God is a condensed or summary version of his character, and so implicitly points to the whole of his character. In a crucial exchange with Moses, God indicates that he will make known to Moses his *name* "the LORD":

> Moses said, "Please show me your glory." And he said, "I will make all my goodness pass before you and will proclaim before you my *name* 'The LORD.' And I will be gracious to whom I will be gracious, and will show mercy on whom I will show mercy. But," he said, "you cannot see my face, for man shall not see me and live" (Ex. 33:18–20).

In the sequel, the Lord comes to Moses as follows:

> The LORD descended in the cloud and stood with him there, and proclaimed the *name* of the LORD. The LORD passed before him and proclaimed, "The LORD, the LORD, a God merciful and gracious, slow to anger, and abounding in steadfast love and faithfulness, keeping steadfast love for thousands, forgiving iniquity and transgression and sin, but who will by no means clear the guilty, visiting the iniquity of the fathers on the children and the children's children, to the third and the fourth generation" (Ex. 34:5–7).

The name "LORD" (*YHWH* in Hebrew) is spoken twice, but a description of his character follows. The description is evidently an expansion of what is implicit in the name. The name of God is to be honored, "hallowed," because it represents God who is holy (Matt. 6:9).

Now when the Son becomes incarnate, we are told, "And the Word became flesh and dwelt among us, and we have seen his glory, glory as of the only Son from the Father, full of grace and truth" (John 1:14). The "Word" communicates who God is. He is "full of... truth." He shows the character of God, and this idea is really very close to the function in the Old Testament of the name of God.

In the Old Testament, God put his *name* on the temple of Solomon (1 Kings 8:29). When the Word "dwelt among us," he was the replacement or antitype for the temple of Solomon. It follows that God's name was on him. He revealed God's character in climactic form.

We can draw a similar conclusion from Philippians 2:9–11:

> [9] Therefore God has highly exalted him [Christ] and bestowed on him the name that is above every name, [10] so that at the name of Jesus every knee should bow, in heaven and on earth and under the earth, [11] and every tongue confess that Jesus Christ is Lord, to the glory of God the Father.

In the context of the Old Testament, the supreme name "above every name" would be the name of God, and specifically the name LORD, the tetragrammaton, the name that God gives himself in Exodus 3:13–15:

> Then Moses said to God, "If I come to the people of Israel and say to them, 'The God of your fathers has sent me to you,' and they ask me, 'What is his name?' what shall I say to them?" God said to Moses, "I AM WHO I AM." And he said, "Say this to the people of Israel, 'I AM has sent me to you.'" God also said to Moses, "Say this to the people of Israel, 'The LORD, the God of your fathers, the God of Abraham, the God of Isaac, and the God of Jacob, has sent me to you.' This is *my name* forever, and thus I am to be remembered throughout all generations."

In Hebrew, "I am" (with Hebrew consonants '*HYH*) is closely related in spelling and meaning to the tetragrammaton, *YHWH*, which is translated "LORD." Isaiah sums it up: "I am the LORD; that is my name" (Isa. 42:8). For Jesus to receive the supreme name is to receive the name "Lord," which is the name of God, as Philippians 2:10–11 indicates. The bowing of every knee mentioned in Philippians 2:10 alludes to Isaiah 45:23, where every knee bows to God the LORD. Jesus the Lord is the name of God.

We can also see the relevance of naming to God's Trinitarian character. The Father is God; the Son is God; and the Holy Spirit is God. As God, they have the same character, that is, the same "name." The baptismal language in Matthew 28:18–19 speaks of the "name" in the singular: "Go therefore and make disciples of all nations, baptizing them in the *name* of the Father and of the Son and of the Holy Spirit, . . ." It is true, of course, that in the literal sense we have distinctive names for each person of the Trinity—"Father," "Son," "Spirit." But they share a common character as God. In fact, when Paul speaks of calling "on the name of the Lord" in Romans 10:13, he quotes a verse from Joel 2:32 that has the tetragrammaton, LORD, and applies that holy name to the Son.

We see, then, that the "name" of God or character of God covers all three persons of the Trinity. We have a particular, key example here of the three interlocking aspects: contrastive-identificational features, variation, and context (distribution). The contrastive-identificational features are the attributes of God, such as lordship, being merciful and gracious, and so on. The variation is the variation among the persons of the Trinity. The features of God's character apply to each person. The context is the context of God's works of creation and redemption, about which whole passages speak. And these contexts in their relationships reflect the original, archetypal relationships among the persons of the Trinity. Each person is not only a particular instance of God and of the character of God, but is such *in relation* to the other persons.

The name of God is thus a particularly apt and intense illustration of the interlocking of aspects—of contrast, variation, and context (distribution). But now observe that God's naming of himself is analogous to God's power to name creatures. God gives names to things he created: "God *called* the light Day, and the darkness he *called* Night" (Gen. 1:5). In addition, God's so-called "communicable" attributes can be shared in an analogical way with creatures. Human beings can be "merciful" and "gracious" by analogy with God's being merciful and gracious (Ex. 34:6).

## The Origin of Words

So we see in God himself the logical origin for the words in language. Words do not come out of nowhere. Out of his bounty, his goodness, God has supplied human beings with all the words in each particular language. He has not given words in isolation, but words that are tied to and related to one another in their meanings, their sounds, and their ability to form constructions that communicate rich truths. And it is not a gift that is unrelated to the Giver. The gift reflects the Giver in mysterious ways. Words, with their ability to describe, reflect God who describes himself, as is hinted at in his self-description, "I am who I am." God describes himself to himself in the communication and communion of the persons of the Trinity, in unity and diversity. And then that unity in diversity is reflected in the unity (contrastive-identificational features), diversity (variation), and interconnectedness (distribution) that exist in any one single word.

When you use a word, you rely on God. Each word shows God's eternal power and divine nature (Rom. 1:20). Each word comes to you in a situation that depends on God's creation of you and of your environment. In its coinherence of aspects, each word images the coinherence in God's Trinitarian character.

# From Words to Perspectives

"The kingdom of heaven is like a grain of mustard seed that a man took and sowed in his field. It is the smallest of all seeds, but when it has grown it is larger than all the garden plants and becomes a tree, so that the birds of the air come and make nests in its branches."

—Matthew 13:31–32

Words are relatively stable in meaning. But words also have flexibility. Over a period of centuries, the meaning of certain words can shift around. Today the English word "gossip" has as one common meaning, "rumor or report of an intimate nature."[1] But in Middle English it was "gossib," a word derived from "god" and "sibb." It was used to designate a godparent. Over the centuries, the idea of intimacy carried over into quite new usages and new meanings.

New meanings can be created not only gradually through shifts in usage, but suddenly through a creative metaphor. I have heard people speak about "gossiping the gospel," where they use the word "gossip" in a creative way. They carry over the connotation of casual conversation and intimacy, but drop the negative associations with the idea of revealing personal secrets that should have been kept secret.

## Associations

How is it that we can "stretch" a word's meaning in this creative way? Let us once again see how this creativity goes back to God.

---

1. *Webster's Ninth New Collegiate Dictionary*, meaning 2a.

When we use the field perspective on meaning, we focus on the relation that a particular word like "gossip" has with various aspects of its normal meaning, as well as further associations that it may have with neighboring meanings and contrasting meanings and "stretched" meanings. We can apply a similar field perspective to words used in describing God. A name for God, or an attribute of God such as "gracious," designates his character. As we saw in the previous chapter, it is a kind of condensation or summary of one aspect of his character. But his character is a whole. God is righteous and gracious and loving and holy and all-powerful. When any name is used to designate God, it designates the God who has all these characteristics.

Thus any one name for God does two things simultaneously. It singles out or focuses on some one characteristic of God, or a small number of related characteristics. And, second, it designates God and *all* that he is, and so invites us to associate with it all the other things that we know about God. A name is like one *perspective* on God.[2]

We stretch or alter what we may normally associate with the meaning "gracious" as applied to human beings when we apply the word to God, in order to bring this one aspect into harmony with everything else that we know about God. God's graciousness is a holy, righteous, all-powerful graciousness. And his righteousness is a gracious, holy, all-powerful righteousness. The word "gracious" is stretched. At the same time, what we already know about God from other verses of the Bible may be deepened when we look at those verses again through the "window" of the "perspective" of graciousness. We ask how those verses show God's graciousness, and how they are consistent with it, and asking such questions deepens our knowledge of those verses.

We can find extensive illustrations of how knowledge can grow by using multiple perspectives. John Frame's books *Perspectives on the Word of God* and *The Doctrine of the Christian Life* illustrate how each of three perspectives—the normative, situational, and existential perspectives—can contribute to our understanding of biblical ethics. Rightly understood, the three supplement and deepen one another. The same holds in principle when we use words like "gracious," "holy," and "righteous" to designate different aspects ("perspectives") on the character of God.

---

2. For further discussion of perspectives, see Vern S. Poythress, *Symphonic Theology: The Validity of Multiple Perspectives in Theology* (Grand Rapids, MI: Zondervan, 1987; reprinted, Phillipsburg, NJ: Presbyterian & Reformed, 2001); John M. Frame, *Perspectives on the Word of God: An Introduction to Christian Ethics* (Phillipsburg, NJ: Presbyterian & Reformed, 1990); Frame, *The Doctrine of the Knowledge of God* (Phillipsburg, NJ: Presbyterian & Reformed, 1987); and other books by John M. Frame.

## Words in General as Perspectives

If a name for God can be used as a perspective on God, can we do the same with words that are not names for God? Take the word "gossip." Can that word's meaning be expanded into a perspective on life? Yes, it can. We start with more or less the literal meaning. The dictionary gives us the definition, "rumor or report of an intimate nature." But intimacy may be a matter of degree. I reveal *something* about myself by everything I say. God's communication includes the aspect of God's presence, and expresses who he is. By analogy, so does communication from a human being. So every human communication is "intimate" in that sense. So "gossip" has expanded into a perspective on all human communication. We say, provocatively, that all human communication is gossip, and we invite readers to adjust to a new, stretched meaning of "gossip." Of course, we have to remove the negative connotations—that gossip is irresponsible revelation of secrets.

Then we can go further by including divine communication. That is even more easily seen to be intimate. If it will not suffice to say that all communication from God *to us* is "intimate," surely the intimate communication among the persons of the Trinity is the final foundation for external communication to us. And so the speech of God is all included when we see that God's speech to us is backed up by internal speech within God.

We can also make one further move, namely, to note that speaking is a perspective on everything God does.[3] The activities of God can be expounded in more than one way, that is, from multiple perspectives that are still faithful to who he is. One of those perspectives is the perspective of speaking, as we see from Hebrews 1:3: "he [the Son] upholds the universe by the *word* of his power." The entire course of God's sustaining activity in providence is here declared to be an operation of his "word," his speech. Thus, we have obtained a verbal perspective on absolutely everything that happens.

## Words and Relations

Making a word into a perspective on everything may be easier with some words than with others. But the potential is there with any word as a starting point, because words exist in *relationships*, as the field perspective emphasizes. Following the relationships out from one point to another connects us with a never-ending web of relationships, and the relationships end up by including everything.

We can rephrase this phenomenon by thinking in terms of the mind of God. The relationships that we see are relationships that we were not the first to create. God is the source for and controller of all relationships. He knows all the relationships in his own mind, as part of his plan for the entirety of history. Our

---

3. I owe this insight to oral lectures by John Frame, heard decades ago.

own knowledge is a partial image of his knowledge. So in using a word as a starting point for exploring relationships, we are tracing in our minds some of the
patterns that exist first of all in God's mind. God's plan is harmonious and coherent, and so all the relationships hold together; everything is genuinely related
to everything else.

Start with the word "dog." What is a dog? We know about dogs in the context
of other animals and in the context of the activities of dogs that show their
dogginess, and in the context of interactions between humans and dogs. Those
contexts represent a host of *relations*. Thinking about dogs leads to thinking
about the creation order, with its kinds of animals. And then there is man in his
relation of dominion to the animals, which is the foundation for the possibility of domesticating dogs and breeding them, which in turn leads to the many
varieties of dogs. And there is the more dynamic context of doggy activities.
Many of these activities—eating, sleeping, chasing, watching, listening—show
analogical similarities to purposes and activities in other higher animals and
to man, and the analogies enable us further to understand what dogs are like
in the kinds of behavior that we expect. The behavior of dogs is analogically
related to human behavior; human behavior in turn is analogically related to
divine action. Hence dogs in some respects reflect God himself. Dogs have
life because God has given them life. And the life that they have is analogically related to divine life. And divine life empowers the entire universe in its
entire course. So the life of a dog is analogically related to the dynamicity of
the entire universe.

Why can a word become the starting point for a perspective on the whole? It is
partly because within the plan of God everything is *related* to everything else. But
perhaps another account can be given. We saw in the previous chapter that God's
name was a special case for understanding words. The name of God is climactically revealed in Christ, who is the Word of God according to John 1:1–3. The
character of God is summed up in Christ. Christ is in this sense a "perspective" on
the whole of God; but the word "perspective" is too weak, since he is himself God.
And the second person of the Trinity, as the Word of God, is also the archetype
for language. So do all words enjoy a structure that is analogically related to the
one archetypal Word? If so, the use of any word as a perspective is an analogical
image of the name of God, who is the Word. The flexibility of words in this way
reflects the original dynamicity of the Word who reveals the Father. "No one has
ever seen God; the only God, who is at the Father's side, he has made him known"
(John 1:18).

When you use a word metaphorically, you are relying on God, who holds
together literal meanings and their metaphorical uses.

## Can We Reduce All Meaning to Literal Meaning?

We can often distinguish literal and metaphorical uses of language. "My dog can roll over" is literal. "Bill leads a dog's life" is metaphorical. One strand of the rich tradition of discussions of metaphor sees metaphor as an "improper" language, for which we can find a literal substitute. Yes, we can often roughly paraphrase a metaphorical statement. But our reflections concerning metaphor and perspectives suggest that reality is richer. Language in its literal and metaphorical capabilities derives from God, who is the infinite source of both the literal and the metaphorical and their relation to one another. In mysterious ways the relation is grounded in the very being of God, in the relation of the Father to the Son through the Spirit. We cannot neatly and perfectly separate out the literal and the metaphorical within language, any more than human thinking can perfectly comprehend the relation of the Son to the Father.

The presence of the Word before the Father is not only the source of human metaphorical language; it is the source of the world. God created the world through his Word. We therefore expect that the world itself is shot through with metaphor.[4] Created things have meaning. And the meanings are analogically related to one another. Not just the word "dog," but dogs themselves are a display of one reflection of the richness of God's divine life. Created dogs are in some sense a metaphor already, according to God's divine purpose.[5]

The cherubim praise God before his throne:

> And around the throne, on each side of the throne, are four living creatures, full of eyes in front and behind: the first living creature like a lion, the second living creature like an ox, the third living creature with the face of a man, and the fourth living creature like an eagle in flight. And the four living creatures, each of them with six wings, are full of eyes all around and within, and day and night they never cease to say,
>
> > "Holy, holy, holy is the Lord God Almighty,
> > who was and is and is to come!" (Rev. 4:6–8).

The cherubim as angelic creatures reflect the splendor and glory of God. They are in turn a model for lions, and oxen, and human beings, and eagles, who reflect the glory of the cherubim. They are also a model for the praise that "every creature" is destined to offer:

---

4. On metaphor in the created world, see Vern S. Poythress, "Science as Allegory," *Journal of the American Scientific Affiliation* 35/2 (1983): 65–71.

5. The metaphorical potential of dogs is dramatically exploited in Francis Thompson's poem "The Hound of Heaven," which compares God's pursuit of the author to tireless pursuit by a hound.

And I heard *every creature* in heaven and on earth and under the earth and in the sea, and all that is in them, saying, "To him who sits on the throne and to the Lamb be blessing and honor and glory and might forever and ever!" And the four living creatures said, "Amen!" and the elders fell down and worshiped (Rev. 5:13–14).

In this picture, there is no level of "pure" literalism to which to descend. Each creature is distinct, but in his very distinctiveness (particularity) enjoys designed relations and rich analogies to the rest of creation and to God himself. Metaphor is a lingual expression of reality, which reflects the metaphorical relations in the mind of God.

# PART 6

# Application

# Truth as a Perspective

"I am the way, and the truth, and the life.
No one comes to the Father except through me."
—John 14:6

We may illustrate the function of perspectives by using truth as a perspective on God's gifts to us.

## Trinitarian Foundations of Truth

Truth has its origin in God. The Father, the Son, and the Holy Spirit know all truth in their mutual knowledge of one another:

> All things have been handed over to me by my Father, and no one knows the Son except the Father, and no one knows the Father except the Son and anyone to whom the Son chooses to reveal him (Matt. 11:27).

The Son is also closely related to truth when he is identified with the wisdom of God:

> ... Christ, in whom are hidden all the treasures of *wisdom* and knowledge (Col. 2:2–3).

And because of him [God] you are in Christ Jesus, who became to us *wisdom* from God, righteousness and sanctification and redemption (1 Cor. 1:30).

The Son is also described as the Word of God (John 1:1; Rev. 19:13). Hence he is the source for the particular words that God speaks to convey truth to us.

Finally, Jesus explicitly claims to be the truth. He says, "I am the way, and *the truth*, and the life. No one comes to the Father except through me" (John 14:6). Jesus makes this claim in a context where he is talking about being the way of redemption, by whom we may know the Father and be reconciled to God after our preceding alienation. But this redemptive role of Jesus is always based on who Jesus has always been as the Word who "was with God, and [who] was God" (John 1:1).

It is appropriate to see the Son, the Word, the second person of the Trinity, as the final, archetypal Truth of God. The truth that we receive comes to us through him. The principle, "No one comes to the Father except through me," is a principle that applies to whatever truth we know, not merely to redemptive truth, because all truth resides first of all in God. And we as creatures have access to the mind of the Father only through the Word who is God.


## Truth Displayed

We can then trace out stages in the display of truth. The Word, the second person of the Trinity, is the archetypal Truth, the Truth of the Father's mind. Jesus as incarnate is the truth. He is still the Word in his incarnation. When incarnate, he does not cease to be God, but continues to be God. In addition, he takes on human nature. "And the Word became flesh [human] and dwelt among us" (John 1:14). John 1:14 continues, "and we have seen his glory, glory as of the only Son from the Father, full of grace and *truth*."

The Son in his incarnation is the perfect image of the Father and accurately displays the Father and his glory. In that accurate imaging of the Father, he also displays full *truth*. This reality agrees with Jesus' later statement in John 14:6, "I am the way, and the *truth*." Jesus displays the truth of the Father not only in his very being but also in his whole life, both words and deeds. For example, the healing of the blind man in John 9, as well as the words that Jesus says about the healing, reveal that Jesus is the light of the world (John 9:5; 8:12), and light and truth are closely related. "The true light, which enlightens everyone, was coming into the world" (John 1:9). When the light comes, namely, Jesus as the incarnate word, he reveals the glory, that is, the light, of the Father, in his fullness of truth (John 1:14).

Hence Jesus' words express truth. Note the close relation between the name, that is, the character of God, the words that the Father has given, the words that Jesus gives, and the fellowship between Father and Son:

I have manifested your *name* to the people whom *you gave me* out of the world. Yours they were, and you gave them to me, and they have kept your *word*. Now they know that everything that *you have given me* is from you. For I have given them the *words* that *you gave me*, and they have received *them* and have come to know in *truth* that I came from you; and they have believed that *you sent me* ( John 17:6–8).

In addition, we learn that the Spirit, sent from Christ, has a role in the truth. The Spirit is given preeminently to the Son, that he may be the means of revelation of the Father: "For he [the Son] whom God has sent utters the *words* of God, for he [God the Father] gives the Spirit without measure. The Father loves the Son and has given all things into his hand" ( John 3:34–35). The Son in turn sends the Spirit, in order that the disciples may receive the truth:

> And I will ask the Father, and he will give you another Helper, to be with you forever, even the Spirit of *truth*, whom the world cannot receive, because it neither sees him nor knows him ( John 14:16–17).

> But the Helper, the Holy Spirit, whom the Father will send in my name, he will teach you all things and bring to your remembrance all that I have said to you ( John 14:26).

> When the Spirit of *truth* comes, he will guide you into all the *truth*, for he will not speak on his own authority, but whatever he hears he will speak, and he will declare to you the things that are to come. He will glorify me, for he will take what is mine and declare it to you. All that the Father has is mine; therefore I said that he will take what is mine and declare it to you ( John 16:13–15).

## The Bible as True

Jesus' words, words from the Father, endorse the truth of God's word as a whole: "Sanctify them in the *truth*; your word is *truth*" ( John 17:17). Jesus indicates also that the Old Testament is the word of God (Matt. 19:4–5; 5:17–20; John 10:35) and submits to the necessity of what it prophesies (Matt. 26:54).

We can see also that the Old Testament comes into being in a way that foreshadows and anticipates Jesus' work. Early in history God spoke to Adam and Eve, and later to Cain, to Noah, to Abraham (Gen. 3:14–19; 4:6, 9, 10–12, 15; 6:13–21; 12:1–3; 13:14–17). Some of his speech may have been written down. But the written canon of the Bible as we now have it began to come into being with the Ten Commandments in written form (Deut. 5:22). There were several stages. First, the Lord spoke to Israel in an audible voice from the top of Mount Sinai (Ex. 20:1, 18–21; Deut. 5:4–5, 22). Second, he wrote the Commandments on tablets, "written with the finger of God" (Deut. 5:22; Ex. 31:18). Moses was involved as a mediating figure even at this early point, as can be seen in that he went up and down the mountain (Ex. 19:21–25; 20:18–21). Then, at the request of the people, God appointed Moses as one who would deliver God's words to the people (Ex. 20:18–21; Deut. 5:24–33). Moses as a mediator of God's word prefigured Christ as the final mediator (1 Tim. 2:5).

The Ten Commandments were deposited in the ark of the covenant (Ex. 25:21; 40:20). Their position in the ark indicated their central role as a covenant document in the covenantal relation between God and Israel. That document deposited in the ark constituted the nucleus of the canon as we now know it.

Later, near the end of his life, Moses added other material to the initial deposit:

When Moses had finished writing the words of this law in a book to the very end, Moses commanded the Levites who carried the ark of the covenant of the LORD, "Take this Book of the Law and put it by the side of the ark of the covenant of the LORD your God, that it may be there for a witness against you" (Deut. 31:24–26).

The later prophets who brought the word of God to the people were seen as following in the pattern of Moses:

The LORD your God will raise up for you a prophet *like me* from among you, from your brothers—it is to him you shall listen—just as you desired of the LORD your God at Horeb [Mt. Sinai] on the day of the assembly, when you said, "Let me not hear again the voice of the LORD my God or see this great fire any more, lest I die." And the LORD said to me, "They are right in what they have spoken. I will raise up for them a prophet *like you* from among their brothers. And I will put my words in his mouth, and he shall speak to them all that I command him. And whoever will not listen to my words that he shall speak in my name, I myself will require it of him" (Deut. 18:15–19).

Since Moses as a mediator prefigures Christ, so do the later prophets. Hence the whole Old Testament comes as the written covenantal word in a manner that prefigures Christ.

At Sinai Christ as the Word speaks from heaven, and enlists Moses as his human channel. The human channel does not diminish the divine authority of the speech, nor obscure the binding character of its claims. The same is true with the prophets ("whoever will not listen to my words, . . . I myself will require it of him" [Deut. 18:19]). The truth, which is the Word, arrives in writing as written truth.

The whole Bible is the word of God, spoken by the Father in the Son, who is the Word, by the power of the Spirit.[1] And so the Bible expresses the truth

---

1. See Benjamin B. Warfield, *The Inspiration and Authority of the Bible* (reprint; Philadelphia: Presbyterian & Reformed, 1967).

that the Son has expressed in his life, and the truth that the Son expresses is in harmony with who he is, namely, the Word and wisdom and truth of God. Every individual truth expressed or implied in each individual verse of Scripture is truth expressing God's mind, in relation to all other truths in God's mind. Each truth is a perspective on Truth. Each truth shines with "his glory, glory as of the only Son from the Father, full of grace and truth" (John 1:14).

## Contrast, Variation, and Context (Distribution) in Truth

There is unity in all truth, deriving from the one Son, the only Son from the Father (John 1:14). There is also diversity in truth. Each truth in each verse has its own texture and its own contrastive-identificational features.[2] Each truth is a particular truth, one instance of the total truth in God. Such diversity reflects the richness of the diversity of the truths in God's mind, which in turn reflects the diversity of the being of God in his three persons.

Such individual truths are not isolated. They are all *distributed* in contexts in the plan of God. We need to remind ourselves that God speaks in his lordship, which involves meaning, control, and presence. God himself is present in each truth, God in his infinity and in the depth of his incomprehensibility. God is present in the clarity of his meaning, and God is present to control and mold our minds, our spirits, and our actions through the Holy Spirit, who is the Spirit of Jesus the Christ, who is the supreme name of God.

Far, then, from depreciating the details of the individual verses of the Bible, a Trinitarian understanding of truth affirms the meticulous significance of every detail, precisely because it manifests the God who speaks.

## Truth in General Revelation

Truth from God comes not only in the written words of God in the Bible, but through the world that God made.

> For what can be known about God is plain to them [unbelievers], because God has shown it to them. For his invisible attributes, namely, his eternal power and divine nature, have been clearly perceived, ever since the creation of the world, in the things that have been made. So they are without excuse (Rom. 1:19–20).

God governs all things "by the word of his power" (Heb. 1:3). In this sense, what God says includes not only the written words in the Bible but the words of power by which God rules the universe. These words also are truthful words. And when human beings observe the created world, they perceive God's attributes

---

2. See chapter 19.

and know God. They have truth about God, because God's word of power in its truthfulness displays truth for them.[3]

We may infer that even among unbelievers there is a general work of the Holy Spirit giving knowledge (Job 32:8).

## An Example of Truth

Consider a particular example. "Bring the cloak that I left with Carpus at Troas" (2 Tim. 4:13).[4] Paul left the cloak there with Carpus. That is a truth. It is a truth

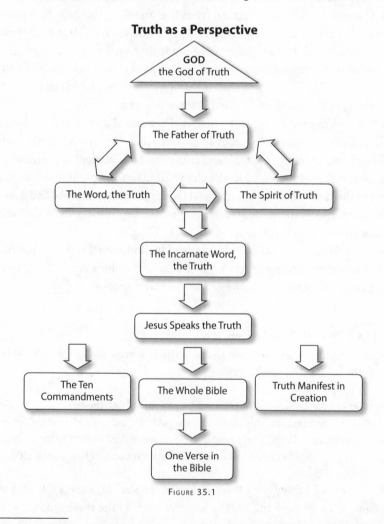

**Truth as a Perspective**

FIGURE 35.1

---

3. See Cornelius Van Til, *Introduction to Systematic Theology* (Phillipsburg, NJ: Presbyterian & Reformed, 1974), especially 62–109 concerning general revelation.

4. Second Timothy 4:13 is a command or request. We consider some of the diversity exhibited by command, assertion, question, and other speech acts in appendix H.

that God has expressed for us to meditate on for the whole history of the church (see fig. 35.1 for how it fits into a larger picture). Here we can only say a few things, as a tentative sample of the outskirts of God's ways.

God caused the cloak to be left not just anywhere, but with Carpus at Troas, in order that God's glory might be manifested. The leaving of that cloak took place with God as primary cause. God worked in concurrence with the secondary causality of Paul and of Timothy. And it is part of God's plan that God's glory might be seen in the manifestation of God's wisdom in the midst of human weakness (1 Cor. 1:18–31; 2 Cor. 12:9). God shows the ordinariness of Paul, God's human instrument. Perhaps Paul was cold in a Roman prison. God shows his care by giving a means by which Paul can get his cloak back. The verse is there because God wanted to show us his care for Paul, and the meticulousness with which he orders the circumstances and the people like Carpus and Timothy, not only for blessing Carpus and Timothy, but for blessing Paul and us. God manifests his truth in the detail of human life, and in the detail that Carpus's life intersected Paul's at a particular point and in a particular way.

God caused the words to be written, in order that we might rejoice in this detail of his wise governance of the galaxies and the molecules and the makings of cloaks and the uncertainties of human possessions of clothing. God spoke his word about a simple cloak, through the Word by whom he rules the world, and through whom he redeemed Paul and Timothy to be his precious children. Those children he cares for by watching out about cloaks through the wisdom of the eternal Word. How could we believe otherwise, unless we are slow to learn, and slow to see his glory?

# Living in the Truth

Speaking the truth in love,
we are to grow up in every way into him who is the head, into Christ.
—Ephesians 4:15

How extensively do we meet with meanings? In all our discussion about language we have been dealing with meanings. But does meaning extend beyond our human use of language?

## Meanings in the World

In a broad sense, meaning belongs to everything that God created. Words and sentences and paragraphs have meaning in a narrower, personal sense, when we use them in conversation in order to achieve human purposes. But God has his divine purposes, not only in the large-scale history of the world but in the little things as well. Paul's cloak. This flower. This bug. This fingernail. This molecule. This instance of the letter "d." Each has meaning within the divine plan.

The world had meaning even before human beings came into it. God started naming things even before he created man. And there was meaning, as ordained according to God's plan, even before he made names explicit. Meaning is everywhere. Meaning is in God's mind. And it is articulate meaning, in accord with the Word, the Logos, the second person of the Trinity. Human thought and human expression never create meanings out of nowhere. They are reflective of divine meanings. God knows every human thought of every human being beforehand:

> You know when I sit down and when I rise up;
>    you discern my thoughts from afar.
> You search out my path and my lying down
>    and are acquainted with all my ways.
> Even before a word is on my tongue,
>    behold, O LORD, you know it altogether (Ps. 139:2–4).

## Attributes of Lordship

Let us remember the three attributes or perspectives on lordship: meaning, control, and presence. God is the Lord. As an attribute of his lordship, he assigns the meaning or significance of everything. Meanings belong even to those things that human beings may never notice: a single ribosome within a single particular cell in your toe; or a peculiarity in one human being's pronunciation as he is recovering from a shot of novocaine and does not yet have full control of motions with his lips and tongue. God also assigns meanings to those things that human beings *do* often notice, such as our own communicative utterances.

Second, God controls the meanings. He controls everything in every language and culture throughout the world. His control is what imparts power to *our human control*, and gives significance and meaning to our human significances.

Third, God is present in his wisdom and truth in the midst of human meanings and human purposes and human attempts at control. He confronts us not only with his goodness and his name, but with his holiness and his requirement of truthfulness and moral responsibility on our part. Language is not something that we are to use as we please, independent of all moral standards. If human beings tried consistently to abandon moral standards with respect to language, no one could be trusted, and communication would be full of failures as well as treacheries. God makes the world of communication livable. But, short of completely reforming and purifying human beings as he will do in the consummation, he rules over a world that still contains lies and treacheries in human language use.

## Use of Language

Concerning this world we have the privilege of speaking. We use language to draw out and make manifest meanings that God has already ordained. We depend on meanings all the time, both the meanings in the words and linguistic constructions, the meanings in the world about which we speak, and even the meanings of imaginary worlds. Imaginary worlds represent something of the creativity of man, which reflects the creativity of God. We can imagine things that do not exist, in imitation of God's comprehension of possibilities that have never come about. God's wisdom exceeds what he has actually created.

And so at every point in language we depend on God. We depend on him even when we are not aware of it. Our duty to God is not to become perfectly aware of everything, which would be impossible anyway. Our duty is to love the Lord our God with all our heart, soul, strength, and mind, and our neighbor as ourselves (Matt. 22:37–40). Love, not knowledge, is our prime duty. But how shall those be reformed who have rebelled against God and turned in hatred against him? We must not pretend that we are not sick with sin and rebellion. We must come to Christ, the source of our redemption, and live from his meaning, control, and presence. We must live in his truth (John 14:6), being sanctified by his word (John 17:17). We must walk in his truth, and speak the truth (2 John 4; 3 John 3–4; Eph. 4:25).

We may express our gratitude to God for the gift of language, not only by praising him when we think of its marvels, but by serving him, even when we are not thinking of those marvels.


## Situations with Non-Christians

We may also grow in our appreciation of the struggle that non-Christians have. They live in God's world, and according to Romans 1:18–25 they know God, in his eternal power and divine nature (1:20). God is present to them in their every breath and every use of language. And that is not pleasant, because they do not want him there.

Language and thought are closely linked. The structures of language that we have explored carry over in many ways into the structures of thought. Human *thinking*, as well as language, depends on God, on his meaning, control, and presence. When we think, "The boy hit the ball," our thinking has the stamp of God's Trinitarian character reflected in it in a host of ways. Non-Christians cannot get God's presence out of their minds. That is something different from the question of whether they can cease consciously to think about God. Clearly they can. But to abolish God's presence would be to abolish thought itself, including every assertion, every question, every doubt, every inference, every category, every word.

Some people have tried to do it. Eastern forms of meditation often involve the practice of emptying the mind, and trying to bring thought to an end. The goal is to be one with the universe, or to experience union with "the All," that is, with a god who is conceived pantheistically. Allegedly, such a union dissolves the restlessness of the human mind, in order to advance toward the goal of final peace. The Buddhists want Nirvana, which is the dissolution of the mind and the person into the cosmic "All."

Yes, the mind is restless. The mind using language is restless. "Our hearts are restless till they find their rest in You."[1] What we need is fellowship with God and reconciliation with God, not Nirvana. The paradox of Eastern mysticism is that it seeks by heroic mental, spiritual, and bodily efforts to arrive at a god, when all along God, the true God, is already there. He is there, right in the structures of language and thought. You do not have to cease to think and you do not have to empty out language to get there. God is already there with language in its fullness, language in its richness. Fill your mind with him, rather than empty it. In fact, emptying it is retreat from God into one more idolatry, where a person pretends that the self is identical with the One, identical with a god.

Non-Christians do not see how to receive God, this God who is closer than thought itself. In fact, no one on his own initiative does. We are rebels. "No one can come to me unless the Father who sent me draws him" (John 6:44). God must give light, through his Son (John 8:12; 9:5). And then, through casting off the darkness and fog in our minds, we may begin to understand how much God was present to us all along, in language as well as other ways. He was present even while we rebelled and hated and fled.

---

1. Updated language, from St. Augustine, *The Confessions of St. Augustin*, 1.1.1, in Philip Schaff, ed., *A Select Library of the Nicene and Post-Nicene Fathers of the Christian Church* (Grand Rapids, MI: Eerdmans, 1979), 1:45.

# Interaction with Other
# Approaches to Language

# Modernism and Postmodernism

My son, be attentive to my words;
incline your ear to my sayings.
Let them not escape from your sight;
keep them within your heart.
For they are life to those who find them,
and healing to all their flesh.
Keep your heart with all vigilance,
for from it flow the springs of life.
Put away from you crooked speech,
and put devious talk far from you.

—Proverbs 4:20–24

My son, if sinners entice you,
do not consent.

—Proverbs 1:10

I n this and the following appendices we consider some of the contributions and limitations in various modern approaches to language.

We begin by looking at some of the influences of modern cultures. All of our modern approaches to language come to us within a cultural environment. The environment does have an influence. It may help to make some approaches seem plausible and natural, while others may seem strange.

In my own approach, I have regularly come back to talking about God, and I have paid attention to instruction about God from the Bible. But our own age is full of doubts about what I am doing. Is it really so? Or am I just biased by my religious beliefs?

The skepticism is quite understandable. Many of us have grown up and live in modern cultures within which claims about God seem weird. We have gone to schools and listened to information sources that have encouraged us to think in certain ways. It has come to seem strange to introduce God at all into a discussion about language. Courses in language, courses in English grammar, courses in foreign languages, and courses in linguistics are typically free of any such discussion. God is irrelevant, it seems. So it seems, but is this seeming itself an illusion?

Human experience is a complex thing, and it is complex to try to grasp how we have come to be who we are, and to think the way we think, and to talk the way we talk. To a certain extent, each of us has his own personal story, which does not match anyone else's. So, for the sake of simplicity I will start with myself. Be patient, please, because I hope in the end to make a broader point.


## My Story

Beginning in 1951, from kindergarten through high school, I went to an American public school. No one had to give an elaborate explanation or justification for school. It was obvious to us as students that the main purpose of school was to impart knowledge, intellectual skills, and some practical skills.

In my experience, the teachers were kind and dedicated and competent. I trusted them. They had a well-defined body of knowledge and skill to impart, and my task was to absorb it.

As I now recognize in looking back, this was a form of "modernism." "Modernism" may have more than one meaning. But in my case it included a basic optimism about human ability to know the truth, and about the progressive accumulation of knowledge over the last few centuries. The knowledge so accumulated, through the powers of reason and experience, was regarded for the most part as unproblematic. We did not worry about the influence of different cultures or different worldviews. Everyone from whatever background was assumed to be capable of sharing in the common pool of knowledge. The knowledge included not only mathematics and the sciences but the humanities. Classes in English and in foreign languages shared this approach. Knowledge of language came as part of the common pool of knowledge.

We did not talk about God in class. Everyone knew that this was partly because we were in a public school in the United States. Over the years, the interpretation of the U.S. Constitution made talking about God a point of tension. Moreover, we knew that people disagreed about God. Bringing up the subject might just produce an argument, without anyone being able to convince anyone else.

As a result, without really wanting to, the school tended to communicate the message that issues about religion were either matters of mere opinion, or were devoid of evidence that could lead to a rational conclusion. What the school taught was what counted as knowledge. Areas about which it did not teach were left dubious or nebulous. And it was supremely easy to believe that, even if truth were to be found somehow in the area of religion, it was irrelevant to the core of knowledge with which we occupied ourselves day after day.

And now I should circle back to an earlier point in time. I did hear about God from another source. My parents went to a church where the Bible was taught, and from an early age I learned about God and about the coming of Jesus Christ into the world to save us from our rebellion against God. When I was nine years old, I recognized my need for Christ, because I saw that I along with everyone else had been a rebel against God. I was convinced that Christ was alive and that he offered me salvation and fellowship with him. I made a public commitment to Christ at a church camp. I became a follower of Christ from that time onward—or perhaps even earlier. I grew in knowing Christ from that time onward.

For my college education I went to Caltech. Richard P. Feynman, Nobel laureate in physics, was a famous and colorful figure on campus. In freshman and sophomore physics we studied Feynman's physics textbook. I thought that his textbook was wonderful, but I also knew that Feynman was well known on campus as an advocate of agnosticism. On the side I read literature that was intended to develop the Christian thinking of college students, and I began to see more potential areas of tension between what the Bible taught and the mind-set of my environment. The typical Caltech student was agnostic or atheistic, and thoroughly modernist. I was a minority, and I did not think like everyone else.

I went to Harvard University for doctoral work in mathematics. At the time (1966–1970) Harvard at the graduate level was just as modernist as Caltech. Again I was a minority, and my sense of the distance between me and the surrounding culture continued to deepen. I need not go into details, but my reading from Abraham Kuyper, Herman Dooyeweerd, Cornelius Van Til, Hendrik van Riessen, D. H. Th. Vollenhoven, and Hendrik G. Stoker convinced me that the foundations of modernism rested on sand. I still appreciated the things that I was learning in my modernist environment. But I did not agree with the foundational assumptions—the worldview—that came along with that environment.

That time, during the latter part of the 1960s, was also the time of the hippie counterculture, and of growing opposition to the Vietnam War. The antiwar movement eventually spilled over into a political blowup at Harvard, when the antiwar activists took over an administration building. I will not go into that story, except to say that it was a harbinger of wider cultural changes in the coming decades.

In the 1990s my story repeated itself through my children, but in a different key. I was now married, with two boys going to public school.[1] In our district the public school teachers, with few exceptions, were kind, dedicated, and competent, as they had been

---

1. Advocates of home schooling and Christian schooling might well ask why my boys went to public school with all its problems. It is a long story. From the standpoint of my principles, I think that ideally a different kind of schooling would be better (see Vern S. Poythress, *Redeeming Science: A God-Centered Approach* [Wheaton, IL: Crossway, 2006], 66–67), but the realities of various situations do not always conform to the ideal. In fact my wife and I used a combination of resources—Christian schooling up through grade 4, and supplemental homeschooling in the summer, and many dinner table conversations about the ideas being circulated in public school.

in my generation. They taught mathematics and science as bodies of knowledge. They were, in that respect, "modernist" about mathematics and science. But in humanities there was a noteworthy shift, in a "postmodernist" direction.

What do I mean by postmodernism? Postmodernism is a diverse movement, with many strands. I cannot hope to cover them all. So I will simplify, and choose one strand, what might be called "relativist postmodernism."[2]

At my boys' school the emphasis in the humanities was no longer on mastering a body of knowledge but on developing your own ideas in interaction with a variety of other people's ideas. The focus was more on the process than on the conclusions.

And hovering over it all was an incessant drumbeat for "tolerance." What did "tolerance" mean? Classes paid much attention to cultural variations. People in different cultures had different ideas and practices, and students were supposed to learn to respect the differences. Did tolerance merely mean respecting harmless variations in culture, as when the Chinese eat with chopsticks and Americans with a fork? Did it mean dispensing with the insidious pride that *assumed* that our own native culture was necessarily superior at every point to all other cultures? Did it mean that we would be willing to revise our own ideas if we learned something that showed we were mistaken at a particular point, or that further advanced our insight? Did it mean respecting other human beings as human, even when their ideas were erroneous or their morals were corrupt?

Or, more questionably, did it mean agreeing that everyone's ideas about religion and morality were equally *valid*? And if the last was meant, ought we to draw the natural conclusion that such ideas are merely social preferences, and have nothing to do with the truth? Would we then be left with only one remaining moral principle, the principle of tolerance itself? And would this one principle show its true power by being the standard by which we condemn any deviation from its dictates?

Would "tolerance" also turn out to be a substitute religion? Does it command our ultimate allegiance (because it is the one remaining principle)? Does it have its own proposal for "salvation," namely, that the inculcation and practice of tolerance is *the* great way by which we will achieve peace among human beings?

In the school system no one consciously colluded to set up a new religion. The teachers did not consciously propagandize the students. Many of them were thinking about racial prejudice, or prejudice against foreigners, or the dangers of pushing around marginalized

---

I am here telling only the most simplified form of the story, in order to make a point about the influence of enculturation.

2. A good introduction to postmodernism can be found in Heath White, *Postmodernism 101: A First Course for the Curious Christian* (Grand Rapids, MI: Brazos, 2006). The suggested follow-up readings at the back of the book offer a good continuation.

I must ask readers with different perceptions of postmodernism to bear with me. I am aware also that advocates of some varieties of relativist postmodernism might dispute the aptness of the term "relativist," because that term belongs to the older thinking of absolutism that they want to redescribe (see, e.g., Richard Rorty, *Contingency, Irony, and Solidarity* [Cambridge: Cambridge University Press, 1989], 75) . In that case, maybe "postmodern contextualism" would be better. My references to postmodernism earlier in this book also have in mind primarily this strand of postmodernism.

people. Or they were thinking about the cruelties that have been committed in past centuries by Europeans motivated by religious zeal. In other words, the teachers were trying to attack real moral failures. As they saw it, they promoted only what was obviously true and helpful for the students and for the future of society.

But in the process the school as a whole fell into a trap. It ended up promoting only one moral value, namely, tolerance. Or at least that was the tendency of the school's practice.[3] The school could not promote other moral values without running into the problem of disagreements over morality. The primary value, the value of tolerance, prescribed that the school teach tolerance about disagreements over morality, and that meant not promoting any particular morality (except, of course, tolerance itself). That left tolerance as the only moral value with any substance. Every other value was demoted and relativized in relation to it. Many students may easily have taken away the message that morality was indeed relative, and that they could make up their own moral standards (see chart A.1 for the contrast between this view and modernism).

| | Modernism | Postmodernism |
|---|---|---|
| *science* | science yields truth | science yields truth (or, more radically, science is social opinion of the scientific guild) |
| *the humanities* | the humanities contain fixed truths | the humanities process opinion |
| *human nature* | humanity the same | humanity diverse |
| *source of knowledge* | reason and experience | socialization |
| *morals* | assumed to be fixed by human nature | variable by society |
| *religion* | not discussed in grade school | variable by society and by individual choice |

CHART A.1

To put it another way, the students took away from the discussion more than the teachers intended. The teachers did not really believe in moral relativism themselves, and they did not directly attack any particular moral stand. (Such an attack, after all, would have been out of step with the principle of tolerance.) Like many postmodernists, the teachers sought agreement on social issues through continuing discussion. They hoped that discussion—the process—would promote a gradual societal evolution of morality. This corporate morality would be what "we" together (in our admittedly limited social and geographical setting) see as appropriate in our society. The high school students who were not completely bored were, I think, willing to begin participating in such discussion.

---

3. The school promoted the avoidance of illegal drugs and the avoidance of practices that run a high risk of transmitting sexual diseases. But even there, the motivation that it gave was not really moral, but pragmatic: "Avoid this because that way you will have a more comfortable life in the long run." The school also from time to time mentioned environmental conservation, but again the ultimate motivation would have been pragmatic: not the comfort of the individual, in this case, but the comfort of the society as a whole.

But they knew that they also had a more private side to their lives. They knew that in any particular area where they had strong desires, they could freely withhold consenting to others' opinions, or could secretly make themselves an exception. Nothing was really binding, and in that sense the whole was tainted with relativism.

So now, how could teachers motivate students who were selfish and who thought they were free to make up their own morality? Particularly at the high school level, how could teachers motivate students who no longer cared and who wondered what was the point of studying? The student thought, "Why should I study if there is no inherent moral obligation to do so, and if no one can say for sure what is the purpose of life?" Little was left, because the school could not appeal to the morals and the human purposes that it had relativized. In their desperate situation, the teachers found the obvious motivation:

> Study this so that you will get good grades. Then you will be able to go to a good college, and from there get a good job paying lots of money. You can live in a big house with three cars and a boat and a swimming pool and the latest electronic gadgets.

The school had created a moral vacuum. The only remaining motivator was material success. The message that came out was that human life is about material success and pleasure. The students were quite ready to accept this message, because it was reinforced by advertising.

And need I say that it was reinforced by some of the students' own desires? They possessed desires toward selfishness, and these desires were nourished and fanned into flame by the subliminal influence of advertising and peer pressure, which like waves of the incoming sea beat ceaselessly against the wall of whatever moral standards they had left within them.

## What Does It Mean to Listen?

Various cultures and various individuals may have various ideas about God, about religion, and about moral standards. That is true enough. But what *kind* of variation is this? According to one form of postmodernism, we are so hemmed in by our cultural environment that we can never find out the truth in an absolute sense, even if it exists. Each culture may have its ideas, and each individual within the culture may have his. But no one really knows.

That is usually where the postmodernist stops his explanation, at the point where his position has a strong appeal to people who value "tolerance." It is not so common for a postmodernist to spell out the logical conclusion. The conclusion is that, since no one knows, we honestly need not bother. No one really needs to take the trouble to find out *in detail* about anyone else's views on such matters, because in the end it is all merely a matter of human opinion, not real knowledge of real, unchangeable truth. Oh, yes, a postmodernist might still listen in a kind of semi-appreciative, selective, ironic way, and try to recover useful insights here and there. But he knows beforehand that the actual views on morality are mistaken, to the degree that they claim to be absolute and universal.

Well, this kind of postmodernism is one view. It is a view held by many. But it is not the only view of the world and its meaning. Other people and other cultures have thought that they had the truth about God and the truth about morals. Think, for instance, of the militant and violent forms of modern Islam or fascism or communism. Some people are fanatically convinced that the acts of terrorism that they are planning are morally right. They think that such acts further the cause of Allah, and contribute to bringing down and destroying American and European "freedoms," which in their sight are only a label for moral corruption, decadence, and disobedience to Allah. Similarly, within Stalinism, some people were fanatically convinced that the oppressive government apparatus was a necessary stage for bringing in the society of communist abundance and peace, and they were willing to sacrifice millions of lives for the sake of that future.

And for postmodernists, that is part of the point. Enormous human damage can be caused by religious fanaticism and moral fanaticism. Not merely traditional religions, but the atheistic fanaticism of communism can be a source of human damage. Fanatics cannot easily be stopped. Their mistaken feeling of certainty drives them forward. And their certainty blinds them to the viewpoints of the other human beings whom they oppress. Postmodernists want us to learn to consider these other human beings sympathetically, rather than with the hostility of fanaticism. One of the major challenges is to enable people to cross cultural barriers and to consider with sympathy people within other cultures and other thought patterns.

I believe there is much to be commended in these postmodernist desires. The Bible itself says, "You shall love your neighbor as yourself" (Gal. 5:14; Lev. 19:18). Loving your neighbor includes loving the neighbor who is culturally different from you. Postmodernists are made in the image of God, and so they, like all human beings, experience in their hearts the force of the command to love. They sense the moral rightness of love,[4] even if they do not read the Bible.

Moreover, postmodernism is fighting against powerful forces of selfishness and pride. Most people, in most cultures, almost automatically assume that their own kind of people and their own kind of culture are superior to everything else. Learning another culture or another language can be frustrating and humiliating. It is easy to transform this frustration into a prejudicial conviction that your own native culture and language always do things "the right way."

But I do not completely agree with the postmodernists about their principle of sympathy. It depends on what "sympathy" means. Does it mean putting away false pride about your own native culture? Does it mean exercising patience in learning a new language or culture? Or does it mean giving up on religion and morals altogether, because no one knows?

Postmodernism thinks it knows before it begins listening to these other cultures that *real* listening to religious views is unnecessary. And why is it unnecessary? Because these other cultures are mistaken. They *must* be mistaken in the fundamental issue of how they assess the status of their alleged knowledge of God and religion and morality. The postmodernists know that others are mistaken because—well, because they have seen the inevitability of the molding effects of culture on what people count as knowledge.

---

4. The Bible indicates that all human beings have a sense of right and wrong (Rom. 1:32). But that sense is distorted by human sin (Eph. 4:17–19).

And is not postmodernism itself a "culture" that has molding effects? Postmodernists might be happy with this. But would they also be happy with an outsider's question? We might ask from outside whether, in the end, postmodernists have "tolerance" only for themselves. Every other culture must in the end submit to their particular vision of how much cultures can actually know. Postmodernists are supremely arrogant, because their postmodernist vision has relieved them of the responsibility really to listen to anyone else.[5] They are "tolerant" of all cultures when all cultures submit to their hegemony.

Many postmodernists are concerned about tolerance toward diverse beliefs not merely because of the beliefs in themselves but because of the impact that beliefs have on communities. It is all too easy for a majority in a community or in a nation to impose their beliefs on minorities, trying to force them into the majority mold, whether in the laws, in business, in entertainment, or in education. Indeed it does happen. It has happened over and over again, and history overflows with the disgraceful wreckage.

Postmodernism tries to address one aspect of this tragedy by encouraging human sympathy. But does it go further than that? Does its idea of "tolerance" dissolve the sharp differences in belief, by implying that they are all mere opinion? And if so, does this dissolution amount to an intolerance for any and every religious or moral absolute?

And so I come back to the question, "What is tolerance?" I wonder whether the term is useful partly because it can mean different things to different people, and even different things to the *same* person at different times. It allows us to think sloppily. Maybe it allows us to approve what we are comfortable with already, and not to impose on ourselves any onerous obligation. If no one really knows, then each person can do what is right in his own eyes. At heart, we can be perfectly selfish. And we escape serious work.

### The Invitation to Think and to Listen

And so I invite my readers not simply to be tolerant, with the "easy" tolerance of modern American civility. I invite them to think. I invite them to engage with my thinking, as someone who belongs to another "culture," namely, the "culture" that tries to follow Jesus Christ, and listens to his instructions in the Bible. The Bible offers a different account, which takes its start from God. "The fear of the LORD is the beginning of wisdom" (Ps. 111:10). If we follow the Bible's account, we take a different approach to language, as well as to other subjects.

---

5. On the godlike claims of this vision, see Vern S. Poythress, "The Quest for Wisdom," in *Resurrection and Eschatology: Theology in Service of the Church*, ed. Lane G. Tipton and Jeffrey C. Waddington (Phillipsburg, NJ: Presbyterian & Reformed, 2008), 109–111.

# Doubt within Postmodernism

But the path of the righteous is like the light of dawn,
which shines brighter and brighter until full day.
—Proverbs 4:18

Once we believe that God exists and that we are made in his image, we can easily come to see that language reflects the character of God. But in a skeptical environment the question inevitably arises as to whether we are simply projecting our ideas about man, and manufacturing a god in our image.

### Is "God" Merely a Human Projection?
One interpretation of Sigmund Freud argues that God is a production of the human mind. A human extrapolates the figure of his father, and God is the father figure projected to infinite size. According to this view, "God" is an illusory copy of the human father. But is this really the way it is? Or is the human father a copy of God the original Father? If God created man in his own image (Gen. 1:26–27), we should expect exactly this type of relationship, except that God is the original rather than the copy.

### The Presence of Language
In fact it is not easy to eliminate God from the situation. Consider first the presence of language and the omnipresence of God. Language is clearly present within the "world" of my own consciousness and the world of my experience. Can we simply stop at that

point? But then do we stop only with our little subjective world of consciousness? Is there an external world?

One of the discussions within postmodernism concerns our access to the larger world. In describing postmodernism within my children's school in the previous appendix, I concentrated on cultures. Postmodernism may appeal to the diversity of cultures, and the influences of our own culture, to raise questions about our access to moral truth. But a similar point can be made by focusing on languages rather than cultures, because language is closely related to culture.

English is my native tongue, and I did not create it. I inherited it in the context of socialization into American culture. It is a part of that culture. It sits in my mind without my having invited it in.

But now a postmodernist reasons: if this is so, how can my knowledge extend beyond the scope of my language? I know only within the bounds of the sphere of language, which means only within the bounds of my consciousness, my personal "world." The external world, the world that is out there, is actually inaccessible to knowledge. I know only what has already undergone the transformation of entering into the inner, subjective world of English. Maybe English is actually not matched to the external world. How do I know? I can never "climb out" from within the encasements of my language, in order to observe the external world as it really is.

Postmodernist reasoning continues: even if I climb into the world of French, by learning French as a second language, I may retain doubts as to whether I have *really* understood French, because I have learned it only through the prior overlay of my English. Maybe English has interfered with my grasp of French.[1] And even if I come to be comfortable in French, how do I know whether French has difficulties analogous to English when it comes to my knowledge of the external world? I can never climb out from under all human languages simultaneously, in order to inspect in an unprejudiced manner the relation between the world as it really is and the world as I receive it within my encasement within English.[2]

On the other hand, if I know that language was a gift from God, I can still be confident. The omnipresence of God guarantees that God himself extends the presence of language beyond my personal world. All the world conforms to God's language, because God created it. By contrast, if I have ceased to believe in God or to rely on him, the situation

---

1. Without getting into technicalities, I may mention that expert study of language learning shows that this interference from a prior language is often subtle, but nonetheless real. On the level of sound patterns, it shows itself in the fact that the English-speaking person who learns French later in life typically retains an English *accent*, betraying the overlay of English on his French. But the effects also occur on the level of meanings, because English meanings are overlaid on French expressions in the learning process.

2. Some postmodernists may see our description as still using the "old terminology" about an external world, rather than just giving up that allegedly unhelpful terminology. But we are talking about how postmodernism looks to those who are still looking from outside at its offerings. People are capable of mentally standing back from their situation, and asking what the world would look like if they could transcend their limitations. For a postmodernist to claim that such "standing back" is unhelpful presupposes godlike insight.

becomes ominous. The very presence of language in all my experience can be seen as something sinister. Maybe it is keeping me from the world as it really is, rather than being a tool for revealing the world as it really is. Skepticism threatens to take hold.

## The Power of Language

Similar observations hold with respect to the power and the meanings of language. First, consider the power of language. When we use it, language gives us power to assimilate new experience. We classify, analyze, and compare that experience to our past grasp of experience, accumulated in the context of language. But does language have this power because it *forces* the new experience into its own preconceived mold?

We have heard about stubborn people who insist on fitting everything into their own mold. They hold to a conspiracy theory about the assassination of John F. Kennedy, or a paranoid fear that people are "out to get them," or a feeling of hopelessness, in which they feel that they are chronically unlucky and that therefore they will never succeed in life. But could these extreme cases show us, by their striking extremity, what is true more subtly *with all of us*? Does our own language force our experience into its mold?

The difficulties increase when we consider the ties between language and culture. Within a particular culture, leaders use language to encourage the loyalty of those under them. Language can become a channel for propaganda, to manipulate people with lies. Through propaganda, Nazism in Germany succeeded in drawing many of the German people into delusions about themselves and their enemies. Militant Islam has succeeded in drawing its adherents into its delusions. Language has helped to captivate people so that they see the world and their own duties in a distorted way.

Immanuel Kant thought that, because human reasoning was uniform, we might be able to show how people everywhere have the same practical, moral use for their ideas about God, morality, and human personality. Kant thought that practical morality might therefore be stable, even though he thought that human beings could never find God himself and have personal communion with him.[3] But if we lose confidence in the uniformity of the human mind, the plausible assumptions about God and morality break up into a diversity of cultures and a diversity of languages and a diversity of cultural opinions. At that point religion and morality become merely subjective opinions.[4] And, according to postmodernism, they become potentially dangerous opinions, because they cause fights between the people whose opinions differ.

Some postmodernists continue to press forward to the conclusions: since no one can really know, the only solution is to propagate postmodernism as the new "gospel,"

---

3. For a critique of Kant, see Vern S. Poythress, "The Quest for Wisdom," in *Resurrection and Eschatology: Theology in Service of the Church*, ed. Lane G. Tipton and Jeffrey C. Waddington (Phillipsburg, NJ: Presbyterian & Reformed, 2008), 100–102.

4. Some sophisticated postmodernists try to go beyond the allegedly unhelpful dichotomy between objective and subjective. Some try to commend and implement their own moral opinions with conviction and vigor, while maintaining at the same time that those convictions are socially constructed. Will they be able to reproduce their morals in society at large, or will the larger society simply fall back on hedonism, consumerism, and selfishness?

the gospel that will redefine and tame the role of traditional religions and show us all how to live together in tolerance. We tolerate one another because, having received the enlightenment of postmodernism, we now know that our earlier fanatical adherence to our religious and moral preferences was an unwarranted dogmatism. Now we know that it is all a mere matter of subjective personal and cultural preferences. You like chocolate ice cream, and I like vanilla. You have one moral opinion and I have another. There is no ultimate moral right or wrong. And we are at peace. So goes man's new gospel of peace on earth among men (see chart B.1 for the relation of postmodernism to other religions).

| Topic | Conventional Religions | The Bible's Message | Postmodernism |
|-------|------------------------|---------------------|---------------|
| ultimate allegiance: | worship a culturally spec-ified "divine" source | follow Jesus Christ as God in the flesh | serve humanity and the principle of tolerance |
| fundamental human problem: | humans are confused and weak | humans are in radical, desperate rebellion and sin | humans absolutize their own perspective |
| solution (way of salvation): | be good; or be enlightened | believe in Jesus Christ | reduce religious beliefs to subjective preferences |
| savior: | self | Jesus Christ | postmodernist insight |

CHART B.1

Postmodernists' new "gospel" may sound like good news to some, but it includes a profound skepticism about our ability to find ultimate truth.

But if we believe in the God presented in the Bible, we can be confident. God om-nipotently determines both the structure of the external world and the structure of the language that we inherit. So our language is not designed by God for manhandling the external world in the process of perceiving it. It is designed to lead to the world rather than to distort it.

And yet there is another part to the story. After man's rebellion against God, wicked-ness multiplied, and at one point God judged human wickedness by confusing human languages (the account is found in Gen. 11:1–9). Human language broke apart into many languages. And because this is a curse from God, there is no guarantee that *any* one human language, or *any* one human culture, has the unique key to access the truth. In fact, none of them do. To be cursed by God is also to be alienated from God, and to be alienated from God is to lose access to the source of all truth. We are wandering in profound darkness, unless God himself mercifully undertakes to cross the barrier that our alienation has erected. We ought to be pleasantly surprised that we have as much insight here and there as we do. So postmodernist suspicion about our access to truth is in part justified, when we focus on human beings who are alienated from God.

And, given our fallen human condition, how do we detect propaganda? How do we detect it if we happen to inhabit a culture filled with it? And how do we decide among multiple cultures, multiple religions, and multiple moral judgments? If God has not spoken, how are human beings *on their own* able to adjudicate between competing views? Postmodernists want us to discuss our views with one another. But what if two people make no progress, but continue to disagree? What if they disagree even more violently than before? And if they make "progress," do they make progress under the influence of some hidden propaganda? Do they merely progress toward a corporate delusion?

And is the postmodernist idea of relativizing religions to their cultures yet one more delusion? Yes, it is. Postmodernism has simply assumed that God cannot reveal himself to human beings in the way that he does, in his work in Christ, in the Bible, and in general revelation as well (Rom. 1:18–23).

### The Meanings in Language

Finally, consider the meanings in language. Meanings, we observed, give access to knowledge and truth, and point to the omniscience of God. But the growth of structural linguistics in the twentieth century confirmed in massive detail what students of literature had long sensed, that meanings within language are not perfectly stable, in and of themselves. The meaning of a particular word or a particular grammatical construction depends partly on relations to other meanings within language.[5]

Language exists in relation to human culture. And human cultures are multiple. This multiplicity can threaten all stability in meaning. We are "in the soup," with the threat of a total collapse of the stability of meaning. Some cultures may perhaps radically differ from the one in which we ourselves have grown up. And will meanings look the same within another culture?

If we are in communion with God, we can still be confident. God governs all the contexts. God is himself the final context for meaning. He is himself the fullness of meaning, and he knows all things. His knowledge is the final context for the possibility of my knowledge. God created man in his own image, so that there remains a commonality to mankind. The languages and customs and patterns of life in other cultures of the world will retain a certain commonality based on the image of God. See chart B.2.

| Postmodernist Doubts about Language | Possible Long-range Implication | Positive Role of Language | God as Original |
|---|---|---|---|
| language is a prison keeping us from reality | loneliness | presence | divine presence bringing language everywhere |
| language "constructs" a world | arbitrariness; or passivity, enslavement | control | divine control of language and world |
| language differences relativize meanings | meaninglessness | meaning | divine impartation of meaning to the world and to our language |

CHART B.2

But if we are alienated from God, we will indeed make difficulties for ourselves. Alienation from God produces in us distortions in our view of God, who is the final context for meaning. And distortions in the context produce distortions in the meanings that we

---

5. See chapter 3.

started with. If we cease to have a stable context at all, the meanings may shift around. But the solution is at hand: to come to God and find communion with him.

## Language about God

Postmodernists have a ready reply to this Christian answer. Some of them might want to ask whether such an answer has really learned anything from the field perspective on language. They would say that all our use of language about God takes place within the sphere of language and meaning. And these meanings shift around, depending on the context, and depending on the perspective that we choose. Since meanings function only within the system of language, they cannot coherently and stably function to delimit the character of God, who is beyond the system. Postmodernist understanding of the character of language relativizes and destabilizes meaning, and so destroys the naïve assumption that we possess stable affirmations about God within language.

Yes, we can understand this reasoning. But we do not need to live within it. The Christian answer has a different view of the world, and does not agree with the assumptions behind this kind of postmodernist reasoning. In particular, postmodernist contextualism has inherited from its modernist cultural ancestors the mistaken assumption that God is irrelevant to the function and character of language. And if it makes that assumption, it will indeed artificially produce a radical destabilizing of the meanings of any language that tries to talk about God.

## Difficulties with a Postmodernist Approach to Language

So postmodernists have unconsciously absorbed at the beginning the conclusion that they reach at the end.

But there are some other difficulties for them. Postmodernists have arrived at their present view of things by a variety of routes and a variety of arguments, including the unconscious effects of education in "tolerance." Though there may be a lot of variety, much of it goes back to ideas flowing out of the social sciences.

Anthropology has revealed not only the variety of cultures but also their internal coherence and self-sustaining powers. Sociology and political study have revealed the power of propaganda. Historical studies have revealed deep differences between the modern era and past centuries. Structural linguistics has played a role in the generation of Lévi-Strauss's structural anthropology, as well as structuralism in the analysis of culture, and from there we have received poststructuralism. In addition, the sociology of knowledge has played a role. Post-Freudian psychology has played a role in raising the awareness of the degree to which our actions are not merely products of rational, intellectual decision making but are influenced by many forces of which we may not be aware. Marxism has shown us ways in which money and power and economic structures influence ideologies.

The first difficulty for postmodernism is that the social sciences are founded on modernism. They grew up largely from the attempt to extend the methods of the natural sciences into the study of human beings and their cultures. They assumed, as did the natural sciences, that the human mind was competent and that the human language used by the social scientist was adequate and stable. Humans were capable of analyzing and understanding the patterns and laws of nature, whether it was subhuman nature or—for the social sciences—human nature itself.

And now postmodernism, building on the insights of the social sciences, has led to the conclusion that knowledge concerning human beings is suspect, because of the distortions of language and culture within which we are immersed. Postmodernism destabilizes not only conventional confidence about religion and morality but confidence in the social sciences as well. And if that confidence is unwarranted, the conclusions of the social sciences are unwarranted, the foundations for postmodernist argument disappear, and the whole edifice collapses.

There are several possible rescue operations that postmodernists can use. One is to say that, though there are personal biases here and there, the social sciences are still sound (more or less), because of their scientific character. They rely on the Kantian distinction between the phenomenal and the noumenal. The phenomenal is what the scientist can observe. The noumenal is what we can conceive of as "really there" behind the phenomena. According to this viewpoint, we can confidently study the phenomenal, through scientific methodology, but the noumenal is inaccessible.

The difficulty that remains here is that the bounds of what is phenomenal seem to shift around for the convenience of the argument. Within this viewpoint students might certainly study external human behavior, insofar as it is visible and audible and reducible to pointer readings on scientific instruments. That is a narrow boundary for what is phenomenal. But could they study *meanings*, either linguistic meanings or the human meanings that belong to cognition and to human social action? That would be a wide boundary. For example, human speech acts, like asserting, promising, commanding, and inquiring, are not merely sound waves in the air produced by human vocal chords, but are intelligible only when we are willing to think about their purposes. And that is a matter of meaning.

When we use language to describe meaningful human actions, we bring along in its trail all the accretions of the fabric of meanings, as well as the trail of our memories and our enculturation.[6] Postmodernism has to talk about these areas of meaning to make its point. And these areas are not pointer readings on scientific instruments. So either postmodernism has made a hidden leap from pointer readings to human meanings, or it should admit that the social sciences need critical revision of their modernist foundations.

The second rescue operation admits that the social sciences are based on unsound foundations. According to this viewpoint, once someone has arrived at the postmodernist conclusion, he looks back at the social sciences and sees that, in the end, there is no well-grounded, objective social science, but only opinions backed up by data that have already been selected according to a cultural mind-set. The social sciences are relativized.

How then does postmodernism credibly establish itself, without the conclusions from the social sciences? How can we have confidence in a position at which we have arrived by untrustworthy means? The reply might be that we are supposed to have confidence because there is no real alternative. We must "muddle through" with a kind

---

6. In fact, these meanings come in the trail even of investigations in natural science.

of pragmatic mind-set, because everything else has been destroyed. In addition, according to this viewpoint, pragmatism or skepticism offers the best means for protecting minorities against oppression. But a question still haunts this worldview: why bother? Concern for the oppressed becomes, according to a sociological account, one more moral value that has been "constructed" into us by enculturation. Why even bother about minorities or about humanity, since we all die in the end? "Let us eat and drink, for tomorrow we die."[7]

Finally, we can look at postmodernist contextualism from outside. The idea that there is no real alternative to postmodernism is an illusory product of cultural conditioning. It is one more culturally authoritative pronouncement that the postmodernist would do well to distrust.

## Dealing with Doubt

Postmodernist questioning concerning language and culture has succeeded in producing uneasiness and doubt and sometimes full-blown pragmatism in people's lives. But such doubt need not be the endpoint. Rather, it can become a starting point for Christians to engage in discussion with postmodernists.

Has everything become doubtful? Not really. Ludwig Wittgenstein observed, "If you tried to doubt everything you would not get as far as doubting anything. The game of doubting itself presupposes certainty."[8]

Wittgenstein makes this statement in the context of his thinking about "language games." Just as ordinary games are played in accordance with rules, so language usage takes place against the background of certain rules, even if, for a particular language, the rules have never been spelled out in an official rule book.[9] There are grammatical rules and rules for pronunciation. There are specific ways in which we ask questions, receive answers, ask counterquestions, and make requests. Use of language involves sharing rules of language with conversation partners.

Doubting is one kind of language game. It presupposes rules, if it is to be a game at all. The game-player cannot doubt the rules themselves. Oh, yes, he could say out loud, "I doubt whether English has any rules, and whether the processes involved in doubting have any rules." But when he says that, he simultaneously relies on the rules. Otherwise,

---

7. First Corinthians 15:32, cited from Isaiah 22:13.

8. Ludwig Wittgenstein, *On Certainty*, ed. G. E. M. Anscombe and G. H. von Wright (New York: Harper & Row, 1969), 18e, proposition 115.

9. The analogy with games is imperfect, because the rules of a game are typically invented and codified in an explicit way, and a person who is teaching a game to someone else may frequently appeal to an explicit rule. Natural languages, by contrast, are learned primarily by examples and by intuition. Only later, in a grammar class, do we hear about rules. The explicit rules in the grammar class are secondary summaries concerning the regularities that are already there in language before the "rules" were explicitly formulated. If the word "rule" suggests an arbitrary rule that human beings consciously invent, the word "regularity" might be better for describing language. Or the word "norm" might serve, to emphasize that we can choose if we want to deviate from a particular regularity. But such deviations stand out *as deviations*, showing that people are still aware of the norm.

within his own utterance the word "doubt" would have no meaning. And for similar reasons the other words in the same sentence, and the sentence as a complete grammatical construction, would have no meaning.

Without social rules for speech acts, the speech act of doubting that a person performs with the sentence would also no longer be identifiable as a coherent speech act.[10] Moreover, without rules the sentence would no longer be identifiable as English, rather than French or Arabic. It would therefore become no better than nonsense syllables: "waheli forshamee paykomah lah." In practice, everyone shows that he does not in fact doubt the rules. Even if his own assertions and his own theories are at variance with his practice, he shows that he knows better.

A person could attempt to perform the game of doubting in the mind alone, without the use of words. But such an attempt would be difficult at best. First, mental contemplations are far from independent of language, even if we do not mentally whisper specific words to ourselves. There is always a background of enculturation and language learning that we do not make conscious to ourselves, but that nevertheless molds the patterns of our thinking. The pattern of doubting is itself a pattern that we have learned from our culture. Second, how does the one who performs the game of doubting assure himself that he is engaged in the game of doubting, rather than some other game, and rather than some other activity that is not a game at all in the normal sense (e.g., sleeping or eating)? He must make reference to the word "doubt" or the rules associated with that word.

And then, even if our hypothetical doubter has succeeded and returned to tell us the tale, he cannot report it without once again submitting to the rules of a language. The ability to doubt is socially and culturally useless unless it can be transmitted. In particular, the postmodernist needs transmission, or else postmodernism would come to life and then also die, all within the bounds of the mind of a single individual.

It has become fashionable among some postmodernists to say that nothing is certain. But saying this is self-defeating. Even in the act of making their claim these people do have certainty concerning the rules of language, the game of doubt, and the meaning of the word "certain." What is actually happening is closer to a proposal for displacing some previous alleged "certainties" of modernism with other, hidden certainties that lie in back of postmodernism. For example, they may be certain about the insights that they have obtained about the molding forces of culture, and about the moral commendability of tolerance. Only such certainty gives them the zeal to promote multicultural tolerance. People live on the basis of certainties, not merely on the basis of an unmotivated program to unmask the difficulties in others' claims to certainty.

Whatever may be the certainties by which people live, they depend on the rules of language. And in doing so they depend on God, even if it is in spite of themselves.[11]

---

10. In a somewhat different context, John R. Searle observes: "But the retreat from the committed use of words ultimately must involve a retreat from language itself, for speaking a language—as has been the main theme of this book—consists of performing speech acts according to rules, and there is no separating those speech acts from the commitments which form essential parts of them" (John R. Searle, *Speech Acts: An Essay in the Philosophy of Language* [Cambridge: Cambridge University Press, 1969], 198). For a discussion of speech acts, see appendix H.

11. See chapters 8–9.

# Non-Christian Thinking

I have seen a limit to all perfection,
but your commandment is exceedingly broad.
—Psalm 119:96

W e need to look more closely at the difference between the truth of God and the counterfeits of Satan, in order to apply this difference to the study of language.

Satan's alternative to serving God involves both antithesis to God and counterfeiting. We can conveniently summarize both aspects in a diagram, the same diagram that John M. Frame has used to summarize Christian and non-Christian views of divine transcendence and immanence. The diagram (fig. C.1), originally labeled "The Square of Religious Opposition," is reproduced here just as it is found in Frame's book on the knowledge of God.[1]

## Understanding Frame's Square

The left-hand side of the square, which includes the corners 1 and 2, represents the Christian position; more precisely, it represents the biblical teaching about the transcendence of God (corner 1) and his immanence (corner 2). In the Bible, God expresses his

---

1. John M. Frame, *The Doctrine of the Knowledge of God* (Phillipsburg, NJ: Presbyterian & Reformed, 1987), 14. As far as I know, John Frame originated this diagrammatic representation, and subsequently it has been called "Frame's square." But many of the ideas represented in the diagram (though not the diagram itself) can also be found in Cornelius Van Til's presuppositional apologetics. See, e.g., Cornelius Van Til, *The Defense of the Faith*, 2nd ed. (Philadelphia: Presbyterian & Reformed, 1963); Van Til, *A Survey of Christian Epistemology*, vol. 2 of In Defense of Biblical Christianity (n.p.: den Dulk Foundation, 1969).

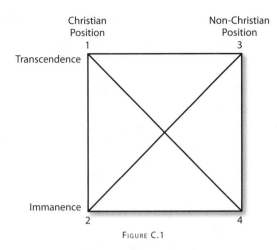

FIGURE C.1

transcendence through his authority and control; he expresses his immanence in presence. Frame relates the traditional categories of transcendence and immanence to his three-fold description of the attributes of lordship, namely, authority, control, and presence.[2] In this book we have chosen to re-express these three aspects as meaning, control, and presence.[3] In fact, meaning can suggest transcendence, because all meaning ultimately originates in God; human thoughts about meanings imitate God's thoughts. And meaning can suggest immanence, because creatures display God's meanings, and because he can make his meanings known to us. So let us for the moment concentrate on control and presence. Control expresses transcendence, and presence expresses immanence. God's word controls what he creates, and thereby expresses God's transcendence. God's word also impinges on the world, and so expresses his presence and his immanence. When God addresses Adam, we see his control in assigning Adam his tasks, and his presence in manifesting his goodness (and other attributes) in his speech. As Frame demonstrates at length, control and presence are not in tension with one another but are two harmonious aspects of God's character. Precisely because God controls the entire universe, he can be present in it, in all its parts. Precisely by being present, he exerts his control.

According to Frame, non-Christian thought has frequently made transcendence and immanence into a problem, by misconstruing them. Transcendence supposedly means that God is far off and unknowable. (This is represented by corner 3 in the square.) Immanence, on the other hand (according to this non-Christian view), means that God becomes immersed in creation and is virtually identical with it (corner 4).[4] Taken together, these two corners are in deep tension. How can God be identical with creation and also be far off? The right-hand side of the square, which includes corners 3 and 4, represents the non-Christian position.

---

2. Frame, *Doctrine of the Knowledge of God*, 15–18.

3. See chapter 3.

4. Frame, *Doctrine of the Knowledge of God*, 15.

We cannot consider all the various kinds of non-Christian positions. Several religious systems, including atheism, Buddhism, and Vedantic Hinduism, deny that there is a personal God at all. But then "God" is replaced by whatever is ontologically ultimate; and that turns out to be inaccessible.

The same diagram can be applied not only to questions of ontology (what exists?) but also to questions of epistemology (what do we know?). In a biblical, Christian view, God's transcendence is expressed by the fact that he controls what we know about him, and that he is the final standard for knowledge about him (meaning and authority). God's immanence is expressed by the fact that he actually makes himself known, both in the creation (Rom. 1:18–23) and by addressing human beings in language (as in Gen. 1:28–30).

By contrast, non-Christian thought tends to say that God is unknowable (non-Christian transcendence, corner 3), and also that when we nevertheless do think about him, we can use ourselves and our own rational powers or our own experience as the final arbiter (non-Christian immanence, corner 4). The view that God or ultimate reality is unknowable has been dubbed non-Christian "irrationalism." The view that our own rationality is the final judge has been dubbed non-Christian "rationalism."[5] Again these two are in tension. How can we confidently use our powers (corner 4) if God is unknowable (corner 3)?

## Antithesis

Now let us relate this square to what we have observed about Satanic deceit. Satan is antithetical to God, and that antithesis is represented by the contrast between the left-hand and the right-hand sides of the square. Satan's speeches to Eve put forward an alternative view of God, and an alternative view concerning knowing God and God's will. The alternative view is represented in the right-hand side of the square.

This alternative view contradicts God's speech in all three aspects: control, meaning, and presence. That is to say, it contradicts God's speech with respect to its view of transcendence (control), and its view of immanence (presence). Satan presents God as someone you cannot trust, which makes God far off and virtually unknowable. This is the non-Christian view of transcendence (corner 3). At the same time, Satan invites man to "play god," to be autonomous, to make up his own mind. He thus implies that human powers should take control of the entire situation. This is the non-Christian view of immanence (corner 4). Both contradict the Christian view, the view on the left-hand side of the square.

We need to add another detail. The diagonal lines that cross the square signify the contradictions. Non-Christian immanence (corner 4) contradicts Christian transcendence (corner 1), while non-Christian transcendence (corner 3) contradicts Christian immanence (corner 2). For man to play god is non-Christian immanence, corner 4, which contradicts God's claim to authority and control (corner 1). For Satan to imply that God cannot be trusted makes God far off or unknowable, which is corner 3. That contradicts the trustworthiness, clarity, and accessibility of God's word in corner 2.

---

5. The terms come from Cornelius Van Til. See, e.g., Van Til, *Defense of the Faith*, 123–128.

## Counterfeiting

In addition, we have observed that Satan is a counterfeiter. In Genesis 3 his distortions of the truth are close to the truth. The counterfeiting is represented by the *horizontal* lines in the square. Satan may use language that seems to be close to the true view of transcendence (corner 1) in order to represent a false view of transcendence (corner 3). Cornelius Van Til describes this similarity as "formal" similarity. That is, the expressions and formulations on the non-Christian side sound similar to those used on the Christian side. In some cases the expressions may even be exactly the same. But in the end they *mean* something different.

The formal similarity is represented by the horizontal line joining corner 1 to corner 3. Similarly, the horizontal line joining corner 2 to corner 4 represents a formal similarity. The language used in corner 4 to describe non-Christian immanence is a counterfeit of the language used in corner 2 to describe Christian immanence. Even the word "immanence" itself illustrates this process. "Immanence" means one thing to a non-Christian and another thing to a Christian. Or consider the word "exalted," which is another word for expressing God's transcendence. Does it mean that God is exalted over human beings and the world in his complete control and authority? Or does it mean that he is far off and unknowable? It could mean different things, depending on whether the context is Christian or non-Christian.

We can see the differences in meaning between the two sides when we look at Satan's expression "you will be like God." Adam and Eve were already like God, because they were made in the image of God and expressed the presence of God in their own persons (corner 2). But Satan intended to put into his words the meaning of autonomy, and of being a self-sufficient judge, which is corner 4.

Now we can apply Frame's square to the area of language. The Christian view says that God can speak clearly (corner 2). When he speaks, his word has authority over us (corner 1). Satan's counterfeiting endeavors to obscure or contradict both aspects. He claims that God does not speak or that his meaning is not clear (corner 3). And he invites human beings to make their own independent judgments about what is said (corner 4).

## The Universality of the Pattern of Deceit

Satan's pattern of opposition is depicted in the book of Revelation, and this pattern is always fundamentally the same. Hence, the pattern depicted in Frame's square is always the same. It will reproduce itself, in one form or another, in all human thought that remains in rebellion against God. The pattern describes not only "Christian atheists" and Barth and Bultmann, whom Frame mentions,[6] but non-Christian world religions, Greek philosophers, and modern atheists.

In particular, the pattern appears in our human use of language and in our attitudes toward language. The rules of language manifest the presence of God. But non-Christians are rebelling against God, and the rebellion will express itself in an altered view with

---

6. Referring to the "God-is-dead" movement, Frame says that "The 'Christian atheists' used to say that God abandoned His divinity and no longer exists as God" (Frame, *Doctrine of the Knowledge of God*, 13–14).

respect to the rules of language. On the one hand, according to a non-Christian view of immanence, the rules of language will become rules to be controlled by man in his would-be autonomy. On the other hand, according to a non-Christian view of transcendence, the source of the rules becomes unknown. The non-Christian will want to conceal from himself how God presents his attributes and his presence in the rules. Though the details may vary, we can expect that rebellion against God, and the attempt to suppress the knowledge of God (Rom. 1:18–23), will always have some effect.

But the non-Christian pattern is not always obvious, because counterfeiting undertakes to conceal the pattern. And people are inconsistent. Every user of language secretly depends on God, the real God described by the left-hand side of the square. At the same time, people are in flight from God, trying to make the right-hand side work. They are relying on the left-hand side while they try to live on the right-hand side.

Traveling between the two sides is a recipe for frustration. In fact, it would be a recipe for complete failure were it not that God shows mercy in some ways even to rebels, and often holds them back from the worst consequences of their rebellion (Gen. 11:6–7; Acts 14:17).

The pattern of counterfeiting also shows itself in our very use of language. Human communication can take the form of half-truths—half-truths about God, or half-truths about other things that we want to manipulate for our own selfish benefit. The mixture of truth and error shows how serious are the difficulties in which we find ourselves.

## Modernism and Postmodernism

The pattern of non-Christian thinking also appears in the relation between modernism and postmodernism. Modernism emphasizes human rationality and its capability. And rationality is a good thing, enabling us to understand God and his communication to us (Christian immanence, corner 2). But what does modernism mean by "rationality"? Modernism slides the meaning over to non-Christian immanence, corner 4. Rationality in practice means the ultimacy of human reasoning, acting independent of fellowship with God. Modernism also has confidence in human language as a tool for understanding. But this confidence turns out to be a form of non-Christian immanence: language is simply human, and can be confidently used in isolation from communion and communication with God.

Postmodernism, by contrast, worries about whether truth is inaccessible. It thinks that truths about God, religion, and morality can never be confidently known. That viewpoint is a form of non-Christian transcendence, corner 3. In part, postmodernism is reacting against the overconfidence in human reason in modernism. If modernism is rationalistic in tendency, postmodernism is irrationalistic. It reacts to the non-Christian immanence in corner 4 by emphasizing non-Christian transcendence in corner 3. And postmodernism also has a view of language. Language is seen as a socially constructed confinement that we cannot escape. So language in its limitations cannot access final truth. That view expresses a non-Christian idea of transcendence, corner 3.

But at a deeper level modernism and postmodernism belong together. They are both cultural movements that cast off dependence on God. Postmodernism, as the later movement, builds on modernism by continuing the practice of independence from God, and, if anything, pushes it further. Both movements, to the degree that they are consistent, share in an essentially non-Christian view about knowledge, and about language as well. Modernism emphasizes rationality and corner 4. But human rationality now and then will begin to inspect itself and admit that human beings are limited. Beyond those limits is the unknown, and this unknown still has the character of non-Christian transcendence, corner 3. Conversely, postmodernism's emphasis on doubt and skepticism about "big" claims is supported underneath by a *rationalistic* analysis of language and culture that thinks it sees the limits. So a principle of non-Christian immanence in corner 4 remains present under the surface.

# Platonic Ideas

Follow the pattern of sound words that you have heard from me,
in the faith and love that are in Christ Jesus.
—2 Timothy 1:13

The Greek philosopher Plato has had much influence on Western civilization, including Western views about thought and about language. We cannot here cover the field, but we may sketch some ways in which a biblically based approach to language differs from Plato.[1]

Plato's dialogues reflect on key ideas, such as the idea of justice, of piety, of beauty, and of truth. Plato thought that the world of the senses was only a shadow of the real world of "forms" or ideal abstractions, such as the ideals of justice and beauty. The supreme form or ideal was the form of the good. And there would also be ideal forms for many kinds of things: a form for dog, horse, cow, goat, and so on. The goal of the philosopher's life was to know these forms or ideals.

## The Connection with Language

Plato discussed not only these ideal forms but also how we could come to know them. He focused on thought. But he wrote in language. And the ideal forms corresponded to key *words* in language, words like "justice" and "goodness."[2] So indirectly Plato suggested implications

---

1. See also John M. Frame, "Greeks Bearing Gifts," in *Revolutions in Worldview: Understanding the Flow of Western Thought*, ed. W. Andrew Hoffecker (Phillipsburg, NJ: Presbyterian & Reformed, 2007), 1–36; Vern S. Poythress, "The Quest for Wisdom," in *Resurrection and Eschatology: Theology in Service of the Church*, ed. Lane G. Tipton and Jeffrey C. Waddington (Phillipsburg, NJ: Presbyterian & Reformed, 2008), 96–100.

2. Of course, Plato used terms in the Greek language; but the challenges are similar in English.

for language. Language and thought are related.

We can make a step in understanding Plato's approach by contrasting it with our own approach to words. Words exist in a multitude of relationships, and can be viewed from a multitude of perspectives, such as the particle, wave, and field perspectives.[3] Plato's view uses the particle perspective as if it were the whole truth. Each form is a particle, essentially independent of everything else.

Like all units of human action, words possess contrastive-identificational features, variation, and context (distribution).[4] Plato wants only the contrastive-identificational features. Pure ideas of a Platonic sort would be like pure contrastive features, pure categories without any necessary connection with the particularities of, for example, particular dogs. Variation would be dispensed with. Of course Plato would have admitted that a particular horse was in a sense a "variation" or a particular manifestation of the ideal form of horse. But the variation was completely secondary in comparison to the ideal. This demotion of the particulars is characteristic of Plato.

In addition, Platonic categories would be without connection to the contexts in which we observe dogs and use whole sentences to talk about them. Context (distribution) would be dispensed with. The result would be an idealization, to be sure. But it would also be unitarian. God is not that way. And God's world is not made that way. We may try to refashion the world to an ideal in our minds, and make the reality conform. But that is a reduction.

## The One and the Many

Many philosophers have struggled with what to do about the relation of particulars to universals.[5] The particulars are the individual horses; the universal is the general idea of *the horse*. How do the two relate? Plato's answer was to emphasize the priority and reality of the one, the universal form. But then how do the particulars ever come about?

The problem of the one and the many finds resolution in Trinitarian doctrine. God is both one and three, with no "priority" of oneness to threeness. God is the archetypal instance of one and many. Created things offer ectypal or derivative instances of one and many. In language, contrastive-identificational features describe the one, the unity of many manifestations. Variation describes the many.

Since the interlocking of identity, variation, and context (distribution) reflects Trinitarian coinherence, the interlocking is not accidental. Nor is it an unfortunate byproduct of our being in the body and being subject to the senses, as Plato might have claimed. Nor is it something that belongs only to words but not to pure thought. It is built into human existence and human experience, to be sure. But it is that way among us humans because it is first of all a pattern in God himself, who is the archetype for the one and the many.

Plato pictured the ideal forms as existing in a realm of pure thought. So how did the material world come to be? In one of his dialogues, the *Timaeus*, Plato introduced a

---

3. See chapter 7.
4. See chapter 19 on behavioremes.
5. See chapter 33.

"demiurge," a kind of god who looked at the forms and created material things using the forms as his model. But this demiurge was in the end inferior to the forms, since the forms dictated the kind of material things that he was supposed to make. Plato's demiurge is godlike, in some ways; but he is a second-rate god, a counterfeit of the true God.

Moreover, Plato's view involves non-Christian thinking about transcendence and immanence.[6] Plato implies that, if and when a human being grasps the ideal forms, he grasps ultimate reality, and he is master of ultimate reality. Human rationality is then the standard for judging everything. This triumph of human reason is a form of non-Christian immanence (corner 4 in Frame's square; see appendix C), where humans are the ultimate judges. At the same time, the forms are in practice inaccessible, since human beings in their bodily existence always contend with the interference of the senses and of the impure particulars, the particular horses or goats or dogs that exist in the material world. This inaccessibility of the forms represents non-Christian transcendence (corner 3 in Frame's square), in which ultimate reality is unknowable.

### Christianized Platonism

Christians adapted Plato's ideas to a Christian framework by placing the ideal forms *within God's mind*. In this version the forms are no longer independent of and superior to God but are simply aspects of God's own thinking. This view is more satisfactory, since it no longer tries to subject God to something outside him that is alleged to be superior to him. We could also translate this view into a view of language, in which words and language are first of all in God's mind, and then in us.

But Christianized Platonism has not yet eliminated Plato's view that the one, the universal, is prior to the many, the particulars. The form of horse, which now exists in God's mind, is prior to the many horses that God creates according to the pattern of the ideal horse that is in his mind. But to say that is a half-truth.

### A Christian View of Horses

God as Creator has planned to create not only each individual horse, but the whole species of horse. God's plan, within his mind, is prior to the horses. His plan is also prior to the creation of the whole species of horses, the universal group. The created world has a universal, namely, the species of horses, and the particulars, namely, individual horses. This is a created one and many. Behind this created one and many lies God's plan for both one and many. The one and the many are equally ultimate in his plan, in his mind. They must be, because both reflect the Trinitarian character of God, who is one and many.

Thinking about one and many is closely related to two perspectives on language that we have considered. The focus on the one, on the universal, corresponds to the contrastive-identificational features belonging to words (or other pieces of language). The word "horse" is one word. It is the same word, every time it occurs. The focus on the many corresponds to variation. Each occurrence of the word "horse" has its own

---

6. See appendix C.

pronunciation, loud or soft. It belongs to a distinct sentence, uttered within a distinct context. But we should not forget context (distribution). Words occur in contexts to which they are related. Analogously, horses occur in contexts—contexts with other horses, contexts in relation to human beings who care for them, and contexts of fields in which they graze and run.

God's plan for horses has a context, namely, his plan for the rest of the world with which horses interact. God's plan for all of history is one. It is unified by the harmony of his own mind—unified, ultimately by the harmony of the three persons of the Trinity in coinherence. Even within God's mind, there is no *isolated* "idea" of horse. It cannot be isolated, because the persons of the Trinity are coinherent. And derivative from this archetypal coinherence, the contrast, variation, and context (distribution) of "horse" are coinherent.

## Cross-cultural Universality and Particularity

Now let us consider the relation of Platonic thought to the diversity of languages and cultures. Plato thought of the ideal forms as ideals that were absolutely the same for all thinking human beings, within all cultures. For Plato, human rationality, when it was sound, was completely universal, with no variation. It was the same for all human beings. According to his view, one universal rationality was trying to grasp one, universal form—let us say, the form of horse. At this level of thought, no room existed for cultural variation. This vision of human unity is, in spirit, unitarian rather than Trinitarian.

What does human unity look like when we try to take into account the Trinitarian character of God? There is still a deep unity in all sound human thinking, since God is one and all human beings are made in his image. But the diversity of persons in God is reflected at a human, ectypal level. Human beings are diverse in their thinking. That can be destructive, when errors and sins and pride corrupt our thinking. But within the body of Christ, renewed by the Holy Spirit, not all diversity is disruptive. Rather, it is enriching.

What does this diversity look like? We may use some simple examples. Let us begin with horses. My wife's friend keeps horses. She trains them. She trains young riders. She knows the individual dispositions and bodily infirmities of each horse. Each horse becomes a friend. For her, the idea of horse is colored by her experience with each horse.

Now compare her experience with a farmer trying to drive wild horses off his farmland. Do the two have the same "concept" of horse? Does either have the same "concept" as a veterinarian who specializes in horses? Or a zoologist who studies the relation of domestic horses to the other members of the horse family (*Equidae*)? Or the specialized researcher who is studying how best to cure horse hoof canker?

All of these people may have some concept of the species of domestic horse. But their concept of the species represents only one aspect of God's knowledge. God's knowledge is comprehensive. It includes all the details that any one of these horse people knows. It includes knowing the entire perspective that one person brings to horses, against the background of his interests and his experience. It is a reduction to smash this into a Platonic universal—horseness.

If the people are all knowledgeable rather than deluded, they carry genuine knowledge. It is all true. They complement one another, rather than fighting over whose concept of horse is "right." Each can learn from the others. In the process, each grows to an enlarged appreciation of God's comprehensive knowledge, which includes knowledge of the relation of horses to the whole of his plan.

The diversity of different views of horses holds even among people who use the same language, say, English. We should expect that inspection of other languages will further highlight diversity. Other languages may have vocabulary that does not match English. They may, for example, make distinctions between colors or tempers or breeds of horses that are not common among English-speaking people. They may have classifications of types of animals that cut across our familiar classifications. But this should not disturb us. We classify whales and dolphins as mammals from the standpoint of technical scientific classification, and we can still classify them colloquially as "fish" from the standpoint of their bodily shape and watery habitat. Partial classifications can be true, as long as they do not make sweeping claims that exclude all other perspectival classifications by automatically pronouncing them "false."

## Perspectives

Diversity in spatial perspectives offers a simple analogy for understanding differences in views of horses, as well as differences in vocabulary and other differences between languages. Suppose we have several people looking at one house. Abe sees my house from an airplane. Barb sees my house from the street. Charlotte sees my house from the backyard. Dorothy sees my house while sitting in my living room. Is what each of them sees false or wrong? Of course not. Mathematically it is possible to "translate" between these perspectives with equations that calculate the differences in angle from any of the vantage points. And we can translate between perspectives in a way that anticipates what objects will be out of sight because they are blocked by some closer object. The perspectives are all valid, and all the people see what is real. They see my house.

God planned all these perspectives. God knows them all exhaustively. God endorses them as genuinely what human beings are supposed to experience. He also planned the relations between perspectives, which we experience when we move from one location to another.

So also, God planned all the perspectives on horses. He planned all the languages. He endorses their use; these languages are genuinely what human beings are supposed to be using. By contrast to this richness, Platonic ideas would allegedly be purely the same for all peoples in all languages. They collapse richness, and reduce it to unity without diversity.

Within language, the difficulties of sinful corruption do enter in. But the removal of sin does not require the removal of other kinds of genuine diversity. Why? Because it is diversity in unity: God is Trinitarian. The diversity of spatial perspectives are unified by our unified human understanding, allowing us to translate between them. The unity of our human understanding reflects the archetypal unity in God's understanding. But it does not wipe out or make unreal the genuineness of Dorothy's particular experience sitting in my living room. The one—the unity of my house—does not contradict the many—the many spatial perspectives. God planned it that way. He did so because he delights to show his glory in harmonious multiple perspectives. He is Trinitarian. That is the ultimate foundation for diverse spatial perspectives; so also for diverse languages. But with language, the potential for rich diversity is so much greater.[7]

---

7. See also Vern S. Poythress, "Reforming Ontology and Logic in the Light of the Trinity: An Application of Van Til's Idea of Analogy," *Westminster Theological Journal* 57/1 (1995): 187–219.

# The Contribution of Structural Linguistics

The tongue of the righteous is choice silver;
the heart of the wicked is of little worth.

—Proverbs 10:20

Now we consider the subject of structural linguistics.[1] Structural linguistics, as a twentieth-century discipline, is to be distinguished from historical linguistics (diachronic linguistics), which has a much longer history, and from earlier attempts at grammatical and phonetic analysis of a single language.

## Simplifications in Structural Linguistics

We need to appreciate the value of linguistics, but also to become aware of its built-in limitations. Human language is so complicated and multidimensional that simplifications had to be made in order to get structural linguistics started. But it is easy along the way, in the excitement of discovery, to forget those simplifications and to make exaggerated or one-sided claims about the implications of a simplified theory.

---

1. Most of this and the next appendix are taken, with modifications, from Vern S. Poythress, "Truth and Fullness of Meaning: Fullness versus Reductionistic Semantics in Biblical Interpretation," *Westminster Theological Journal* 67/2 (2005): 211–227; also appearing in Wayne Grudem et al., *Translating Truth: The Case for Essentially Literal Bible Translation* (Wheaton, IL: Crossway, 2005), 113–134. Used with permission. For implications for Bible translation, see also the other essays in Grudem et al., *Translating Truth*.

In considering the development of structural linguistics, I have to make some simplifications myself, and confine myself to some high points illustrating the trends.[2] I focus particularly on the issue of how linguistics treats *meaning*.

### Ferdinand de Saussure, 1906–1911

Many consider that structural linguistics had its origin in the lectures of Ferdinand de Saussure in 1906–1907, 1908–1909, and 1910–1911, which were later compiled into the book *Course in General Linguistics*.[3] After some historical observations, Saussure introduced the main body of discussion by delineating the object of linguistics. Linguistics will study language as a system, instead of studying speech.[4] That is, it will study the systematic regularities common to all native speakers of a language, rather than the particularities of every individual speech by every individual speaker. It will study the fact that "moved" is the past tense of "move," but not the occurrence of "moved" within a single particular utterance.

The focus on the system of language decisively contributed to the delineation of linguistics as a subject distinct from textual analysis and exegesis. But the advance came with a cost. Any reasonable approach to the meaning of a specific communication must take into account the speaker, the audience, and the circumstances, since all three affect the nuances of a particular speech or text. The meaning of a particular communication naturally depends on the particular words and their meanings. However, the meaning of a longer communication is not simply a mechanical product of word meanings, but includes a complex particular texture that varies with circumstance. Saussure deliberately cut off the variations in order to study "the system."

Second, Saussure largely cut off the influence of communicative context by focusing on word meanings.[5] Like his earlier move, this one flattens out the complexity of meaning. We may illustrate by considering a sample sentence: "The boy fed his dog." This sentence, composed of five words, utilizes the word meaning belonging to each of its words. But the sentence conveys more than the mechanical sum of those meanings. The sentence as a whole represents a larger construction, in which two noun phrases ("the boy" and "his dog") indicate the subject and the object, and in which a verb, "fed," indicates the action. Word meanings by themselves do not capture this complexity.

---

2. See the historical accounts in Leonard Bloomfield, *Language* (London: George Allen & Unwin, 1933), 4–19; Peter Matthews, *A Short History of Structural Linguistics* (Cambridge: Cambridge University Press, 2001). For an introduction to the whole discipline, see John Lyons, *Introduction to Theoretical Linguistics* (Cambridge: Cambridge University Press, 1969).

3. Ferdinand de Saussure, *Course in General Linguistics* (New York/Toronto/London: McGraw-Hill, 1959). The English text is a translation from *Cours de linguistique générale* (1916).

4. Saussure, lecturing in French, used the French word "langue" to designate the language system. By contrast, he used "parole" to designate particular speeches. Subsequent discussions frequently pick up this key distinction, and the two terms "langue" and "parole" have become technical terms to describe it.

5. Ibid., 65, "The Nature of the Linguistic Sign."

Saussure was aware of this difficulty. In later discussion he added context back in by introducing a key distinction between *syntagmatic* and *associative* (or paradigmatic) relations.[6] A *syntagmatic* relation is a relation among the parts within a larger construction like a sentence. For example, in the sentence "The boy fed his dog," the definite article "the" is related to "boy," and both are related to "fed." In general a *syntagmatic* relation is a side-by-side relation between the particular words that build up a single sentence, or between the sentences that make up a paragraph. By contrast, an *associative* relation is a relation between a particular word like "fed" and other words that could have fit in its place: "feeds," "is feeding," "loved," "saw," and so on. This second kind of relation has also been called a "paradigmatic relation."

By discussing these relations, Saussure acknowledged the complexity of actual communication. But damage has still been done, since the consideration of larger constructions with words still relies on words as its starting point. In many ways this reduction is quite understandable, because words are stable in relation to the surrounding speech, and we must start with some simplifications in order to get linguistics off the ground.

Third, Saussure introduced a model for linguistic signs with three parts: (1) the "sound-image" or signifier, (2) the "concept" or signified, and (3) the "sign" that consists of both parts combined together in a single whole. For example, the word *arbor* in Latin, which means "tree," is made up of (1) the sound-image consisting in a sequence of sounds a+r+b+o+r, (2) the concept of "tree," and (3) the "sign," namely, the word *arbor*, which associates the sound with the concept.[7] The form of the word consists in the sound-image, while the meaning can be equated with the concept.

This move makes sense as a way of defining more rigorously the distinction between form and meaning. But it introduces a subtle reductionism in the thinking about meaning. Children learning a language often learn the meanings of words through their occurrences in social situations where there is reference to a real-world object. Words for milk and soup, chair and table come to have meaning through the help of occurrences of milk and soup and chairs and tables in the environment. In the long run, referential functions have an indispensable role in meaning. Saussure has left out reference, and settled on "concept," which suggests a purely mental phenomenon. This restriction is once again understandable, given his earlier decision to focus on the language system. The language system does not directly refer to objects in the world in the same way that specific speakers refer to such objects in specific speeches. Within a dictionary, that is, within the language system, "arbor" means "tree," any tree. But in a specific speech a speaker may refer to one particular tree in his backyard. We can never understand meaning in its fullness if we leave out reference.

The omission of reference offers an open door for later reductionisms. For example, certain forms of structuralism have treated language as a closed system of signs that refer only to other signs. In the hands of certain practitioners, the "meaning" of any one particular text got reduced to the central truth that meaning is a function of the system.

6. Ibid., 124–127.
7. Ibid., 65.

Saussure proposed still another reduction when he shifted from "meaning" to "value." By "value" he means the significance that a particular unit has by virtue of its oppositions or contrasts to neighboring units. He says, "Language is a system of interdependent terms in which the value of each term results solely from the simultaneous presence of the others."[8] The word "solely" signals the reduction. It ignores both reference and the historical accumulation of potential for literary allusion to earlier occurrences of the same expression. Among linguists the benefits of focusing on the system of interdependent terms are now well known and undeniable. But we should not conceal from ourselves that these benefits derive partly from ignoring intractable complexities in what is left out.

## Leonard Bloomfield, 1933

A second milestone in the development of structural linguistics occurred with Leonard Bloomfield's publication of *Language* in 1933. Like Saussure, Bloomfield considered the correlation between sound and meaning to be fundamental.[9] And initially he introduced meaning in connection with life situations in which language is used to accomplish practical tasks. ("I am going to the store to get some bananas.") But simplifications entered in as he focused on the concerns of linguistics. For one thing, Bloomfield used a simple stimulus-response model for understanding human behavior.[10] He stated bluntly, ". . . in all sciences like linguistics, which observe some specific type of human activity, the worker must proceed exactly as if he held the materialistic view."[11]

Though Bloomfield in his early discussion equated meaning with the entire situation in which an utterance occurs, he soon reduced the task to "constant and definite meaning" for any one form.[12] This move—again, an understandable and convenient simplification to facilitate early progress in linguistics—ignored the influence of context. Meaning was effectively reduced to the meaning of an expression independent of the larger context.

## Noam Chomsky, 1957

As our next milestone we may conveniently take Noam Chomsky's *Syntactic Structures* in 1957.[13] Chomsky's book laid the foundation for what came to be known as *generative grammar*. Together with Chomsky's later work *Aspects of the Theory of Syntax*,[14] this book had enormous influence on the direction of linguistic research, especially in the United States, partly because it offered rigor and formalization. It achieved an impressive conclusion: certain simple types of formal grammar could be proved by mathematically rigorous means to be inadequate for the complexities of natural language.

---

8. Ibid., 114. On the same page Saussure explicitly distinguishes "value" from "signification." Likewise he says, "In a language-state everything is based on relations" (122).

9. Bloomfield, *Language*, 27.

10. Ibid., 23–31, 33–34.

11. Ibid., 38.

12. Ibid., 158.

13. Noam Chomsky, *Syntactic Structures* (The Hague: Mouton, 1957).

14. Noam Chomsky, *Aspects of the Theory of Syntax* (Cambridge, MA: MIT Press, 1965).

But rigor and formalization came, as usual, with a price. Chomsky stipulated that a *language* was "a set (finite or infinite) of sentences, each finite in length and constructed out of a finite set of elements."[15] This definition, which allows for a language to be subjected to a rigorous mathematically based analysis of syntax, ignores the role of context, both the context of a situation and the context of a discourse in paragraphs and larger sections. It is a vast simplification, but unfortunately Chomsky did not overtly acknowledge how much it simplifies. In the next sentence after this definition, he simply declared that "All natural languages in their spoken or written form are languages in this sense, . . ." We also hear hints that grammaticality is independent of meaning, which is true only as a first approximation.[16] In the long run grammatical categories make sense only in the service of meaningful communication.

Chomsky also introduced the significant distinction between *kernel* sentences and nonkernel sentences.[17] Roughly speaking, kernel sentences are simple, active-voice sentences like "The boy fed the dog." These sentences arise within Chomsky's formalism by the application of phrase structure rules and obligatory transformations.[18] Nonkernel sentences include passive sentences, such as "The dog was fed by the boy," and derived expressions like "It was the boy who fed the dog." Optional transformations specify how to move from an active clause structure like "The boy fed the dog" to the related passive structure, "The dog was fed by the boy." We should also consider expressions like "The boy's feeding the dog." The sentence "The boy fed the dog because it was mealtime" derives from two kernel sentences, namely, "The boy fed the dog" and "It was mealtime." These derivations use optional "transformations." All complex sentences, as well as other sentence types that derive from kernel sentences, arise from applying optional transformational rules to the original set of kernel sentences.[19]

This schema opens the door to the possibility of a semantic analysis in which the meaning of a sentence is the sum of the meanings of the kernel sentences from which it is derived, plus the semantic relations between kernels that are specified by the grammatical links between them. Such an analysis is tempting precisely because in many

---

15. Chomsky, *Syntactic Structures*, 13. Chomsky also assumed that sequences of words fall neatly into *grammatical* and *ungrammatical* types, which he acknowledged is an idealization (14). To achieve the impressive formal result of showing that finite state grammars are inadequate for natural language, he also had to introduce the idealization that says that sentences may be indefinitely complex—though the finiteness of human memory, in practice, puts a limit on the length of sentences (23).

16. Ibid., 15; see also the more extended discussion, 92–105.

17. Ibid., 45.

18. The *phrase structure rules* are a series of simple rules that, when used together, produce the most basic clause structures with subject and verb and sometimes an object. *Transformations* are specific formal rules that specify how to move from one grammatical structure to a "transformed" structure. One example is the "passive transformation," which converts "The boy fed the dog" into "The dog was fed by the boy." Technically, the transformations operate not on a sequence of words, but on tree structures, which include extra grammatical labels. For further explanation, see Chomsky, *Syntactic Structures*, 34–48; Lyons, *Introduction to Theoretical Linguistics*.

19. Technically, the optional transformations are applied to "forms that underlie kernel sentences . . . or prior transforms" (Chomsky, *Syntactic Structures*, 45).

cases it approximates the truth, and captures some of the core meaning or basic meaning that we associate with a sentence. But as a total account of meaning it is obviously reductionistic.

Linguistics has continued to develop since the Chomskyan revolution in 1957 and 1965. Chomsky's generative grammar eventually mutated into the theory of government and binding, and then into the minimalist program.[20] Though the detailed structure of the theories has changed markedly, the spirit of formalization and reductionism remains in place. But we also see challenges from competing theories. Cognitive linguistics, with its meaning-centered approach, challenges the grammar-centered approach of generative grammar and its successors.[21] Other alternative linguistic theories continue to attract followers.[22] Semantic theory has attracted continuing interest, sometimes without any strong dependence on a particular theory of grammar or sound.[23] The possibility of coherent alternative theoretical approaches suggests that any one approach is selective (and therefore potentially reductionistic) in its understanding.[24]

20. See, e.g., Noam Chomsky, *Rules and Representations* (New York: Columbia University Press, 1980); Chomsky, *Lectures on Government and Binding* (Dordrecht/Cinnaminson, NJ: Foris, 1981); Chomsky, *Some Concepts and Consequences of the Theory of Government and Binding* (Cambridge, MA: MIT Press, 1982); Chomsky, *Language and Problems of Knowledge* (Cambridge, MA: MIT Press, 1988); Liliane Haegeman, *Introduction to Government and Binding Theory* (Oxford: Blackwell, 1991); Andrew Radford, *Syntax: A Minimalist Introduction* (Cambridge: Cambridge University Press, 1997); David Adger, *Core Syntax: A Minimalist Approach* (Oxford: Oxford University Press, 2003).

21. See, e.g., David Lee, *Cognitive Linguistics: An Introduction* (Oxford: Oxford University Press, 2002); William Croft and D. Alan Cruse, *Cognitive Linguistics* (Cambridge: Cambridge University Press, 2004).

22. See, e.g., Mary Dalrymple, *Lexical-Functional Grammar* (San Diego: Academic Press, 2001); René Kager, *Optimality Theory* (Cambridge: Cambridge University Press, 1999). And I believe there is still value in the more nonformalized, discovery oriented, antireductive approach of tagmemic theory (Kenneth L. Pike, *Linguistic Concepts: An Introduction to Tagmemics* [Lincoln: University of Nebraska Press, 1982]).

23. See John Lyons, *Semantics*, 2 vols. (Cambridge: Cambridge University Press, 1977); D. Alan Cruse, *Meaning in Language: An Introduction to Semantics and Pragmatics* (Oxford: Oxford University Press, 2000).

24. See Pike, *Linguistic Concepts*, 5–9, on the role of theory in language analysis.

# Translation Theory

Also Jeshua, Bani, Sherebiah, Jamin, Akkub, Shabbethai, Hodiah,
Maaseiah, Kelita, Azariah, Jozabad, Hanan, Pelaiah, the Levites, helped
the people to understand the Law, while the people remained in their places.
They read from the book, from the Law of God, clearly, and they gave the sense,
so that the people understood the reading.

—Nehemiah 8:7–8

And they were amazed and astonished, saying, "Are not all these who are speaking Galileans? And how is it that we hear, each of us in his own native language?
Parthians and Medes and Elamites and residents of Mesopotamia, Judea and
Cappadocia, Pontus and Asia, Phrygia and Pamphylia, Egypt and the parts of
Libya belonging to Cyrene, and visitors from Rome, both Jews
and proselytes, Cretans and Arabians—we hear them telling in our own tongues
the mighty works of God."

—Acts 2:7–11

In the twentieth century a theory of Bible translation developed in tandem with linguistics and tried to profit in a multitude of ways from the developments in structural linguistics.[1] But while linguistics initially focused largely on issues of sound

---

1. For a broader context, see L. G. Kelly, *The True Interpreter: A History of Translation Theory and Practice in the West* (New York: St. Martin's, 1979). This and the previous appendix are taken, with some alterations, from Vern S. Poythress, "Truth and Fullness of Meaning: Fullness versus Reductionistic Semantics in Biblical Interpretation," *Westminster Theological Journal* 67/2 (2005): 211–227. Used with permission.

and grammar, translation had to deal directly with meaning and all its complexities. Bible translators confronted the task of translating the biblical message into thousands of tribal languages.

## Eugene Nida

Eugene Nida, in consultation with other pioneers in the field, developed the theory of "dynamic equivalence" or "functional equivalence," which stressed the importance of transferring meaning, not grammatical form.[2] Nida discussed various kinds of complexity in meaning even at a comparatively early date, beginning with his 1947 publication of *Bible Translating*.[3] He explicitly spoke about translating "fullest meaning" instead of a bare minimum.[4]

In 1964, Nida published the fuller and more theoretically advanced work, *Toward a Science of Translating*.[5] By this time, he was aware of the formalistic approach in generative grammar, not only Chomsky's *Syntactic Structures* but also Katz and Fodor's groundbreaking article, "The Structure of a Semantic Theory."[6] Nevertheless, in the first three chapters of his book he refused to be reductionistic. He spoke explicitly about many dimensions of meaning, and referred favorably to Roman Jakobson's classification of meaning into emotive, conative, referential, poetic, phatic, and metalingual dimensions.[7] He was so bold as to say:

> ... no word ever has precisely the same meaning twice, for each speech event is in a sense unique, involving participants who are constantly changing and referents which are never fixed. Bloomfield (1933, p. 407) describes this problem by saying that "every utterance of a speech form involves a minute semantic innovation."[8]

And again:

> In any discussion of communication and meaning, one must recognize at the start, each source and each receptor differs from all others, not only in the way the formal aspects of

---

2. See the discussion in Vern S. Poythress and Wayne A. Grudem, *The Gender-Neutral Bible Controversy: Muting the Masculinity of God's Words* (Nashville: Broadman & Holman, 2000), 57–90; or. Poythress and Grudem, *The TNIV and the Gender-Neutral Bible Controversy* (Nashville: Broadman & Holman, 2004), 169–202.

3. Eugene Nida, *Bible Translating* (New York: American Bible Society, 1947).

4. Ibid., 23.

5. Eugene Nida, *Toward a Science of Translating: With Special Reference to Principles Involved in Bible Translating* (Leiden: Brill, 1964).

6. Jerrold J. Katz and Jerry Fodor, "The Structure of a Semantic Theory," *Language* 39 (1963): 170–210. On the developments in structural linguistics, including Chomsky's work, see the previous appendix.

7. Nida, *Toward a Science of Translating*, 40–46. Page 45n3 refers to Roman Jakobson, "Closing Statement: Linguistics and Poetics," in *Style in Language*, ed. Thomas A. Sebeok (Cambridge, MA: Technology Press, M.I.T., 1960), 350–377. On Jakobson's six dimensions, see appendix H.

8. Nida, *Toward a Science of Translating*, 48.

the language are handled, but also in the manner in which symbols are used to designate certain referents. If, as is obviously true, each person employs language on the basis of his background and no two individuals ever have precisely the same background, then it is also obvious that no two persons ever mean exactly the same thing by the use of the same language symbols. At the same time, however, there is an amazing degree of similarity in the use of language . . .[9]

But Nida was also determined to use whatever insights he could obtain from Chomsky's generative grammar. So in chapter 4 he focused on what he called "linguistic meaning." Here he looked at the meanings associated with distribution of a word within larger contexts and within grammatical structures.[10] According to Nida, linguistic meaning often appears on "two levels":

> First, that meaning which is derived from the kernel construction by way of the transformations, and secondly that meaning which is supplied by the particular terminal construction (the end result in the process of transformation from the kernel to the resulting expression).[11]

In using the key terms *kernel* and *transformations*, Nida was clearly adopting the framework of Chomsky's generative grammar. Meaning was now to be seen within this framework.[12]

The concentration on "linguistic meaning" involves a reduction. Nida was aware of this, and so in the following chapter he supplemented this account with a discussion of "referential and emotive meanings."[13] But someone less aware than Nida can easily use the schema reductionistically to think that all or almost all of the really significant meaning is linguistic meaning, and that this meaning comes to light exclusively through the Chomskyan framework. The temptation is all the stronger because Nida himself suggested that his scheme could serve as the basis for a translation procedure:

> . . . it is most efficient for us to develop an approach to translation which takes these facts fully into consideration. Instead of attempting to set up transfers from one language to another by working out long series of equivalent formal structures which are presumably adequate to "translate" from one language into another, it is both scientifically and practically more efficient (1) to reduce the source text to its structurally simplest and most semantically evident kernels, (2) to transfer the meaning from source language to receptor language on

---

9. Ibid., 51.

10. The initial discussion of "linguistic meaning" occurs in ibid., 41–42.

11. Ibid., 65.

12. The terminology occurs also in Eugene A. Nida and Charles R. Taber, *The Theory and Practice of Translation* (Leiden: Brill, 1969), 39. It originates from Chomsky, *Syntactic Structures* (The Hague: Mouton, 1957).

13. Nida, *Toward a Science of Translating*, 70–119; note the earlier delineation of kinds of meaning, 41–43; see also Nida and Taber, *Theory and Practice of Translation*, 56–98.

a structurally simple level, and (3) to generate the stylistically and semantically equivalent expression in the receptor language.[14]

As Nida indicates in the surrounding discussion, an approach of this type looks promising particularly for languages whose formal, grammatical structures do not match well those of Indo-European languages such as English, German, Greek, and Latin. All languages show "remarkably similar kernel structures."[15] So if we can decompose meaning into these kernels, we can transfer it more easily from one language to another. In addition, the nonkernel structures do not necessarily reveal directly the underlying semantic relations. For example, the sentence "he hit the man with a stick"[16] may mean either that he used the stick as an instrument, or that the man who received the blow had a stick in hand. Such ambiguous constructions often have to be translated differently depending on the underlying meaning. Nida therefore proposed a three-stage process, in which the first stage involves decomposition into underlying kernel meanings.

The three-stage process promises benefits. But it comes at the cost of leaving out much of the richness of meaning that Nida expounded in the immediately preceding chapter. We have a breathtaking reduction here. Let us list some of its features.

First, we engage in reduction by ignoring all the idiosyncrasies of an individual speaker.

Second, we reduce meaning to the meaning of sentences, and no longer consider the interaction with situational context or the larger textual context of discourse. It should be noted in Nida's favor that elsewhere he explicitly called for attention to the larger contexts of paragraphs and discourse.[17] But this sound advice of his is at odds with the transformational generative model of his day, which confined its analysis to the sentence and its constituents. The reduction to considering only sentence meaning, and to considering sentences one by one, leads to ignoring discourse cohesion, including cohesion achieved through the repetition of key words. This reduction then inhibits the reader from seeing meaning relations not only within individual books of the Bible but in later allusions to earlier passages. The important theme of promise and fulfillment in the Bible is damaged.

Third, we reduce all figurative expressions to a literal level, since the core formal structures in transformational generative grammar deal only with literal meanings.

Fourth, we reduce meaning from a richness including referential, emotive, expressive, and other dimensions to the single plane of "linguistic meaning."

Fifth, we assume that meanings in the original are all clear and transparent. This assumption may be approximately true with some types of source texts on technical subjects

---

14. Nida, *Toward a Science of Translating*, 68. We can see the three-stage process worked out more explicitly and practically in Nida and Taber, *Theory and Practice of Translation*, 104.

15. Nida, *Toward a Science of Translating*, 68. These kernel structures are similar to some of what we discussed earlier when we focused on sentences.

16. An example used in ibid., 61.

17. ". . . expert translators and linguists have been able to demonstrate that the individual sentence in turn is not enough. The focus should be on the paragraph, and to some extent on the total discourse" (Nida and Taber, *Theory and Practice of Translation*, 102).

or on mundane affairs; but it is far from being true with the Bible, which contains both obscurities and depths.[18]

Sixth, we reduce the meaning of a complex nonkernel sentence to its constituent kernels.[19] This move is a genuine reduction, since meanings in fact do not reduce in a simple way to the meanings of kernel structures. Consider the expression "God's love." Can we reduce this expression to the kernel structure "God loves you"? In many contexts, this involves a decided change of meaning, since the expression "God's love" does not indicate the object of his love. Supplying an object such as "you" or "people," as we must do in a kernel sentence, forces upon us greater definiteness than the original expression.[20]

A similar problem often occurs with passives. "Bill was overwhelmed" is less definite than "Something overwhelmed Bill." For one thing, the passive expression does not indicate whether or not some one particular thing did the overwhelming. Maybe Bill felt overwhelmed, but there was no easily identifiable source for the feeling. Or maybe some other person, rather than some circumstance, overwhelmed Bill. The running back charged into him and overwhelmed him on the football field.

Similar problems occur when the back-transformation into a kernel requires us to supply an object. For example, the expression "Charlotte's kiss" gets transformed into the kernel sentence "Charlotte kissed someone." But did she kiss her dog? The "someone" in question may be an animal rather than a human being. The word *someone* does not then represent the possibilities quite adequately. Or did she throw a kiss to a large audience? Or did she just make a kissing sound, without directing her lips toward any particular someone? If we produce a kernel sentence to represent meaning, we expect it to have an object. But with any object we supply, such as "someone," we change the meaning by introducing assumptions that are not contained in the vaguer expression, "Charlotte's kiss."[21]

The reduction arises partly from reductive moves that have already taken place within the theory of transformational generative grammar, which Nida was using as a

---

18. The point about depth versus transparency is made eloquently by Stephen Prickett, *Words and the Word* (Cambridge: Cambridge University Press, 1986), 4–36.

19. Compare Noam Chomsky, *Aspects of the Theory of Syntax* (Cambridge, MA: MIT Press, 1965), 132.

20. Still another problem exists with an expression like "the love of God." This expression may indicate either the love that God has toward someone, or the love that someone has toward God, depending on the context. And some contexts may deliberately play on the potential ambiguity.

21. Generative grammar in 1965 could potentially handle some of this kind of complexity using so-called "subcategorization rules." But such rules were still an abstraction that exists several steps away from the particular changes in meaning-nuances that we may observe in actual sentences in natural languages.

Linguists can escape this problem temporarily by conceiving of the kernel sentences not as sentences in English but as abstract representations. But they are still on the horns of a dilemma. Either they try to represent every nuance of meaning in the abstract representation, which would make it intolerably complex and defeat the purpose of having it be a generalized representation, or else they admit that fully concrete English has nuances of meaning not captured in the abstract representation.

model. They also occur because somewhere along the line people may begin to assume that the transformations in question are meaning-preserving. But they actually change meaning, as Nida admitted when he talked about "two levels of linguistic meaning," the second of which is "supplied by the particular terminal construction."[22] Moreover, from a semantic point of view, the speaker does not necessarily start psychologically with a kernel sentence.[23] The speaker may not know or may not be concerned to supply semantically absent information that would have to be supplied in order to construct a kernel structure.

In fact, generative grammar originated as an attempt to describe grammar, not meaning. It so happened that generative transformations connected sentences with analogous meanings. But no one could guarantee that the meanings would be identical. Sometimes differences in meaning are obvious. Compare the question "Did you feed the dog?" with the analogous statement "You fed the dog." These two are transformationally related. But they differ in meaning because one is a question. By that very fact it has a different function in communication than the corresponding statement.

To insist that the meanings must be identical constitutes a reduction.[24] It may still be a useful reduction. The linguist who uses the reductive process achieves rigor and insight of various kinds. But he also puts himself and his disciples in a position where they may forget the reduction, or refuse to acknowledge it. They then force meaning in human discourse to match their "scientific" results, rather than forcing their science to acknowledge the full reality of human communication.

---

22. Nida, *Toward a Science of Translating*, 65.

23. In fact, Chomsky warned against understanding generative grammar as a psychological theory (Chomsky, *Aspects of the Theory of Syntax*, 9).

24. There are complexities about how we might treat transformations. In *Syntactic Structures* (1957) Chomsky postulated a simple system of phrase structure rules leading to a relatively simple set of kernel sentences. Under this schema, questions were to be derived from statements by applying the optional transformation "$T_q$" (p. 63). But by 1965 Chomsky had incorporated the question marker into the base structure, and the question transformation became obligatory, so that a transformation analogous to $T_q$ could preserve the additional meaning involved in asking a question (see Chomsky, *Aspects of the Theory of Syntax*, 132).

Obviously, over a period of time we could incorporate more and more previously neglected meaning aspects into the base grammar, in hopes of achieving a more adequate account of meaning. But the cost is increasing complexity in the base. In the most extreme case, we might imagine a situation where all the lost meaning has been reintegrated; but the cost would likely be a horrendous complexity. In fact, for the sake of rigorous testability, generative grammar chooses in spirit to seek reduction rather than fullness of meaning.

In 1964 Nida did not fully endorse Chomsky's later (1965) view that transformations must be meaning-preserving. Whether because he was working with Chomsky's 1957 view in *Syntactic Structures*, or because he saw the reductionism inherent in generative grammar, he affirmed that some extra meaning is contributed by the "particular terminal construction" (*Toward a Science of Translating*, 65). But if so, it vitiates the attempt to translate by reducing meaning to the underlying kernel structures (as Nida proposed in *Toward a Science of Translating*, 68).

## Scientific Rigor

The occurrence of the words "science" and "scientific" in the discussions can also signal a difficulty. Many have observed that social scientists have often envied the rigor and prestige of natural sciences, and have struggled to achieve the same level of rigor within their own fields. But a field dealing with human beings contains innate complexities and multidimensional relations. In such a situation, rigor and fullness of meaning will often be like two ends of a seesaw. If one goes up, the other must go down.[25]

Nida's 1964 book shows some telltale symptoms of this difficulty. He entitles the book, *Toward a Science of Translating.* Its title already introduces a tension: will we have "science," so-called, with its ever-increasing rigor? If so, will we put ourselves at odds with the centuries-old philological and hermeneutical instinct that interpretation and translation alike are arts, not sciences?

Yes, we may have maxims for interpretation or translation. At points, we may have highly technical procedures for checking out our instincts, and for searching ever more minutely the meaning of particular words in particular contexts, and the meanings of various grammatical constructions. But in the end the process of translation is so complex and multidimensional that it must remain an art; it involves technique, to be sure, as all good art does, but it is never reducible to a merely mechanical or formal process.[26]

Now Nida's title does not say, "The Science of Translating," but "*Toward* a Science of Translating." The word "toward" signals that we are still feeling our way. We have not yet arrived at a full-fledged science. But the title nevertheless holds out as a goal the reduction of translation to science. And this, I believe, contains a built-in bias in favor of formalism, and with it an invitation to move toward a reductionist approach to meaning. It suggests in particular that all figurative, allusive, and metaphorical language must be reduced to the level of the literal, in order to be fit for processing by the scientific machinery.

In contrast to this reductionistic movement, Nida himself displays in his chapter 3 a great deal of sensitivity and understanding concerning the multidimensional character of the meaning of texts. The problem, if you will, is not with Nida's own personal awareness of meaning, but with the program he proposes to others—others who may be less aware of the complexities.

We can see the problem coming to life if we look at Nida's description of translation after his discussion of generative grammar and kernel sentences:

> Instead of attempting to set up transfers from one language to another by working out long series of equivalent formal structures which are presumably adequate to "translate" from one language into another, it is both scientifically and practically more efficient (1) to reduce the source text to its structurally simplest and most semantically evident kernels,

---

25. Kelly delineates the problem: "Linguists' models assume that translation is essentially transmission of data, while hermeneutic theorists take it to be an interpretative re-creation of text. It is hardly surprising then, that each group, sure that it has the whole truth, lives in isolation from the other" (Kelly, *True Interpreter*, 34).

26. Note the duality that Kelly sees in theories of translation: "For the majority, translation is a literary craft . . ." "In contrast, linguists and grammarians have identified theory with analysis of semantic and grammatical operations" (Kelly, *True Interpreter*, 2).

(2) to transfer the meaning from source language to receptor language on a structurally simple level, and (3) to generate the stylistically and semantically equivalent expression in the receptor language.[27]

This key sentence contrasts two kinds of approach, both of which are utterly *formalistic* and mechanical about the translation process. The first approach would match surface grammatical structures between two languages, using an interminably long list. The second approach matches underlying kernels instead of surface structures.

But Nida has here presupposed that the only alternative to one formalistic approach is another formalistic one. He has not even mentioned the possibility of an *art*—the art of translation.[28] What if by art we have someone translate who has a high level of comprehension of complex meanings in both languages? Is not this nonformal, nonmechanistic approach superior to both of Nida's alternatives? Nida in his excitement over the potential of linguistics has lost sight of the complementary perspectives offered in the centuries-long traditions of hermeneutical theorists and literary analysts.[29]

The inclusion of the word "scientifically" in the middle of the sentence from Nida that is quoted above increases the difficulty. It biases readers to understand translation as a formal, mechanical process. It suggests that once the appropriate transformational rules are known for the two languages in question, we can simply apply the mechanical process in order to produce the appropriate result.

We should say in Nida's defense that he is partly thinking of the practical constraints on Bible translations into exotic languages. The professionally trained missionary Bible translator cannot hope to have the native speaker's competence in Mazotec or Quechua. Given the translator's limitations, thinking in terms of kernel sentences and transformations can provide genuine insights into differences between languages, and suggest ways in which the verses of Scripture may have to be re-expressed in Mazotec.

But, as Nida stresses elsewhere, there is no good substitute for testing a proposed translation with native speakers.[30] The translator must take into account the full effects of connotative and affective meanings, of context, of previous enculturation, and so on. There can be no *science* of translation in the strict sense, and Nida's own practical discussions are proof of it. The formalization of meaning constitutes a danger, because it can lead to a reductionistic approach to translation by those who do not see the partial

---

27. Nida, *Toward a Science of Translating*, 68.

28. Further down on the same page (ibid.) Nida mentions "the really competent translator," by which he presumably means someone who knows both languages intimately. But Nida uses this temporary tip of the hat toward competence only as evidence that restructuring is sometimes legitimate; he does not consider whether the existence of this competent translator also shows the limitations in the reductionism and formalism that Nida proposes everywhere else on the page.

29. See Kelly, *True Interpreter*, 2–4, 36. "In the polemic between these three groups of theorists, only a few individuals have perceived that their approaches are complementary" (pp. 3–4). "Where linguistics concentrates on the means of expression, the complementary hermeneutic approach analyses the goal of linguistic interactions. The focus here is anti-empiricist: the central reality is not the observable expression, but the understanding of the cognitive and affective levels of language through which communication takes place" (7).

30. Nida and Taber, *Theory and Practice of Translation*, 163–182.

and one-sided character of Nida's proposed procedure. A wide human sensitivity and comprehension is needed, and this larger human involvement complements technical study of language and linguistics.[31] And I should underline the complementarity here. The technical study of language and linguistics does have much to contribute. I am not advocating an ignorance of linguistics, or a minimization of its value, but an awareness of the specialized character of its foci and consequent limitations in the vision of any one linguistic approach.

In considering Nida's approach and its subsequent development, we should also bear in mind the practical limitations that arise in many situations where the target for translation is a tribal culture with no previous literacy. Cultures with no previous knowledge of the Bible or Christianity, and sometimes with little or no previous knowledge of worldwide cultures, create special difficulties for communicating religious truths. The extra barriers put a heavy premium on making everything simple and clear. Without this simplicity—which itself constitutes a kind of reduction—the target readers, with minimal skills in literacy, may give up altogether and not read the message at all. In such a situation the missionary wants primarily to spread the basic message of the gospel to a new culture, not to produce a Bible translation for an already mature church. We can sympathize with the goals of utmost simplicity and clarity in such cases without converting these goals into general standards for Bible translation or for discourse meaning and semantics.

## Componential Analysis of Meaning

We can see a similar encroachment of reductionism in the componential analysis of meaning. In the approach called componential analysis, the meaning of a word gets reduced to a series of binary components. A "bachelor" is (1) human, (2) male, and (3) unmarried. Linguists have a formal notation to describe these components. The first component, "human," is denoted "[+ human]." The plus sign indicates that it is human as opposed to nonhuman. The meaning "nonhuman" would be denoted "[- human]." Similarly, "[+ male]" indicates the meaning "male." "[- male]" would mean "female." "[- married]" means "unmarried." We can then summarize the meaning of "bachelor" by listing three binary components: [+ human], [+ male], and [- married].

Componential analysis has a considerable history in the area of analyzing sound ("phonology"). Here it works reasonably and insightfully, because the sound system of a language offers a small, limited system of sounds whose significance depends largely on contrasts with other elements in the system. Thus in English the sound (phoneme) "p" is distinguished from "b" by the role of the vocal chords.[32] With "p" the vocal chords do not vibrate, and so "p" is called an "unvoiced" consonant. "P" differs from "f" and "v" by the fact that with "p" the air stream is at one point completely stopped. Thus, "p" can be characterized both as "unvoiced" and as stopping the air stream. In the formal notation of linguistics, we may say that "p" is [- voiced] (unvoiced) and [+ stop] (it stops the flow of air). In keeping with its formalistic and reductionistic program, generative

---

31. Kelly notes the complementarity in *True Interpreter*, 3–4.
32. Technically, in some contexts aspiration is also a factor.

grammar soon adopted the use of componential analysis in its study of meaning. By analogy with the procedure of decomposing sounds into distinctive binary features for sound, it decomposed meanings into distinctive binary meaning components such as [+ male] or [- married].

When we deal with kinship terms and certain other well-defined, limited areas of meanings,[33] an analysis into meaning components may yield significant insight. And it may be of value more broadly for the language learner who is trying to appreciate key meaning contrasts in a new language. Nida rightly saw the value and introduced "componential analysis" of meaning in connection with his instruction about translation.[34] But Nida also indicated some limitations:

> By analyzing only the minimal features of distinctiveness, many supplementary and connotative elements of meaning are disregarded, . . .[35]

The danger here is that careless practitioners may later overlook the reductionistic character of componential analysis, and consider it to be *the definitive* statement about meaning.

The reductionism in componential analysis can get added to other reductionisms that we have observed in Nida's use of kernel sentences. As a result, reductionistic approaches to meaning may enter the process of Bible translation. Anthony H. Nichols, in his extended analysis of dynamic equivalence translation, has shown that dangers of this kind are not merely hypothetical but have had a baleful effect on some sample translations.[36]

Unfortunately, the formalistic, "scientific" cast of the theory may make it difficult to take criticism. Theorists tell themselves that science is superior to the rabble's naïveté. Once they have a scientific theory, criticism from outside can easily be dismissed as uninformed, because it does not bow before the power and insight of the theory. Theorists have then discovered a means for self-protection. When an outside observer complains about losses of meaning in a sample translation,[37] he may be told that he is not competent to judge, because he is not initiated into the mysteries of componential analysis

---

33. Modern linguistic theory speaks of "semantic domains" or "semantic fields." See, e.g., John Lyons, *Semantics*, 2 vols. (Cambridge: Cambridge University Press, 1977), 1:250–269. For an application to Greek lexicography, see Johannes P. Louw and Eugene A. Nida, *Greek-English Lexicon of the New Testament Based on Semantic Domains*, 2 vols. (New York: United Bible Societies, 1988). For an example using kinship terms, see Nida, *Toward a Science of Translating*, 90–93.

34. Ibid., 82–87.

35. Ibid., 87; other limitations are listed on the same page.

36. Anthony Howard Nichols, "Translating the Bible: A Critical Analysis of E. A. Nida's Theory of Dynamic Equivalence and Its Impact upon Recent Bible Translations," Ph.D. dissertation, University of Sheffield, 1996. As we might have guessed from the nature of Nida's dynamic equivalence model, one of the effects is a flattening or elimination of figurative speech. Figurative speech poses a genuine challenge for translation, because a word-for-word rendering of a figure into another language may be difficult to understand or may invite misunderstanding. But this is not to say that we must go to the opposite extreme and systematically eliminate figurative expressions because of an aversion to anything that is not transparently clear.

37. For an eloquent complaint by such an "outsider," see Leland Ryken, *The Word of God in English: Criteria for Excellence in Bible Translation* (Wheaton, IL: Crossway, 2002). Note the

and translation theory. What the translation theorist's net does not catch is summarily judged not to be fish!

Decades ago, Bible translators learned that they must listen carefully to the judgments of native speakers about meaning. It would be ironic if now, as translation theory grows more mature, it were used in reverse to pronounce "expert" judgments about which kinds of meaning native speakers may be allowed to worry about.

## Continued Development

Linguistically based translation theory has continued to develop since Nida wrote in 1964.[38] Analysis of propositional relations and discourse has enriched the early model.[39] Translators like Ernst-August Gutt have explicitly criticized over-simple approaches to meaning that characterized the early days of translation theory.[40] Kenneth L. Pike early recognized the complexity of the interlocking between form and meaning, and the embedding of language meaning in a larger human context.[41] Textlinguistics emphasizes the role of a full discourse, including paragraphs and larger cohesive structures, rather than confining attention only to individual sentences in isolation.[42]

Above all, better translators have always known that translation is an art; Nida's and others' technical tools are properly used only as one dimension in the process of trying to do justice to total meaning.[43]

---

appendix (ibid., 295–327) by C. John Collins, who has more of an "insider's" understanding of the issues.

38. See, e.g., the extensive bibliography at <http://www.ethnologue.com/bibliography. asp>.

39. John Beekman and John Callow, *Translating the Word of God: With Scripture and Topical Indexes* (Grand Rapids, MI: Zondervan, 1974), especially 267–342; Kathleen Callow, *Discourse Considerations in Translating the Word of God* (Grand Rapids, MI: Zondervan, 1974). For a framework that acknowledges still more dimensions of meaning, see Vern S. Poythress, "A Framework for Discourse Analysis: The Components of a Discourse, from a Tagmemic Viewpoint," *Semiotica* 38/3–4 (1982): 277–298; Poythress, "Hierarchy in Discourse Analysis: A Revision of Tagmemics," *Semiotica* 40/1–2 (1982): 107–137.

40. Ernst-August Gutt, *Relevance Theory: A Guide to Successful Communication in Translation* (Dallas: Summer Institute of Linguistics, 1992); Gutt, *Translation and Relevance: Cognition and Context* (Oxford/Cambridge: Blackwell, 1991).

41. Kenneth L. Pike, *Language in Relation to a Unified Theory of the Structure of Human Behavior* (The Hague/Paris: Mouton, 1967), especially 62–63; Vern S. Poythress, "Gender and Generic Pronouns in English Bible Translation," in *Language and Life: Essays in Memory of Kenneth L. Pike*, ed. Mary Ruth Wise, Thomas N. Headland, and Ruth M. Brend (Dallas: SIL International and the University of Texas at Arlington, 2003), 371–380.

42. See, in particular, Robert E. Longacre, *The Grammar of Discourse*, 2nd ed. (New York: Plenum, 1996); Longacre, "Holistic Textlinguistics," SIL, 2003 (available at <http://www.sil. org/silewp/2003/silewp2003-004.pdf>).

43. But Nichols, "Translating the Bible," demonstrates that in practice translators adhering to the "dynamic equivalence" approach associated with Eugene Nida have too seldom risen above the limitations of a reductionistic theory of meaning.

All this is good news. But the dangers of reductionism remain as long as linguists and translation theorists experience pressure from the prestige of scientific rigor. Rigor is possible in linguistics and in translation when we isolate a sufficiently small piece of language, or one dimension of language, and temporarily ignore the residue that does not cleanly fit into a formalized model. Such models do offer insights, but they can be misused in a clumsy or arrogant manner.

## Language in the Context of Divine Speech and Divine Sovereignty

As we have seen, from the beginning God's speaking plays a key role in human life. We may put it provocatively: God is a native speaker of each human language, and a member—the key member—of the linguistic community. Given that reality, we must take care not to use linguistic insights in a reductionistic fashion. Rather, we must rethink the nature of language itself, free from the assumption that it involves only horizontal communication between human beings and that its meanings can be completely and definitively captured under the microscope of linguistic technique.

The principle of avoiding reductionism applies especially to the character of God's speech. But it applies derivatively to the speech of human beings, who are made in the image of God and who therefore have the capability of thinking God's thoughts after him.

What does it mean to think God's thoughts after him? We are creatures and never become God. But we can know truth. Any truth that we know is first of all in God's mind. We are not the first to have thought about it. God thinks it first. And because our mind is made *like* his, we can imitate him, and can know truths. God can express truths by speaking. Likewise, human beings, in imitation of God, can express truths by speaking.

Linguistics is useful in analyzing speech, because it does make evident some of the structural regularities belonging to language. But any particular approach within linguistics will have limitations because it is selective in its focus.

# Symbolic Logic and Logical Positivism

I speak as to sensible people; judge for yourselves what I say.

—1 Corinthians 10:15

Let us now consider developments in symbolic logic. Reflection about logic goes all the way back to Aristotle. But formal symbolic logic blossomed in the late nineteenth and early twentieth centuries with the work of Gottlob Frege, Bertrand Russell, and others.[1] Symbolic logic made more rigorous the idea of a valid proof. And it proves useful in uncovering logical fallacies in informal reasoning. But what of its limitations?

For the most part, the use of symbolic logic requires that we begin with isolated sentences. This step already involves a reduction of the full richness of human communication as it occurs in long discourses and social interaction. It also requires that a sentence be isolated from its situational context, that is, the context surrounding human beings when they communicate with one another at a particular time and place. Logic isolates the sentence into a "proposition" (without context) and then treats the sentence almost wholly in terms of its truth value.[2]

---

1. For an introduction, see Susanne K. K. Langer, *An Introduction to Symbolic Logic* (New York: Dover, 1953); Irving M. Copi, *Introduction to Logic*, 4th ed. (New York: Macmillan, 1972).

2. A part of these comments on logic is taken, with modifications, from Vern S. Poythress, "Truth and Fullness of Meaning: Fullness versus Reductionistic Semantics in Biblical Interpretation," *Westminster Theological Journal* 67/2 (2005): 211–227; also appearing in Wayne Grudem et al., *Translating Truth: The Case for Essentially Literal Bible Translation* (Wheaton, IL: Crossway,

Symbolic logic affords valuable opportunities to make hidden assumptions explicit, and to detect fallacies in reasoning. In its attempt to grasp truth and truthful reasoning, it depends on the rationality of the human mind, which is made in the image of God. Logic thus reflects the rationality of God himself. But the human mind is not God, and so there are limitations. Symbolic logic, to be rigorous, has to reduce seriously the full richness of human communication, in its focus on isolated propositions and their truth values. It is so obviously reductive in its approach to meaning that perhaps we do not need so much to remind ourselves of its reductive character.


## Logical Positivism

And yet one philosophical movement, logical positivism, did fall into a reductionism closely related to logic. Logical positivism saw the rigor of symbolic logic, along with the rigor of mathematics and the lesser rigor in hard sciences, as the model for all truth. It thought in terms of propositions isolated from human discourses and focused on truth value. It said that only two kinds of propositions had cognitive meaning and truth value, namely, tautologies and empirically verifiable statements. All other propositions had only "emotive" significance.

Tautologies are statements that can be seen to be true by virtue of an inspection of their meaning: "A is A"; "What is white is white"; and "Bachelors are unmarried." In contrast to tautologies, empirically verifiable statements are statements whose truth can be checked out by empirical means, by inspecting or measuring something within the environment. Thus, "The moon is made of green cheese" is empirically verifiable and false. "An apple seed can be planted and sometimes grows into an apple tree" is empirically verifiable and true. "Being negates itself" (a famous statement from Heidegger) is not empirically verifiable.

Logical positivism blossomed and flourished for a while, especially among people who admired the rigor of science and who felt impatient with or skeptical about general philosophical and religious statements ("God is love"). It is a significant movement from the point of view of language, because it was hoping to clean up language and concentrate on the proper and fruitful uses of language for empirical science, while discarding the allegedly fruitless and meaningless uses having to do with philosophy, metaphysics, and religion.


## The Demise of Positivism

Yet logical positivism died because of its own internal problems. Consider its fundamental thesis:

A statement is cognitively meaningful only if it is either tautologous or empirically verifiable.

2005), 113–134. Used with permission. See also Poythress, "Reforming Ontology and Logic in the Light of the Trinity: An Application of Van Til's Idea of Analogy," *Westminster Theological Journal* 57/1 (1995): 187–219.

Is this thesis itself a tautology? If so, it can only be because the expression "cognitively meaningful" has already been secretly redefined to *mean* "tautologous or empirically verifiable," in which case it is trivially true. But then it is useless for the practical task of assigning *genuine* meaning (as opposed to its own hothouse definition of meaning). Or is the thesis empirically verifiable? No, because it is a claim about cognitive meaning, not about the phenomenal world. We cannot specify a series of scientific procedures that would lead to a definitive test of its truthfulness.

So now apply the thesis to itself:

> The thesis of logical positivism is cognitively meaningful only if it is either tautologous or empirically verifiable.

Since the thesis is neither tautologous nor empirically verifiable, it is not cognitively meaningful. Hence the thesis has destroyed its own meaning, and the movement of logical positivism cannot be sustained.

In looking back over the collapse of logical positivism, we can see in the movement the desire to save language from confusion. By so doing, the logical positivists also hoped to save human beings from confusion and from the allure of false religion. At root, this was a "redemptive" program. The central thesis, the thesis about tautology and verifiability, offered a seemingly universal vision about the nature of meaning. But it had to exceed its own bounds—it had to ascend to heaven—in order to obtain this vision.[3] It was in fact a kind of substitute religion. It declared, on the basis of godlike insight into the nature of truth and verifiability, that all conventional religions and philosophies were meaningless. With that declaration it offered to its adherents godlike wisdom, and freed them from the alleged deceits of conventional religion. But in the long run it undermined itself, since it could give no coherent account of the basis for its own claim.

---

3. On the theme of ascent to heaven, see Vern S. Poythress, "The Quest for Wisdom," in *Resurrection and Eschatology: Theology in Service of the Church*, ed. Lane G. Tipton and Jeffrey C. Waddington (Phillipsburg, NJ: Presbyterian & Reformed, 2008), 86–114.

# The Theory of Speech Acts

All the ways of a man are pure in his own eyes,
but the Lord weighs the spirit.

—Proverbs 16:2

N ow we consider the theory of speech acts, as developed by John Austin and John R. Searle.[1]

## Classification of Speech Acts

What is the theory of speech acts? It describes and classifies the different kinds of things that people do when they use sentences in actual speech. According to John Searle's classification, there are five general categories.[2] (1) "Assertives," such as "I went to town

---

1. The foundational works are John L. Austin, *How to Do Things with Words* (Cambridge, MA: Harvard University Press, 1962); and John R. Searle, *Speech Acts: An Essay in the Philosophy of Language* (London: Cambridge University Press, 1969). See also Searle, *Expression and Meaning: Studies in the Theory of Speech Acts* (Cambridge: Cambridge University Press, 1979); Searle, *Intentionality: An Essay in the Philosophy of Mind* (Cambridge/New York: Cambridge University Press, 1983); William P. Alston, *Philosophy of Language* (Englewood Cliffs, NJ: Prentice-Hall, 1964); and critique in Armin Burkhard, ed., *Speech Acts, Meaning, and Intentions: Critical Approaches to the Philosophy of John R. Searle* (Berlin/New York: de Gruyter, 1990). Speech-act theory has roots in the later writings of Ludwig Wittgenstein. This appendix appeared in an earlier form in Vern S. Poythress, "Canon and Speech Act: Limitations in Speech-Act Theory, with Implications for a Putative Theory of Canonical Speech Acts," *Westminster Theological Journal* 70/2 (Fall 2008): 337–354; used with permission.

2. Searle, *Expression and Meaning*, viii, 12–20. Compare this classification with that of John Austin in *How to Do Things with Words*, 150–163, and note Searle's expression of dissatisfaction with Austin's classification (Searle, *Expression and Meaning*, 8–12). Speech-act theory concerns itself not only with classification but also with making some key distinctions among sentences, utterances, and the social commitments made using utterances.

yesterday," "commit the speaker . . . to the truth of the expressed proposition."[3] (2) "Directives," such as "Go to town," "are attempts . . . to get the hearer to do something."[4] (3) "Commissives," such as "I promise to go to town," "committ [sic] the speaker . . . to some future course of action."[5] (4) "Expressives," such as "I apologize," express a "psychological state" about a situation.[6] (5) "Declarations," such as "I resign," "bring about the correspondence between the propositional content and reality."[7] One of the points of speech-act theory is to awaken us to the fact that assertions of fact are only one of a number of kinds of speech act.

## Speech-act Theory in Relation to Behavioremes

Speech-act theory has affinities with what we have said about human action and behavioremes, especially human *verbal* action.[8] Among the kinds of verbal behavioremes Kenneth Pike lists the following: a judge's giving sentence, a lawyer's argument, the President's annual message to Congress, a sermon, an umpire's decision; greetings, calls, questions; requests, commands; statements; singing a song, chorus, vocal solo, cantata, oratorio, aria, chant, participation in a choir practice session; giving a joke, limerick, parody, pun, or comedy; and others.[9] All of these are similar in some ways to speech acts.

Speech-act theory thus has some of the same purposes as Pike's theory of the behavioreme. Both draw attention to ways in which human beings use language in actual situations. Language use is human use within a context, with various purposes.[10] Speech-act theory has enriched the understanding of language by pushing analysts away from merely analyzing a sample sentence in isolation from its actual use by human beings (and potential use by God and angels).

Now let us look at some of the limitations of speech-act theory. Inevitably a focus on limitations is going to sound negative. So I should say at the beginning that I am not really criticizing speech-act theory at its best, but rather attempting to head off misuses

---

3. Searle, *Expression and Meaning*, 12.

4. Ibid., 13.

5. Ibid., 14.

6. Ibid., 15.

7. Ibid., 16–17.

8. See chapter 19.

9. Kenneth L. Pike, *Language in Relation to a Unified Theory of the Structure of Human Behavior*, 2nd ed. (The Hague: Mouton, 1967), 138–139.

10. In reflecting on speech acts, J. L. Austin has these things to say:

> We must consider the total situation in which the utterance is issued—the total speech act—if we are to see the parallel between statements and performative utterances, and how each can go wrong (Austin, *How to Do Things with Words*, 52).

> . . . for some years we have been realizing more and more clearly that the occasion of an utterance matters seriously, and that the words used are to some extent to be 'explained' by the 'context' in which they are designed to be or have actually been spoken in a linguistic interchange. Yet still perhaps we are too prone to give these explanations in terms of 'the meanings of words' (ibid., 100).

and oversimplifications, as well as lack of awareness concerning the simplifications that enter into the formation of the theory.

## Starting with the Simple

Speech-act theory, like any theory, is selective in its attention to human behavior. What are the consequent strengths and weaknesses? What does it leave out, or at least put in the background?

John Searle specifically acknowledges some simplifications:

> I am ignoring more complex types of subject expressions, field predicate expressions, and molecular propositions. Until we can get clear about the simple cases we are hardly likely to get clear about the more complicated ones.[11]

Yes, the standard procedure in many kinds of modern analysis starts with simple, "atomic" cases. The atomic cases are the simplest, and the analyst can hardly hope "to get clear" about complex cases without a basis in simple cases. He builds up from atoms to molecules to macroscopic structures.

The difficulty lies in the assumption that such analysis leaves nothing essential aside. But of course it does. It leaves aside context. Even within the field of chemistry, the behavior of atoms depends strongly on how they are bonded to other atoms. So it is with human communication. The decision to start with atomic propositions is a decontextualizing move, and all such moves are problematic when, as is the case with human language, context is essential to meaning. In this case, the context includes the complexity of human beings, who are the speakers and conversationalists, and the complexity of their environment, which includes world history and the God who rules it.[12]

People can still achieve impressive results with this kind of analysis, because it does observe features of language and communication that are actually there. But will they along the way forget the initial simplifications? Let us suppose that they become "clear" about simple cases—because they have systematically ignored sources of complexity. Will they then take pride in their alleged deep insight? And then will they, out of pride, *impose* the same "clarity" on complexity, by simply smashing out the complexity and forcing it into the mold crafted by their "clarity"? The fault here would not be with speech-act theory itself, narrowly conceived, but with the practitioners who forget its innate limitations.

## Issues of Hierarchy

So let us consider how smaller, "atomic" speech acts are embedded in larger contexts.

---

11. Searle, *Speech Acts*, 33.

12. Note how, in discussing indirect speech acts, which are one form of complexity, Searle rightly appeals to many dimensions of human knowledge both about the environment and about the assumptions and commitments of other human beings. This context is not formalizable, nor does Searle suggest that it is (Searle, *Expression and Meaning*, 34–35).

Speech-act theory classifies speech acts into various kinds. Speech acts include asking a question, making a promise, pronouncing a verdict, or issuing a command. These are all classes of verbal behavioremes. Speech-act theory focuses on the contrastive-identificational features that characterize a particular kind of speech.[13] But what becomes of the contextual (distributional) aspect of these speeches?[14] Small speeches are embedded ("distributed") within larger groupings of human behavior. Speech-act theory does encourage reflection about contextual conditions that may be necessary for the happy execution of a speech.[15] The condition of being an umpire is necessary in order to call a strike in a baseball game. But because of the focus on atomic propositions, there is little attention to the way in which speeches can be embedded in larger speeches, and how several smaller purposeful human actions may together accomplish a larger purpose.

The choral singer, for example, not only has the purpose of singing a song, but of singing in concert with others to produce a harmonious and elegant result. Within the context of a worship service, the choral singer has the larger purpose of praising God and leading the people in such praise. Moreover, the choral singer participates in a *corporate* speech act with the other singers. Speech-act theory, by its exclusive focus on individual actions, puts in the background the reality of corporate cooperative actions, corporate competitive and antagonistic actions, and the corporate purpose of speech behavior in contexts like group discussions.

Even within a monologue we find complexities in human purpose, partly because smaller pieces of language are embedded in bigger ones. Suppose that a political speaker makes a request. That is one kind of speech act. But his request can occur in a larger context. Let us imagine a situation in which the request occurs as part of an apology, which is part of an explanation, which is part of a whole political speech.[16] The speech

---

13. The focus on classificational features is especially obvious in Searle, "A Taxonomy of Illocutionary Acts," in *Expression and Meaning*, 1–19. But it is evident more widely in the concern for distinguishing major *kinds* of speech acts.

14. See the discussion of contrast, variation, and context (distribution) in chapter 19.

15. See especially Searle, *Expression and Meaning*, 12–45.

16. In J. L. Austin's exposition of speech acts (*How to Do Things with Words*), it is not clear whether he is intending to analyze only single sentences that are also complete utterances (monologues), or to include all single sentences whether or not they are complete utterances, or to include all complete utterances, or to include paragraphs or sections within larger complete utterances. For simplicity he focuses on the utterance of single sentences that are also complete utterances, leaving to one side the additional complexities with larger groupings.

John Searle, in his foundational exposition concerning speech acts, is also not clear about the role of larger speeches in human action. It appears that he simplifies by focusing on sentence-level speech acts: "The characteristic grammatical form of the illocutionary act is the complete sentence (it can be a one-word sentence); . . ." (Searle, *Speech Acts*, 25). Most of the time Searle further simplifies to sentences with a single clause (cf. ibid., 33).

By contrast, a verbal behavioreme, also called an "uttereme" (see chapter 19), is a unit that allows for embedding. When they appear in conversation, phonemes, morphemes, words, phrases, clauses, sentences, paragraphs, and whole monologues are all utteremes. The speaker "does something" with purpose when he utters them. Thus Pike's category of "uttereme" is better adapted to include the full range of purposeful verbal action, both at lower levels (word, phrase) and higher levels (paragraph). See also Kevin Vanhoozer's discussion of a hierarchy of acts in "From Speech

as a whole rhetorically has several purposes: to praise his party, to justify its policies, to rally and encourage the faithful, to raise funds, and to promote his own election.[17] The embedded request represents not just a simple request but also an utterance that serves the several larger purposes. Description in terms of speech acts may sometimes stop with saying, "he is making a request." That is technically correct. But it focuses on only one aspect (the contrastive-identificational aspect of a particular verbal behavioreme).

Next, are we attending to *variation*? Suppose the particular politician's request runs, "Please do not judge me harshly." That is a request. So far so good. But it is also a particular *kind* of request. It is a request with respect to audience behavior in moral and judicial evaluation, not a request to donate money, or to cheer more loudly, or to talk to their friends about the campaign, or to take heart. More specifically still, it is a request that indirectly warns the audience against the temptation to be harsh in judgment. It suggests a plea for mercy, but avoids an overt admission that the speaker *needs* mercy (which might in turn suggest that what he did is actually quite wicked). More specifically still, it is a request of this kind that politely asks ("Please"), and thereby indicates respect for the audience and for social graces.

Does an analysis in terms of speech acts merely say, "He is making a request"? A generality may be true enough, but it focuses on the general rather than all the specifics. The specifics are also a meaningful part of human action. The difficulty here is that meaning in the world of persons and personal action is so rich and multidimensional that no theory can master it. Therefore analysts, in their desire to be "scientific" and precise, run the risk of neglecting all but some single dimension, or a small number of dimensions, that can be selected out and flattened enough so that the analysis can be "rigorous."[18]

The classification of speech acts into different types, such as assertion, promise, and command, helps us to notice the variety of ways in which human beings use language. That is most helpful in broadening the field, and correcting an earlier philosophical viewpoint that thought of the essence of language as consisting in propositions that were used to make assertive claims about the facts of the world. Promises and commands do different things than do assertions. Assertions endeavor to fit words to the world, while

---

Acts to Scripture Acts," in *First Theology: God, Scripture, and Hermeneutics* (Downers Grove, IL: InterVarsity, 2002), 191–194.

17. The actual *bringing about* of the intended goals may in many cases be classified as "perlocutionary effect" rather than "illocutionary act" (see the distinction introduced by J. L. Austin, *How to Do Things with Words*, 94–107). But when certain intentions concerning effects are made manifest in a particular speech, the manifestation of those intentions—though not their effects on the audience—is often one aspect of what the speaker does in speaking. The speaker can be held responsible for commitments that he makes in speech with respect to effects on the audience. On occasion, he can even be held partly responsible for a response that he incites in the audience—or fails to incite when he is in a position to do so. So the line between illocution and perlocution is delicate. And a given verbal behavioreme (speech act) will often be embedded in sequence in a still larger behavioreme, which may include the audience consequences within it.

18. J. L. Austin states the problem well with respect to philosophical analysis: "And we must at all costs avoid over-simplification, which one might be tempted to call the occupational disease of philosophers if it were not their occupation" (Austin, *How to Do Things with Words*, 38).

commands propose new actions in the world that will fit the words in the command. The direction of fit is different.[19]

But now can there be more complex cases? Can human verbal actions have purposes and make commitments in multiple dimensions? Surely they can, because human actions are capable of having multiple interlocking purposes and making complex commitments. Consider the request, "Please tell me what you read yesterday, and what you thought of it." This request may have complex purposes. Like other requests, it proposes an action that fits the words. But a request, in distinction from a command, invites the respondent to have a certain flexibility that matches his personality and needs. In this respect, the requester wishes his words to fit the person. And so the subsequent action—or decision not to act—will fit the person as well. And the request also asks to be informed about the world, the world of the person, and the world of the book he read. In addition, if a mother asks her child a question like this one, she may be more interested in finding out about her child than about the book he read. This complexity arises even with a request that grammatically is fairly simple. What about sarcasm? What about jokes, used to teach or persuade?

To his credit, Searle acknowledges at the conclusion of his taxonomy of speech acts that, "Often, we do more than one of these [kinds of acts] at once in the same utterance."[20] It is easy for later students to overlook that qualification.

We can enrich the picture being developed in speech-act theory by noting, as Roman Jakobson does, that any one use of language has multiple purposeful dimensions. Jakobson distinguishes emotive, conative, referential, poetic, phatic, and metalingual dimensions.[21] Roughly speaking, the emotive dimension concerns what the speaker reveals about his attitudes; the conative concerns the impact on recipients; the referential concerns information about the world; the phatic concerns the way in which the communication expresses and affects the social bond between speaker and hearer; the metalingual concerns what the speech reveals about language as a code; and the poetic concerns ways in which a message focuses on itself, perhaps by rhythm or alliteration. All of these dimensions are present in all communication, but one or more may be more prominent in a particular act of communication.[22]

---

19. See Searle, *Expression and Meaning*, 3–4.

20. Ibid., 29.

21. Roman Jakobson, "Closing Statement: Linguistics and Poetics," in *Style in Language*, ed. Thomas A. Sebeok (Cambridge, MA: Technology Press, M.I.T., 1960), 353–358.

22. Ibid., 353: "Although we distinguish six basic aspects of language, we could, however, hardly find verbal messages that would fulfill only one function. The diversity lies not in a monopoly of some one of these several functions but in a different hierarchical order of functions. . . . the accessory participation of the other functions in such messages must be taken into account by the observant linguist." We may compare this approach with Searle's. Searle's "taxonomy" (*Expression and Meaning*, viii, 12–20) includes "Assertives," corresponding to Jakobson's referential function; "Directives," corresponding to the conative function; "Commissives," corresponding most closely to the phatic function; "Expressives," corresponding to the emotive function; and "Declarations," corresponding to both referential and phatic functions. Searle wants a clean separation between different types of speech act, whereas Jakobson emphasizes the presence of multiple simultaneous functions for any one speech act.

## Implications for Biblical Interpretation

Now let us explore possible implications of speech-act theory for biblical interpretation. Speech-act theory has been employed by some to throw light on biblical interpretation. Focusing on the human purposes (and also divine purposes) manifested in various pieces of text is one legitimate kind of focus, and it may succeed many times in drawing our attention to a dimension of textual communication that we have previously overlooked. This danger of overlooking confronts "professional" interpreters as much as anyone else, precisely because the methodical and self-conscious approach of the professional pushes him strongly in the direction of paying attention *only* to those things that his method and his self-conscious reflection tell him to notice.

On the other hand, speech-act theory, or genre theory, or any other theory, is not comprehensive in its attentiveness. So the danger arises that it too may overoptimistically be used as if it were the key to understanding, rather than simply a reminder of one more dimension in communication.

We may illustrate by considering an exhortation: "And walk in love, as Christ loved us and gave himself up for us, a fragrant offering and sacrifice to God" (Eph. 5:2). The first clause, "walk in love," is command-like. The subsequent parts are assertion-like, in that they discuss past events and their significance. We might argue that the sentence as a whole is a command, since the main clause, "walk in love," is imperatival in form. But suppose we break the one complex sentence into four separate sentences: "Walk in love. For Christ loved us. He gave himself up for us. In that way he was a fragrant offering and sacrifice to God." Now we have one command and three assertion-like sentences that back up and motivate the command. Was their assertion-like force already implied when we had only one sentence? Presumably so. In addition, even when we have four sentences, they are not independent of one another. Expressions like "for" and "in that way" link the sentences, and the distinct sentences are subtly linked by the fact that they are juxtaposed. So none of the three assertive sentences is *merely* an isolated assertion.

When we consider Ephesians 5:2 in the larger context of the whole New Testament, more complexities arise. In New Testament teaching we regularly find two sides, the "indicative" of what God has done in Christ and the "imperative" of what Christians are to do as a result. The two sides interlock and at a deep level imply one another. The word "as" in Ephesians 5:2 briefly hints at this relation.

Some people have summed up Christian life in the aphorism, "Be what you are." We are to act in accordance with the new life that God has given us in Christ, and Christ himself is the supreme embodiment of that new life. This situation has a factual dimension to it: not only has Christ lived and died and risen from the dead; he has also through the Holy Spirit given us new life animated by his resurrection power (Rom. 8:9–13). But there is also an aspect of command: these realities, which have already become true for anyone who trusts in Christ, are to be worked out in our behavior and our attitudes.

The relation between command and assertion is intimate. Explicit commands presuppose and imply corresponding assertions. And the assertions imply corresponding commands. The first half of Ephesians focuses more on what God has accomplished (Ephesians 1–3), while the second half focuses more on what we are to do in response (Ephesians 4–6). But the two hold together ("therefore," Eph. 4:1). Any one sentence,

taken in context, has multiple purposes, which include affirming facts, enjoining behavior, promising God's blessing, and directing and strengthening belief. Typically one
purpose, such as commanding, may be most prominent. But others are implied. A simple
division between assertion, command, and promise not only simplifies but all too easily
oversimplifies the rich reinforcement present in New Testament letters.

John Searle acknowledges the possibility of richness when he discusses "indirect
speech acts," that is, "cases in which one illocutionary act is performed indirectly by
way of performing another."[23] But it is easy for less sophisticated users of the theory
to overlook this possibility of complexity. And it is easy to think that such complexity
is exceptional. But Jakobson's classification of multiple dimensions of communication
suggests that it is pervasive.[24]

We can put it another way. Speech-act theory, used simplistically, tends to make people
think that each sentence-level act makes a single, simple speech commitment, defined
as its "illocutionary force": it either asserts, promises, commands, wishes, or the like.
But a sentence in the Bible may often have, in addition to one more obvious and direct
commitment, multiple, interlocking purposes, related in multiple ways to its literary
context and its addressees. Speech-act theory, seen by some of its advocates as a way for
enhancing our appreciation of multiple kinds of speech in the Bible, may at the same
time artificially flatten and restrict the implications of any one kind of speech.

The dangers are not merely hypothetical. As an example, consider Nicholas Wolterstorff's observation that many parts of the Bible, such as the Psalms, contain addresses
to God in the second person. ("But *you*, O LORD, are a shield about me, . . ." Ps. 3:3.)
Therefore, he claims, they cannot be God's address to us in the prophetic mode.[25] On
an elementary level, parts of the Bible are indeed distinct, in genre, in addressees, and
in kinds of speech acts. But this observation easily becomes reductionistic if it is used
to classify songs as *not* divine address. A song that is supposed to be sung to God can be
embedded in the divine-address discourse of Deuteronomy, by God's own command
(Deut. 31:19–32:47). It is thus *both* God's address to man and, when sung, man's address to God. And the song, when sung, is God's witness against Israel as well as Israel's
address to God: ". . . this song shall confront them as a witness (for it will live unforgot-
ten in the mouths of their offspring)" (Deut. 31:21). Deuteronomy 31 is especially
significant because it lays out the significance of the deposit of written divine words as
a part of a growing canon: "Take this Book of the Law and put it by the side of the ark
of the covenant of the LORD your God, that it may be there for a witness against you"

---

23. Searle, *Expression and Meaning*, 31. See the full discussion in ibid., 30–57, and note also
Searle, *Speech Acts*, 68–70.

24. Searle's discussion of indirect speech acts deals with cases where the context makes it
clear that the main point is something other than the literal meaning. But even when the main
point is closer to the literal meaning of a sentence, other dimensions affect the total impact of
the communication.

25. Nicholas Wolterstorff, *Divine Discourse: Philosophical Reflections on the Claim that God Speaks*
(Cambridge: Cambridge University Press, 1995), 52–54, 186–189; building on Paul Ricoeur,
"Toward a Hermeneutic of the Idea of Revelation," *Essays on Biblical Interpretation* (Philadelphia:
Fortress, 1980).

(Deut. 31:26). What is deposited is part of the written documents of the covenant or treaty between God and Israel.[26] The later songs in the book of Psalms and elsewhere in the canon are thus to be seen as a continuation of this kind of complex, embedded, multipurpose and multivocal speech in Deuteronomy 32.

The covenant and canon given through Moses involve rich communication. The covenant through Moses begins with direct speech of God at Mount Sinai and then the Ten Commandments written with the finger of God (Ex. 31:18; Deut. 9:10). Next God commissions Moses to speak his words (Deut. 5:22–33).[27] Later Moses writes God's law in a book (Deut. 31:9–29). This writing continues the earlier commission. At the same time, the writing uses what has already been spoken; that is, it appropriates earlier discourse, including God's direct writing of the Ten Commandments.[28] Commissioned speech, commissioned writing, and appropriation of earlier discourse all have the same authority as direct speech and give us unfettered access to what God says. Hence the different modes of speech and writing turn out to be perspectives on the same total process of God's speech and communication, rather than being completely distinct brands of speech act and acts of writing, such as a neatly pigeonholed classification might like to have.[29]

We can illustrate the same complexity if we summarize the entire covenantal relation between God and Israel in a single simple declaration: "You are my people." As a summary, this sentence condenses a multifaceted relationship. The sentence is a declarative sentence, and so is most obviously to be classified as an "Assertive" within Searle's taxonomy. It states a true fact. But the fact has become true because of God's declaration that it is to be. Hence, the sentence is also like a "Declaration." It is also a promise, since God commits himself, and so is a "Commissive." It expresses God's attitude ("Expressives") and implies an obligation of loyalty on the part of the people ("Directives"). It combines into one all five major kinds of speech acts in Searle's classification.[30]

## Focus on the Sentence

We may observe in more detail some of the simplifications and narrowing in focus that occur in John Searle's exploration of speech-act theory in his book *Speech Acts*. Fairly early, he chooses to focus on sentence-level speech acts, rather than longer speeches:

> Since every meaningful sentence in virtue of its meaning can be used to perform a particular speech act (or range of speech acts), and since every possible speech act can in principle

---

26. Meredith G. Kline, *The Structure of Biblical Authority* (Grand Rapids, MI: Eerdmans, 1972).

27. In the terminology of Nicholas Wolterstorff, this kind of commissioned speech is "deputized" (Wolterstorff, *Divine Discourse*, 42–46).

28. Wolterstorff (ibid., 51–54) discusses "appropriated" discourse.

29. See also Vern S. Poythress, "Divine Meaning of Scripture," *Westminster Theological Journal* 48 (1986): 241–279; Poythress, "The Presence of God Qualifying Our Notions of Grammatical-Historical Interpretation: Genesis 3:15 as a Test Case," *Journal of the Evangelical Theological Society* 50/1 (2007): 87–103.

30. See Searle, *Expression and Meaning*, 12–20.

be given an exact formulation in a sentence or sentences [does this mean several alternative sentences, any one of which could be used to manifest or illustrate the same speech act, or does it mean a paragraph or longer discourse?] (assuming an appropriate context of utterance), the study of the meanings of sentences and the study of speech acts are not two independent studies but one study from two different points of view.[31]

The first and most obvious simplification here is the move to focus on sentence-level speeches; Searle leaves aside more complex actions that can be built up using many sentences linked together in one or more paragraphs within a monologue.[32] The text also simplifies by apparently assuming that any one sentence has only one meaning, "its meaning." In fact, we frequently find instances in which a sentence is ambiguous and could sponsor more than one meaning, depending on the context.[33] "Bob hit the man with a stick." Was the stick the instrument that Bob used, or was it in possession of "the man"? "Bob feared him." Was the fear dread of a fellow human being, or reverential fear of God? This illustration with respect to language for God is particularly significant. Do words like "fear" have quite the same meaning when used with respect to a human being as when used with respect to God?

## The Ideal of Complete Knowledge

The essay also speaks about supplying for "every possible speech act" "an exact formulation in a sentence or sentences," and says that this is possible "in principle." But it is only "in principle." The larger context in Searle's book shows awareness of the fact that any one particular human language may have to be expanded or adjusted to make such a formulation possible:

> I can in principle if not in fact increase my knowledge of the language, or more radically, if the existing language or existing languages are not adequate to the task, if they simply lack the resources for saying what I mean, I can in principle at least enrich the language by introducing new terms or other devices into it.[34]

---

31. Searle, *Speech Acts*, 18 (the question in brackets is my own addition to Searle's text). See also 25. In a more technical discussion, 30–31, Searle introduces specific technical terms—"deep structure," "phrase marker," and "deletion transformations"—which belong to Chomskyan transformational generative grammar (note also the expression "generative grammar," 120). As we observed in appendix E, the Chomskyan approach simplifies in a host of ways for the sake of rigor. Among these is the decision to treat sentences without considering their larger context in discourse.

32. Searle's statement excluding "molecular propositions" and concentrating on atomic ones occurs later in the book (ibid., 33). But we can see its influence even at this early point. Mary Louise Pratt recognizes the focus on sentences and endeavors to extend the analysis to longer discourses (Pratt, *Toward a Speech Act Theory of Literary Discourse* [Bloomington: Indiana University Press, 1977], 85, 141–142).

33. Elsewhere, Searle indicates his awareness of ambiguity (Searle, *Expression and Meaning*, 117).

34. Searle, *Speech Acts*, 19–20.

Thus Searle is not in the end interested in any particular natural language. Rather, he considers a hypothetically enriched language that would have whatever resources the speaker needs. This move to a hypothetical language is certainly an idealization.

We may note another idealization in the sentence just quoted. Searle says, "... if they simply lack the resources for saying what I mean." The "I" whom he mentions is assumed already to know exactly what he means, independent of any and every linguistic resource for expressing what he means. He then only needs to look around for the convenient means, or to invent them if they do not yet exist.

But real people sometimes have the experience of struggling toward what they mean. They may grope for words, not completely knowing what they are after until they find a way of saying it. Or, even after they have said it, they may sometimes have a dim sense that they expressed themselves inadequately, but they have no idea how to proceed to "invent" ideal linguistic resources that would allow them to grasp even for their own benefit what they are groping after. They are experiencing the limitations of their finiteness and of their own grasp of language.

But perhaps Searle did not mean to overlook the existence of such struggles. Rather, in Searle's key paragraph the "I" could be something like a corporate "I": it tacitly includes all investigators and language innovators, who might together introduce further distinctions and clarifications in the way that we talk. The limitations of any individual are then supposed to be overcome by an ongoing corporate program of improvement. Searle is right that any language has potential for innovation.

But if that is all that he means, his wording is infelicitous. The use of the singular "I" suggests that any limitations can be overcome by a single individual who unproblematically knows what he means. There is a real danger that some readers will understand Searle's statement in a way that ignores the limitations that belong to actual speakers. The "I" in question then becomes a superhuman "I," an "I" who magically ascends above all the influences and limitations of any particular culture or language. This "I" has achieved a godlike, masterful position. This "I" has risen above the limitations of any one language, and knows what is cross-culturally universal merely from rationally clarifying its vision from within one language and culture.[35]

## Plurality of Languages and Cultures

By speaking about the possible inadequacy of "existing languages,"[36] Searle has also bypassed another important question, the question of *differences* in cultures and languages,

---

35. In fairness we should note that John Searle's book, *Speech Acts*, links itself with Chomskyan transformational generative grammar, which has a strong interest in linguistic universals. Speech-act theory might then appeal to the work of linguists as the basis for its assurance of its own cross-cultural universality. But, as seen in appendix E, generative grammar in the tradition of Chomsky has its own limitations, due primarily to its preference for rigor instead of complexity. Its internal structure minimizes the role of context, including context in larger bodies of discourse and context in culture. And so it is not suited for wrestling with the full complexities of cross-cultural understanding. It too cannot achieve a full, true transcendence above the limitations of cultures.

36. Ibid., 19–20.

and the difference that they might make. To put it in another way, speech-act theory bypasses the distinction between insiders' and outsiders' views of language and culture.[37] That simplification can have potentially disastrous consequences, because a person is undertaking to analyze all languages by analyzing only one (in this case, English). All the discussion is intended to be completely universal. But it conveniently uses English and the broader context of scholarship in the Western tradition as its context for what it hopes will be culturally universal truths.[38] The results are stimulating and suggestive. But the method is unsound anthropologically. We need to check other languages and cultures, in order to find out whether some feature that appears to be salient from our insider's cultural standpoint within English is indeed universal rather than being limited to English.

## Exactitude

Next, we can observe an idealization in the expression "exact formulation."[39] Whether or not Searle's book intends it, such an expression opens the door to the idealization in which we conveniently forget or suppress variation and context (distribution), and retain only contrastive-identificational features in an idealized sentence. "Exactness" in philosophical circles too easily connotes perfect precision in concepts (no variation), and perfect isolation from context (no distributional influence), both of which are idealizations for the sake of a certain kind of cleanness or neatness.[40] More rigorous results can then follow. But the rigor is obtained at the price of certain forms of artificiality.

## Sentences and Speech Acts

Searle's book also simplifies by correlating a single sentence with a single kind of speech act. For example, the book says that a speaker in uttering the sentence "Sam smokes habitually" is characteristically making an assertion.[41] This act of asserting then contrasts with the act of asking a question, using the sentence "Does Sam smoke habitually?" That certainly makes sense, but it lays aside the way in which particular contexts help to determine the nature of a particular speech act. "Sam smokes habitually" might be said by a speaker to a listener within a context where both know very well what Sam's smoking habits are, but where the main topic of discussion is the foolishness of habitual smoking, and its effects on health. "Sam smokes habitually" is then not exactly an "assertion," as if it were intended to inform the listener of something he probably does not yet know, but

---

37. See chapter 19, and the discussion of the difference between "etic" (outsider) and "emic" (insider) viewpoints.

38. See Umberto Eco, *The Search for the Perfect Language* (Oxford: Blackwell, 1995), 312–316.

39. Searle, *Speech Acts*, 18.

40. In fairness to Searle, it should be noted that several times he indicates awareness of fuzzy boundaries in the meaning of key concepts.

41. Searle, *Speech Acts*, 22–23.

more a reproach, or a comment on Sam's lack of foresight.[42] Or the speaker might use the same sentence in another context, in which he and his conversation partner have been talking about various ways in which they might honor Sam as their leader and exemplar. What habits should they adopt in imitation of him, in order to solidify their comradeship? Then the sentence is not an "assertion" as much as an indirect proposal about one such habit that they might adopt.

The exact force of an utterance does depend on context. Searle's book protects itself to some extent by noting that these phenomena appear not with complete and utter uniformity, but "characteristically," and "in appropriate circumstances."[43] It specifies at one point that the speaker "is speaking literally."[44] It later acknowledges the possibility that "one and the same utterance may constitute the performance of several different illocutionary acts."[45] And Searle's discussion of "indirect speech acts" supplements the analysis of simple, direct speech acts.[46]

But it is easy for less skilled practitioners to forget indirect speech acts, and to suppress the multitude of possibilities for contextual influence. This is not a trivial simplification, since one of the points of speech-act theory is to see particular sentences in the *context* of human action.

## The Isolation of Illocutionary Force

Next, Searle introduces a key distinction between propositions and illocutionary acts:

> Since the same proposition can be common to different kinds of illocutionary acts, we can separate our analysis of the proposition from our analysis of kinds of illocutionary acts.[47]

The key example, which Searle has already introduced, involves the same "proposition" about Sam and his smoking, but with four possible illocutionary acts:

1. Sam smokes habitually. [asserting]
2. Does Sam smoke habitually? [asking a question]
3. Sam, smoke habitually! [giving an order]
4. Would that Sam smoked habitually. [expressing a wish or desire][48]

---

42. In the circumstances I have envisioned, would the speaker be likely to say, "I assert that Sam smokes habitually"? No, I think not. The speaker does imply the truth of the proposition that Sam smokes habitually. But he typically would not use the word "assert" if he intends his remark as a reproach.

43. Searle, *Speech Acts*, 22.

44. Ibid., 18.

45. Ibid., 70.

46. Searle, *Expression and Meaning*, 30–57.

47. Searle, *Speech Acts*, 31.

48. Ibid., 22. The remarks in brackets are my own explanatory additions to Searle's text.

The distinction between propositions and illocutionary acts does make sense, since we can see the distinction in action in this and any number of other cases. It is a valuable distinction. But it is not "pure"; that is, it does not *separate* two aspects perfectly, in such a way that there is no longer interaction or entanglement.

This area of entanglement needs some explanation. Consider first a simple yes-no question: "Does Sam smoke habitually?" According to Searle's analysis, a speech like this one can be broken up into two separate aspects: the underlying proposition and the "illocutionary force." The illocutionary force is the character of the speaker's commitment in the act of delivering the utterance. In this case, the illocutionary force is asking a question, and can be symbolized by the question marker, "?". The underlying proposition is "Sam smokes habitually," but without the force of an assertion, a question, or any other particular action on the part of the speaker. These two, the proposition and the speech action, can be roughly separated. But is the separation "pure" and complete?

Searle himself recognizes a remaining impurity when he notes that with questions that ask "how?" or "what?" or "why?" the "propositional" aspect consists not in a full proposition but in an *incomplete* proposition. For example, consider the question, "Why did he do it?" The illocutionary force is to ask a question, and is represented by the question marker, "?". The underlying proposition, freed from the influence of the act of asking, would be "He did it because . . ." But we have to supply something else. The proposition in this case is incomplete, because the word "why" within the question asks the respondent to supply some particular reason, which will form part of the proposition when it is given assertive force.[49]

In addition there are other, subtle interactions. Assertions are typically made about states of affairs from the past, whereas commands and requests are typically made concerning potential states of affairs in the future. In assertions, the reference and the predication can often be made quite definite: "This tree branch fell down in the last storm." But an order concerning the future may sometimes presuppose conditions that affect the ability of the order to refer and to predicate. "Tomorrow cut down the bottom tree branch on this tree" presupposes that you will still be alive tomorrow to perform the task, and that the tree branch in question will be there waiting (rather than having fallen down in a storm tonight, or having been cut down by someone else during the night).

In his sample case about Sam smoking, Searle neatly avoids some of the difficulties about time by making the proposition "habitual." "Sam smokes *habitually*." It is not about past or future time, but it is a general affirmation about all times. But there are still subtle influences. Typically, an assertion that "Sam smokes habitually" focuses on the past, about which the speaker knows. By contrast, the command "Sam, smoke habitually!" focuses on the future, and is unlikely to be given as an order to Sam if Sam already smokes habitually. So the predication "smokes habitually" is not quite the same in its temporal relation to the real world in the two cases. In other words, when we try to reduce these two propositional expressions to completely atemporal propositions, we must spell out explicitly the temporal conditions, and we end up with two distinct propositions in the two cases. "Smokes habitually" as an assertion means "smokes habitually (looking

---

49. Ibid., 31.

backward in time)." "Smoke habitually" as a command means "smoke habitually (looking forward in time)."[50]

For the sake of rigor, Searle wants an exact separation of the two components, as can be seen from the fact that he introduces a rigorous symbolic notation:

The general form of (very many kinds of) illocutionary acts is
$$F(p)$$
where the variable "$F$" takes illocutionary force indicating devices as values and "$p$" takes expressions for propositions.[51]

The point is that "$F$" is notationally separated perfectly from "$p$." Rigor is achieved by ignoring the subtleties in natural language that involve entanglement of the two.

## The Ordinary Reader

And here, does the "ordinary" reader or listener often have the advantage? Perhaps many ordinary readers have tacitly known all along about speech acts. That is, they know the difference between questions, requests, commands, songs, sermons, parables, and reports.[52] Of course, these categories are "insider" categories that may then differ from one language to another. But human nature has sufficient unity so that the ordinary reader still appreciates to a considerable extent how different kinds of utterances differ in their purposes. And then he probably does *better* than the theoretical analyst, because he responds as a whole person, who appreciates multidimensional purposes, rather than as an analyst, who stands one step removed from full interaction with the textual communication.

The analyst, by stepping back, achieves a kind of human analogue to transcendence. But he remains finite, a flesh and blood human being. His own analytical activity is part

---

50. Searle may escape using the route of idealization already mentioned: he is not actually talking about any actual language, including English, but about idealized propositions that are exact in meaning. But now we are traveling into the area of artificial language that may have no implications for any actual language.

Another kind of idealization takes place when we move from live performative expressions like "I promise . . ." to the theoretical idea of illocutionary force. If we wish, we may make explicit what kind of speech act we are performing, by adding a "performative" expression such as "I assert," "I promise," or "I ask." But in these cases, the performative expression is itself qualified by a larger context, so that it is not perfectly "pure" and isolatable. "I ask you, 'Are you going?'" does not usually mean exactly the same thing as "Are you going?" It may connote by its explicitness that the speaker is being more formal or official. He already knows the answer, or he is trying to force an answer from a reluctant addressee, or he indicates that in some other way the relation between speaker and addressee is peculiar. His main commitment is still to ask a question, but the way that he asks has additional emotive, conative, and phatic implications (see Jakobson, "Closing Statement," 353–358).

51. Searle, *Speech Acts*, 31.

52. J. L. Austin, introducing his lectures on speech acts, modestly comments, "What I shall have to say here is neither difficult nor contentious; the only merit I should like to claim for it is that of being true, at least in parts" (Austin, *How to Do Things with Words*, 1).

of a larger situation, which is in turn subject to analysis that uncovers purposes and assumptions and sins of which he is not yet aware.[53]

## Philosophical Purposes in Speech-act Theory

We may also consider the more long-range purposes of speech-act theory. One of its short-range purposes, as we said, is to focus on and make clear the context of utterances in human action. At that point its purposes overlap with those of linguists, especially sociolinguists and linguists who focus on "pragmatics," that is, the use of language in the context of human action.[54] Are there then any notable differences that differentiate speech-act theory from the work of linguists?

Nowadays there are many interdisciplinary crossovers. So we would be oversimplifying to say that speech-act theory belongs to the tradition of philosophical investigation of language. But there is still something to be learned here. Ludwig Wittgenstein did not use the terminology of "speech acts," but in his later period his examination of "language games" shows attention to language use in a context of human action, and in the broader context of "forms of life." "Forms of life" are next door to what we have discussed concerning the diversity of human cultures. Wittgenstein, then, begins reflection on speech acts without using the terminology. And what is his purpose? There may be many purposes, but one is to dissolve philosophical conundrums by examining the ways language is used in ordinary life and in philosophy.[55]

And so we come again to the problem of transcendence. Philosophy sometimes asks deep and searching questions about wisdom. It asks the big questions about reality, knowledge, and the human condition. One way that we might approach such questions is through reflection that focuses on metaphysics; that is, we focus on what is, and on what is reality. Classical Greek philosophy primarily followed this route. But Immanuel Kant declared this route to be impossible because of the limits of human reason. For Kant, epistemology, that is, the study of what can be known and how it can be known, becomes the primary key for answering the other big questions, and—significantly—for showing which questions are impossible to answer because of the limitations of our finite condition.

Contemporary philosophy shows a turn from epistemology to language. If we know how language functions, we may be able to dissolve or dispense with questions that arise from ill-use of language. Limitations in language play a role here analogous to the role played in Kantian philosophy by limitations in human reason.

---

53. The best forms of deconstruction have a profound awareness of this problem of analysis. Human analysis can never be complete, and human beings never have a final point of view that terminates the possibility of a further step of standing back.

54. Gabriel Falkenberg notes that, mainly due to Searle's work, "problems such as those of illocutionary forces, utterance meaning and context interpretation are in safe keeping in linguistics proper today [1990]" (Falkenberg, "Searle on Sincerity," in Burkhard, ed., *Speech Acts, Meaning, and Intentions*, 130).

55. We may observe a similar interest in J. L. Austin, *How to Do Things with Words*, in that he explicitly addresses philosophers (2, 38); and in John R. Searle, in the very title of his book: *Speech Acts: An Essay in the Philosophy of Language*.

Speech-act theory, as used in the philosophical tradition, can then potentially serve as a key to understanding language. Speech-act theory is richer than the earlier tendency to think only in terms of disembodied propositional truths. But it can be a key only if it does not truncate the full richness of language. Truncating that richness would be likely to have the long-range effect in philosophical reasoning of truncating the world about which language can be used to speak. And so speech-act theory, precisely because it does not capture the full richness of language, cannot capture either the full richness of personhood, or the full richness of God the infinite person in whose image we human persons are made. No, if we expect speech-act theory to provide the first few steps, if not the complete ladder, to transcendence, we will either be disappointed or will delude ourselves into accepting a counterfeit claim to transcendence.

The danger also arises that some people may treat speech-act theory as if it were an *alternative* rather than an added dimension that would supplement a focus on propositional truth.[56] For many people who want to avoid the responsibility of submitting to objective truth, it would be convenient if all questions about truth could be transformed into a subdivision of sociological analysis, where we look at what people do to other people through words. Unfortunately, questions about truth will not go away. Truth claims occur directly within the common speech act of *assertion*, where a person makes a claim about truth.[57]

At its best, speech-act theory can be an insightful contribution to a larger whole, by focusing on one dimension of human action. But it runs up against limitations when we try to make it into a tool for achieving philosophical wisdom. The genius of speech-act theory is to teach us to pay attention to the meaning that utterances receive through embedding in a larger context of human purposeful action. But context, its strength, is also its weakness. Sentence-level utterances occur in the context of larger discourses. Discourse takes place in the context of human action. Human purposeful action takes place within the context of culture, and culture in the context of cultures, in the plural. And cultures occur in the context of a world and a world history whose interpretation differs from culture to culture. And that, as the postmodern relativists have seen, can lead to an ultimate relativism in the whole human project. In the end, such relativism at a high level, relativism generated by multiple cultures, injects relativism back down into the meaning of any speech act—unless there is a transcendent adjudication of truth. God gives wisdom; God brings reconciliation between man and God and between cultures.

---

56. Paul Helm expresses this concern eloquently in an Internet posting, "Propositions and Speech Acts," <http://paulhelmsdeep.blogspot.com/2007/05/analysis-2-propositions-and-speech-acts.html, May 1, 2007. J. L. Austin makes it clear that in his view particular speech acts presuppose or imply a host of truths (Austin, *How to Do Things with Words*, 45–46). So Austin clearly does not make his approach an *alternative* to a concern for truth, but rather a supplement or complement to it.

57. Moreover, the sociological analysis concerning what people do to one another has a deep interest only because it makes definite claims. These claims, either tacitly or explicitly, are claims concerning truth.

# Reaching Out to Deconstruction

Look carefully then how you walk, not as unwise but as wise,
making the best use of the time, because the days are evil.

—Ephesians 5:15–16

How can we use our appreciation of language as we interact with other people, including those outside the Christian faith? How do we talk with people who have thought hard about language, but have denied its relation to God?

## Deconstruction

For example, what would it be like to reach out to one particular group, namely, the advocates and practitioners of "deconstruction"? I pick them because they have thought about language and have much to say about language. At the same time, many of them do not believe in the God of the Bible. Many of their views are akin to what we have seen in postmodern contextualism.[1]

Deconstruction is notoriously hard to define.[2] For our purposes, we do not need a definition, because we are not trying to capture the whole of deconstruction but only to single out a few concerns and to indicate points of contact that a dialogue could pursue.

---

1. See appendices A and B.

2. For a helpful introduction, see Heath White, *Postmodernism 101: A First Course for the Curious Christian* (Grand Rapids, MI: Brazos, 2006); John D. Caputo in Jacques Derrida, *Deconstruction in a Nutshell: A Conversation with Jacques Derrida*, edited with a commentary by John D. Caputo (New York: Fordham University Press, 1997).

## Our Attitudes

When Bible-believing Christians have read about deconstruction, most of them have reacted very critically. And there are some good reasons for this. Christians have thought, "These people are out to destroy stable meaning, including the meaning of the Bible. They are wrong." Yes, they are wrong if they reject God; and if they reject God they will fall into other errors. They will in many respects oppose the Christian faith and the Bible.

Even so, they still live in God's world. They use a language that God gave them. By common grace they may have some genuine insights. Even if their claims are counterfeit, counterfeiting is a distortion of truth. So can we endeavor to find what their insights are?

Separating the good and bad can be a complex task. With respect to deconstruction, we can only make a beginning here. But, using the resources developed in the earlier parts of this book, we *can* make a beginning. We can see how some points in deconstruction have some similarity with genuine truths about language. I will focus more on the similarities than on the differences, precisely because the differences are often more obvious. Both the similarities and the differences can be possible starting points for dialogue.

## Deconstruction as a Field Perspective

First, deconstruction often uses a field perspective on meaning. That is, it focuses on how meaning exists within a network of relations.[3] Rather than considering either a word or a sentence or a text in isolation, as a stable unit or "particle," it follows outward the multitude of relations that contribute to the function of the word or sentence. One such context is often the language system, whether English or French or some other. And the system, as we have seen, allows creativity in meaning. If a person simply follows the relations out "horizontally," with no ultimate root in God and his meaning, everything may seem to be in motion. There is no final whole among finite human beings. It is easy to leave God out and conclude that there is no final whole, period. And so the less-than-final partial context that the person chooses might produce a meaning that depends on his choice.

## A Motto of Deconstruction: "Nothing Outside the Text"

Now let us go on to some particulars. The deconstructor Jacques Derrida has said that "there is nothing outside the text."[4] This motto sounds like the concern about whether we can get outside language in order to see the world as it really is. Is language, and the cultural deposits carried by language, a prison that conceals the real world?

Deconstructors do not mean that everything is "text" in a literal sense. They realize that people talk orally, and that they talk about foods, buildings, and objects in their

---

3. See chapter 3.
4. Jacques Derrida, *Of Grammatology* (Baltimore: Johns Hopkins University Press, 1976), 158.

"world." But they want to make the point that in an extended sense this whole world about which they talk is "text" because, culturally, it has already been processed and as-similated to human meanings. According to them, the same applies to what we say about "God" or "gods." That too is allegedly part of the constructed world of human meanings. So a deconstructor might infer that he never actually has access to God, and that such access is impossible in principle.

If God does not exist, and if we are faced with multiple cultures, then relativism or pluralism would seem to follow.

But within a biblical worldview, we have seen that God is a language user; indeed, he is the prime user. Meanings are not simply humanly generated but are generated by God. In fact, his plan encompasses all meanings, and anticipates all the meanings that human beings begin to see in the course of time. All meaning derives from God. And creation itself derives from God. Everything exists because he *spoke* it into existence (Genesis 1). Created things owe their very existence, as well as their particular qualities, to God's speech. God calls them into existence, sustains them (he "upholds the universe by the word of his power," Heb. 1:3). He defines their nature ("God called the light Day," Gen. 1:5). In a sense there is nothing outside the "text" of God's speech. Creatures exist, but they are not God. For these creatures, there is no meaning that God does not give, and no existence that does not depend on his signifying word.

Thus, the deconstructive motto is true when we apply it to God's word governing creation. We never get outside God's meanings.[5] And then the motto is also true for communication in language that includes human beings, because such communication can never leave God out. God is a member of the "language community" that speaks English or any other human language. And his general revelation, spoken of in Romans 1, is continually imparting meanings to human beings in every language community.

## A Motto of Deconstruction: "The Death of the Author"

A second principle or motto found with some deconstructors is that the author is dead.[6] What is meant is a little hard to discern. But one main goal seems to be to free readers from the idea that there is one authoritative meaning, namely, the author's, which the author comprehensively controls, and which is the unique target for textual interpreta-tion. The "death" of the author is a dramatic way of summing up the difficulties with

---

5. Cornelius Van Til repeatedly makes the point that all facts and all meanings derive from God's plan and his omnipotence. Non-Christian thought tends to think of facts and meanings as just "there," independent of God (if God even exists). The universe and its meanings are ultimately impersonal. But a world in which God is present, and which he controls, has all its meanings in relation to God, and to God's plan for the world. See, e.g., Cornelius Van Til, *The Defense of the Faith*, 2nd ed. (Philadelphia: Presbyterian & Reformed, 1963), 37–46; Van Til, *A Survey of Christian Epistemology*, vol. 2 of In Defense of Biblical Christianity (n.p.: den Dulk Foundation, 1969), 12–18, 34–37. There are no "brute facts," that is, nothing separated from the "text" of God's plan.

6. In particular, see Roland Barthes, "The Death of the Author," reprinted in William Irwin, ed., *The Death and Resurrection of the Author?* (New York: Hill & Wang, 2002), 3–7, together with the surrounding discussion in the other pieces in the same book.

the idea of an author's total control. For some people the expression probably links itself intentionally with the "death" of God as the supreme Author. But for others it is a protest against making human authors into godlike beings with godlike control over their language, over the origins of their meanings, and over their expressions. That is, it attacks the idolatry that would make poets into gods.

In what way do authors "die" within deconstruction? There are at least three related ways of making them die. One way is to demonstrate that interpreters can multiply interpretations of a single text, and that the text itself does not impose only one completely unified meaning. A second is to show that authors are not sovereign, free creators of meaning, but are enmeshed in contexts of language and culture that precede them. And a third is to show that readers are enmeshed in their own contexts of language and culture that accompany them. So even if we could stabilize authorial meaning, readers would not perfectly access it, but would read in terms of their own contexts.

The arguments that deconstructors give are intended to hold for any text whatsoever, including the biblical text. Hence, with respect to the biblical text, this approach might seem to imply that readers are free to abandon the authority of the human author. And if there is a divine author, his authority also would be abandoned. The death of the human author is thus linked to the death of God, the divine author.

One of the main missing pieces in this view of texts is a concept of history as divinely planned. A text without a context in human action and human history can indeed be taken in more than one way, and so interpreters can multiply meanings. And even if a text is seen in its historical contexts, readers can always decide to go in their own autonomous directions, unless they have an ethical norm constraining them. We need God as the source of our ethical norms, and we need God as the final context constraining choices of meanings.

But in addition, deconstruction's approaches to meaning can easily be understood as producing a polarity between two alternatives: (1) stable meaning, which they fear may become tyrannical; and (2) creative interpretation, which is freeing. Within a biblical worldview the two are not at odds with one another. Fellowship with God leads to creativity, because the stable meaning of God's word encompassing the whole of history is indefinitely rich and leads to increase in knowledge. Diversity of interpretations within the body of Christ is not always bad (though distortion of the truth is), because when the body functions properly the members encourage one another in growing in the truth. One person contributes a genuine insight here, and another there. Multiple perspectives from multiple people within the body of Christ enrich that body.[7]

In addition, merely human authors are not perfectly in control of themselves.[8] They are finite. They rely on a past, which developed under the sovereignty of God, and on a future, which they do not completely understand. Their meanings at one moment in time are linked both to past and to future. In such ways, the meanings of a human author

---

7. See chapter 18; and Vern S. Poythress, *Symphonic Theology: The Validity of Multiple Perspectives in Theology* (Grand Rapids, MI: Zondervan, 1987; reprinted, Phillipsburg, NJ: Presbyterian & Reformed, 2001).

8. See chapter 20.

are not sealed up into an airtight container. They are meanings within many-dimensional relationships.

Moreover, human beings are contaminated by sin. They do not write with one mind. Products of human meaning are not completely well-defined and integrated. Deconstruction is right to call into question assumptions to the contrary, and to warn us to be suspicious about political agenda and power struggles that may corrupt human communication.

In fact, deconstruction in its critique of unexamined assumptions has curious affinities with the transcendental apologetics inaugurated by Cornelius Van Til.[9] Deconstruction undertakes to bring to the surface ways in which a given piece of writing tacitly relies on a background involving language and thought, and how the unfathomability of that background ultimately undermines or at least de-centers the explicit theses in a piece of writing. By analogy, all sinful human beings undermine their own theses through the tension between their own sinful intentions and their tacit reliance on God. We earlier used the illustration of the small girl who had to sit on her grandfather's lap in order to slap him in the face. Figuratively, the rebel against God has to sit on the "lap" of God's gift of language in order to speak against his truth. And because rebels use language, the gift of God, they may end up like Caiaphas (John 11:49–53), speaking better than they know. Deconstruction tries to uncover ways in which a writing's own language reveals undermining tensions. Is deconstruction perhaps part counterfeit, part construal of the truth about fallen human beings in rebellion?

The language of deconstruction also shows an affinity to the Christian story. The death of the author takes place in order that the reader may live, that is, that he may not simply submit to the past but may explore a fresh future. Christ's death took place in order that we may live a new life for God's glory: "he [Christ] died for all, that those who live might no longer live for themselves but for him who for their sake died and was raised" (2 Cor. 5:15). The connection between Christ's work and authorial death is not far-fetched. Christ's death included his surrendering his human powers to the will of God. In so doing, he reversed the sinful human tendency to seek autonomy, to seek to master every situation for selfish benefit. Sinful human authors fall into the pattern of seeking to master absolutely the meanings of their writings, and to master absolutely the thinking of those to whom they communicate. To that desire they ought to die. And readers also are called on to die to the desire for absolute mastery of fixed authorial meaning. Such death is death to autonomy, death to wanting to be "like God."

Moreover, Jesus' willingness to die has an analogical relation to the willingness of God to send his word out in the world of sin, where his word will be mocked, corrupted, twisted, abused, and "killed." The Bible to this day is mocked and abused, not only by its

---

9. See, e.g., Van Til, *Defense of the Faith*; John M. Frame, *Cornelius Van Til: An Analysis of His Thought* (Phillipsburg, NJ: Presbyterian & Reformed, 1995). The link is probably not accidental, but arises from the relation between Christian and non-Christian views of transcendence (appendix C). Van Til's approach represents a Christian approach to knowledge. Deconstruction is a non-Christian analogue (a counterfeit).

overt enemies but also sometimes most painfully by God's would-be "friends," who claim to serve him and yet twist his word to serve their own power or pride or comfort:

> "Which of the prophets did your fathers not persecute? And they killed those who announced beforehand the coming of the Righteous One, whom you have now betrayed and murdered, you who received the law as delivered by angels and did not keep it" (Acts 7:52–53).

> "Woe to you, scribes and Pharisees, hypocrites! For you are like whitewashed tombs, which outwardly appear beautiful, but within are full of dead people's bones and all uncleanness. So you also outwardly appear righteous to others, but within you are full of hypocrisy and lawlessness" (Matt. 23:27–28).

The killing that happened literally to some of the Old Testament prophets and New Testament apostles happens figuratively to the message that they delivered. The message is "killed" and trampled by sinful listening and responses. The message submits to these indignities in order that, on the far side, beyond the death of the message, resurrection life may come to the very ones like Paul the apostle who earlier vilified the message.

Death and resurrection took place once in history in the person of Christ. But then they are mirrored repeatedly in history in the life of his followers and of the message they bear. We may therefore suspect that, by analogy, the same story of death and resurrection produces its image in all interpretive struggles concerning human communication. Truth seems to struggle to win its way in the midst of human resistance to truth.

### A Motto of Deconstruction: Deferral of the Signified

Next, deconstruction claims that interpreters never arrive at a final stable "signified." What does that mean?

To understand, we must go back to Ferdinand de Saussure, who introduced the terms "signifier" and "signified."[10] In Saussure's analysis each linguistic sign, like the word "dog," has two sides, the signifier and the signified. The signifier is the "sound image," the sequence of sounds, d + o + g (not the written alphabetic symbols, but the spoken sound of "d," of "o," and of "g"). The signified is the "concept," in this case the concept of a dog.

Deconstruction claims that each signified becomes in turn a signifier that points beyond itself. That is to say, there is a chain of references or allusions. A alludes to B, and B to C, and C to D, and so on. For example, thinking about "dog" leads to "animal," which leads to "life," which leads to instances of life like this oak tree, which leads on indefinitely. There is no final termination for reference. This claim is closely related to a field perspective. Yes, any one word or one sentence leads by relations to others. There is no "final" stopping point in that sense.

Deconstruction claims that we cannot find a final rest, an end to the chain, a single final signified. This is sometimes applied to a statement about God as a final Signified. Deconstruction argues that there can be no such final signified, with or without the

---

10. See appendix E.

capital S, because signs always have relationships to more signs. We never come to an end that is outside the system (outside "the text").

Deconstruction is attacking the picture of an alleged final rest in a single, undifferentiated signified. This signified would be final, with no relationships. The quest for knowledge in classical philosophy would seem to demand such a final rest in perfect knowledge of a particular object. The same quest can be focused on desired knowledge of a god. This picture of the final signified implies an essentially unitarian concept of a god. Such a god has no differentiation or inner dynamic. There is no such unitarian god. In that respect, deconstruction is nearly right: it rejects this kind of idolatrous conclusion.

When we come to consider the true God, our human access to him is through the Word. There is a final Reference in God. God the Father is in a sense the ultimate Signified. But the Father exists in eternal relation to the other persons in the Trinity. The Father is known through the Son. By analogy with the subsystems of language,[11] we can say that the Father is like the Signified, the Spirit is like the Signifier, and the Son is the Word, in whom Signified and Signifier are eternally united and mutually indwelling. The three persons exist in unity and diversity, in fellowship with one another rather than in conceptual isolation.

Thus there is no end to the relationships, because relationships are included in the deepest reality of who God is. We *do* find in God the Father the final Signified. But we find simultaneously final relations: the relation of Signification among the Father and the Son and the Holy Spirit. Deconstruction is right, in a way deeper than what it intends.

Moreover, deconstruction is right that human intention is not final. Rather, God's intention is. But our human dependence on God does not imply that we can find no rest. God has made himself accessible to us in Christ, through the work of the Holy Spirit.

Behind the discussion in deconstruction lies a profundity in language. Relations of signification within language derive from the final relation of signification among the persons of the Trinity.[12] Therefore, relations within language never stop in a single final term, short of God himself. Deconstructors are wrestling with profundities, but they will have no satisfaction if they merely destroy unitarian ontology while ignoring the God who is really there.

---

11. See chapter 32.

12. More precisely, the concept, the signified, belongs to the referential subsystem of language. The signifier or "sound image," by contrast, belongs to the phonological subsystem of language. By speaking of signifier and signified Saussure proposed analytically to isolate the two sides of a word like "dog." But in fact "dog" is a form-meaning composite, and the two sides cannot be perfectly isolated in practice. They interlock, as an aspect of the interlocking of the two subsystems, phonological and referential. In chapter 32 we saw that these subsystems analogically derive from the mystery of the Trinity. They coinhere by analogy with the coinherence of the Father and the Spirit. The plan of the Father corresponds to the referential aspect, while the Spirit as the "breath" of God corresponds to the phonological aspect.

## A Motto of Deconstruction: Absence

Deconstruction also has a polemic against "presence." According to deconstruction, meaning never arrives as a presence that we fully embrace, without remainder. We never exhaustively understand meaning. That kind of description is closely related to the previous concern about deferral, where one element points to another through signification, or where successive readings of a text continue to generate new insights. In face-to-face conversation, a human speaker may seem simply to be "present" to us in an unproblematic way. But when we start thinking explicitly about the way in which the conversation tacitly uses the medium of language, we become aware that the ideas of the speaker do not "immediately" enter our minds, but rather they do so *mediately*. The speaker employs language as his medium, and what he says enjoys a multitude of relations to a language system.

Deconstruction then generalizes this principle, to claim that no idea is simply "present" in the mind apart from the medium of language.[13] And language leads to the blurring or destabilizing of any allegedly "perfect" vision of a clear and distinct idea.

Deconstruction then applies the same principle to God as well. God is not "present," because our ideas about him are mediated through language.

The conclusion that God is absent would indeed follow were it not for the fundamental fact that God is present throughout language, in all its aspects. That is, he is "present," not in the sense that deconstruction criticizes autonomous philosophy for desiring, but in the sense that his presence is expounded in Scripture. He is present while remaining transcendent, incomprehensible. We do not need to "make" him present by going through linguistic gymnastics.

Once again, deconstruction has appropriated part of a truth. God does not come to man apart from mediation—specifically, the mediation of the Son, who is the Word. And there is the mediation of the Holy Spirit, who indwells those who trust in Christ, and who in fellowship with the human spirit illumines us to know God and call him "Father" (Rom. 8:15). Our God is Trinitarian, not unitarian in the way that deconstruction tries to combat. God is present as "Immanuel," "God with us," in the person of his Son (Matt. 1:23).

## A Critique of "Logocentrism"

Next, deconstruction offers a critique of "logocentrism." What does that mean? The word "logocentrism" by its etymology denotes the idea of the centrality of the word,

---

13. Jacques Derrida, *Positions* (Chicago: University of Chicago Press, 1981), 26: "The play of differences supposes, in effect, syntheses and referrals which forbid at any moment, or in any sense, that a simple element be *present* in and of itself, referring only to itself. Whether in the order of spoken or written discourse, no element can function as a sign without referring [partly by relations in the language system] to another element which itself is not simply present. This interweaving results in each 'element'—phoneme or grapheme—being constituted on the basis of the trace within it of the other elements of the chain or system. This interweaving, this textile, is the *text* produced only in the transformation of another text. Nothing, neither among the elements nor within the system, is anywhere ever simply present or absent."

since "logos" is the Greek term for "word." In some of its uses, the term "logocentrism" may include an allusion to the Christian idea of the centrality of Christ, whom John 1:1 identifies as "the Word."[14] It may sound as if deconstruction is directly attacking Christian doctrine. But that impression in superficial. Rather, deconstruction plays on the different possible allusions of the term "logocentrism." The target of its critique is first of all the practice in Western philosophy of using reason as the way to conduct a quest for final wisdom. The quest has the aim of attaining a godlike, transparent, rational, final vision of truth, a truth of pure thought. In this context, the Greek word "logos" is associated with reason rather than specifically with Christian thought. The philosophical quest relies on reason and has reason at its center. At the same time, the term "logocentrism," by alluding to Christian thought, suggests that this Western quest is a secular transmutation of religion. Deconstruction uses the term as a provocative label, and intends to suggest that the rationalist tradition in the West is a substitute religion.

Moreover, the critique of "logocentrism" has an affinity to the themes that we just discussed concerning the final signified and final presence. Western philosophy wants a final, rational vision that is independent of the alleged "impurity" belonging to the form-meaning character of language. Thus deconstruction has appealed to some of the truths that we have articulated.[15]

One concern in the practice of deconstruction has been to "deconstruct" parts of Western philosophy and metaphysics. Deconstruction has explored critically some of the assumptions in the Western philosophical tradition. And well it might. Much in that tradition has sought man-made wisdom.[16] And in many cases philosophers have tried to use language, or at least key terms in their philosophy, as if those terms had an infinite precision and stability: terms were to be infinitely precise in contrastive-identificational features, with no interference from variation and context (distribution).[17] Terms were to make the truth "present" unproblematically and completely, as if man could have a godlike vision.

### De-centering or Reversing Polarities

Deconstruction also engages in the practice of de-centering or reversing various polarities such as normal/abnormal, man/woman, objective/subjective, literal/figurative, meaning/interpretation, inside/outside. Such polarities have traditionally been understood

---

14. The Greek of John 1:1 uses the term "logos."

15. See also the discussion of the limitations of speech-act theory in appendix H. In the desire for human control over meaning on the part of speakers, we can see reflected some of the Western tradition of reason. Similarly, the desire for superhuman, final mastery of meaning infects verbal interpretation (chapter 21).

16. See Vern S. Poythress, "The Quest for Wisdom," in *Resurrection and Eschatology: Theology in Service of the Church*, ed. Lane G. Tipton and Jeffrey C. Waddington (Phillipsburg, NJ: Presbyterian & Reformed, 2008), 86–114.

17. See chapter 19; appendix D; and Vern S. Poythress, "Reforming Ontology and Logic in the Light of the Trinity: An Application of Van Til's Idea of Analogy," *Westminster Theological Journal* 57/1 (1995): 187–219.

in a hierarchical relation, where the first term is primary and the second is derivative. Sophisticated deconstructors are not trying to abolish these distinctions but to make visible and put in question the cultural assumptions and power structures to which they are related. To accomplish this, they often rely on a process similar to the perspectival process in which a word is stretched in meaning until it is a perspective on the whole.[18] And indeed, that can be done, because a perspectival process exploits relations of one meaning to another. Everything enjoys relations to other meanings. Even in God, the persons of the Trinity enjoy eternal relations to one another.

But the perspectival process can also be distorted. If we lose sight of God, the process can be used to advocate half-truths and falsehoods. That is why this deconstruction process can in practice contain insights, but at the same time, depending on the practitioners, can also include distortions and falsehoods in a complex mixture.

## The Undermining of Conventional Assumptions

Deconstruction has affinities with the suspicious, upsetting approaches to human existence that have arisen in Friedrich Nietzsche, in Marxism, in Freudianism, and in French existentialism. For many people these are deeply upsetting. In various ways these philosophical views do involve the reconstrual of the whole world of thought. Meeting these new views may be similar to meeting foreigners and trying to understand a new culture. The foreigners cut across conventional assumptions. For Bible-believing Christians, these "foreigners" have been doubly upsetting because they have been anti-Christian in their roots.

But there is another aspect. These people are introducing the upsets partly because they are suspicious about the conventional, about the status quo, about complacent assumptions that all is normal and healthy. That is one reason why deconstructors undertake to "reverse" polarized contrasts. They are radically dissatisfied. Spiritually speaking, they are desperate, and desperation drives people to radical remedies.[19] In particular, deconstruction may at times push up against and stretch the limits of language. The writing becomes

---

18. See chapters 34–35.
19. Jonathan Culler puts it thus:

> If "sawing off the branch on which one is sitting" seems foolhardy to men of common sense, it is not so for Nietzsche, Freud, Heidegger, and Derrida; for they suspect that if they fall there is no "ground" to hit and that the most clear-sighted act may be a certain reckless sawing, a calculated dismemberment or deconstruction of the great cathedral-like trees in which Man has taken shelter for millennia (Culler, *On Deconstruction: Theory and Criticism after Structuralism* [Ithaca, NY: Cornell University Press, 1982], 149).

> . . . the [pragmatist] notion of truth as what is validated is used to criticize what passes for truth. Since deconstruction attempts to view systems from the outside as well as the inside, it tries to keep alive the possibility that the eccentricity of women, poets, prophets, and madmen might yield truths about the system to which they are marginal—truths contradicting the consensus and not demonstrable within a framework yet developed (ibid., 153–154).

difficult to understand because it breaks conventions of writing that are typical within rationalistic philosophy, in order to draw attention to those conventions and limits.[20]

The desperation and radical suspicion are understandable, because these viewpoints have grasped a half-truth: we are not by nature either normal or spiritually healthy. The most radical remedy of all is the Christian gospel. It is a gigantic reversal of polarities in which fallen human beings have taken refuge (Luke 1:51–53), and people are not likely to consider it seriously unless they are desperate.

The crucifixion of Christ is the supreme reversal. Out of death comes life forever (Rev. 1:18). Out of humiliation comes honor (Phil. 2:8–10). Out of weakness comes power (2 Cor. 12:9–10; 13:4). Out of defeat comes victory (Luke 24:20). Out of suffering comes glory (Luke 24:26). Out of darkness comes light (Luke 23:44; 22:53; John 9:4–5; 12:31–36). Out of judicial execution comes vindication (Rom. 4:25). Out of folly comes wisdom (1 Cor. 1:25). In its interest in reversal, deconstruction has come close indeed, without arriving at the central secret of history.

We might even say that the suspicious approaches of deconstruction and its predecessors are not nearly suspicious enough, nor desperate enough, nor radical enough. They have not yet become suspicious of the root desire for human autonomy, nor desperate enough to cast themselves on God's mercy, nor radical enough to embrace the radicality of the cross. No one does unless God overcomes his resistance (John 6:44, 65).

And if Christians themselves have become complacent and compromised in their placid acceptance of the status quo within a surrounding mainstream modernity, they too need to be shaken up and criticized for their complicity—our complicity. We all fall victim here and there, and the critical voice of others, even if it should contain only a grain of truth in the midst of error, may reveal sin.


## Wisdom Again

The desire for wisdom is deep in human beings; it is one aspect of their being created in the image of God. But it gets perverted through sin. Through the desire for wisdom, much benefit has come to us all. By common grace we benefit from the work and insight of many others—including practitioners of deconstruction. The desire leads people toward fresh insights, fresh depths, fresh mysteries.

---

20. In this push against the limits of language, deconstruction has affinities with "negative theology," as some commentators have observed. But both deconstruction and negative theology go astray into a non-Christian view of transcendence, corner 3 of Frame's square (see appendix C). They search for answers at the limit of autonomous intelligibility and the limit of meaning, rather than surrendering to the simplicity and availability of the message of the Bible (corner 2):

> The testimony of the Lord is sure,
> making wise *the simple* (Ps. 19:7).

> We refuse to practice cunning or to tamper with God's word, but by the *open statement* of the truth we would commend ourselves to everyone's conscience in the sight of God (2 Cor. 4:2).

But because we have rebelled against God, the desire for wisdom takes the twisted form of desiring to be a god, to have a superhuman, rationally transparent mastery of meaning. Of this desire deconstruction is rightly suspicious; and it rightly desires to unmask it. But insight alone does not bring deliverance. Autonomy does not disappear merely through our becoming aware of our sin, intellectually or otherwise—but only by the work of Christ. In fact, deconstruction runs the same danger that is common to all, namely, that its own desire to unmask may turn out to be yet another form of the desire to be godlike. "The heart is deceitful above all things, and desperately sick; who can understand it?" (Jer. 17:9).

We see the temptation in many forms. A desire to be godlike may motivate not only modernist confidence in reason and postmodernist promotion of tolerance. It may also sometimes motivate the desire to use linguistics or symbolic logic to master language, or to use speech-act theory as a universal rational platform for understanding language, or to master meaning in verbal interpretation, or to invent a replacement for redemptive stories.

We who are Christians are still contaminated by sin ourselves, and we may find forms of this sinful desire cropping up in unlikely places. We can desire to master in a godlike fashion the Bible itself, and end up with a self-righteous attitude toward those who disagree with us.

Postmodernists, as we have observed, fear dogmatism. And indeed dogmatism of a sinful kind has power to creep in even among those who have come to know the truth, to know Christ who is the truth. If so, it makes us the more guilty, because "everyone to whom much was given, of him will much be required" (Luke 12:48). The solution, however, does not lie in a kind of false humility that renounces truth. Rather, we should boldly rely on the truth of what we have received from God. We are to love truth as a pathway to ever richer enjoyment of truth and to expansion of knowledge beyond our present imagining (Eph. 3:18–21).

Postmodernists also see dogmatism in the attempt to possess a final narrative explanation, a "metanarrative," that is, an overarching account of history that would convince us by its rational power.[21] Such a narrative, they fear, represents yet another false human claim to the ability to attain final wisdom. To surrender to it is to surrender autonomy, and to be taken captive by the rhetorical trickery of someone else's story. But in its understandable fear of being taken in, has postmodernism created its own dogmatism, the dogmatism of claiming, as a second-order knowledge, that metanarratives are always deceptive maskings for human power? And then is it held captive still, to the final and most inexorable captivity, the desire for human autonomy, the desire to be free from God?[22]

---

21. "Simplifying to the extreme, I define *postmodern* as incredulity toward metanarratives" (Jean-François Lyotard, *The Postmodern Condition: A Report on Knowledge* [Minneapolis: University of Minnesota Press, 1984], xxiv). See the discussion of postmodernism's redemptive stories in chapter 27.

22. Two pictures come to my mind, both from C. S. Lewis. In Lewis's story *The Last Battle: A Story for Children* (Harmondsworth: Penguin, 1956), the dwarfs "refused to be taken in." Having been deceived so many times, they were determined to live by suspicion and critique. The other picture comes from Lewis's *The Pilgrim's Regress: An Allegorical Apology for Christianity, Reason,*

The Bible does offer a metanarrative, in a sense, but it is multitextured,[23] multilayered, and as yet incomplete: we still await the second coming. The Bible invites us to a willing, freeing, and glorious captivity to the living Christ. Out of captivity comes freedom. And the captivity itself, captivity to God, overtakes us not through human strength but through weakness. The Bible's story convinces us not by its superior transparency to fallen human rational powers, but by the power of the Holy Spirit, who opens spiritually blind eyes:

> And I, when I came to you, brothers, did not come proclaiming to you the testimony of God with lofty speech or wisdom. For I decided to know nothing among you except Jesus Christ and him crucified. And I was with you in weakness and in fear and much trembling, and my speech and my message were not in plausible words of wisdom, but in demonstration of the Spirit and of power, that your faith might not rest in the *wisdom of men* but in the power of God (1 Cor. 2:1–5).

---

*and Romanticism* (reprint, pocket edition; Grand Rapids, MI: Eerdmans, 1958), book 4, chapter 1, p. 66, where prisoners in the dungeon of Freudianism refuse to come out, telling themselves that their perception of deliverance "is one more wish-fulfilment dream. Don't be taken in again." Among the saddest of the chains of captivity are those self-imposed by the determination to be autonomously critical and suspicious.

23. There are multiple genres in the Bible, and four Gospels, not one. On the implications of the four Gospels, see Poythress, *Symphonic Theology*, 47–51.

# Supplementary Reflections

# Special Cases of Human Speech

For no prophecy was ever produced by the will of man,
but men spoke from God as they were carried along by the Holy Spirit.

—2 Peter 1:21

We now look at two special cases of human speech, namely, speech by inspired spokesmen of God, and evil speech.

### The Word of God through Human Spokesmen

All people who belong to Christ are expected to walk in harmony with him. And so their speech is to be empowered by the Holy Spirit:

> . . . be filled with the Spirit, addressing one another in psalms and hymns and spiritual songs, singing and making melody to the Lord with your heart, giving thanks always and for everything to God the Father in the name of our Lord Jesus Christ, submitting to one another out of reverence for Christ (Eph. 5:18–21).

But with the apostles and with the people whom God appointed to write the Bible, we have a special case, where the product is completely what God says, as well as being the product of the human instrument.

The Old Testament prophets served as "mediators" between God and man, by bringing God's word from God to man. Christ is the final mediator (1 Tim. 2:5). Hence, the prophets and other human writers of Scripture are analogous to Christ, who is the final prophet (Heb. 1:1–2; Acts 3:21–26). The prophets foreshadowed or looked forward to the coming of Christ as the final Prophet.

Now let us think about the role of choice in language. The prophet Isaiah continually made decisions concerning what words and what sentences and what discourses to write in the book of Isaiah. He made *choices*. At the same time, God chose to have exactly those words in Isaiah, and to speak them to his people. Isaiah's human choices and decisions matched the choices and decisions that God made as divine author.

The biblical prophets and spokesmen for God were so molded by God that they *desired* to carry out God's will and to utter what God wanted them to say. Their will was in harmony with God's will. In this respect, they reflect by analogy the harmony between the will of the Son and the will of the Father.[1] The Son is the model for human creativity. Human creativity does not mean *independence* in the human will, but creativity in fellowship with God.

We may also consider the fact that Christ is one person with two natures: a divine nature and a human nature. His divine will is in harmony with his human will. His speech is both divine speech and human speech. The choices with respect to his human nature are in harmony with the choices with respect to his divine nature. Genuine choice involves harmony between the two natures.

Every part of the Bible is the word of God, given through human spokesmen. "For no prophecy was ever produced by the will of man, but men spoke from God as they were carried along by the Holy Spirit" (2 Pet. 1:21). The mention of "the will of man" does not mean that men had no part at all. Rather, it is saying that they had no *independent* part. The initiative lay not with them but with God, so that the product completely expressed God's will, not merely man's. The Holy Spirit used human wills, which were in harmony with God's will.

To have a robust, biblical doctrine of Scripture, we must also have a robust, biblical doctrine of the human will and human speech.

### Another Kind of Freedom?

Some people oppose this view. These opponents want a picture of independent human wills—for the sake, they may think, of protecting human freedom. They may claim that the human spokesmen who wrote the Bible were an exception. These opponents may say that, in the case of the Bible, God overrode the normal "freedom" of the will of the human writers in order to make sure that the product was exactly what he wished it to be. My response would be that the human writers were indeed fully "free," but not in the sense that the opponents mean it. The biblical writers were free with a freedom that imitates the freedom of the decisions of the Son of God, who is at the Father's side (John 1:18). We do not need to take away the authors' "freedom" in the proper sense of the word.

But if the opponents are willing to dispense with what they call human "freedom" in the case of writers of Scripture, they have put themselves in a dilemma.

On the one hand, suppose that this alleged "freedom" is dispensable. Then we can dispense with it. No human being needs it, any more than the writers of Scripture. It is not necessary for human dignity. Only a freedom in harmony with God's will is necessary.

---

1. See chapter 6; and Vern S. Poythress, "Divine Meaning of Scripture," *Westminster Theological Journal* 48 (1986): 241–279.

On the other hand, suppose that this "freedom" is so valuable that ordinary human beings must be allowed to have it. Then the opponents, by suggesting that God sometimes takes away freedom, are in danger of charging God with underhandedness. The end, namely, the production of Scripture, does not justify the means, namely, the annihilation of freedom.

There remains still another alternative: for opponents to claim that what we have in Scripture is not fully what God would wish, but is a compromise worked out by God as he wrestled with the human wills of the human writers. Allegedly, God refused to take away their freedom of independence, and so he was not fully master of the end product. This too is an unsatisfactory result, and a dangerous one as well, because it depreciates the trustworthiness of Scripture, at least in its details. In this view the Scripture ends up being, not the word of God, but the best approximation to an expression of God's will that he could achieve in the circumstances.

### Transcendence and Immanence

The difficulties over this issue are not unique. In essence we have seen them before. They have to do with Christian and non-Christian understandings of transcendence and immanence.[2] A Christian view of God's transcendence is a Christian view of God's control. In the area of language, it implies that God fully controls the language that he speaks. In particular, he fully controls the discourses found in the Bible. More broadly, he controls the whole course of history, not only in its general outlines but also in its details. Pilate gave his sentence and the soldiers cast their lots because God planned it.

Now consider a Christian view of God's immanence. We affirm God's personal presence. He is present as a person, in communion with human persons. God-designed communion between persons does not crush individual human personality, but includes the design of diversity, individuality, and genuine choice and creativity on the part of each individual. Such choices need not be *isolated* from the presence of God, or the presence of other human beings, in order to be genuine. To the contrary, they receive meaning from the presence of God, before whose presence we serve.

Now consider a non-Christian view of transcendence. God must be far off, in order for a human being to be himself, to be autonomous. And, according to non-Christian immanence, human beings are sufficient in themselves to act as final and exclusive decision makers. In this kind of thinking, for God to have control is for humans to lose their own autonomous control. According to the diagonal line that runs from corner 1 to corner 4 of Frame's square, a non-Christian view of human control (corner 4) contradicts God's control (corner 1).[3]

---

2. See appendix C.
3. On Frame's square, see appendix C.

## *Transcendence and Immanence in the Arena of Knowledge*

The struggle for a healthy understanding of transcendence and immanence takes place in the sphere of knowledge as well as the sphere of power. What kind of knowledge do we expect human beings to have concerning the character of God's sovereignty and its relation to human responsibility? Do we as human beings desire to make an exact model, to make transparently clear to ourselves exactly how divine control relates to human responsibility? Then we are really desiring to move to corner 4 in Frame's square, that is, to human autonomy. Under this arrangement, man will be the standard for knowledge. Or will we trust God's superior knowledge of freedom (Christian transcendence, corner 1), and his instruction to us in Scripture (Christian immanence, corner 2)?

## Evil Human Wills

Christians are to obey God willingly. But what about those who disobey God? They too carry out his will, that is, his plan. We can see this in the case of Caiaphas:

> So [after the raising of Lazarus] the chief priests and the Pharisees gathered the Council and said, "What are we to do? For this man performs many signs. If we let him go on like this, everyone will believe in him, and the Romans will come and take away both our place [the temple] and our nation." But one of them, Caiaphas, who was high priest that year, said to them, "You know nothing at all. Nor do you understand that it is better for you that one man should die for the people, not that the whole nation should perish." He did not say this of his own accord, but being high priest that year he *prophesied* that Jesus would die for the nation, and not for the nation only, but also to gather into one the children of God who are scattered abroad. So from that day on they made plans to put him to death (John 11:47–53).

Caiaphas made choices to speak the words he did. And he had evil motives in doing so. He was encouraging the Jewish council unjustly to seek Jesus' death. God made choices that Caiaphas would speak exactly these words, and in doing so God had wise plans not only to reveal Caiaphas's motives but also to reveal his own plan for bringing good out of the crucifixion. God even spoke a *prophecy* through Caiaphas, namely, that "Jesus would die for the nation, and not for the nation only, but also to gather into one the children of God who are scattered abroad" (John 11:51–52).

God preserved his goodness throughout this process. His motives for what he said were good, while Caiaphas's motives were evil. And God's meaning in what he said was edifying, whereas Caiaphas's meaning was corrupting for those who heard it. It is a remarkable illustration of God's control and his goodness, as well as human decision making on the part of Caiaphas.

Caiaphas's speech *prophesied*. Even though it took place unwillingly, he became a spokesman for God. And so at this point he was analogous to Christ, who is the final spokesman for God. But his unwillingness contrasts with Christ's willingness. The details about how God brought about his speech through Caiaphas's speech will remain mysterious. But we can be sure that we have here a case where God brought good out of evil (compare Gen. 50:20). In the most outstanding case, God brought good out of evil in the crucifixion. Christ the mediator worked out the good will of God in the midst of human evil wills. By analogy, we infer that Christ the mediator was present even in God's speech to us through Caiaphas.

Admittedly, Caiaphas's speech is a special case. But it nevertheless illustrates a broader principle about how God can speak in connection with evil human speech.

We can also illustrate with the example of Herod and Pontius Pilate. Acts 4 indicates quite pointedly that their actions were prophesied beforehand:

> And when they [the Christians] heard it [the opposition of Jewish leaders], they lifted their voices together to God and said, "Sovereign Lord, who made the heaven and the earth and the sea and everything in them, who through the mouth of our father David, your servant, said by the Holy Spirit,
>
>> "'Why did the Gentiles rage,
>>     and the peoples plot in vain?
>> The kings of the earth set themselves,
>>     and the rulers were gathered together,
>>     against the Lord and against his Anointed'— [quoted from Psalm 2:1]
>
> for truly in this city there were gathered together against your holy servant Jesus, whom you anointed, both Herod and Pontius Pilate, along with the Gentiles and the peoples of Israel, to do *whatever your hand and your plan had predestined to take place*" (Acts 4:24–28).

Since Psalm 2 offers a prophecy of these events,[4] we can reformulate the situation from the perspective of speaking. In Psalm 2 God spoke his prophetic word, a choice to speak one thing rather than many possible alternatives. His word had power to bring about the effects. Herod and Pontius Pilate then acted in accordance with what God spoke. Herod and Pontius Pilate, during the course of events, also spoke their own words, and in doing so they made their own choices and their own decisions. For example, rather than acquitting Jesus, as Pilate morally should have done, he gave sentence for Jesus to be crucified. "Pilate *decided* that their demand should be granted" (Luke 23:24). For this he bears moral guilt, because it was his own decision. He made his own decision. And God as primary cause made a decision to decree and prophesy that Pilate should issue this sentence. God had good purposes, while Pilate had corrupt purposes. There is no moral compromise here to God's goodness.

We can see other illustrations of a similar kind. God chose to speak in Psalm 22 and chose to prophesy in 22:18 about the soldiers who divided Christ's garments. When the events actually unfolded, the soldiers had their discussion as to what to do with the garments, and made their *decision*:

---

4. Psalm 2 in its original historical and literary context within the book of Psalms probably speaks generically about the Davidic king, and moves from there to encouraging readers to anticipate the final messianic king. All the kings in the line of David foreshadowed the coming of the great, final king in the line of David, namely, the Messiah (see Isa. 9:6–7). Thus, in the purpose of God, he designed that Psalm 2 should be connected both to the kings who foreshadowed the Messiah and to the Messiah himself. In this complex sense, Psalm 2 prophesies the events of Christ's life.

When the soldiers had crucified Jesus, they took his garments and divided them into four parts, one part for each soldier; also his tunic. But the tunic was seamless, woven in one piece from top to bottom, so they said to one another, "Let us not tear it, but cast lots for it to see whose it shall be." This was to fulfill the Scripture which says,

> "They divided my garments among them,
> and for my clothing they cast lots."

So the soldiers did these things (John 19:23–24).

God decided what to speak. The soldiers also decided, on their own level.

In human decision making in general, human beings exercise a creativity analogous to divine creativity, because they are made in the image of God (chapter 6). So also in these special cases. Human corruption does not free people from dependence on God or from the control of God, which is necessary for their own subordinate human control. God remains completely good and morally incorruptible, as can be seen from the goodness of his purposes with Caiaphas, Pilate, and the soldiers at the cross.

# Bibliography

R eaders who are just beginning to explore theology or philosophy should note that I include books in this bibliography because I have cited them or used them in the course of writing this book. I do not approve of all of them. Readers who are interested in my evaluation should consult the places in this book where I make citations or comments. And even then, I may sometimes cite a book where I approve one thing that it says, but do not approve of the whole book. What I have said about non-Christian thinking (appendix C) needs to be applied to the reading of books.

Adam, A. K. M. *What Is Postmodern Biblical Criticism?* Minneapolis: Fortress, 1995.

Adger, David. *Core Syntax: A Minimalist Approach.* Oxford: Oxford University Press, 2003.

Alston, William P. *Philosophy of Language.* Englewood Cliffs, NJ: Prentice-Hall, 1964.

Anderson, Stephen R. *Doctor Dolittle's Delusion: Animals and the Uniqueness of Human Language.* New Haven, CT: Yale University Press, 2004.

Austin, John L. *How to Do Things with Words.* Cambridge, MA: Harvard University Press, 1962.

Barr, James. *Semantics of Biblical Language.* London: Oxford University Press, 1961.

Barthes, Roland. "The Death of the Author." In Roland Barthes, *Image/Music/Text.* New York: Hill & Wang, 1977. Reprinted in William Irwin, ed. *The Death and Resurrection of the Author?* Westport, CT/London: Greenwood, 2002. 3–7.

———. *Elements of Semiology.* New York: Hill & Wang, 1968.

———. *Mythologies.* London: Jonathan Cape, 1972.

———. *S/Z: An Essay.* Translated by Richard Miller. New York: Hill & Wang, 1974.

———. *Writing Degree Zero.* London: Jonathan Cape, 1967.

Bartholomew, Craig, Colin Greene, and Karl Möller, eds. *After Pentecost: Language and Biblical Interpretation.* Carlisle, UK: Paternoster; Grand Rapids, MI: Zondervan, 2001.

Bartsch, Hans Werner, ed. *Kerygma and Myth: A Theological Debate.* Rev. ed. New York: Harper & Row, 1961.

Beekman, John. "Toward an Understanding of Narrative Structure." Dallas: Summer Institute of Linguistics, 1978.

Beekman, John, and John Callow. *Translating the Word of God: With Scripture and Topical Indexes.* Grand Rapids, MI: Zondervan, 1974.

Berger, Peter L., and Thomas Luckmann. *The Social Construction of Reality: A Treatise in the Sociology of Knowledge.* Garden City, NY: Doubleday, 1967.

Black, David Alan. *Linguistics for Students of New Testament Greek.* Grand Rapids, MI: Zondervan, 1988.

391

Bloomfield, Leonard. *Language*. London: George Allen & Unwin, 1933.

Boa, Kenneth D., and Robert M. Bowman Jr. *Faith Has Its Reasons: Integrative Approaches to Defending the Christian Faith*. 2nd ed. Waynesboro, GA/Bletchley, UK: Paternoster, 2005.

Bruce, F. F. *The Acts of the Apostles: The Greek Text with Introduction and Commentary*. 2nd ed. Grand Rapids, MI: Eerdmans, 1952.

Bultmann, Rudolf. "New Testament and Mythology: The Mythological Element in the Message of the New Testament and the Problem of Its Re-interpretation." In *Kerygma and Myth: A Theological Debate*. Edited by Hans Werner Bartsch. Rev. ed. New York: Harper & Row, 1961. 1–44.

Burkhardt, Armin, ed. *Speech Acts, Meaning, and Intentions: Critical Approaches to the Philosophy of John R. Searle*. Berlin/New York: de Gruyter, 1990.

Byl, John. *The Divine Challenge: On Matter, Mind, Math, and Meaning*. Edinburgh: Banner of Truth Trust, 2004.

Callow, Kathleen. *Discourse Considerations in Translating the Word of God*. Grand Rapids, MI: Zondervan, 1974.

Carroll, Lewis. *Through the Looking Glass and What Alice Found There*. 1871.

Carson, D. A., and John Woodbridge, eds. *Hermeneutics, Authority, and Canon*. Grand Rapids, MI: Zondervan, 1986.

———. *Scripture and Truth*. Grand Rapids, MI: Zondervan, 1983.

Chomsky, Noam. *Aspects of the Theory of Syntax*. Cambridge, MA: MIT Press, 1965.

———. *Language and Problems of Knowledge: The Managua Lectures*. Cambridge, MA: MIT Press, 1988.

———. *Lectures on Government and Binding*. Dordrecht/Cinnaminson, NJ: Foris, 1981.

———. *Rules and Representations*. New York: Columbia University Press, 1980.

———. *Some Concepts and Consequences of the Theory of Government and Binding*. Cambridge, MA: MIT Press, 1982.

———. *Syntactic Structures*. The Hague: Mouton, 1957. Second printing, 1962.

Clowney, Edmund P. *Preaching and Biblical Theology*. Grand Rapids, MI: Eerdmans, 1961.

———. *The Unfolding Mystery: Discovering Christ in the Old Testament*. Colorado Springs: NavPress, 1988.

Collins, C. John. *The God of Miracles: An Exegetical Examination of God's Action in the World*. Wheaton, IL: Crossway, 2000.

Conn, Harvie M. *Eternal Word and Changing Worlds: Theology, Anthropology, and Mission in Trialogue*. Grand Rapids, MI: Zondervan, 1984.

Cotterell, Peter, and Max Turner. *Linguistics and Biblical Interpretation*. Downers Grove, IL: InterVarsity, 1989.

Croft, William, and D. Alan Cruse. *Cognitive Linguistics*. Cambridge: Cambridge University Press, 2004.

Cruse, D. Alan. *Meaning in Language: An Introduction to Semantics and Pragmatics*. Oxford: Oxford University Press, 2000.

Culler, Jonathan. *On Deconstruction: Theory and Criticism after Structuralism*. Ithaca, NY: Cornell University Press, 1982.

Dalrymple, Mary. *Lexical-Functional Grammar*. San Diego: Academic Press, 2001.

Davies, Brian. *Language, Meaning, and God: Essays in Honour of Herbert McCabe OP*. London: Chapman, 1987.

Derrida, Jacques. *Deconstruction in a Nutshell: A Conversation with Jacques Derrida*. Edited with a Commentary by John D. Caputo. New York: Fordham University Press, 1997.

———. *Of Grammatology*. Baltimore: Johns Hopkins University Press, 1976.

———. *On the Name*. Stanford, CA: Stanford University Press, 1995.

———. *Positions*. Chicago: University of Chicago Press, 1981.

de Saussure, Ferdinand. *Course in General Linguistics*. New York/Toronto/London: McGraw-Hill, 1959.

Eagleton, Terry. *The Illusions of Postmodernism*. Cambridge, MA: Blackwell, 1996.

Eco, Umberto. *The Search for the Perfect Language*. Oxford: Blackwell, 1995.

Erickson, Millard J., Paul Kjoss Helseth, and Justin Taylor, eds. *Reclaiming the Center: Confronting Evangelical Accommodation in Postmodern Times*. Wheaton, IL: Crossway, 2004.

Falkenberg, Gabriel. "Searle on Sincerity." In *Speech Acts, Meaning, and Intentions: Critical Approaches to the Philosophy of John R. Searle*. Edited by Armin Burkhardt. Berlin/New York: de Gruyter, 1990. 129–146.

Frame, John M. *Apologetics to the Glory of God: An Introduction*. Phillipsburg, NJ: Presbyterian & Reformed, 1994.

———. *Cornelius Van Til: An Analysis of His Thought*. Phillipsburg, NJ: Presbyterian & Reformed, 1995.

———. *The Doctrine of God*. Phillipsburg, NJ: Presbyterian & Reformed, 2002.

———. *The Doctrine of the Christian Life*. Phillipsburg, NJ: Presbyterian & Reformed, 2008.

———. *The Doctrine of the Knowledge of God*. Phillipsburg, NJ: Presbyterian & Reformed, 1987.

———. "God and Biblical Language: Transcendence and Immanence." In *God's Inerrant Word*. Edited by John Warwick Montgomery. Minneapolis: Bethany Fellowship, 1974. 159–177.

———. "Greeks Bearing Gifts." In *Revolutions in Worldview: Understanding the Flow of Western Thought*. Edited by W. Andrew Hoffecker. Phillipsburg, NJ: Presbyterian & Reformed, 2007. 1–36.

———. *Perspectives on the Word of God: An Introduction to Christian Ethics*. Phillipsburg, NJ: Presbyterian & Reformed, 1990.

———. "Scripture Speaks for Itself." In *God's Inerrant Word*. Edited by John Warwick Montgomery. Minneapolis: Bethany Fellowship, 1974. 178–200.

Frei, Hans W. *The Eclipse of Biblical Narrative: A Study in Eighteenth and Nineteenth Century Hermeneutics*. New Haven/London: Yale University Press, 1974.

Gadamer, Hans Georg. *Truth and Method*. 2nd rev. ed. New York: Crossroad, 1989.

Gaffin, Richard B. Jr. *"By Faith, Not by Sight": Paul and the Order of Salvation*. Bletcher, UK/ Waynesboro, GA: Paternoster, 2006.

Gaussen, Louis. *Theopneustia: The Bible: Its Divine Origin and Entire Inspiration*. Reprint (as *The Divine Inspiration of the Bible*), Grand Rapids, MI: Kregel, 1971.

Gordon, Raymond G. Jr., ed. *Ethnologue: Languages of the World*. 15th ed. Dallas: SIL International, 2005. See also <http://www.ethnologue.com>.

Graham, Billy. *Peace with God*. Waco, TX: Word, 1984.

Greimas, Algirdas J. *Structural Semantics: An Attempt at a Method*. Lincoln: University of Nebraska Press, 1984.

Grudem, Wayne, et al. *Translating Truth: The Case for Essentially Literal Bible Translation*. Wheaton, IL: Crossway, 2005.

Gutt, Ernst-August. *Relevance Theory: A Guide to Successful Communication in Translation*. Dallas: Summer Institute of Linguistics, 1992.

———. *Translation and Relevance: Cognition and Context*. Oxford/Cambridge: Blackwell, 1991.

Haegeman, Liliane. *Introduction to Government and Binding Theory*. Oxford: Blackwell, 1991.

Hirsch, E. D. *The Aims of Interpretation*. Chicago: University of Chicago Press, 1976.

———. *Validity in Interpretation*. New Haven, CT: Yale University Press, 1967.

Hoffecker, W. Andrew, ed. *Revolutions in Worldview: Understanding the Flow of Western Thought*. Phillipsburg, NJ: Presbyterian & Reformed, 2007.

Irwin, William, ed. *The Death and Resurrection of the Author?* Westport, CT/London: Greenwood, 2002.

Jakobson, Roman. "Closing Statement: Linguistics and Poetics." In *Style in Language*. Edited by Thomas A. Sebeok. Cambridge, MA: Technology Press, M.I.T., 1960. 350–377.

Jakobson, Roman, and Morris Halle. *Fundamentals of Language*. The Hague: Mouton, 1956.

Johnson, Dennis E. *Him We Proclaim: Preaching Christ from All the Scriptures*. Phillipsburg, NJ: Presbyterian & Reformed, 2007.

Kager, René. *Optimality Theory*. Cambridge: Cambridge University Press, 1999.

Katz, Jerrold J., and Jerry Fodor. "The Structure of a Semantic Theory." *Language* 39 (1963): 170–210.

Kelly, L. G. *The True Interpreter: A History of Translation Theory and Practice in the West*. New York: St. Martin's, 1979.

Kendrick, Graham. *This Is Your God (Meekness and Majesty)*. Kingsway's Thankyou Music, 1986.

Kline, Meredith G. *Images of the Spirit*. Grand Rapids, MI: Baker, 1980.

———. *The Structure of Biblical Authority*. Grand Rapids, MI: Eerdmans, 1972.

Kline, Meredith M. "The Holy Spirit as Covenant Witness." Th.M. thesis, Westminster Theological Seminary, 1972.

Kuhn, Thomas S. *The Structure of Scientific Revolutions*. 2nd ed. Chicago: University of Chicago Press, 1970.

Kuno, Susumu, and Etsuko Kaburaki. "Empathy and Syntax." *Linguistic Inquiry* 8 (1977): 627–672.

Lakoff, George, and Mark Johnson. *Metaphors We Live By*. Chicago: University of Chicago Press, 1980.

Lane, Michael, ed. *Introduction to Structuralism*. New York: Basic, 1970.

Larson, Edward J., and Larry Witham. "Scientists and Religion in America." *Scientific American* 281/3 (September 1999): 88–93.

Lee, David. *Cognitive Linguistics: An Introduction*. Oxford: Oxford University Press, 2002.

Lévi-Strauss, Claude. *The Elementary Structures of Kinship*. Boston: Beacon, 1969.

———. *The Raw and the Cooked: Introduction to a Science of Mythology*. New York: Harper & Row, 1970.

———. *The Savage Mind*. Chicago: University of Chicago Press, 1966.

———. *Structural Anthropology*. New York: Basic, 1976.

Lewis, C. S. *Christian Reflections*. Grand Rapids, MI: Eerdmans, 1967.

———, ed. *Essays Presented to Charles Williams*. Reprint, Grand Rapids, MI: Eerdmans, 1966.

———. *The Last Battle: A Story for Children*. Harmondsworth: Penguin, 1956.

———. "On Stories." In *Essays Presented to Charles Williams*. Edited by C. S. Lewis. Reprint, Grand Rapids, MI: Eerdmans, 1966. 90–105.

———. *The Pilgrim's Regress: An Allegorical Apology for Christianity, Reason, and Romanticism*. 3rd ed. Grand Rapids, MI: Eerdmans, 1958.

———. *The Screwtape Letters*. New York: Macmillan, 1943.

Longacre, Robert E. *Anatomy of Speech Notions*. Lisse, Netherlands: de Ridder, 1976.

———. *Grammar Discovery Procedures*. The Hague/Paris: Mouton, 1968.

———. *The Grammar of Discourse*. New York/London: Plenum, 1983.

———. "Holistic Textlinguistics." SIL, 2003. Available at <http://www.sil.org/silewp/2003/silewp2003-004.pdf>.

Louw, Johannes P., and Eugene A. Nida. *Greek-English Lexicon of the New Testament Based on Semantic Domains*. 2 vols. New York: United Bible Societies, 1988.

Lyons, John. *Introduction to Theoretical Linguistics*. Cambridge: Cambridge University Press, 1969.

———. *Semantics*. 2 vols. Cambridge: Cambridge University Press, 1977.

Lyotard, Jean-François. *The Postmodern Condition: A Report on Knowledge*. Minneapolis: University of Minnesota Press, 1984.

———. *The Postmodern Explained*. Minneapolis: University of Minnesota Press, 1993.

Mannheim, Karl. *Ideology and Utopia: An Introduction to the Sociology of Knowledge*. New York: Harcourt, Brace, & World, 1968.

Marshall, Bruce D. *Trinity and Truth*. Cambridge: Cambridge University Press, 2000.

Matthews, Peter. *A Short History of Structural Linguistics*. Cambridge: Cambridge University Press, 2001.

Milbank, John. *Theology and Social Theory: Beyond Secular Reason*. Oxford/Cambridge: Blackwell, 1990.

———. *The Word Made Strange: Theology, Language, Culture*. Oxford/Cambridge: Blackwell, 1997.

Montgomery, John W., ed. *God's Inerrant Word*. Minneapolis: Bethany Fellowship, 1974.

Nichols, Anthony Howard. "Translating the Bible: A Critical Analysis of E. A. Nida's Theory of Dynamic Equivalence and Its Impact upon Recent Bible Translations." Ph.D. dissertation, University of Sheffield, 1996.

Nida, Eugene A. *Bible Translating*. New York: American Bible Society, 1947.

———. *Toward a Science of Translating: With Special Reference to Principles Involved in Bible Translating*. Leiden: Brill, 1964.

Nida, Eugene A., and Charles R. Taber. *The Theory and Practice of Translation*. Leiden: Brill, 1969.

Owen, John. *Communion with the Triune God*. Edited by Kelly M. Kapic and Justin Taylor. Wheaton, IL: Crossway, 2007.

Pike, Kenneth L. *Language in Relation to a Unified Theory of the Structure of Human Behavior*. 2nd ed. The Hague: Mouton, 1967.

———. *Linguistic Concepts: An Introduction to Tagmemics*. Lincoln and London: University of Nebraska Press, 1982.

————. *Talk, Thought, and Thing: The Emic Road toward Conscious Knowledge*. Dallas: Summer Institute of Linguistics, 1993.

Pike, Kenneth L., and Evelyn G. Pike. *Grammatical Analysis*. Dallas: Summer Institute of Linguistics, 1977.

Piper, John. *The Future of Justification: A Response to N. T. Wright*. Wheaton, IL: Crossway, 2006.

Piper, John, and Justin Taylor, eds. *The Supremacy of Christ in a Postmodern World*. Wheaton, IL: Crossway, 2007.

Polanyi, Michael. *Personal Knowledge: Towards a Post-critical Philosophy*. Chicago: University of Chicago Press, 1964.

————. *The Tacit Dimension*. Garden City, NY: Anchor, 1967.

Poythress, Vern S. "Canon and Speech Act: Limitations in Speech-Act Theory, with Implications for a Putative Theory of Canonical Speech Acts." *Westminster Theological Journal* 70/2 (Fall 2008): 337–354.

————. "Christ the Only Savior of Interpretation." *Westminster Theological Journal* 50/2 (Fall 1988): 161–173.

————. "Counterfeiting in the Book of Revelation as a Perspective on Non-Christian Culture." *Journal of the Evangelical Theological Society* 40/3 (September 1997): 411–418.

————. "Divine Meaning of Scripture." *Westminster Theological Journal* 48 (1986): 241–279.

————. "A Framework for Discourse Analysis: The Components of a Discourse, from a Tagmemic Viewpoint." *Semiotica* 38/3–4 (1982): 277–298.

————. "Gender and Generic Pronouns in English Bible Translation." In *Language and Life: Essays in Memory of Kenneth L. Pike*. Edited by Mary Ruth Wise, Thomas N. Headland, and Ruth M. Brend. Dallas: SIL International and the University of Texas at Arlington, 2003. 371–380.

————. "God's Lordship in Interpretation." *Westminster Theological Journal* 50/1 (1988): 27–64.

————. *God-Centered Biblical Interpretation*. Phillipsburg, NJ: Presbyterian & Reformed, 1999.

————. "Hierarchy in Discourse Analysis: A Revision of Tagmemics." *Semiotica* 40/1–2 (1982): 107–137.

————. "Mathematics as Rhyme." *Journal of the American Scientific Affiliation* 35/4 (1983): 196–203.

————. "Newton's Laws as Allegory." *Journal of the American Scientific Affiliation* 35/3 (1983): 156–161.

————. "The Presence of God Qualifying Our Notions of Grammatical-Historical Interpretation: Genesis 3:15 as a Test Case." *Journal of the Evangelical Theological Society* 50/1 (2007): 87–103.

————. "The Quest for Wisdom." In *Resurrection and Eschatology: Theology in Service of the Church: Essays in Honor of Richard B. Gaffin, Jr.* Edited by Lane G. Tipton and Jeffrey C. Waddington. Phillipsburg, NJ: Presbyterian & Reformed, 2008. 86–114.

————. *Redeeming Science: A God-Centered Approach*. Wheaton, IL: Crossway, 2006.

————. "Reforming Ontology and Logic in the Light of the Trinity: An Application of Van Til's Idea of Analogy." *Westminster Theological Journal* 57/1 (1995): 187–219.

————. *The Returning King: A Guide to the Book of Revelation*. Phillipsburg, NJ: Presbyterian & Reformed, 2000.

————. "Science as Allegory." *Journal of the American Scientific Affiliation* 35/2 (1983): 65–71.

———. *The Shadow of Christ in the Law of Moses*. Phillipsburg, NJ: Presbyterian & Reformed, 1995.

———. *Symphonic Theology: The Validity of Multiple Perspectives in Theology*. Grand Rapids, MI: Zondervan, 1987; reprint, Phillipsburg, NJ: Presbyterian & Reformed, 2001.

———. "Truth and Fullness of Meaning: Fullness versus Reductionistic Semantics in Biblical Interpretation." *Westminster Theological Journal* 67/2 (2005): 211–227. Also appearing in Wayne Grudem et al., *Translating Truth: The Case for Essentially Literal Bible Translation*. Wheaton, IL: Crossway, 2005. 113–134.

Poythress, Vern S., and Wayne A. Grudem. *The Gender-Neutral Bible Controversy: Muting the Masculinity of God's Words*. Nashville: Broadman & Holman, 2000.

———. *The TNIV and the Gender-Neutral Bible Controversy*. Nashville: Broadman & Holman, 2004.

Pratt, Mary Louise. *Toward a Speech Act Theory of Literary Discourse*. Bloomington/London: Indiana University Press, 1977.

Prickett, Stephen. *Narrative, Religion, and Science: Fundamentalism versus Irony, 1700–1999*. Cambridge: Cambridge University Press, 2002.

———. *Words and the Word: Language, Poetics, and Biblical Interpretation*. Cambridge: Cambridge University Press, 1986.

Propp, Vladimir. *Morphology of the Folktale*. 2nd ed. Austin/London: University of Texas Press, 1968.

Radford, Andrew. *Syntax: A Minimalist Introduction*. Cambridge: Cambridge University Press, 1997.

Ricoeur, Paul. *Essays on Biblical Interpretation*. Philadelphia: Fortress, 1980.

———. *The Rule of Metaphor: Multi-disciplinary Studies of the Creation of Meaning in Language*. Toronto/Buffalo: University of Toronto Press, 1977.

———. *Time and Narrative*. 3 vols. Chicago: University of Chicago Press, 1984–1988.

Ridderbos, Herman N. *Redemptive History and the New Testament Scriptures*. Phillipsburg, NJ: Presbyterian & Reformed, 1988.

Robinson, John A. T. *Honest to God*. Philadelphia: Westminster, 1963.

Rorty, Richard. *Contingency, Irony, and Solidarity*. Cambridge: Cambridge University Press, 1989.

———. *Philosophy and the Mirror of Nature*. Princeton, NJ: Princeton University Press, 1980.

Rosenstock-Huessy, Eugen. *Speech and Reality*. Norwich, VT: Argo, 1970.

Ross, Stephen David. *The Limits of Language*. New York: Fordham University Press, 1994.

Ryken, Leland. *The Word of God in English: Criteria for Excellence in Bible Translation*. Wheaton, IL: Crossway, 2002.

Sapir, Edward. *Language: An Introduction to the Study of Speech*. New York: Harcourt, Brace, 1921.

———. *Selected Writings of Edward Sapir in Language, Culture, and Personality*. Edited by David G. Mandelbaum. Berkeley: University of California Press, 1949.

Sayers, Dorothy L. *The Mind of the Maker*. New York: Harcourt, Brace, 1941.

Schaff, Philip, ed. *A Select Library of the Nicene and Post-Nicene Fathers of the Christian Church*. Grand Rapids, MI: Eerdmans, 1979.

Searle, John R. *Expression and Meaning: Studies in the Theory of Speech Acts*. Cambridge: Cambridge University Press, 1979.

———. *Intentionality: An Essay in the Philosophy of Mind*. Cambridge/New York: Cambridge University Press, 1983.

———. *Speech Acts: An Essay in the Philosophy of Language*. London: Cambridge University Press, 1969.

———. "A Taxonomy of Illocutionary Acts." In *Language, Mind, and Knowledge*. Edited by Keith Gunderson, Minneapolis: University of Minnesota Press, 1975. 344–369.

Silva, Moisés. *Biblical Words and Their Meaning: An Introduction to Lexical Semantics*. Grand Rapids, MI: Zondervan, 1983.

———. *God, Language, and Scripture: Reading the Bible in the Light of General Linguistics*. Grand Rapids, MI: Zondervan, 1990.

Simpson, J. A., and E. S. C. Weiner, eds. *Oxford English Dictionary*. 2nd ed. Oxford/New York: Oxford University Press, 1989.

Souriau, Étienne. *Les deux cent milles situations dramatiques*. Paris: Flammarion, 1950.

Steiner, George. *After Babel: Aspects of Language and Translation*. 2nd ed. Oxford/New York: Oxford University Press, 1998.

———. *Real Presences*. London/Boston: Faber & Faber, 1989.

Stonehouse, Ned B., and Paul Woolley, eds. *The Infallible Word*. Reprint, Grand Rapids, MI: Eerdmans, 1953.

Thiselton, Anthony C. *Interpreting God and the Postmodern Self: On Meaning, Manipulation and Promise*. Grand Rapids, MI: Eerdmans, 1995.

———. *New Horizons in Hermeneutics*. Grand Rapids, MI: Zondervan, 1992.

———. *The Two Horizons: New Testament Hermeneutics and Philosophical Description with Special Reference to Heidegger, Bultmann, Gadamer, and Wittgenstein*. Grand Rapids, MI: Eerdmans, 1980.

Tipton, Lane G., and Jeffrey C. Waddington, eds. *Resurrection and Eschatology: Theology in Service of the Church: Essays in Honor of Richard B. Gaffin, Jr.* Phillipsburg, NJ: Presbyterian & Reformed, 2008.

Tolkien, J. R. R. "On Fairy-Stories." In *Essays Presented to Charles Williams*. Edited by C. S. Lewis. Reprint, Grand Rapids, MI: Eerdmans, 1966. 38–89.

*Trinity Hymnal*. Philadelphia: Great Commission, 1990.

Van Til, Cornelius. *The Defense of the Faith*. 2nd ed. Philadelphia: Presbyterian & Reformed, 1963.

———. *An Introduction to Systematic Theology*. Phillipsburg, NJ: Presbyterian & Reformed, 1974.

———. *A Survey of Christian Epistemology*. Vol. 2 of In Defense of Biblical Christianity. n.p.: den Dulk Foundation, 1969.

———. *Why I Believe in God*. Philadelphia: Committee on Christian Education, Orthodox Presbyterian Church, 1966.

Vanhoozer, Kevin J. *The Drama of Doctrine: A Canonical-Linguistic Approach to Christian Theology*. Louisville: Westminster John Knox, 2005.

———. *First Theology: God, Scripture, and Hermeneutics*. Downers Grove, IL: InterVarsity, 2002.

———. *Is There a Meaning in This Text? The Bible, the Reader, and the Morality of Literary Knowledge.* Grand Rapids, MI: Zondervan, 1998.

Vos, Geerhardus. *The Self-Disclosure of Jesus: The Modern Debate about the Messianic Consciousness.* Reprint, Phillipsburg, NJ: Presbyterian & Reformed, 2002.

Warfield, Benjamin B. *The Inspiration and Authority of the Bible.* Reprint, Philadelphia: Presbyterian & Reformed, 1967.

White, Heath. *Postmodernism 101: A First Course for the Curious Christian.* Grand Rapids, MI: Brazos, 2006.

Whorf, Benjamin Lee. *Language, Thought, and Reality: Selected Writings.* Edited by John B. Carroll. Cambridge, MA: Technology Press of Massachusetts Institute of Technology; New York: Wiley, 1956.

Wittgenstein, Ludwig. *On Certainty.* Edited by G. E. M. Anscombe and G. H. von Wright. New York: Harper & Row, 1969.

———. *Tractatus Logico-Philosophicus.* London: Routledge & Kegan Paul, 1922.

Wolterstorff, Nicholas. *Divine Discourse: Philosophical Reflections on the Claim that God Speaks.* Cambridge: Cambridge University Press, 1995.

———. "The Promise of Speech-act Theory for Biblical Interpretation." In *After Pentecost: Language and Biblical Interpretation.* Edited by Craig Bartholomew, Colin Greene, and Karl Möller. Grand Rapids, MI: Zondervan, 2001. 73–90.

Wright, Nicholas T. *Jesus and the Victory of God.* Minneapolis: Fortress, 1996.

———. The Resurrection of the Son of God. Minneapolis: Fortress, 2003.

# Index

# Scripture Index